BOSWELL'S CLAP AND OTHER ESSAYS

Also by William B. Ober

BOTTOMS UP!
A PATHOLOGIST'S ESSAYS ON
MEDICINE AND THE HUMANITIES

BOSWELL'S CLAP AND OTHER ESSAYS

Medical Analyses of Literary Men's Afflictions

BY WILLIAM B. OBER, M.D.

ALLISON & BUSBY

The author would like to express gratitude to the following journals:

Bulletin of the New York Academy of Medicine for permission to reprint "Boswell's Gonorrhea," 45, No. 6 (June 1969), 587–636; "Drowsed with the Fume of Poppies: Opium and John Keats," 44, No. 7 (July 1968), 862–81; "Madness and Poetry: A Note on Collins, Cowper, and Smart," 46, No. 4 (Apr. 1970), 203–66; "Chekhov among the Doctors: The Doctor's Dilemma," 49, No. 1 (Jan. 1973), 62–76.

New York State Journal of Medicine for permission to reprint "William Carlos Williams: The Physican as Poet," 69, No. 8 (Apr. 1969), 1084–98; "Did Socrates Die of Hemlock Poisoning?" 77, No. 2 (Feb. 1977), 254–58.

Bulletin of the Menninger Clinic for permission to reprint "Swinburne's Masochism: Neuropathology and Psychopathology," 39, No. 6 (Nov. 1975), 500–555.

Academy of Medicine of New Jersey Bulletin for permission to reprint "Lady Chatterley's What?" 65, No. 1 (Mar. 1969), 41–63.

Annals of Internal Medicine for permission to reprint "Thomas Shadwell: His Exitus Revis'd," 74, No. 1 (Jan. 1971), 126–30.

An Allison & Busby book
Published in 1990 by
W.H. Allen & Co. PLC
Sekforde House
175/9 St John Street
London EC1V 4LL

First paperback edition 1988

Printed in Great Britain by
Courier International Ltd, Tiptree, Essex

ISBN 0 85031 856 4 (hardback)
ISBN 0 074900 011 2 (paperback)

CONTENTS

LIST OF ILLUSTRATIONS

PREFACE

These collected essays, written over the past decade, show a number of ways whereby medical information and insights can illuminate and perhaps resolve certain literary problems. This does not imply that every reader should read with a medical eye nor need any given writer be viewed as a "case." That would be presumptuous and would defeat the aims of literature.

Many literary critics claim that the text itself is sufficient and extraneous biographical considerations irrelevant: I am not of this company. I am unable, perhaps unwilling, to dissociate a statement or a literary work from its context. I like to know who wrote it, when he wrote it, why he wrote it, and what audience he addresses; beyond that, something of the circumstances, immediate and remote, that gave rise to the work. Such knowledge may not be essential to enjoyment or understanding, but I find it helpful. People who find such knowledge useless or gratuitous ought not read this book. I fear that members of the antibiographical school would happily dismiss Johnson's *Lives of the Poets* because they place small value on "the common sense of readers uncorrupted by literary prejudices."

On first blush it seems a reasonable position to claim that literature ought not be examined in the light of nonliterary events. But does literature exist as an entity entire unto itself, independent of other parts of life, untouched by any other reality? Textual and structural critics of recent decades claim this is so, that literature lives within the frame of language alone. True enough, but only up to a point, and nice molecular analysis does not help. We do not test the consecrated wine for hemoglobin content, nor would Carême's recipe for a madeleine give us insight into the workings of Proust's imagination. But literature is often a transformation of experience, and it can be illuminating to find out just what the experience was and how the writer used it.

No apologia has much value unless it defends against anticipated critical attacks. One cannot ward off every blow, but a few parries are obvious. Some will say that applying medical reasoning to literature is "reductive," a now fashionable word for what in my youth we called oversimplification. A medical point of view is reductive if and only if one claims that is the only way to read and stops. It is merely one way of looking at a blackbird, one form of evidence, one element to be taken into account in a final synthesis. A reader may adopt a medical stance to find out what added information it can bring to an established literary and critical corpus.

Another objection might be the bland assertion that I have "psychoanalyzed" my subjects, carrying with it a pejorative tone to the very idea of psychoanalysis. Psychoanalysis is a clinical discipline to which a subject or patient comes voluntarily for a therapeutic purpose. My subjects did not come to me; I chose them and make no pretense to cure them. What's more, they are all safely dead. The cardinal technique of psychoanalysis is for the analyst to listen to the patient's free associations, and there is a continuing dialogue between doctor and patient. When associations are made in these essays, they were made by me and not my subjects, and there is no dialogue. But it is true that when I have found concepts developed by psychoanalysis and other schools useful and appropriate, I have tried to apply them. Does anyone in the eighth decade of the twentieth century deny the existence of unconscious mental processes, that dreams and fantasies reveal something about these processes, or that a writer's psyche is present in his work and examination of such work can help ideas reveal the man? Surely, by this date psychoanalytic ideas are part of the mainstream of medical thought. I have been eclectic in my choice of concepts applying to mental processes, and in these essays, with one exception (Williams), the focus is on the particular rather than the general.

I am a pathologist by training and practice, specifically a histopathologist, and spend much of my time trying to diagnose diseases and analyze disease processes by looking through a microscope at pieces of tissue removed from the human body by biopsy, at surgery, or autopsy. Using tissue sliced extremely thin so that it will transmit light, pathologists examine carefully selected, sharply delimited objects in an evenly illuminated field. Up to a point we can control illumination, but the lens system does limit the degree of resolution. From such microcosms we construct macrocosms. There is nothing mysterious or esoteric about this method; daily, in every hospital, pathologists look at tissues and the cells that comprise them. No sensible pathologist believes that his microscopic examination tells him everything he needs to know about a specific patient or a specific disease. He has to take into account the patient's personal history, the sequence of events, and to apply evidence from other disciplines such as physiology, biochemistry, and the like, to produce a rounded view of the problem at issue.

By applying the retrospectoscope I have tried to scrutinize selected literary subjects much in the fashion that a pathologist examines tissues and cells, fitting them into a frame he hopes will provide a satisfactory explanation. Whether an explanation is satisfactory depends partly on its internal consistency, partly on how much it explains, and partly on what questions it leaves unanswered. Internal consistency is established in part by the congruity between various bits of evidence and in part by congruity with our own experience of what is possible. But it is rash to extrapolate from such explanations into sweeping generalizations.

A pathologist is a physician, and like every other physician, he takes into account both physical and psychological data. At this late date one need not argue the close interrelation and reciprocal effects of organic processes upon mental ones, or conversely. Most of these essays are examples of the mind-body problem, specimens of the old-fashioned nineteenth-century term, "medical psychology." I have been eclectic, taking both evidence and theory where found, testing them for reliability and validity, and assessing where and how they apply. I propose no methodological innovations.

One must, of course, choose one's subjects with care. For example, Byron's clubfoot is not a good subject. Too much has been written to determine whether it was his right foot or his left foot, but the evidence is inconclusive and no firm answer can be given. Nor is it an important point per se. We shall never be satisfied that we know the cause of Shakespeare's death. But Pope's "long disease, my life" is an excellent subject, because his infirmities colored not only his life but his work. What is required for this type of medical analysis is adequate biographical information and a substantial corpus of literary material. Preferably, the writer should have sufficient merit to make his work worth reading. A writer's journals (Boswell) provide invaluable clues, and if voluminous correspondence survives (Swinburne, Keats), one is fortunate indeed. Autobiographical material may be misleading by virture of what is omitted and because of the need for self-justification. Comments from contemporary sources are useful but must be checked for accuracy, opportunity to observe, and possible bias. Best of all is documentation of a wealth of physical and psychological symptoms that bear directly upon the writer's work.

From such criteria it can be argued that the essay on Shadwell was an ill-considered venture. To read his complete works was a labor and not one of love; he is not a writer of great importance; neither is there a wealth of data, nor does the cause of his death bear upon his work. The essay has no more profound a purpose than to set the record straight and show how simple medical analysis can be applied two centuries later to reconstruct the scene and assign a more probable cause of death. It does have its cautionary point for the literary historian: when there is a medical question, consult a doctor.

I shall not comment on the content of the other essays, but I do note two matters relating to form. The essays on *Lady Chatterley* and William Carlos Williams were originally lectures, and I have chosen to retain the first person singular in which they were delivered. The essay on Keats's use of opium is much abbreviated. Its first version contained more extensive comments on the use of narcotics by other writers, including the literary experiences based on contemporary psychedelic drugs. It was painful to take the advice of a much respected editor and cut it to size, but I think his judgment was sound.

We all remember Socrates' last words, "Crito, I owe a cock to Aesculapius," but few of us remember what follows—"Will you remember to pay the debt?" In many ways this collection is a cock to Aesculapius, offered in oblation to a profession that has been kind to me, and I do have a few debts to acknowledge. No man searches the literature unaided, and I have had the advantage of being in close proximity to many fine libraries. I must single out for special mention the Library of the New York Academy of Medicine with its extensive historical collection and its two distinguished librarians, Gertrude L. Annan and Alfred N. Brandon, to say nothing of the many skilled and dedicated librarians on its staff. The reading room of the British Museum (now the British Library) has sheltered me on many occasions, and contrary to popular belief, its service has been prompt and perceptive.

I have had the benefit of sound and sensible advice as well as encouragement from many scholars. Professor Frederick A. Pottle of Yale vetted my essay on Boswell, saw it through several drafts, gently pointing out errors of omission and commission, and placed new material in my hands. His colleague, Professor Frank Brady, also read the manuscript and gave me practical suggestions. I acknowledge the kind permission of Yale University and the McGraw-Hill Book Company to quote extensively from Boswell's *Journals* and other papers.

Professor Cecil Y. Lang of the University of Virginia supplied information about Swinburne previously inaccessible to me and resolved several problems. That essay could not have been attempted without his scholarly edition of Swinburne's letters. Professor Harry T. Moore of Southern Illinois University debated many points about D. H. Lawrence and *Lady Chatterley* with me and was helpful in sorting out fact from fiction in the Lawrence legend. I am indebted to Professor Emile Delavenay of the University of Nice for tracing the filiation of many of Lawrence's ideas from those developed by Edwin Carpenter. Professor Jacques Barzun of Columbia University gave me encouragement when I encountered difficulties, and I have tried to heed his cautions about historiography written from the point of view of a specialist. My friend of long standing, Professor Howard Nemerov of Washington University, Saint Louis, has been a never failing source of support and advice. It was kind of Professor Reed Whittemore of the University of Maryland to invite me in 1966 to address the English Institute on William Carlos Williams, where I was probably a nonprophetic Daniel among the lions (or Donatello au milieu des fauves?), and I hope I may claim that on that occasion *non sine gloria militavi*.

Several of my fellow pathologists have taken the time and trouble to read these essays in typescript and have given me the benefit of their experience, notably Dr. Harold L. Stewart of Bethesda, Maryland, Dr. Hugh G. Grady of Philadelphia, Pennsylvania, Dr. William D. Sharpe of New York, Dr. Paul F. Cranefield of New York, Dr. John H. Edgcomb of New York, and Dr. Melvin B. Black of San Francisco. I have consulted freely two friends who are psychiatrists, Dr. Harold E. Mann of Berkeley, California, and Dr. Robert A. Senescu of Albuquerque, New Mexico.

Those essays that appeared in the *Bulletin of the New York Academy of Medicine* have been improved by the editorial judgment of Dr. Saul Jarcho. Dr. Sydney Smith and his colleagues at the *Bulletin of the Menninger Clinic* applied their skills to the essay on Swinburne. To one accustomed to the form of citation used in medical and scientific journals the conversion to the niceties and complexities of "MLA style" was a challenge, and I acknowledge with thanks the kind offices of Mr. Richard Steins of New York who helped me prepare final copy for publication. It has been a pleasure to work with Mr. Vernon Sternberg and his colleagues at the Southern Illinois University Press.

My indebtedness to my wife is incalculable, not only for time stolen from her society (the sweet rubato of reading and writing) but for providing a well-ordered household in which I could pursue my avocation. But I dedicate this book to my children, Elaine who will read it and Stephen who cannot. And to the reader's judgment I recall the aphorism of Alexander Pope: "For what I have published I can only hope to be pardoned; for what I have burned I deserve to be praised."

William B. Ober, M.D.
Tenafly, N.J.
April 1978

CHAPTER 1

Boswell's Clap

The world will certainly receive with glee
The slightest bit of history of Me.

John Wolcot (Peter Pindar)

James Boswell as a journalist and biographer is a valued friend; as a patient he is at first unfortunate and finally tragic. The discovery and publication of his journals and other papers, and more recently a sympathetic biography dealing with his early years, furnish the medical historian with a unique chronicle notable for its frankness and accuracy.[1] Neither reticence nor prudery prevented Boswell from recording his vices along with his virtues, his failures with his successes. One might wish for closer attention to the details of symptoms and treatment, but Boswell was trained as a lawyer, not as a doctor. Only in his later years was there any attempt on his part to withhold information which might be construed as derogatory. It was not until the end of his fourth decade that he even considered—in his private journals—the idea of his being *retenu*.

Boswell records nineteen attacks of urethritis, almost all of them acute, almost all following sexual exposure and almost certainly gonococcal in origin (see table, pp. 40–42). As his experiences multiplied, it is not always easy to distinguish recrudescence of an old infection from a fresh infection incurred by recent exposure. In some instances Boswell's allusions to his illness are not amplified by details of symptoms and treatment; consequently the diagnosis is sometimes inferential.

But there can be no doubt that he had repeated attacks of gonorrhea between 1760 and 1790, and that he probably died of complications of that disease. Singularly, Macaulay's two essays (1832, 1856) which damned Boswell were inaccurate to the point of calumny but glossed over his venereal disease superficially. By contrast Pottle, who is warmly sympathetic to Boswell, takes scrupulous pains to see that each venereal episode is documented as fully as the canon permits, a testimony to the relative enlightenment of the mid-twentieth century and equally to the scrupulosity of inspired scholarship. Inevitably the question arises why Boswell, a man of good family, considerable education, adequate professional status, and prominent social connections should deliberately expose himself to the risk of gonorrhea, not only deliberately but even compulsively. As one reads his journals consecutively, it is difficult to escape the conclusion that Boswell was driven by forces beyond his conscious knowledge and control. The frank revelations of his journals furnish clues to the motives for his behavior, supply insight into the psychogenic background of his venery and its infections, and explain some of the contrarieties of his character.

Boswell's first attack of gonorrhea was incurred when he was almost twenty years old. He had matriculated at the University of Edinburgh at the age of thirteen and completed his undergraduate education at eighteen in 1758. During his last years at the university he had become interested in the theater and had fallen in love with an actress who was a Roman Catholic. Conversion to Catholicism would have debarred him from inheriting his father's estate and from becoming a member of the bar. To break up this romance, an amour that was never consummated, his father packed him off to Glasgow to study under Adam Smith. Glasgow had no theater and was even more tedious for Boswell than Edinburgh; he escaped on horseback to London in the spring of 1760. His brief conversion to Catholicism and a vague plan for becoming a monk were speedily rejected when he got his first taste of the city's pleasures through the dubious good offices of Samuel Derrick, an Irish literary hack, and Lord Eglinton (Alexander Montgomerie), his father's Ayrshire neighbor, who had a town house in Mayfair. Derrick introduced him to lesser actresses and some prostitutes. Pottle relates: "He [Boswell] experienced for the first time what he elegantly calls the melting and transporting rites of love in a room in the Blue Periwig, Southampton Street, Strand, his priestess a Miss Sally Forrester. He was at that time well advanced in his twentieth year."[2]

Lord Eglinton moved in somewhat higher circles. He invited Boswell to be a guest at his home in Mayfair, supplied him with money, and "rescued him from religious error by making him a libertine in every sense of that word." Again, we may rely on Pottle for a description of Boswell's introduction to high life: "Fine clothes, the bustle and glitter of the metropolis, endless parties, the opportunity to combine gross physical pleasure with the refined intellectual delights of the theatre and of high conversation—these, Boswell was convinced, were what he was made for, and these were London."[3]

It was the beginning of a love affair that lasted for thirty-five years: Boswell fell in love with London, and neither conjugal love nor the promise of success at the Edinburgh bar, not to mention the quiet dignity of being Laird of Auchinleck, could stop him from returning again and again to the city that had captured his mind and heart. To use a term now in vogue, for Boswell, London was "where the action is."

By the time Lord Auchinleck, his father, came to claim his wandering boy, Boswell had contracted his first case of gonorrhea, presumably from a prostitute. For this he was treated by Andrew Douglas, a fellow Scot who, having served as a naval surgeon, had opened a practice in Pall Mall, though not admitted to the Company of Surgeons. In all probability Douglas had no degree but had trained by apprenticeship in Scotland. Boswell gives us no details of treatment; in fact, he had not yet begun to keep his journal, and we know of this episode only incidentally through his account of his third attack, written two years later; all we are told is that it lasted ten weeks. On his return to Edinburgh he continued to patronize prostitutes, and the result was a second attack of urethritis which lasted four months. Again, Boswell supplies no details of symptoms or treatment. Our information about this attack comes chiefly from a letter written the following spring to his friend and classmate at the university, William Temple: "Last summer, indeed, I went to a house of recreation in this place, and catch'd a Tartar, too, with a vengeance. But I hope you don't call passing some hours with an infamous creature—when hurried on by the heat of youth—a *connection*. This season, I have never been, nor do I intend again to be a guest in the mansions of gross sensuality.[4]

It is not unlikely that this second attack may have been a recurrence of an incompletely treated and unresolved first infection, aggravated by continued sexual activity; however, there were apparently several exposures to sources of new infection. Boswell must have suffered the indignity of being treated for this infection while living in his father's house.

One might view these first two attacks as merely the price paid for the exuberance of delayed fulfillment of adolescent sexuality, and dismiss them as nothing more. It is even difficult to fault Boswell for incurring his third attack, as he took reasonable precautions. But during the two years he passed in Edinburgh studying law, he managed to have affairs with four women and to father an illegitimate child on Peggy Doig, a servant girl. Having passed his examination in civil law at the end of July 1762, Boswell persuaded his father to let him have a year in London to see if he could obtain a commission in the Foot Guards through influence. It was at this time that Boswell began to keep a fully written chronological journal, and this year saw the famous *London Journal,* 1762–1763, the manuscript of which was discovered at Fettercairn House in 1930. In one sense Boswell's journals were a substitute for the confessional. True, Boswell as a monk would be unimaginable, but he did have religious interests, even though he seems to have been incapable of using religious teaching as a guide for conduct. Pottle makes two penetrating remarks about the journals: "he enjoyed confessing so much that . . . the sacrament of penance might have been only another opportunity for self-indulgence."[5] And, shifting from psychological to literary values: "Boswell's power as a writer developed surprisingly little after his twenty-second year."[6]

Boswell's virtue for the medical historian is one of his limitations as a writer: he lacked creative imagination. Adept at recreating a scene based on real events, he could not create one out of whole cloth. Though he achieved distinction as a belle lettrist, journalist, and biographer, success as a poet or dramatist was beyond him. As a corrective to those who would rate his literary gift too highly, may one modestly suggest that the Recording Angel, albeit a thoroughly worthy and competent angel, was not on the same level as the Creator? Such a comparison may not be quite fair. The Creator made *things,* not a fabric of *words,* and we are not told that the Recording Angel attempted a *literary* record. A more equitable comparison might be between Boswell and Sir Walter Scott. Boswell did have his own distinctive skill with words, but he was not angelic. His journals, as his wife complained, left him "embowelled to posterity," but they did so in an objective, uninflected fashion; Boswell was an antihero long before the term came into vogue. No account of any love affair and its sequelae quite matches the nonheroic stance in Boswell's account of his brief affair with Louisa.

On his arrival in London in November 1761, Boswell hastened to seek out his previous sexual partners, but the nymphs had departed. One cannot deny a touch of exhibitionism in his account; the journal (unlike his later ones which were private) was being sent in weekly packets to his university friend, John Johnston, at Edinburgh. The entry dated November 25 tells us:

I had now been some time in town without female sport, I determined to have nothing to do with whores, as my health was of great consequence to me. I went to a girl with whom I had had an intrigue at Edinburgh [Mrs. Love] . . . and tried to obtain my former favours, but in vain . . . I was really unhappy for want of women . . . I picked up a girl in the Strand; went into a court with intention to enjoy her in armour [i.e., using a condom]. But she had none. I toyed with her. She wondered at my size, and said if I ever took a girl's maidenhead, I would make her squeak. I gave her a shilling and had enough command of myself to go without touching her. I afterwards trembled at the danger I had escaped. I resolved to wait cheerfully till I got some safe girl or was liked by some woman of fashion.[7]

The "safe girl" appeared in the person of an actress he had known casually in Edinburgh, immortalized in his journal as Louisa, now identified as Anne Lewis.[8] By this time she had been separated from her husband Charles Standen, a strolling player, and was a woman Boswell knew to be neither celibate nor promiscuous, but for himself, possibly, "available." Boswell first called on her on December 14, 1762. By December 20 he had lent her two guineas to meet a dun. By December 26 she permitted liberties and consented to a proposed affair but postponed consummation. Louisa was prepared to yield, but on January 2 Boswell was impotent:

I felt dispirited and languid. I approached Louisa with a kind of uneasy tremor. I sat down. I toyed with her. Yet I was not inspired by Venus. I felt rather a delicate sensation of love than a violent amorous inclination . . . I thought myself feeble as a gallant, although I had experienced the reverse many a time. Louisa knew not my powers. She might imagine me impotent. I sweated almost with anxiety, which made me worse. . . . When I began to feel that I was still a man . . . and was just making a triumphal entry . . . we heard her landlady coming up. . . . I was unhappy at being prevented from the completion of my wishes, and yet I thought I had saved my credit for prowess, that I might through anxiety have not acted a vigorous part.[9]

Boswell now experienced loss of potentia and attributed it to "anxiety"—the word is repeated twice. He also tells us that in his judgment anxiety aggravated his inability to achieve erection. This vocabulary and insight in 1763 anticipates our twentieth-century usage, a tribute to Boswell's skill with words. Boswell did not pursue the question more deeply and examine himself for a mechanism which caused his anxiety.

Boswell and Louisa fulfilled their destiny ten days later, after a brief postponement necessitated by Louisa's menses. The event did not take place in her lodgings but in a tavern to which they repaired to spend the night. Boswell's account (written for Johnston's eyes) anticipates the sexual athleticism and vocabulary conventions of the purportedly salacious literature hawked surreptitiously in the early 1900s:

I came softly into the room, and in a sweet delirium slipped into bed and was immediately clasped in her snowy arms and pressed to her milk-white bosom.... The friendly curtain of darkness concealed our blushes. In a moment I felt myself animated with the strongest powers of love, and, from my dearest creature's kindness, had a most luscious feast. Proud of my godlike vigour, I soon resumed the noble game. I was in full glow of health. Sobriety had preserved me from effeminacy and weakness, and my bounding blood beat quick and high alarms. A more voluptuous night I never enjoyed. Five times was I fairly lost in supreme rapture. Louisa was madly fond of me; she declared I was a prodigy, and asked me if this was not extraordinary for human nature. I said twice as much might be, but this was not, although in my own mind I was somewhat proud of my performance.[10]

One senses that Boswell is "writing up" for Johnston's benefit. In no entry in his later journals does he affect the florid, orotund, adjectival style to describe his concupiscence. It is Boswell's more usual, substantive style which prompted Fussell to write that he had so much in common with twentieth-century writers: "Boswell is also one of us in his sexual ambitiousness and self-consciousness. Except for Boswell, few before the age of Dr. Kinsey and Wilhelm Reich can have bothered to record for posterity the number of their sequential orgasms on given occasions. Pepys and William Hickey sometimes come close to Boswell in erotic frankness, but their enjoyments of the flesh are not, like Boswell's, a function of the delights of documentation."[11]

Boswell records his own history more precisely than Jean Jacques Rousseau, for all the latter's much vaunted self-revelation. With Rousseau one senses a need for self-justification; his *Confessions* are largely a self-serving declaration.

As a lover Boswell was variable. His next session with Louisa was four days later at her lodgings. His response was quite different: "*January 16:* I ... was permitted the rites of love with great complacency; yet I felt my passion for Louisa much gone. ... I had a strong proof of my own inconstancy of disposition, and I considered that any woman who married me must be miserable."[12]

Two days later, on January 18, six days after his first exposure to Louisa, Boswell developed symptoms of his third attack of gonorrhea. He had been symptom-free for over two years; reinfection is far more probable than a recrudescence of his infections of 1760. He "began to feel an unaccountable alarm of unexpected evil; a little heat in the members of my body sacred to Cupid, very like a symptom of that distemper with which Venus, when cross, takes it into her head to plague her votaries. But then I had run no risks. I had been with no woman but Louisa; and sure she could not have such a thing. . . . When I came to Louisa's, I felt myself stout and well, and most courageously did I plunge into the fount of love, and had vast pleasure as I enjoyed her as an actress who had played many a fine lady's part."[13]

Boswell was not so suspicious of the import of his symptoms that evening that he inquired of Louisa whether she might be infected, and he did not hesitate to expose himself again. But it was to be his last evening of such vast pleasure for several weeks. The following evening he went to the theater, supped with friends, but "When I got home, though, then came sorrow. Too, too plain was Signor Gonorrhea. Yet I could scarce believe it, and determined to go to friend Douglas next day."[14] This dashed his hopes for "a winter's safe copulation." Boswell's account may not stir a reader to compassion. His solution to the problem of finding a safe and satisfactory sexual outlet is too calculating, too much the product of the rational notions of the age of sensibility to engage one's emotions. Two centuries later we can read about it with as much detachment as he wrote about it. Boswell provides only a few details of Douglas's method of treatment, but the acute phase of the infection lasted about six weeks. His initial symptoms of urethritis appeared on January 19, and he was confined to his quarters in Downing Street from January 22 to February 27, 1763. He had plenty of time to write in his journal, and we are rewarded with a revealing account of his reaction to this illness.

His attitude toward Douglas is typical of the ambivalence of the doctor-patient relation; even on the day Douglas examined him Boswell records: "*January 20:* . . . the same man as a friend and as a surgeon exhibits two very opposite characters. Douglas as a friend is most kind, most anxious for my interest . . . but Douglas a surgeon will be as ready to keep me long under his hands, and as desirous to lay hold of my money, as any man. . . . I have to do not with him but with his profession."[15] Douglas's treatment consisted chiefly of having Boswell keep to his room, rest, take a low calorie diet, electuaries to keep his bowels free, medications not otherwise described and, on one occasion (January 30), bloodletting. It is inferred that Douglas did not recommend instillation of medication into the urethra by syringe.

After consulting Douglas, Boswell went that day to Louisa's to tax her with being the cause of his infection. She admitted to having been infected three years previously but said she had been in good health for the past fifteen months. With the benefit of today's knowledge that gonorrhea may lurk latent and asymptomatic in women as a low-grade endocervicitis, it is easy to account for Louisa's belief that she was not infectious, and one is willing to take her word that she had had no lover but Boswell for six months. Boswell was less charitable: "There is scarcely a possibility that she could be innocent of the crime of horrid imposition. And yet her positive asseverations really stunned me. But she is in all probability a most consummate dissembling whore."[16] Unwilling to accept his own share of responsibility, he then rationalized his position: "It is indeed very hard. I cannot say, like young fellows who get themselves clapped in a bawdy-house, that I will take better care again. For I really did take care. However, since I am fairly trapped, let me make the best of it. I have not got it from imprudence. It is merely the chance of war"[17]

But Boswell could not chalk his experience up to profit and loss for very long. His conscience bothered him; where there was guilt, there had been a wrongful act, and his miscreant had to be punished. On February 3, two weeks after his infection began, his prudence went so far as to induce him to write to Louisa:

Madam:—My surgeon will soon have a demand upon me of five guineas for curing the disease which you have given me. I must therefore remind you of the little sum which you had of me some time ago. You cannot have forgotten upon what footing I let you have it. I neither *paid* it for prostitution nor *gave* it in charity. It was fairly borrowed, and you promised to return it. I give you notice that I expect to have it before Saturday sennight.

I have been very bad, but I scorn to upbraid you. I think it below me. If you are not rendered callous by a long course of disguised wickedness, I should think the consideration of your deceit and baseness, your corruption both of body and mind, would be a very severe punishment. Call not that a misfortune which is the consequence of your own unworthiness. I desire no mean evasions. I want no letters. Send the money sealed up. I have nothing more to say to you.[18]

This is one of the great "end of the affair" letters of all time. Boswell copied the text in full in his journal and subjoined this prim comment: "Am not I too vindictive? It appears so; but upon better consideration I am only sacrificing at the shrine of Justice; and sure I have chosen a victim that deserves it"[19] Precisely one week later, February 10, Louisa's maidservant left a small pocket for Boswell containing the two guineas, carefully sealed, no note enclosed.

One can only marvel at the nicety with which Boswell allocated financial responsibility for the by-products of sexual intercourse; scarcely six months previously he had given Peggy Doig £10 to cover the cost of her confinement with his illegitimate child and had made equitable provision for the infant's maintenance. His legal training had made him conscious that the needs of justice must be served by properly apportioned punishment. It was at about this period of his life that he began to take a deep interest in witnessing public executions. Boswell records passing many sleepless, haunted nights after seeing such hangings, but he persisted in attending them all the same. In later years when he would lose a client to the gallows, he would visit the condemned man frequently in his cell and talk with him about the fear of death, punishment in the life hereafter, and similar cheerful topics. Viewed in this context, there is considerable significance in his own statement in the autobiographical sketch he later wrote for Rousseau: "The eternity of punishment was the first great idea I ever formed."[20] It was an idea which was to remain with him, consciously and unconsciously, all the rest of his life, and much of his behavior can be interpreted in the light of his ideas about punishment.

The night after he wrote to Louisa he developed pain and swelling in a testicle; presumably this was a transient epididymitis, as it subsided by morning. He does not record whether he interpreted it as a punishment, but he had suffered from this unpleasant complication in one of his previous infections, presumably the second. By February 27 he recorded in his journal that his disorder was over and nothing but a gleet (i.e., a clear urethral discharge, indicative of subsiding posterior urethritis and prostatitis) remained. By March 25 he was again active sexually and picked up a girl in St. James's Park.

The remainder of Boswell's stay in London was devoted to unsuccessful efforts to procure a commission in the Foot Guards through patronage. On May 16 he met Samuel Johnson; though he did not know it then, it was the most significant encounter of his life. He punctuated these last few months in London with almost a dozen incidents of intercourse with streetwalkers. They gave him physical satisfaction for the nonce; after they were over, he was filled with regrets and self-reproach, vide:

"*March 31:* . . . I had a low opinion of this gross practice and resolved to do it no more.[21]

"*May 10:* Yet after the brutish appetite was sated, I could not but despise myself for being so closely united with such a low wretch."[22]

On most of these occasions (but not all) he would use "armour." At the time condoms were made from the dried intestines (usually the cecum, which ends as a blind pouch) of sheep, lambs, calves, goats, and perhaps other animals. They were thick and tended to dull the sensation in coitus. Such condoms were rather stiff and became brittle unless stored in containers of water. Boswell records his own surreptitious practice: "*March 30:* If Molly [the maidservant] be gone, take out . . . from pot & put up in paper."[23]

It was often necessary to rewet the condom before putting it on. It was not uncommon for condoms used by army officers to be decorated with their regimental colors. One can only speculate whether this was an added inducement for Boswell in his choice of a military career. However, he did not contract gonorrhea again for two years.

Having failed to secure the commission he wanted, Boswell yielded to his father's pressure and agreed to spend the next year in Utrecht to study civil law more intensively under Professor Christian Heinrich Trotz. It is unnecessary to relate the details of the manipulations which went back and forth in correspondence between father and son, but it was agreed that he would spend one winter in Utrecht, then be allowed to visit Paris and some of the German courts. Boswell's year at Utrecht was marked by steadfast application to his studies and complete continence. Utrecht was dull and confining; Boswell was depressed. But he did establish an emotional entanglement with a young lady of good family, Belle de Zuylen. Boswell was seriously attracted and considered marriage; they continued to correspond for several years. Belle de Zuylen was intelligent and well educated, a keen student of mathematics and metaphysics. Boswell may have delighted in the company of intellectually inclined women, but he did not choose them as sexual partners. The woman he later chose as his wife was intelligent, sympathetic, and tolerant, but had no intellectual pretensions.

Boswell's continence came to an end on September 11, 1764, at Berlin, and thereafter in Germany he had recourse to prostitutes but successfully avoided venereal infection.[24] He persuaded his father to let him travel through Switzerland and Italy. In December 1764 he gained entree to Rousseau. He was able to convince the famed philosopher of his sincerity in seeking guidance, and the recorded conversations in Boswell's journal are rich in self-revelation. One important passage follows upon Boswell's request for advice regarding participation in sex affairs with married women:

"*December 14: Rousseau:* . . . you have no right to do evil for the sake of good.

"*Boswell:* True. None the less, I can imagine some very embarrassing situations. And pray tell me how I can expiate the evil I have done?

"*Rousseau:* Oh, sir, there is no expiation for evil except good."[25]

To this interchange Boswell was later to append some characteristic reflections of his own: "A beautiful thought this: Nevertheless, I maintained my doctrine of satisfaction by punishment. . . . Immutable justice require atonement to be made for transgressions, and this atonement is to be made by suffering. This is the universal idea of all nations, and seems to be a leading principle of Christianity."[26]

Sin and atonement, guilt and expiation by punishment—these were Boswell's moral heritage inculcated by the Calvinistic doctrines of the Church of Scotland. At the time of Boswell's visit, Rousseau was suffering severely from urinary difficulties, chiefly painful and frequent micturition, the result of urethral stricture. It does not seem to have occurred to Boswell, at least he did not record it, that he too some day might be suffering from a stricture as a sequel of gonorrhea or that the lesion might be construed as a punishment. Within two weeks Boswell was at Ferney visiting Voltaire. Their conversation was brilliant, but Voltaire was too wily a dialectician to let himself be trapped into melodramatic antitheses between good and evil.

Boswell's travels in Italy brought him his fourth and fifth episodes of urethritis. Much of his time was spend in the company of Lord John Stuart Mountstuart, son of the earl of Bute, then George III's prime minister. Boswell picked up his new infection in Rome late in April 1765. Unpublished memoranda and an expense account for April 8, 11, and 15 record *"badinages à différentes réprises,"* and the memoranda record definite symptoms on April 29.[27] He was treated by James Murray, the Old Pretender's personal physician, who prescribed instillation of an unspecified medication into the urethra by syringe. The treatment was not very effective because Boswell did not follow Murray's advice in other matters. He continued to be sexually active though infected, never a wise course for a man suffering from urethritis or prostatitis. On May 1 he noticed that he had also contracted infection with crab lice; the entry is terse: "Discovered beasts. Shaved; ludicrous distress."[28]

Boswell's symptoms subsided and he set out for Venice with Lord Mountstuart in mid-June. He was probably not completely well, for he stopped off en route at Padua and consulted with Giovanni Battista Morgagni. The founder of the present day discipline of morbid anatomy, then eighty-three, conversed with Boswell in both Latin and Italian:

"Medicus, ut Natura, qui gradatim facit, et nihil per saltus!" [He was] quite against [my using] syringe. Sober living, little exercise, and let it heal up itself, and so [be] sure. For scurvy reburba [rhubarb] and goat milk. [Morgagni]: Nimis studui. Libris et cadaveribus versatus sum. Affect[io] hypochond [riaca]. Sumsi; equitans curavi. Ne sis solus. Posses vel curare vel fere idem. Ego 83 ann[os],—little drugs; never bled."[29]

Morgagni's leading principle was that a physician takes his cue from Nature, which proceeds step by step, never by leaps and bounds. The aged savant also remarked that he had studied too hard, having passed his life among his books and dissecting cadavers. This, he claimed, had induced hypochondria, one of Boswell's recurrent complaints, which he had cured by horseback riding. Boswell may have followed Morgagni's advice about discontinuing use of the inconvenient syringe, but he did not live soberly. He and Lord Mountstuart continued to swive their way through Italy. On arriving in Venice, they resumed their reckless habits. Writing to Rousseau a few months later (October 5) he recounts: "My fancy was stirred by the brilliant stories I had heard of Venetian courtesans. I went to see them, *et militavi non sine gloria*, but the wounds of my Roman wars were scarcely healed before I received fresh ones at Venice."[30]

Lord Mountstuart also contracted gonorrhea at the same debauch, probably from the same courtesan, an opera dancer.[31] Boswell considered his Venetian infection as a new one. The number of his exposures makes superinfection a strong possibility; certainly his Roman infection was not completely healed. Urethral discharge must have persisted until Boswell reached Florence, where there were further incidents of venereal exposure. At Florence he records: "Sent for Dr. Tyrrell who came and said you could not as man of honour (?) see a woman, as you would infect."[32] Tyrrell had been practicing in Florence for more than two decades and is mentioned in Sir Horace Mann's correspondence with Horace Walpole. Boswell summoned him two days later to order cassia and pay a fee of two zechins. Symptoms of urethritis persisted until after Boswell arrived at Siena on or about August 24, but there is not further mention of them.

At Siena Boswell managed to have an affair with Girolama Piccolomini, the wife of the Capitano di Popolo, an office equivalent to that of mayor, a scion of one of Siena's most honored families. His initial excursion with her was a failure; he could not have an erection. But later sessions must have been satisfactory, and they maintained a correspondence for some time. Boswell stayed in Siena until the end of September. In October he made his fortunate and politically important trip to Corsica. He identified himself with the cause of Corsican independence, became a confidant of General Pascal Paoli, and laid the foundation for his book, *An Account of Corsica* (1768), which thrust him into some public prominence. The chief medical complication of the Corsican trip was that Boswell developed ingrown toenails from hiking through the rough, mountainous terrain in tight-fitting boots. Recurrent infections of the toes were to plague him for many years thereafter.

Boswell returned to the mainland, where he was confronted with angry, sarcastic letters from his father, who demanded that he return home from his unauthorized jaunts. He returned by way of Paris, where he learned of his mother's death. *"January 27:* At Wilkes's saw in *St. James Chronicle,* mother's death. Quite stunned; tried to dissipate [grief]. Dined Dutch Ambassador's; much of Corsica. At six Mme. Hecquet's as in fever. Constance elegant."[33]

Madame Hecquet's was a fashionable bordello in Paris at the time. Boswell had a much different reaction when his father died about seventeen years later (see below). A letter confirming the sad news that Lady Auchinleck had died on January 11 arrived from home the next day. Boswell returned to England, ironically in the company of Thérèse Le Vasseur, Rousseau's "housekeeper" and mother of his four or five illegitimate children, who was on her way to join Rousseau during his visit to London. The pages of the journal describing their relation have been destroyed, but there is no doubt that Boswell and Thérèse carried on an affair.

On his return home Boswell spent the next three months studying Scots law and preparing his Latin thesis. He passed the examination in Scots Law on July 11, successfully defended his thesis on July 26, was admitted advocate that day, and put on his gown on July 29, 1766. His sixth attack of urethritis occurred in Edinburgh and began in March 1767, more than a year after he had begun to practice law. Shortly after finding himself a mistress in the person of a Mrs. Dodds and setting her up in her own establishment, he recorded giving a supper party for *"March 8:* . . . two or three of my acquaintances, having before I left Scotland laid a guinea that I should not catch the venereal disorder for three years. . . . We drank a great deal till I was so much intoxicated. . . . I went to a low house . . . where I knew a common girl lodged, and like a brute as I was lay all night with her. . . . Next morning I was like a man ordered for ignominious execution. But by noon I was worse, for I discovered that some infection had reached me."[34]

An incubation period of less than one day is not consistent with gonorrhea, and Boswell must have had some other form of urethritis. It was a year and a half since his Italian infection had subsided, and it seems unlikely that recrudescence of that infection would develop in half a day. Presumably, this attack of urethritis was "nonspecific." Boswell first consulted Peter Adie, an Edinburgh surgeon; then, on removing to Auchinleck after the Court of Session rose, Daniel Johnstone, a physician at Ayr. He records no data about treatment and was symptom free by April 17.

There seems little doubt that a seventh attack of urethritis was truly a new gonorrheal infection. A letter to Temple dated June 26, 1767, tells us that "I got myself quite intoxicated, went to a bawdy-house, and passed a whole night in the arms of a whore. She indeed was a fine, strong, spirited girl, a whore worthy of Boswell if Boswell must have a whore, and I apprehend no bad consequences."[35] His lack of apprehension was unjustified; a month later he had to confess to Temple: "*July 29:* . . . I shall stay a month here after the Session rises, and be cured. I am patient under it, as a just retribution for my licentiousness. But I greatly fear that Mrs. [Dodds] is infected, for I have been with her several times since my debauch and once within less than a week of the full appearance of mischief."[36]

In spite of Boswell's fears, Mrs. Dodds appears not to have become infected, as she later gave birth to Boswell's second illegitimate child. Though the little girl is thought to have died in infancy, there is no record that she was born with gonorrheal ophthalmitis, a strong probability were her mother actively infected. Also, Boswell continued his relation with Mrs. Dodds after the child was born, and there seems to have been no illness traceable to her.

The sixth and seventh episodes of urethritis mark an important change in Boswell's pattern of behavior. Up to this time we hear little about his drinking; though not a teetotaler—what sensible Scot is?—judged by the standards of his day, he had been relatively abstemious. The Edinburgh bar to which Boswell had been admitted advocate in 1766 was composed of some hearty drinkers, and for the first time Boswell began to drink to excess. The incident with the "common girl" while drunk was the first of many. Time and again in later years Boswell would get drunk at dinner with friends or colleagues, then roam the streets and wind up in bed with a whore. Boswell drank partly to demonstrate his conviviality and manliness and partly to mask his anxiety at being in such close propinquity with his father, living in his house, practicing in his courtroom. The conscience is that part of the psyche which is soluble in alcohol. The well-known effects of alcohol as a short term antidepressant and its ability to release inhibition may also have played a role in Boswell's increasing alcohol usage. But Pottle sums up Boswell's behavior with regard to liquor and sex: "For nothing is clearer in the repeated episodes in which Boswell whores while drunk than that he let himself get drunk in order to have a defence for whoring."[37] The syndrome is not unique to Boswell.

Boswell's seventh attack of urethritis seems to have begun early in July 1767; it continued into October of that year. He makes few allusions to it in his memoranda, notes, or journal, and it may have been symptomatically mild though prolonged in course. He was treated by Mr. Duncan Forbes, an Edinburgh surgeon, who was also

the medical officer of the Horse Guards. His eighth episode of urethritis is likewise only vaguely documented. Boswell seems to have
become so accustomed to this disease that he scarcely bothers to comment on it by this stage of his career, a striking contrast to the detail in
which he reports some of his earlier attacks. He was in Edinburgh for
the winter session of the court; by December 1767 Mrs. Dodds was far
advanced in her pregnancy, and he had recourse to prostitutes. A letter
to Temple dated December 24 tells us that "Amidst all this love I have
been as wild as ever. I have catched another memorandum of vice, but
a very slight one." His journal for January 16, 1768 records that "I was
ill of a venereal disorder."[38] But on that day he had intercourse with a
streetwalker "to try the experiment of cooling myself when ill." This
seems a singular form of self-treatment. He does not make the source
of his eighth infection explicit, nor does he mention his medical attendants and their suggested remedies. It is difficult to judge whether
this eighth episode was a recurrence of the seventh or a nonspecific
urethritis. Boswell had intercourse again on January 19 with Jenny
Kinnaird, an illegitimate daughter of Charles, sixth Lord Kinnaird,
after drinking malaga; he "was most amorous, being so well that no
infection remained."[39] He renewed sexual relations with Mrs. Dodds
on January 31 and February 2. Presumably whatever infection he
suffered had subsided into a gleet; on March 26 he writes: "I was still
apprehensive of some venereal mischief, and at any rate had the
remains of an old one, though without infection."[40] By this time his
urethral infection was so firmly established in its chronicity that he was
probably never without some form of discharge, usually clear. Boswell
believed that he had three separate and distinct attacks of gonorrhea
from 1767 to 1768 with complete recovery between them, a conclusion
which contemporary knowledge of gonorrhea untreated with antibi-
otics makes it difficult to assert with confidence.

When the winter session rose in March 1768, Boswell hastened to
London to renew his many friendships. The journal for this period was
not kept so regularly as before, but by April 21 he was suffering from a
new attack of gonorrhea, his ninth, contracted as the result of "roaring." Entries in his journal record relations with prostitutes on March
22, 23, 25, 29, and 30, but twelve pages of text have been torn out after
this date, and the next relevant, datable information comes from a
letter to his friend John Johnston dated April 25 in which he writes that
"Last year's evil was nothing to this."[41] The next day he wrote to
Temple that he was confined to his rooms "suffering severely for
immorality" and that his surgeon says "my distemper is one of the worst
he has seen."[42] A journal entry dated May 12 informs us that Scottish

acquaintance, Mr. Home of Billy, advised him to consult the famous Percivall Pott, whose eponym survives in a disease of the vertebrae, a fracture of the ankle, and a scrotal tumor of chimney sweeps.[43] Boswell did so, but failed to record Pott's recommendations. He was confined to his rooms in Half Moon Street, prevented from reaping the social kudos which was justly his, since his book on Corsica had been published the preceding winter and had occasioned much political stir. Indirect evidence suggests that this ninth attack of urethritis had cleared by June. Ironically, it was at the Green Canister in Half Moon Street that a Mrs. Philips offered condoms for sale in 1776; she sold out to a Mrs. Perkins, but soon reopened at a new location; their "war of handbills" is one of the more droll episodes in the history of contraception in England.[44]

Boswell returned to Edinburgh at the beginning of June 1768. During the two years he had been paying court to a number of eligible young ladies with a view to marriage. In the spring of 1769 he journeyed to Ireland to court Mary Anne Boyd, an attractive young heiress. He was accompanied on this errand of love by his first cousin, Margaret Montgomerie of Lainshaw, his father's niece. Neither the nature of his mission nor his companion was able to prevent him from contracting in May a new case of gonorrhea, the result of exposure in a brothel at Dublin, "one night of Irish extravagance" in the company of two army officers.[45] His symptoms began some time before May 29 and persisted through October, a period of five months. This illness came at an extremely awkward time for Boswell. He finally managed to resolve his emotional instability, and the acquaintanceship and camaraderie between him and Margaret Montgomerie matured into love; by August they were informally engaged. With much anxiety Boswell consulted a large number of medical men between May and October: his old friends Douglas, Forbes, and Pott, also John Gregory, then professor of medicine at the University of Edinburgh, and Sir John Pringle, the distinguished Scottish pioneer in military hygiene, who was a close friend and advisor. To make certain he had no lingering trace of venereal infection before marriage, he returned to London to take the "cure" offered by a much-advertised nostrum known as Kennedy's Lisbon Diet Drink. Professor Gregory did not rate it highly; he consented to Boswell's trip to London only "to put his mind at rest." Sir John Pringle advised against it, but Boswell was more impressed by the testimonial of a friend, Colin Campbell, who said the Lisbon Diet Drink had cured him after he had spent more than £300 in vain at Edinburgh.[46]

The Lisbon Diet Drink consisted chiefly of sarsaparilla with a little sassafras, licorice, and guaiac wood. It cost half a guinea for a pint bottle, a rather expensive medication considering that Boswell drank a bottle a day. The Gilbert Kennedy who profited by this medicament was a graduate of Rheims and Oxford, a pompous man then in his late seventies who had served for many years as physician to the British Factory at Lisbon. In addition to taking Kennedy's decoction, Boswell also followed the advice of Forbes and Pott to undergo a minor surgical procedure, probably a small incision in the prepuce to relieve paraphimosis. The journal records: *"October 16:* Yesterday morning Duncan Forbes came, and with kindness to save dire forebodings *cut. . . .* Then called Kennedy; nonsense. Then Pott; sensible, neat, and fine."[47]

There were no complications. Boswell returned to Scotland later that month and was married to Margaret Montgomerie on November 25, 1769. During the decade before his marriage, from the age of nineteen to almost twenty-nine, Boswell had had no less than ten attacks of urethritis; at least six of them were fresh primary attacks of gonorrhea. He did not contract a new infection for more than six years.

Boswell remained faithful to his wife for almost three years. She proved to be an excellent spouse—responsive, sympathetic, sensible, even economical. He worked hard at his legal practice; his articulacy won him a good reputation as a pleader; his income was fair and improving. His wife did not try to dissuade him from going to London between terms of court, but she preferred to remain in Scotland. In March 1772 we find Boswell in London after the winter Session: *"March 19:* As I walked up the Strand and passed through a variety of fine girls, genteelly dressed, all wearing Venus's girdle, all inviting me to amorous intercourse, I confess I was a good deal uneasy. . . . I resolved never again to come to London without bringing my wife along with me."[48]

Like so many of Boswell's high resolves this was never kept. His first lapse from marital fidelity occurred that autumn in Edinburgh. His wife had made a slow recovery from a miscarriage and was pregnant again. Though he was not keeping a daily journal at the time, his notes suggest cryptically another attack of urethritis; "after too much wine" he had resorted to a woman of the town and had "dire uneasiness" and "dreary fears" of the consequence.[49] His valuable wife knew all and made him send for a doctor. Without more documentation, this cannot be enumerated as a real attack; it was a "scare."

Despite his relative continence during the first few years of marriage, the journal records an ever-increasing number of episodes of intoxication. Boswell began to drink seriously in 1766, never alone, always with friends or colleagues; by 1774 he could have been fairly described as a regular drinker. To drinking he added gambling as an additional vice, albeit never for ruinous stakes. On occasion he would stay out all night, drinking and playing cards with fellow attorneys, while his wife waited up for him anxiously. Stormy scenes at home were inevitable; Boswell, contrite, would promise to reform, but never did. By the spring of 1775 he was readying his mind for fresh adventures: "I thought of my valuable spouse with the highest regard and warmest affection, but had a confused notion that my corporeal connexion with whores did not interfere with my love for her."[50] To which Ryskamp and Pottle subjoin the editorial comment that "Literature perhaps affords no fuller record of that slow process of self-deceit by which men of strong passions and weak wills prepare justification for indulging their appetites. With Boswell words were everything. Promiscuity . . . had an ugly sound in his ear, but concubinage was biblical."[51]

Accordingly, when Boswell visited London in April 1775, he pleaded this case with Sir John Pringle, who would have none of it, and with Dr. Johnson, who pointed out its sophistry. The precise score of his conquests in the spring of 1775 is not known, but he took precautions and did not contract infection.

Boswell was not so lucky when he visited London in March of the following year. He indulged in a compulsively riotous outburst of sexual activity; his journal records intercourse with prostitutes on March 29, 30, 31, and April 1. Symptoms, "though moderate ones," appeared on April 4. Two pages of the journal manuscript have been removed at this point, but enough remains to indicate that Boswell purchased some medication at an apothecary's, presumably in an attempt of self-treatment. The symptoms must have persisted, for on April 10 he consulted Sir John Pringle, who confirmed the diagnosis of a new episode of gonorrhea and referred him to Andrew Douglas for treatment. Douglas's ideas of therapy had changed since 1760 and 1763. He now prescribed an electuary, medication in a pill with added sweetening, rather than his customary lenitive, a mild laxative. Boswell adds: "He said there was now an injection which produced a speedy cure with great safety; that he had altered his opinion as to injections, and that Sir John Pringle approved of this, but it was a secret known only to a few."[52] By "injection" Boswell meant a urethral irrigant instilled by syringe; the hypodermic syringe had not yet been invented, and parenteral medication was unknown. The composition of the new safe irrigant remains unknown.[53] The usual urethral irrigants of the latter half of the eighteenth century were variously a dilute solution of vitriol, dilute nitrous acid, mercury salts (possibly because at that time gonorrhea was confused with the early stages of syphilis), a mixture of lead salts known as Goulard's extract, and any number of other acid or heavy-metal salt solutions. Doubtless each doctor had his favorite solution, and there must have been an almost infinite number of personal variations. One can only imagine the discomfort caused by instilling acid into an already inflamed, pus-producing urethra. If purulent exudate or coagula blocked the urethra, surgeons were accustomed to maintain its patency by inserting bougies and cannulas. Not uncommonly such instillations and instrumentation succeeded in forcing infected material from the anterior urethra into the posterior segment, thence into the prostrate. One can scarcely be astonished at the frequency with which chronic prostatitis developed or at the high rate of urethral stricture. (A century later Louis Napoleon died of uremia, the result of urinary calculi which formed as a complication of gonorrheal stricture of the urethra with urinary outflow-tract obstruction and secondary infection.) If all went well, the acute infection would subside, usually in four to six weeks, but an appalling number of cases became chronic.

Boswell began seeing Douglas on April 11; he records visits to both Pringle and Douglas through May 13, but makes no mention of his illness. The new treatment was probably fairly effective, as the disease lasted no more than six weeks. During this, his eleventh attack Boswell was again confined to his lodgings, a sad trial, for Boswell must be numbered among those who would far rather walk hand in hand with Thackeray through Vanity Fair than sail with Yeats to Byzantium. His infection probably had subsided when he returned to Scotland toward the end of May, but neither the journal nor extant notes specify when he resumed conjugal relations. It is reasonable to infer that he would not have approached his wife if he thought himself actively infected, but he did not uniformly record his relations with her.

Boswell's next two episodes of urethritis were contracted in Edinburgh, the twelfth in February 1778, the thirteenth in July 1780. Documentation is fragmentary, as his journal entries for the intervals in question are terse, but in both instances he had gone whoring while drunk[54] and developed symptoms a few days later. The episode of February 1778 was associated with fever, weakness, headache, and general malaise.[55] Such constitutional symptoms suggest more than a simple recurrent urethritis; they might indicate a severe prostatitis, but he may equally well have contracted a respiratory infection while wandering drunk in the streets of Edinburgh on a cold February night. Boswell consulted Alexander Wood and was apparently sick enough for Wood to see him three times on February 15. His constitutional symptoms seem to have abated by the eighteenth, but he was "not quite so well as to *morbus*" on the nineteenth.[56] Symptoms of urethritis must have persisted into March, as on March 5 he notes that he had had nothing but water to drink and on March 12 Wood advised him to use the post chaise instead of the coach to London.[57] He arrived in London on March 17, and his journal records his plans phrased with a metaphor which can be described only as singular in a man suffering from a venereal disorder: "I resolved to take London as one takes mercury; to intermit the use of it whenever I should feel it affect my brain, as one intermits the use of mercury when it affects the mouth."[58] There is no evidence that Boswell was ever treated with mercury or that he ever contracted syphilis, which would require it. Later (see below) he did develop what he calls "scurvy," i.e., some form of scorbuticlike skin lesions, but they do not suggest luetic origin. His choice of the clinical effects of mercury as a metaphor suggests that he may have unconsciously feared that his promiscuity might indeed expose him to the pox.

Unfortunately Boswell never wrote formal journal entries for the period of March 22 to May 23, and the course of his twelfth attack of urethritis can be followed only from rough, unpublished notes. On April 2 he consulted Sir John Pringle "and was made patient." He resumed relations with an old partner in extramarital relations; the notes refer to her cryptically as "36," probably the number of her house. On April 10 he notes: "Then hastened to 36. Not quite whole yet, but Sir John had said no ill, so was to try *balsamum femineum*. Not in." The following day the lady was at home when Boswell called, but "Sat awhile 36. Luckily was refused, as not certain yet." Two weeks later there was no problem; a note for April 25 states: "Away and met 36, vastly snug. . . . Twice refreshed." And on the following day: ". . . 36 said I was *better* than formerly." If this marks the end of his attack, it had lasted ten weeks.

Over two years elapsed between the twelfth and thirteenth attacks. Symptoms followed swiftly after he confessed to his wife that he had "wandered." He was exposed on July 14, 1780, told his wife the next day, and Alexander Wood was called on the seventeenth.[59] Boswell saw Wood on July 19, 23, and 29.[60] He took a dose of salts on July 30 and two days later walked to call on Sir John Pringle, who was visiting in Edinburgh. The exertion brought on a headache and possible recurrence of urinary symptoms, and he went to bed when he came home and summoned Wood. Boswell records visits to Wood on August 6 and 14. By September 17 his health was almost fully restored but he did not resume conjugal relations until December 28, when Wood assured him he was free of infection.[61] Margaret Boswell seems to have escaped gonorrheal infection only because she was aware of her husband's disease and proclivities and because he did have enough good sense to abstain from sexual relations with her when there was a chance of infection.

The next infection, Boswell's fourteenth, is not materially different in quality. He had gone to London in March 1781, had pursued his usual run of intellectual and physical pleasures, and on May 1 had had intercourse with a prostitute while drunk.[62] The journal is somewhat mutilated, but symptoms began on May 7. There is no record of his consulting any of his usual physicians, but there are notes of self-medication; he took salts on May 14 and peppermint drops for headache and giddiness on May 17.[63] Fragmentary jottings indicate that he was "not well" from May 7 through 25, but on that day he "ventured again" with a girl just the other side of Westminster Bridge.[64] By June 19 he was back in Edinburgh and uneasy that his indisposition was not abating, but Boswell then believed himself noninfective.[65]

It is easy enough to round out the history. Boswell's father died in 1782 and he became the ninth Laird of Auchinleck. His wife began to develop signs and symptoms of pulmonary tuberculosis in 1777, had well-established disease by 1779, and by the middle of the 1780s was ill more often than well. In 1786 Boswell made an ill-advised move to leave the Edinburgh bar and try to practice law in London. He attracted no clients and his income was sharply reduced. Samuel Johnson had died in December 1784, and there was no one left to brake his downhill course. His fifteenth attack of urethritis was contracted at Edinburgh in December 1783. Documentary evidence of exposure, onset of symptoms, and medical treatment is lacking because pages of the journal for November 26 through December 12 have been removed. The last previous entry is ironic: *"November 25:* This being my wedding day, I most sincerely renewed my most affectionate vows to my valuable Spouse."[66] A number of jottings testify to his illness and confinement to his home; those include advice on January 18 from Alexander Wood to continue medication for twelve more days.[67] His health was almost restored by February 4, and on February 14 he resumed conjugal relations with his ailing wife.[68]

Boswell remained wholly free of new disease for a year and a half. He contracted no infection in 1784, the year of Dr. Johnson's death, but in May 1785 he paid his annual visit to London and, while there, established a continuing relation with Betsey Smith, a prostitute. His first contact with her was after an evening of drinking on May 12, but he

visited her again on the next two days.[69] Symptoms of urethritis developed on May 16, and Boswell sought medical advice from Giuseppe,
General Paoli's servant.[70] Boswell must have felt either an attachment
or responsibility for Betsey Smith quite different from his usual post-
coital regrets for, on learning that she too was ill, he called on James
Ware, a surgeon, and arranged for her to enter St. Thomas's Hospital.
His expense account shows that he paid her entrance fee: "Admission,
Betsey, to St. Thomas's . . .10/6," and he gave her some pocket money
as well.[71] The same expense account shows that he too was still having
symptoms. The day after Betsey crossed Westminster Bridge and
entered St. Thomas's, Boswell records the purchase of sulphurated
pills for 2/8 and mercurial pills for 6d., a more specific clue to the
nature of his disease than a previous entry on May 27 for unspecified
"Medicines."[72] This sounds suspiciously like self-medication based on
long personal experience with the disease. The medical record is
somewhat confused by Boswell's libertinism. Boswell had relations with
another prostitute on June 22 while Betsey was still in hospital, and six
days later he was taken ill in the street with sudden chills and fever.[73]
The following day he consulted "Mr. Hayward" (doubtfully identified
as John Heawood, a surgeon in Southwark) who prescribed an ape-
rient. Boswell took physic on June 30; it operated briskly, and he was
relieved by July 1 and "vastly well" by July 5.[74]

After Betsey Smith was discharged from St. Thomas's, Boswell tried
to persuade her to seek employment in domestic service; this was his
first effort at reforming any of the prostitutes he had used. His own
symptoms abated gradually; an entry in his expense account for July 22
shows that he paid Percivall Pott one guinea; Pott declared him free
from infection, but on August 1 Boswell dutifully enters the purchase
of "Medecines [sic]," but there is no clue as to the use for which they
were intended.[75]

Less than a year later Boswell was back in London trying to initiate a
practice as a lawyer. His wife had not yet come down to London; that
disastrous journey lay a year ahead. Boswell had been carrying on an
affair with Margaret Caroline Rudd, a woman of some notoriety who
had been acquitted of forgery in 1775; Boswell had first met her the
following year, but their liaison did not begin until the autumn of 1785;
it continued through the winter and spring.[76] At this time Boswell was
beginning to work on his *Life of Johnson;* the combination of lack of legal
business and a literary task left him abundant free time. Precisely how
he developed his seventeenth episode of urethritis is not certain. It may
have come from Mrs. Rudd, but it may equally have been the result of
sexual contacts not otherwise recorded. The journal entry for Febru-

ary 22, 1786, records that he "took an impatient fit to see M. C. Visited there. Not well. No meeting for some time."[77] One cannot decide whether it was Boswell or Mrs. Rudd who was not well, but the next relevant entry on February 24 makes it seem as if she were the one who was ill: "Sat two hours [with M. C.], and was assured this was a very flattering attention, when, on account of certain reasons best known to *our*selves, there could be no gratification of one kind."[78]

The journal and notes for the next six or seven weeks are silent about symptoms suggesting urethral disease, but by April 14 Boswell is certainly suffering from urethritis: "Had resisted seeing M.C. Winter [i.e., George Winter, a surgeon] called and gave advice as to medicines. Was comforted. . . . Then [strange prescription for illness!] Polly Wilson."[79] Polly Wilson was a prostitute with whom Boswell had had connection before, and one wonders whether the "strange prescription" was an idea which occurred to him on the spur of the moment when he met her by chance in the street. Precisely what Winter prescribed is not known, nor can any date be assigned to the subsidence of Boswell's seventeenth episode of urethritis. We do know that on April 20 he read John Hunter's newly published *A Treatise on the Venereal Disease* and was depressed for several weeks.[80]

The next four years slipped by rapidly and Boswell's fortunes slowly declined. He continued to work on his *Life of Johnson,* tried to add to his income by legal work and political preferment, but without much success. In 1786 his faithful wife moved down to London and shared his squalid house in Great Queen Street, but her health broke and she returned to Auchinleck, where she died in 1789; she left Boswell five adolescent children to rear and educate. By this time he was a habitual drinker and, apart from his great work on the *Life,* his last decade was one of tragic failure. To be sure, Boswell was not a solitary drinker, but he regularly drank to excess when in society and to such an extent that he could not control his conduct. Like most members of the upper class of his day, he rarely drank whiskey. Most of his references indicate that port, claret, malaga, and other wines were his customary fare.[81]

Innumerable entries in Boswell's journal testify that he could foresee his debacle but was powerless to stop it. His only triumphs were literary: he published the *Journal of a Tour to the Hebrides with Samuel Johnson, LL.D.* in 1785, less than a year after his great friend and father figure died. But the frank disclosures and accurate reporting of real conversations made him socially suspect, and even, in some quarters, unwelcome. Without the sympathetic encouragement and practical editorial help of Edmond Malone—sometimes given almost daily—he would never have finished the *Life of Johnson,* which finally appeared in 1791.

Even in the hour of his triumph he could see his end: "I was as on a board on which fine figures had been painted, but which some corrosive application had reduced to its original nakedness."[82] The medically prescient reader will not be surprised to learn that Boswell's urethra finally developed a stricture. A brief, pathetic journal entry for January 31, 1790 records: "Earle's; was sounded; almost fainted."[83]

There were several visits to Earle in Hanover Square at this time: Boswell must have suffered dolefully. James Earle was Percivall Pott's son-in-law, the most adroit surgeon at St. Bartholomew's at the time, famous for his skill at lithotomy, later a Master of the College of Surgeons. He succeeded to his father-in-law's practice after Pott died in 1788. Boswell first records consulting Earle on January 28, and Earle, in accordance with accepted surgical principles, saw Boswell again on February 2, three days after the sounding. As usual Boswell became something more than a patient. He had counted many of his doctors as his friends, and Earle too must have found his lively conversation stimulating, for Boswell's list of social engagements notes that he had dinner at Mr. Earle's on March 18 and again on May 1.[84] By this time his inevitable *descensus Averni* was plain. The diagnosis of post-gonorrheal urethral stricture and the passage of a sound took place only three weeks after Boswell had been arrested and confined over-night by the guard for being "riotous," i.e., making a public disturbance while drunk, a fate more suitable for attendants upon a saloon bar than the courtroom bar.

Boswell's nineteenth episode of urethral disease, his last before his final illness, took place less than six months after the sounding. He contracted his disease in London from a prostitute after drinking: "I had eat and drunk a little at Lord Lonsdale's . . . I was heated. I rashly went three times in the course of this day to a stranger. I was feverish."[85]

Boswell slept poorly that night and was hot and feverish the next day. This does not suggest gonorrheal urethritis either newly acquired or recurrent, but it is consistent with ascending infection of the urinary tract with prostatic or renal involvement. Boswell was trying to obtain political preferment and public office through Lord Lonsdale, whose political machinations made it necessary for Boswell, ill though he was, to accompany him to Carlisle. His illness persisted and he debated over a number of remedies.[86] By June 22 he had difficulty in walking, great pain, and a "sore," presumably on his genitalia. On June 26 he wrote to Earle for advice and on June 30 wrote to Malone, "I am again unfortunate enough to have *one* sore of a certain nature, contracted, I think, Monday fortnight, which *alone* gives me more pain and alarm than several which I had lately. . . . I have for twelve days followed Mr. Earle's method, without any seeming effect."[87] Precisely what this "sore" was is not certain. It was inflammatory and tended to mortification, but it was probably not a primary chancre of syphilis in view of the fact that he had had several like it before.[88] On July 4 Boswell went to a local barber and operated on his own sore; he may have repeated the operation the following day.[89] Whatever the nature of his complaint was, he was somewhat improved when he returned to London on July 15, records that he "lived generously" on July 19, and by August 1 was having sexual intercourse again.[90] The most likely explanation is that his sexual activity in June aggravated his chronic prostatitis, that secondary infection supervened, and that the "sore" was some form of local pyogenic abscess.

Precisely how Boswell apparently escaped syphilis is unknown, a matter of luck more than caution or cerebration. He did suffer from a succession of cutaneous complaints from the age of thirty-nine, and he was often worried that a given lesion might be "a taint from my Pleasance adventure."[91] But the lesion of July 1779 is described as an excoriation and in November as a "scurvy" covering his thighs and legs.[92] In December 1784 the "scurvy" involved his scalp, and the scorbutic complaint recurred in November 1792; it involved different parts of the body.[93] Although dermatologic complications of syphilis may mimic almost any lesion, recurrent skin eruptions from 1779 to 1792 and a series of genital and possibly perineal "sores" in 1790 form a slender thread upon which to diagnose syphilis, especially in a man who consulted many well-trained physicians and whose propensity for venery and its disorders was known to them.

Over the next five years Boswell's position slowly deteriorated. Publication of the *Life* gave him his day of glory. It may have ensured his reputation for posterity, but it did little for his immediate personal problems. Slowly he sank in fortune and men's eyes until on April 14, 1795, he collapsed at a dinner of the Literary Club. According to Farington's diary he had to be carried home: "Boswell this day attended the Literary Club, and went from thence too ill to walk home."[94] The initial symptoms were chills and fever, violent headache, and nausea. Boswell survived until May 19 in a state of great weakness and pain; the location and character of the pain are nowhere stated. Some clues to the nature of Boswell's last illness can be found in his last correspondence, and these must be viewed in the light of his past history, especially as neither he nor his son James, Jr., who was in attendance, was a trained medical observer or even attempted an objective analysis of signs and symptoms.

Boswell recognized that his illness was serious, and the letter he dictated to his friend William Temples strikes a note of guarded optimism. He dictated it to his son, James, Jr., on April 17, three days after the onset of illness: "My father desires me to tell you 'that on Tuesday evening he was taken ill with a fever of cold attended with a severe shivering and violent headache, disorder and throwing up. He has been close confined to bed ever since. He thinks himself better today but cannot conjecture when he shall recover.' "[95]

Under the ministrations of Richard Warren, Boswell improved somewhat but continued weak. His mind was clear, but he was not strong enough to write in his own hand a letter congratulating Warren Hastings on his acquittal; it was dictated to an amanuensis on April 24. Boswell apologizes for not having been able to pay his compliments in person inasmuch as "He has ever since Tuesday se'night been close confined to bed with a severe and alarming fever. . . . Dr. Warren now gives him the pleasing assurance that his sufferings are nearly at an end."[96] One trusts that the ambiguity implicit in the phrase attributed to Dr. Warren was unintentional. Whatever his doctors told him, Boswell must have interpreted optimistically. Apparently, he felt better and seemed to be improving.

An ominous note is sounded in a letter from Thomas David Boswell, Boswell's younger brother, to Temple, dated May 4, 1790, three weeks after the illness began: "I am sorry to say my poor brother is in the most imminent danger; a swelling in his bladder has mortified, but he is yet alive, and God Almighty may restore him to us."[97] This letter localizes Boswell's illness to his lower urinary tract, which suggests urinary retention with heavy contamination of the retained urine producing gross pyuria, but prostatic abscess cannot be excluded. Viewed in terms of the onset of illness—chills, fever, headache, nausea—the most likely diagnosis is acute hematogenous pyelonephritis complicating urethral stricture; this entity seems to dominate the picture. Needless to say, this disease could not have been diagnosed clinically in 1795 nor for the next century or more.

Silence masks the events of the next four days. Boswell may even have rallied a little; the "mortification" his brother described may have been the passage of coagula of purulent urine, affording some measure of relief. If this conjecture is correct, Boswell presumably had pyoureter and pyonephrosis in addition to the acute and chronic cystitis and the all-important pyelonephritis. On May 8 his son, James, Jr., wrote again to Temple:

My father still being unable to write I again give you what information I can, which is only that he continued for a considerable time since I wrote last to be in a state of extraordinary pain and weakness.

He is now, I thank God, a great deal recovered and the pain has almost gone. The greatest care is taken of him. The advice of Dr. Warren, Mr. Earle the surgeon, Mr. Devaynes the apothecary, and Mr. Hingston who has been bred up under him, have all in their different departments contributed towards the recovery.[98]

The tone is optimistic, and latter-day readers will be pleased that Boswell received the benefit of four professional medical advisers; he did not die neglected. Boswell made a gallant but feeble attempt to add a few words to Temple in his own hand; he bravely began the salutation and opening sentence, but the writing is barely legible. Boswell recognized this and dictated the rest to his son. The manuscript is touching to see, the scrawl of a dying man, the last words that inveterate and diligent scrivener committed to paper.

I would fain write you with my own hand, but realy canot [*sic*] [Boswell's hand breaks off here]. My son James is to write for me what remains of this letter, and I am to dictate. The pain which continued for so many weeks was very severe indeed and when it went off I thought myself quite well; but I soon felt a conviction that I was by no means as I should be, being exceedingly weak, as my miserable attempt to write you afforded full proof. All, then, that can be said is that I must wait with patience. . . . I feel myself a good deal stronger today, notwithstanding the scrawl.[99]

Boswell's façade of optimism was not justified, and a postscript by his son to Temple on the same sheet reveals an important point: "You will find by the foregoing . . . that he is ignorant of the dangerous situation in which he was and, I am sorry to say, still continues to be.—Yesterday and today he has been somewhat better, and we trust that the nourishment which he is now able to take and his strong constitution will see him through."[100]

Apparently, Boswell had been suffering from persistent nausea and vomiting. His son and medical attendants could appreciate the dangers of prolonged malnourishment even though the subtleties of dehydration and electrolyte imbalance were not yet known. That the vomiting was persistent indicates that uremia had developed as the kidneys were being destroyed by pressure and infection. Boswell seems to have held his temporary improvement of May 8 for a few days longer, for five days after the letter of James, Jr., to Temple,[101] Thomas David Boswell wrote to him on May 13:

I wrote to you on the 4th instant when my Brother was in very great danger; I have now the pleasure of acquainting you that he is better, and that good hopes are entertained of his recovery; the nature of the disease will render it tedious, particularly as he is very weak.

[P.S.] My Brother has not been so well this last night; I hope by my next to give you better accounts.[102]

The night of May 12 probably marked a crisis in Boswell's disease; one infers that he relapsed, never to recover, and the postscript to his brother's letter can be taken as a prognostic guide. Nausea and vomiting recurred, and Boswell grew rapidly weaker. Two further letters from James, Jr., to Temple dated May 16 and May 18 respectively indicate the progressive downhill course and rapid clinical deterioration:

May 16, 1795: My father received your letter yesterday which I read to him as he was unable to do it himself. He continues much in the same state as he was when I wrote last. He is very weak, but it is to be hoped that, by taking a sufficient quantity of nourishment, he will recover strength and health.[103]

May 18, 1795: I am sorry to inform you that, since I wrote last, my father is considerably worse; he is weaker, and almost all the nourishment he takes comes off his stomach again. He has expressed a very earnest desire to be lifted out of bed, and Mr. Earle, the surgeon, though it might be done with safety. But his strength was not equal to it, and he fainted away. Since then he has been in a very bad way indeed, and there are now, I fear, little or no hopes of his recovery.[104]

Uncontrolled vomiting and retching are consistent with terminal uremia, and the profound weakness was the result of both. There is no comment about urinary output; we may infer oliguria from decreased intake. Not even the strongest constitution is proof against progressive renal failure. Boswell died on May 19, 1795; a letter from his brother to Temple gives the hour: "*May 19, 1795:* I have now the painful task of informing you that my dear brother expired this morning at two o'clock; we have both lost a kind, affectionate friend, and I shall never have such another."[105]

The paleodiagnosis based on literary remains is uremia, the result of acute and chronic urinary tract infection, secondary to postgonorrheal urethral stricture. In the absence of an autopsy the precise anatomic changes remain uncertain; one cannot exclude the possibility of prostatic abscess or renal abscess as the precipitating event for the terminal illness, but there is no need to postulate such relatively infrequent complications. Chronic urinary tract infection may smolder insidiously for a number of years accompanied only by intermittent low-grade fever and malaise until the terminal stage. Renal function becomes gradually impaired as the process continues. The patient may seem in fairly good health despite elevated blood pressure and moderate nitrogen retention, neither of which could be estimated in Boswell's day. Customarily an acute episode presages the final phase. Boswell's collapse at the Literary Club with chills and fever, a violent headache, nausea, and vomiting suggests an acute recrudescence of the smoldering infection, and the swelling in (or of) the bladder with mortification two or three weeks later substantiates the clinical suspicion of urinary retention and acute sepsis behind it. By the time this stage is reached, the entire urinary outflow tract is infected and the renal parenchyma irretrievably compromised. It is not inaccurate to say that Boswell died of the complications of his many episodes of gonorrhea.

We have followed Boswell through nineteen episodes of urethral disease, of which at least twelve must be reckoned as new primary cases of gonorrhea, one a nonspecific urethritis, one the development of a urethral stricture about thirty years after his first attack, and the others as recrudescences of subsiding recent infections. With this medical history in mind we must return to the original question: Why should a man of good family, considerable education, adequate professional status, a satisfactory wife, and prominent social connections deliberately expose himself to the risk of gonorrhea? His journals, candid in so many respects, furnish a number of clues which permit an approximate answer. The decisive, determining elements were his relation with his father, his religious upbringing, and his own psychosexual development.

Boswell's father, Alexander Boswell, eighth laird of Auchinleck, was a distinguished Scottish jurist in addition to being one of the landed gentry. In 1754, when he was forty-seven years old, he was appointed one of the fifteen judges of the Court of Session, the highest civil bench in Scotland, and in 1755, in addition, one of the six judges comprising the High Court of Justiciary, the highest criminal bench in Scotland. Though this conferred no hereditary patent of nobility, he was entitled to style himself Lord Auchinleck. He was a conservative Whig and a staunch Presbyterian, eminently respectable and highly respected. He was a man of great rigidities, unerringly certain of what was right and what was wrong, what was proper and what was improper. Though he had a strong sense of family, especially his family's status, he was unloving as a parent. Stiff and unbending, he wore his red judicial robes within the bosom of his family. He had a strong sense of both property and propriety; his chief fear was that his eldest son would squander his inheritance or by light-hearted conduct disgrace the family, or both.

There was little doubt in Lord Auchinleck's mind about his prescriptive right to control his son and decide what pattern young Boswell's life would take. He had long determined that his son and heir would be a lawyer, and a lawyer he made him. Boswell's flight from Glasgow to London in 1760 and his flirtation with Roman Catholicism were the first overt symptoms of his effort to throw off the paternal yoke. Boswell's reluctance to choose the law as a career may very well have stemmed from a feeling of insecurity, a sense of inadequacy to compete with his father in the profession in which the latter had been so successful. There is sufficient evidence of "instability" dating from his childhood to make such a suggestion plausible. As a child he suffered severely from many terrors, notably the fear of ghosts. Many of his fears were tinged with religious fantasies, especially those connected with punishment and eternal damnation, even before the age of ten. Boswell records that until his eighteenth year he was unable to sleep alone at night. At the age of five he had been sent to a day school but had to be withdrawn and tutored at home because of his "delicate health," a term which fails to define any recognizable symptoms or syndrome, but which might be construed to imply excessive timidity and dependence on his mother. When the subject of metaphysics was introduced into the course of logic he took as an undergraduate at the University of Edinburgh in 1756–57, the introspection it initiated served to send Boswell, then no more than seventeen, into a serious depression, which he later described under the then fashionable term, hypochondria. Young Boswell recovered without psychotherapy—there was none in those days—and was able to finish his formal education in 1758 without further evidence of "delicacy."

Boswell suffered from this "hypochondria" intermittently for the rest of his life. Today we should probably describe it as episodic depression. This does not imply that Boswell was psychotic; such recurrent depressions of moderate degree are not uncommon in neuroses. Boswell's "hypochondria" implies a lability of mood; his affect was easily depressed for no apparent external cause. His journals are filled with allusions to it and, in later life, when he was part owner of the *London Magazine*, he contributed to it a series of monthly essays titled *The Hypochondriack*, seventy in all, from 1777 to 1783. Boswell's emotional lability did not always take the form of depression; he records instances of boisterous good spirits, even elation, again for inadequate external cause, but his predominant deviation from even humor was depressive. It is possible that Boswell cultivated his "hypochondria" to some extent; it was in literary vogue at the time, so much so that it was called by some "the English sickness." However, he did have reason to fear mental breakdown. His younger brother John (born 1743) became a lieutenant in the army but became mentally ill in his twenties. Boswell's uncle, John Boswell, his father's younger brother and a physician in Edinburgh, also suffered from similar episodic depressions, and the two would frequently exchange gloomy views on the notion of a family taint. Later, one of Boswell's daughters suffered from a form of mental aberration characterized by paranoid ideas, possibly a form of paranoid schizophrenia.

Boswell's relations with his father deteriorated over the years. True, his father had generously given him a year in London (1762–63) after he had completed the first part of his legal qualifications. But Lord Auchinleck was firm in his resolve about his son's career and would do nothing to back Boswell's hope of getting a commission in the Guards. There is even a suggestion that he may have used his influence sub rosa to frustrate the young man's hopes. But the fact that the eldest son of a prominent judge and landholder could not buy his commission was prima facie evidence that the father was opposed to the scheme. After Boswell faithfully pursued and completed his studies in Utrecht, Lord Auchinleck generously gave him permission to make a somewhat limited tour of northern Europe. True, Boswell used this experience to good advantage, but he extended the tour unduly and at no inconsiderable expense, putting off to the bitter end his return to Scotland and a career at the bar. One must admit that the end of Boswell's grand tour was sordid: after learning of his mother's death he repaired to a bordello; on his trip from Paris to London he carried on an affair with Rousseau's ex-mistress.

Even in the interval between his admission to the Scottish bar and his marriage, Boswell's conduct was designed to demonstrate his independence of his father and his disregard for his father's standards. He dabbled in literature, anathema to his father. He consorted with "gay blades" and acquired a reputation as a "man about town," a reputation for semipublic intoxication and furtive whoring late at night. In a small city with an upper class which was both self-limited and self-perpetuating, as Edinburgh was in the 1760s, his behavior could scarcely have been unknown to his father, and even our own tolerant age cannot find Lord Auchinleck's distrust of his son unjustified. Boswell showed little inclination to conform to the image of what his father wanted him to be.

Boswell's marriage marked a major crisis in the father-son relation. Lord Auchinleck had always wanted his son to marry a sound and sensible girl of good family and fair fortune. He could not complain about "family" when Boswell announced his intention of marrying

Margaret Montgomerie, his first cousin. She was sound and sensible, and she was Lord Auchinleck's own niece. Unfortunately, she was almost penniless, and this was, for him, a disqualifying defect. All the more so as his Lordship, then sixty-two years old, a widower for more than three years, was contemplating remarriage (despite a recent attack of obstructive prostatic disease) and wanted to see his son financially independent. Boswell was aware of his father's plans and had remonstrated with him, not only out of deference to his late mother, but from the feeling that such a parade of an old man's sexuality would reduce his father to *turpe senilis amor, peccet ad extremum ridendum*— (nothing is so ridiculous as an old man's passion).[106]

There were also material considerations. On many previous occasions Lord Auchinleck had threatened to sell off his estate and disinherit all his sons. To be sure, he could not do that, as the estate was entailed. But he had added considerable land to it by his own purchase, and this portion he could have sold or bequeathed to a child of a second marriage. Moreover, Boswell's expected income could be materially reduced by his father's provision for his widow's jointure and annuities for her children. Not only was this a real threat but it was made by a distinguished lawyer and judge. Boswell did not recognize that there was a legal limitation upon his father's control of his inheritance until he was permitted to see the marriage contract between his father and mother which had never been registered at Register House. He did not make this discovery until October 1778, by which time he had been married for nine years and was the father of four children.[107] The occasion of Boswell's marriage was neither the first nor the last time that Lord Auchinleck threatened disinheritance.

Lord Auchinleck did not attend his son's wedding to Margaret Montgomerie at her family's home at Lainshaw on November 25, 1769. That day he was fulfilling a previous engagement at Edinburgh by marrying as his second wife Elizabeth Boswell, a spinster of forty who was also his first cousin, the daughter of his father's younger brother, John Boswell of Balmuto. History records few more striking examples of the use of synchronous sexual competition by a father to perpetuate castration anxiety in his son.

Boswell's unsatisfactory relations with his father were not an unmixed curse. Much of his young manhood was spent in an unconscious search for a father substitute, an older man who, unlike Lord Auchinleck, would advise him unselfishly and uncensoriously. One has but to mention his visits to Rousseau and Voltaire, his long attachment to General Paoli, and his profoundly deferential attachment to Dr. Johnson. Men of even less fame could serve him in this role, and serve him well; Sir David Dalrymple, later Lord Hailes, a famous Scottish jurist, advised him on many occasions about his conduct in legal affairs, and Sir John Pringle was another man of distinction in a learned profession to whom he often turned. Boswell had written to Pringle about his affair with Mrs. Dodds and his gonorrhea. Sir John knew Boswell's character and gave him sound fatherly advice, but in a tone whereby the advice might be heeded, vide a letter in December 1767:

I was amused, as I have been before on the like occasion, with your confidence about your success. I have commonly observed that vanity is for the most part punished by mortifying the person in the very thing in which he most prides himself. . . . You have had, it seems, too much success upon less honorable terms with a weak one of the fair sex. I hope you have as sincerely repented of that action, as you must have done of that act which brought you into the condition in which Mr. Forbes saw you—[viz., gonorrhea contracted from the "common girl" while drunk]. If you have not repented, and with great compunction too, be assured that your misfortunes are not at an end, and that Providence . . . will not cease to chastise you till you cry *peccavi*.[108]

Sound advice indeed, but Boswell did not take Sir John's strictures to heart. Apparently, he felt that to cry *peccavi* to the pages of his journal was sufficient to absolve him. Page after page records his self-reproach for his errors and sins, but he did not modify his conduct. Such constantly repeated self-mortification is a frequent device used by a neurotic depressive personality to exteriorize guilt by shamelessly exposing misdeeds to scrutiny.

Boswell's religious upbringing had taught him that gambling, drinking, and whoring were wrong. It is not necessary to parade the theology and ethic of Scottish Calvinism and the High Church of Scotland. Boswell's mother was pietistic to the point of superstition. He records that on almost every Sunday as a little boy he went to church with his family, sometimes as often as three times during the day, hearing three sermons, each no doubt filled with its promise of fire and brimstone. Again we return to his statement to Rousseau that "the eternity of punishment was the first great idea I ever formed." Again we note the vocabulary in which he judged Louisa guilty of sin and deserving of punishment. Again we note his morbid interest in hangings. But even religious teaching could not inhibit Boswell's gonadal urges. Shortly after his reception into the Roman Catholic church on his first visit to London in 1760 he was initiated into sexual intercourse. On his second trip in 1762 he went to divine service on his second Sunday in the city. At Saint James's Church in Piccadilly he heard a sermon on the text "Wherewithal shall a young man cleanse his way?"[109] His journal records that "In the midst of divine service I was laying plans for having women, and yet I had a most sincere feeling of religion. . . . I have a warm heart and a vivacious fancy."[110] So much for the Church of England as a guide for Boswell's perplexities! Or for that matter the Kirk of Scotland, or any other church. His was a "piety that seldom issues in righteousness."

The religious ideas inculcated in Boswell as a youth are almost inextricable from his account of his psychosexual development. The information comes from the autobiographic sketch he wrote for Rousseau in 1765. The completed sketch was preceded by two outlines; parts of a discarded first draft and several discarded leaves from the final draft also survive. Boswell tells us: "At thirteen I was sent to the University. There I had more freedom. . . . My youthful desires became strong. I was horrified because of the fear that I would sin and be damned. It came into my troubled mind that I ought to follow the example of Origen. But that madness passed."[111] Boswell is not the only young man to have had night terrors, anxiety about sin, and thoughts of self-castration as the result of Calvinism. Two centuries later, after hundreds of "confessions" and case histories this has become a familiar tale. But there is even more information in portions of the autobiographical sketch which Boswell discarded: "Already (age 12–13) in climbing trees, pleasure. Could not conceive what it was. Thought of heaven. Returned often, climbed, felt, allowed myself to fall from high branches in ecstasy—all natural. Spoke of it to the gardener. He, rigid, did not explain."[112] This seems to be a relatively clear description of early orgasms at puberty induced by friction against a tree trunk, not an uncommon experience. That the orgasms were spontaneous is attested by the phrase "all natural." At about this time Boswell fell deeply in love with a Miss Mackay, but his tutor ridiculed him. He informs us: "I knew about the rites of Venus. But unfortunately I learned from a playmate the fatal practice [viz., masturbation]. I was always in fear of damnation. I thought that what I was doing was but a small sin, whereas fornication was horrible."[113]

When this is viewed with mid-twentieth-century "enlightenment," one cannot help feeling a certain pity for the guilt-ridden boy, but his predicament was not only far from unique but extremely frequent in pious and observant households with strict views on sexual morality. The stock example of the minister's son springs readily to mind, and Boswell, the judge's son, conducted himself in the tradition of that cliche. One additional inference seems plausible: Boswell's knowledge of the "rites of Venus" was probably imperfect and inaccurate; whatever he knew, he did not learn it from his mother or father.

Boswell retained his guilt about masturbation and probably practiced it infrequently as an adult. The journal alludes to it only infrequently and indirectly. A memorandum written at Geneva on December 26, 1764, shortly after leaving Voltaire, reads: "Yesterday . . . at night low lasciviousness. Have a care. Swear with drawn sword never *pleasure* but with a woman's aid."[114] Significantly, this passage remained in memoranda and he did not transcribe it into his journal proper. Few such hints are to be found. Like so many individuals who feel guilt about a specific sexual act, Boswell could not even mention masturbation without adding a self-exculpatory pejorative comment. Even as early as 1758 in a letter to Temple he wrote: "When at London, please buy for me the little pamphlet against Onania, a crime too little regarded. The title is curious. I should like to see it."[115]

Quite correctly, in his account of his affair with Louisa, Boswell describes his *anxiety* and assigns it as the cause of his temporary lack of potentia. His journals record a few subsequent instances of difficulty in this respect, but most of them seem to have occurred after drinking. Not long after he had recovered from the gonorrhea he contracted from Louisa he was introduced to a Miss Temple, who was being kept by a man of means but who dispensed her favors freely as the spirit moved her. Boswell relates the *chagrin d'amour* he felt in the following entry:

June 5, 1763. She was in fine spirits; gave me strawberries and cream, and used every endearing amorous blandishment. But alas! my last night's rioting and this morning's indulgence, joined with my really being in love with her, had quite enervated me, and I had no tender inclinations. I made an apology very easily; and she was very good, and said it happened very commonly after drinking. However, I was much vexed.[116]

He made use of the same rationalization when he could not get an erection with Girolama Piccolomini some two years later: "*September 10, 1765.* Then Jirol [ama]—quite agitated—put on Cund[um] enter'd—heart beat fell—quite sorry—but said *segno ver[a] Pass[ione]*."[117] This time he had not been drinking, and his protestation that it was true love which had rendered him impotent sounds a bit thin. The same argument had been used almost a century before by the earl of Rochester in *The Imperfect Enjoyment.* But the most pathetic instance of Boswell's occasional lack of potentia occurs at the beginning of that volume of his journal so aptly titled *The Ominous Years. October 5, 1774:* "Dined at Sir George Preston's. . . . I sauntered awhile in the streets, returned to Sir George's for supper. Had heated myself and catched cold. Drank to intoxication. *conat."[118]

The note "*conat" signifies a failed attempt at coitus with his wife when he returned home that night. One speculated whether this was the first of many such instances and that Boswell did not bother to record them. He came home drunk so many nights! The last reference to his own impotence occurred again in Edinburgh. He had dined at Baron Gordon's; there was much noise and drinking. Boswell concludes his account of the day's events with: *"December 14, 1777. Sat till near 12. Wandered but incapax. Home about 1."*[119]

It is tempting to assign Boswell's occasional impotence to anxiety in relation to sexual activity, a product of a set of complex psychological forces in which his father's admonitions and threats, inextricably intermingled with a sense of sin and guilt engendered by religious teaching, combined to inhibit his sexual performance. He could not get an erection because he felt his conscience sting. If we accept the notion that religious teaching is at least in part a set of ideas engrafted by fathers (or father-equivalents) upon their sons, it is not difficult to take the next step, namely, that punishment for sin is meted out by the father (or his substitute). For the sin of forbidden sexuality the punishment is castration, and even at the age of thirteen Boswell had thought of emulating Origen by castrating himself. Even in death Boswell's father inhibited him. Less than forty-eight hours after Lord Auchinleck died, Boswell attempted conjugal relations, but ruefully had to record: *"September 1, 1782.* What! When he who gave you being is lying a corpse? Checked."[120] One may contrast this with his unbridled conduct on learning of his mother's death, but he was sixteen years younger then.

Yet intrapsychic conflicts and anxieties are not the exclusive cause of sexual impotence. Boswell's failures with Louisa, Miss Temple, and Girolama Piccolomini can be explained by bashfulness and the fear of not being able to live up to his gallant professions. Certainly, the social aspects of his sexual relations were important. The episodes with these ladies were all planned assignations, and Boswell had time to reflect on a matter which is often better performed spontaneously. The night before he failed with Miss Temple he had had relations with two different women, had drunk heavily, and had gone "roaring" all the way from Green Park to St. Paul's. It is possible to overestimate the significance of impotence as a symptom in Boswell's case. He records only five instances of lack of potentia between the ages of twenty and fifty-five. The general impression is one of overwhelming potency and episodic debauches of compulsive sexual athleticism, as in Rome during February 1765 in London during March 1768, and again in London during March and April 1776.[121] Boswell had a "rage" for whoring until he was exhausted, much like his drinking until he was senseless.

A significant element in Boswell's unconscious motivation in continuing his promiscuous sexual behavior must have been a need to reassure himself of his masculinity, his ability to perform. At this remove one cannot decide to what extent his compulsive whoring was the product of a denial of unconscious homosexual impulses or a form of competition with his father. To serve such ends he had intercourse time and again with women who were otherwise repulsive to him. To be sure, on occasion, as with Louisa, with Mrs. Dodds, with Girolama Piccolomini, and several others he was able to achieve a continuing relation. But for the most part his extramarital encounters were devoid of emotional content and unrewarding. The analogy with Don Giovanni and his *"in Italia son già mille e tre"* is obvious and requires no amplification. But Boswell was unable to conceive of sex without guilt; hence the repeated episodes of getting drunk before he could screw his courage to the sticking point. The alcohol dissolved his guilt, albeit only in part and for a short time. He still felt the need for punishment, but not necessarily as an integral part of the sexual act; that would have made him a masochist. What he unconsciously sought was the *risk* of punishment.

We can relate this type of motivation to that seen in some (but not necessarily all) compulsive gamblers, and Boswell's gambling was as compulsive as his drinking and fornication. Such characters have as strong a drive to lose as to win. A typical example of this self-destructive pattern was Dostoevsky, whose incentive to write was chiefly to obtain money for gambling. He would boast that when he had it, he would give Fate "a punch in the nose." Fate usually struck back and Dostoevsky lost. In one sense Fate represented a father image from whom he was asking, or courting, punishment. That was the risk he took.

In like fashion, when Boswell got drunk he too would court punishment to expiate his sexual guilt. One penalty for sexual guilt is castration. To contract venereal disease is equivalent to castration, as it involves mutilation and impairment of the sexual organs. One can overlook Boswell's first two episodes of urethritis at the age of twenty; they can be explained away as youthful folly and fecklessness. One can even exculpate him in his affair with Louisa; his stated aim was "a winter's safe copulation." But after that one would think that consciously he "knew better." Instead, his medical record grew worse. When sober and in full possession of his faculties, he would usually wear "armour" and protect himself. When drunk, he was at the mercy of an unconscious force which drove him to self-destruction.

The acceptance of punishment implies forgiveness. One doubts that Boswell even unconsciously sought forgiveness from Lord Auchinleck, at least not after he was half grown. Lord Auchinleck meted out justice. Boswell's need for absolution was supplied by two sources, both close to his heart; his journal and his wife. To confess his sins to his journal and reproach himself in word was a partial expiation, but it was also a self-indulgence. After a few years of marriage, remission of sins *per litteras* no longer sufficed. Shortly after he began to transgress his marriage vows, he began to enter key words into his journal by trans-literating them into their Greek phonetic equivalents, a simple sub-stitution cipher which could easily be read by anyone acquainted with the Greek alphabet. He would leave his journal lying in his study so that his faithful wife might read it, as she eventually did. Forever the accurate recorder, Boswell would then note in a later entry that his wife was outraged, had reproached him bitterly, had sworn that henceforth she would be his wife in name only, etc., etc. Then, a few days later, he would record with satisfaction that she had forgiven him and conjugal relations had been resumed. Another ploy he used was simple confes-sion after the fact; on more than one occasion he pictures himself coming home after a night of drunken whoring, admitting it to his patient wife, and waiting for her forgiveness. Whatever the picture lacks in grace, it more than makes up for in psychopathology.

Yet sexual guilt did not seem to interfere with his attitude toward sexual relations with his wife. Boswell managed to compartmentalize his attitude toward other women from his strong emotional and physi-cal attraction to Margaret. There is no indication that he had recourse to prostitutes when she was accessible. At such times he entertained fantasies of "Asiatic satisfactions" with concubines. On one such occa-sion, after an interval of coolness following his promiscuous behavior he records that his wife was "averse to hymeneal rites" and that "when I was sure that she was in earnest to allow me to go to other women without risk either of hurting my health or diminishing my affection for her, I would go. . . . I considered indulgence with women to be like any other indulgence of nature."[122]

But between 1769 and 1780 Margaret Boswell had nine pregnancies (including three miscarriages) during which Boswell did have transient liaisons with other women in Edinburgh, and when he and his wife were separated during his absence in London, *voi sapete quel che fa*. It is not fair to judge Boswell's relations with his wife by the standard of a later age when woman's status is more egalitarian, but it is sad to reflect that she was a better wife to him than he a husband.[123]

Boswell foresaw his fate but was powerless to stop it. The forces which propelled him were unconscious and uncontrollable. The jour-nal records a dream in January 1784, a year before Johnson died, two years before his disastrous move to London, five years before Margaret died: "*January 6, 1784:* I awaked in horrour, having dreamt I saw a poor wretch lying naked on a dunghill in London, and a blackguard ruffian taking his skin off with a knife in the way that an ox is flead [i.e., flayed]; and that the poor wretch was alive and complained woefully."[124]

It is as close as Boswell came to self-pity, and it was prophetic of his last miserable decade and final punishment: failure and disgrace in London. A century and a half were to elapse before his personal reputation was reestablished by the publication of his journals and other papers which served to explain his character. The journals, which had been his confessional, proved to be the instrument of his redemption. But redemption and salvation postmortem are elusive grails. Boswell was too much of a realist to count on them. He was more concerned with his daily life than with what fame the future might bring him. Thus we leave him, a man trapped by forces beyond his control, with motivation deeper than his insight, driven to a life marked by mental depression, chronic anxiety, a continuing sense of guilt and need for punishment, intemperate and incontinent, impairing his manhood by courting (and receiving) venereal disease in expiation, and finally seen "lying naked on a dunghill in London."

Boswell's attacks of urethritis

Attack No.	Location	Date of onset	Boswell's age	Duration	Physicians	Comment
1	London	March 1760	19 yr. 5 mo.	10 weeks?	Douglas?	Contracted from prostitute. Information from entries made 2 to 3 years later in *London Journal*.
2	Edinburgh	July–August 1760	19 yr. 10 mo.	4 months?	Unstated	Possibly a recurrence of incompletely resolved first infection. Possibly complicated by epididymitis.
3	London	January 18, 1763	22 yr. 3 mo.	6 weeks	Douglas	Contracted from "Louisa." Complicated by transient epididymitis February 4. Gleet on February 27.

Boswell remained chaste and continent during his stay in Utrecht, July 1763 to September 1764

Attack No.	Location	Date of onset	Boswell's age	Duration	Physicians	Comment
4	Rome	April 29, 1765	24 yr. 6 mo.	6 to 8 weeks	Murray Morgagni (in Padua)	Information based chiefly on *Memoranda* (unpubl.). Journal entries for 26–29 April disappeared. B. writes of *badinages* and the extraordinary sum of 4 sequins. Use of syringe. Complicated by crab lice. Consulted Morgagni in Padua en route to Venice.
5	Venice	July–August 1765	24 yr. 8 mo.	6 to 8 weeks	Unstated	Possibly a recurrence of fourth infection. No mention of physician or treatment at Venice. Later, in Florence, consulted Dr. Tyrrell who prescribed cassia. Contracted infection from a dancer; convalesced at General Graeme's country villa. Notes for 10 and 11 July missing from memoranda; these may have recorded appearance of symptoms.
6	Edinburgh	March 8, 1767	26 yr. 4 mo.	5 weeks	Adie (Edinburgh) Johnstone (Ayr)	Probably nonspecific urethritis; symptoms began too soon after exposure to a whore. Court of Session rose on March 11 and B. went to Auchinleck; no chance to infect Mrs. Dodds.

7	Edinburgh	Early July 1767	26 yr. 9 mo.	9 weeks	Forbes	No details of symptoms or treatment. Contracted infection night of June 23; drunk, went to a bawdy house. Infection cleared by October 8, 1767.
8	Edinburgh	December 1767 or January 1768	26 yr. 2 mo.	4 to 8 weeks	Unstated Forbes?	Limited data about exposure, symptoms or treatment. B. apparently free of external signs of infection by March 26, 1768.
9	London	April 1768	27 yr. 6 mo.	4 to 6 weeks	Forbes Pott	Possibly an exacerbation of the three previous infections contracted at Edinburgh. Details lacking; several pages of ms. torn from *Journal*.
10	Dublin	May 1769	28 yr. 7 mo.	5 months	Forbes, Pott, Pringle, Gregory, Douglas, Kennedy *et al.*	Exposure in Dublin brothel between May 8 and May 26, continued under medical care all summer. Kennedy's Lisbon Diet Drink in September. Surgery by Forbes paraphimosis? October 16.

Boswell married Margaret Montgomery November 25, 1769. No extramarital contacts until autumn 1772.

11	London	April 1776	35 yr. 5 mo.	4 to 6 weeks	Pringle Douglas	Intercourse with prostitutes March 29, 30, 31 and April 1. Referred by Pringle to Douglas, who prescribed urethral irrigation with a *new* medication. No clear statement when attack subsided, but no mention of illness or visits to doctor after May.
12	Edinburgh	February 1778	37 yr. 4 mo.	10 weeks	Wood Pringle	Intercourse with prostitute January 24, 25. Notes missing January 31 to February 12, but symptoms present on February 13. Disease persisted through March, when Boswell left for London, where he consulted Pringle. Improved slowly; asymptomatic by end of April.
13	Edinburgh	July 1780	39 yr. 9 mo.	10 weeks	Wood	"Wandered" July 14; confessed to wife next day. Wood called July 17. Symptoms almost negligible August 16; health almost fully restored September 17; resumed conjugal relations December 28.

	Location	Date	Age	Duration	Attending	Notes
14	London	May 1781	40 yr. 6 mo.	8 to 9 weeks	Not stated	Intercourse with prostitute May 1, with Fanny Bates May 5. Symptoms began May 7. Self-medication. Illness not abating June 19. Happy reconciliation with wife July 16.
15	Edinburgh	December 1783	43 yr. 1 mo.	8 weeks	Wood	Source of infection and dates uncertain; six pages of *Journal* removed (November 26 to December 12). Under Wood's care and confined to house December 20 to January 16. Health almost restored by February 4; conjugal relations resumed February 14.
16	London	May 1785	44 yr. 7 mo.	5 to 10 weeks	Ware "Guiseppe" Pott Hayward	Continuing relations with Betsy Smith, a prostitute. Suspicious symptoms May 16. Arranges for Betsy Smith's treatment at St. Thomas's Hospital. Intercurrent relations with other prostitutes. Pott declares him free of infection July 22.
17	London	February 1786	45 yr. 4 mo.	8 weeks	Winter	Carrying on affair with Mrs. Rudd since autumn of 1785. Symptoms noted February 22, 1786. Relations with Polly Wilson, a prostitute, in April though symptomatic. Reads John Hunter *On the Venereal Disorder* April 20. No record when infection terminated.
18	London	January 1790	50 yr. 3 mo.	—	Earle	Sounded by Earle for urethral stricture January 31, 1790.
19	London	June 1790	50 yr. 9 mo.	6 weeks	Not stated(?)	Contracted from prostitute after drinking. Illness developed while in Carlisle on political business. Developed a "sore," presumably on genitalia. Self-medication. Resumed sexual activity August 1.

CHAPTER 2

Swinburne's Masochism: Neuropathology and Psychopathology

Rousseau may have been the first writer to describe the erotic pleasure he experienced while being spanked as a child, but his *Confessions* do not develop this theme in detail. By contrast, masochistic behavior dominated much of the daily life experiences of Algernon Charles Swinburne, and masochistic fantasies are ubiquitous in his poems, dramas, and personal correspondence. Every reader will recognize him instantly as ready to

> change in a trice
> The lilies and languors of virtue
> For the raptures and roses of vice
> (*Dolores*, 1866)[1]

Swinburne defines his predominant vice in another familiar poem:

> "If you were queen of pleasure,
> And I were king of pain"
> (*A Match*, 1866).

Although Swinburne took pleasure in depicting his fantasies in verse, most of this material is not available to the general reader, and details of his actual practices are largely unrecorded and are therefore irretrievable.

Despite voluminous analyses after the fact, no medical study of Swinburne's masochism had been conducted. Two early studies erroneously treated him as a sadist, but they were based on incomplete evidence.[2] In general, early explorations of Swinburne's masochism have been descriptive, anecdotal, literary, and even psychological. But their insights were perforce limited because the most detailed outline of Swinburne's behavior was not available until 1962 when Cecil Y. Lang published, as an appendix to his edition of Swinburne's letters, Sir Edmund Gosse's essay "Swinburne's Agitation."[3] Gosse could not have published this manuscript in his biography of Swinburne in 1917 while some of Swinburne's relatives were still alive, but he did deposit it in the British Museum.[4] The earlier accounts need not be deprecated since they furnish raw material for a case history, but they neither synthesize data nor provide a psychobiological framework against which the pathogenesis and symptomatology of the poet's plight can be examined.

My intent is to demonstrate that Swinburne's psychopathology had its root in neuropathology, that the specific primary event was anoxic brain damage incurred at birth, and that his masochism and other abnormal behavior developed as a psychological overlay. The modifying factors can be traced to his family constellation, to a special relationship with a female cousin, Mary Gordon, to the social and environmental factors surrounding his education and ultimately to the crisis that confronted him when he passed from adolescence into manhood. In addition, I shall mention his interpersonal relations with members of his peer group—his friends and literary associates. And finally, I believe it useful to understand Swinburne's position in the history of English flagellatory and sadomasochistic verse, a literary and cultural phenomenon to which he was a major contributor.

To define masochism as aggressive impulses directed inwardly is so simplistic as to be a tautology. The dichotomy between pain and pleasure as opposite poles of a spectrum may furnish a convenient scale for quantifying observations in a psychological experiment; but, in practice, sadism and masochism are usually inextricably intermingled. Too arbitrary a distinction, carried to its logical conclusion, would lead to the position that a complete sadist could never achieve satisfaction if his victim were a complete masochist because the consummation of the act would give the latter pleasure. Yet the converse need not be true: No semantic difficulty arises for the masochist, who is indifferent to whether the individual inflicting pain derives pleasure from it or not.

Because its outer surface is continuous with its inner surface, the Moebius strip has been suggested as a useful symbol for the mental processes in schizophrenia.[5] In the psychotic patient there is often no clear demarcation between conscious and unconscious, between inner and outer reality. The same geometric form may well symbolize the

The

Flogging-Block.

An Heroic Poem.

By Rufus Rodworthy, Esq.
(A. Hernon Clavering)
With Annotations
By Barebum Birchingham, Esq.
(Bertram Bellingham)

London:

1777.

I sing the Flogging-block. Thou, red-cheek'd Muse,
Whose Hand the Blood of smarting Boys imbrues,
Scholastic Dame, revered of State & Church,
Whose Lords to be have writhed beneath the Birch,
Thou that canst see, & smile, before thy Frown
A budding Bishop take his Breeches down,
And, tingling at the Terrors of thy Nod,
A Judge that shall be Strip to taste the Rod,
And ere his Brow be ripe for Bays to come
Birch, Birch enshrine the beardless Poet's Bum,
Birch, Birch alone embrace his brawnier Part,
Birch, Birch inflame his Flesh with constant Smart,
Birch, daily Birch, ring Music in his Ears,
Birch, hourly Birch, renew his recent Tears,
Birch, Birch, incessant Birch, fill all his Days with Fears.

Facsimile of the first page of Swinburne's *The Flogging-Block.*
Courtesy of the Trustees of the British Library

sadomasochistic state, a condition in which neither the observer nor the participant can readily distinguish subjective fantasy from its objective realization, a condition in which a given individual can assume either role as the circumstances dictate. Both sadism and masochism are a fusion of sexual and aggressive impulses; the masochist is passively receptive to aggressive behavior and manipulation by others.

Swinburne was somewhat exceptional in that he identified almost exclusively with the passive masochistic role in both fantasy and fact. There is suggestive evidence that on one occasion he tried to initiate a friend into the pleasures of masochism, but apart from that poorly documented incident his only sadistic trait was at the level of literary polemics. For clinical purposes we may consider him as an example of the pure masochist.

Current theories of masochism derive from Freud's essay *A Child Is Being Beaten* (1919), in which he describes three phases in the evolution of the fantasy, the first and third being conscious and sadistic. The second phase is masochistic and unconscious, and there is a significant difference between boys and girls in its development.

In the case of the girl the unconscious masochistic phantasy starts from the normal Oedipus attitudes; in that of the boy it starts from the inverted attitude, in which the father is taken as the object of love. . . . In her transition to the conscious phantasy . . . the girl retains the figure of her father, and in that way keeps unchanged the sex of the person beating; but she changes the figure and sex of the person being beaten, so that eventually a man is beating male children. The boy, on the contrary, changes the figure and sex of the person beating, by putting his mother in the place of his father; but he retains his own figure, with the result that the person beating and the person being beaten are of opposite sexes. In the case of the girl what was originally a masochistic (passive) situation is transformed into a sadistic one by means of repression, and its sexual quality is almost effaced. In the case of the boy the situation remains masochistic, and shows a greater resemblance to the original phantasy with its genital significance, since there is a difference of sex between the person beating and the person being beaten. *The boy evades his homosexuality by repressing and remodelling his unconscious phantasy; and the remarkable thing about his later conscious phantasy is that it has for its content a feminine attitude without a homosexual object-choice.* (Italics added)[6]

Much of the above theory is evident in Swinburne's youthful development, but there is a separation between life and letters as well as a compartmentalization within his literary output. In his published poems and plays there is a persistent theme of a cruel dominant woman for whom young boys or pages willingly suffer torture, even death, or for whom lovers pine in pain. Conversely, in his unpublished (and largely unpublishable, at least during his lifetime) poems the constant theme is that of a naughty schoolboy being birched by a schoolmaster. It is easy enough to identify Swinburne with the boy on the flogging block; but when it came to seeking flagellation in real life, he had to resort to being beaten by female prostitutes in a flagellation brothel.

Most of Swinburne's biographers have decided the corporal punishment he received at Eton was the determining factor in his subsequent practices as a passive flagellant. While many of his masochistic fantasies doubtless centered around these pubertal experiences at Eton, it is only fair to point out that even until recent years thousands of boys were regularly birched in the public schools, yet only a few became sadists or masochists in adult life. Flagellation has been called *le vice anglais* with some justification; in England it was tacitly licit, part of the psychosexual ambience. Even such an agreeable novelist as Anthony Trollope wrote in casual correspondence to his brother in 1862: "I am glad you are to have a child. . . . The pleasures of paternity have been considerably abridged, since the good old Roman privilege of slaying their offspring at pleasure, has been taken from fathers. But the delights of flagellation, though less keen, are more enduring. One can kill but once; but one may flog daily, and always quote Scripture to prove that it is a duty. . . . A daughter, I fear, does not offer so much innocent enjoyment."[7]

Trollope may have been writing in a partly jocular vein, but there is no reason to doubt that he occasionally disciplined his two sons in the manner then conventional. To cite another example, even so august a person as Prime Minister Gladstone indulged in self-flagellation in an attempt to expiate his sense of guilt at being aroused sexually by seeing prostitutes in the street or by reading pornographic literature. Even before Gladstone, Melbourne, who was Queen Victoria's first prime minister, wrote a letter to his mistress, Lady Brandon, in which he commented that "a few twigs of a birch applied to the naked skin of a young lady produces with very little effort a very considerable sensation."[8]

As the flogging block was part of the standard furniture of the Victorian public school, so surreptitious homosexual practices were common. Yet relatively few persons who were products of that educational system became exclusively homosexual as adults. Perversions do make headlines, and unusual cases becomes *causes célèbres*, but one cannot construct a general rule from exceptions. Most boys at Eton found being birched a painful, unpleasant experience. Why it was not so in Swinburne's case requires investigation of his physiological and psychological background before he entered Eton in 1849 at the age of twelve.

To reconstruct a subject's medical history in the light of a concept of disease that was not recognized until a century after the subject's birth poses the question of reliability of data. To be sure, observations of symptomatology were not collected or recorded with the new concept in mind, and such data as are preserved are often fragmentary, often made by unskilled observers, and often recorded in terms that do not permit precise judgment. An element of conjecture is inevitable; but in Swinburne's case, evidence from independent sources is consistent and corroborative, including information about his physical condition. By coupling the evidence for anoxic brain damage incurred at birth with Swinburne's behavior as a child, as an adolescent, and as an adult, one can see an internally consistent pattern. As further evidence, his psychopathology is clearly evident in his writings.

Reviewing the concept of minimal cerebral dysfunction, C. R. Strother placed emphasis on the clinical observation of "symptoms of antisocial behavior, irritability, impulsiveness, emotional lability and hyperactivity, but . . . no significant cognitive impairment."[9] Even so, there is not unanimous agreement regarding which children with a heterogeneity of behavioral signs ought to be included under the rubric of minimal brain dysfunction. A considerable number of syndromes have been suggested: hyperkinetic syndrome, developmental clumsiness, choreiform syndrome, hypokinetic behavior disorder, congenital aphasia, congenital auditory imperception, dyslexia, dysgraphia, and so forth. In individual cases a noticeable degree of overlap exists as there seems to be in Swinburne's case. Evidence that Swinburne suffered brain damage includes hyperkinetic behavior, dysgraphia, choreiform movements and tics; there is also physical evidence for arrested hydrocephalus.

However, Herbert G. Birch presents the view that disturbed behavior is not the *direct* consequence of brain damage: "Instead, we see individuals with damage to the nervous system, which may have resulted in some primary disorganization, who have developed patterns of behavior in the course of atypical relations with the developmental environment."[10] The point is that minimal brain damage may be a necessary cause for disturbed behavior in some cases but in and of itself is not a sufficient cause. Of course, there is abundant evidence that Swinburne's relations with his environment were "atypical."

Just one of the difficulties I encountered as a medical historian was to establish the circumstances of Swinburne's birth. Needless to say, his mother's obstetrical history is not available, if indeed it was ever recorded. The only first hand account is Swinburne's own; and although he was among those present, he cannot, of course, be accounted a competent witness. Writing in 1875, some thirty-eight years after the event, to E. C. Stedman, the American editor and writer, Swinburne stated that he was born "all but dead, and certainly not expected to live an hour."[11] Perhaps Swinburne exaggerated the gravity of his condition—he often indulged in self-dramatization—but his statement in a letter to a stranger must have some nidus of fact in what he had been told by his mother or father.

In the absence of medical documentation, secondary data may help support or refute the point. Swinburne was the firstborn child of Captain (later Admiral) Charles Henry Swinburne and Lady Jane Hamilton, daughter of the third earl of Ashburnham and many years her husband's junior. At the time of Algernon's birth, his parents had been married for two years, were already comfortably established at East Dene in Bonchurch on the Isle of Wight, and, since they were wellborn, had ample means and were in a position to make advance preparations for a delivery at home. Since primiparous deliveries are more often associated with difficult labor than later ones, a primigravida of Lady Jane's position would not, at that time, be likely to be far from home near her expected date of confinement. But the curious fact is that Swinburne was delivered in 1837 in London, far from his parents' home on the Isle of Wight. Without an obstetrical history, the question of premature rupture of membranes and an unexpected premature delivery cannot be evaluated; on the other hand, Lady Jane may have felt that obstetrical care was better in London and that she wished to bear her first child near her family and friends. Swinburne's later neurological symptoms and musculoskeletal development are consistent with a difficult, possibly premature, delivery accompanied by some degree of cerebral anoxia. If so, resuscitation may have been difficult and the first few hours risky and uncertain. "Not expected to live an hour" may be dramatic exaggeration, but circumstantial evidence seems to favor Swinburne's version.

Anoxia, more accurately hypoxia, during the perinatal period is well recognized as a proximate cause for such gross neurological disorders as hemiplegia, hemiparesis, epilepsy, cerebral palsy, and mental retardation. In recent years the clinical concept of minimal cerebral dysfunction has been matched by the neuropathological demonstration of minimal brain damage. Many children with behavioral disturbances, learning disabilities such as dyslexia and dysgraphia, hyperkinetic behavior, and poor motor coordination are thought to have suffered hypoxic brain damage. This concept is reinforced by the finding of minor neurological abnormalities and electroencephalographic irregularities in a large proportion of such children. Histopathological studies of the brain in institutionalized children in this category have shown such lesions as selective neuronal necrosis, periventricular leukomalacia, and matrix infarction.[12] Such small lesions are random and occasionally widely distributed; consequently, the range of possible manifestations is wide and variable. There can be no question about Swinburne's emotional and behavioral disturbances; evidence from a number of sources strongly suggest that he did suffer from neurological disabilities.

Considerable evidence bearing on Swinburne's neurological status is cited by Gosse, Swinburne's first biographer and a personal friend. To be sure, Gosse's reputation for accuracy is clouded because, homosexual himself, he suppressed important information about Swinburne's alcoholism and masochism. But in all fairness, the truth could not have been published in 1917 while some of Swinburne's relatives were still alive, and Gosse did deposit a manuscript account in the British Museum containing such facts as would have been discreditable to publish at the time.[13] It is unlikely that Gosse invented the following account; its main points are supported by independent observers:

From earliest childhood he had the trick, whenever he grew the least excited, of stiffly drawing down his arms from his shoulders and giving quick vibrating jerks with his hands. . . . If he happened to be seated at a moment of excitement, he would jerk his legs and twist his feet also, though with less violence. . . . All this developed itself in early childhood, and alarmed his mother, who applied to a specialist for advice. . . . [His] report was that these motions resulted from 'an excess of electric vitality,' and that any attempt to stop them would be harmful . . . to the very end of his life, whenever Swinburne was happy, or interested, or amused, he jerked his arms and fluttered his little delicate hands.[14]

At other points in his narrative, Gosse supplies confirmatory observations from Lady Burne-Jones's description of Swinburne's visits to herself and her husband when they lived on Russell Street in the 1860s: "He was restless beyond words, hopping about the room unceasingly, 'seeming to keep time, by a swift movement of the hands at the wrists, and sometimes of the feet also, with some inner rhythm of excitement.' "[15] To which can be added A. C. Bradley's observation based upon a recollection dating back to 1869–70: " 'When he became animated—and he was so for most of the time—he flapped his hands continuously, even reminding me . . . of a man I once saw who suffered from a mild form of St. Vitus's dance. ' "[16] In a more extended account of a visit to The Pines in 1902, A. C. Benson refers to Swinburne's "drumming impatiently on the ground with his feet" and "many little whistles and fingertaps on the table" during luncheon.[17] While reading aloud to his guest after luncheon, "his little feet drummed under the chair, and he kept up a brisk battery of taps on the table."[18]

Such uncoordinated, involuntary, stereotyped movements of the extremities are best classified as tics, a type of choreiform movement; their perseveration into adult life indicates the continuing nature of the neural discharge that evoked them. To the phenomenon of bizarre, uncontrolled movements can be added innumerable observations of Swinburne's peculiar gait, described by his cousin Mrs. Disney Leith as "that springy, dancing step which he never entirely lost" and by others as a skipping type of locomotion—convincing evidence of defective neuromotor coordination.[19]

Once the idea is advanced that Swinburne suffered anoxic brain damage with neurological sequelae, other evidence falls into place. Iconographic evidence suggests his head was disproportionately large for his small, five foot four inch body. Despite a luxuriant growth of red hair in his youthful pictures, one can see the high cranial vault, an inference confirmed by photographs taken later in life when he had become bald. His frontal bones are conspicuously prominent, and phrenological skill is not necessary to diagnose mild arrested internal hydrocephalus. Gosse informs us that: "The disproportionate size of his head—which was noticeable all through his life, although ridiculously denied after his death—was an object of amazement at Eton. His hat was the largest in the school, when he was only twelve years of age."[20] Fortunately, the process was stable and not progressive.

Swinburne's handwriting affords further evidence of neuromuscular disability, although it probably falls short of dysgraphia. Writing in 1862 to William Rossetti after reading a letter autographed by the Marquis de Sade in Richard Monckton Milnes's collection at Fryston, he compares himself to his hero: "The handwriting I flatter myself with thinking not unlike that of *this note*."[21] Both de Sade's and Swinburne's penmanship were messy scrawls, but Mrs. Leith comments that "Swinburne's handwriting underwent a considerable change during his lifetime. As a schoolboy and even in his Oxford days, it is small and cramped, requiring some trouble in deciphering. Later, it becomes larger and distincter, though often exceedingly rugged—especially after he had sustained an injury to the wrist."[22] Gosse says nothing about an injury to the wrist; he implies some form of developmental effect:

[His] manner of work ... was modified by his extreme dislike to the physical act of writing. What he called "the curse of penmanship" weighed heavily upon him. This was due to a weakness of the wrist which began to show itself quite early in life. ... It developed, however, very slowly ... but it made the act of holding a pen very irksome. The process of this weakness may be traced in Swinburne's handwriting, which about 1862 became so feeble and illegible that he altered his style of holding the pen, his manuscript thereby becoming easier to read, but still more wearisome to write.[23]

Gosse's explanation seems to be based partly on conversations with Swinburne and partly on examination of the many manuscripts Thomas J. Wise had purchased from Swinburne's estate. Mrs. Leith's account seems based on her recollection of letters she had received over the years. Foregoing graphological analysis, one may conclude that Swinburne's handwriting indicates poor motor coordination until, as an adult, he consciously tried to improve it.

A minor piece of evidence concerns Swinburne's eyesight, not his visual acuity but his ocular control. Gosse tells us: "[William] Morris described . . . how Swinburne would read his poems aloud, covering up one eye with his hand as he did so. This curious trick I also recollect, without exactly understanding the object of it; Swinburne often seemed to have a difficulty in focussing his sight, which I have no doubt was astigmatic."[24] Gosse might have been better advised to doubt astigmia. The mechanism for this refractive error and means for correcting it had been discovered by Thomas Young in the first decade of the nineteenth century. By Swinburne's time, except for extreme cases, astigmatism was corrected by lenses, even as today. Furthermore, the condition is usually bilateral, and covering one eye would not have helped Swinburne to read. A more plausible explanation for his covering one eye would be either a weakness of the extraocular muscles or unilateral nystagmus, both of which can result from neurological damage, albeit not exclusively so, and cause difficulty in focusing.

An ambiguous and less decisive point is raised by Swinburne's so-called fainting fits. No record of them exists in his childhood or youth; they occurred chiefly in the 1860s and 1870s from about age twenty-five to forty. His family referred to them as "epileptic," but this term may have been a euphemism to conceal his alcoholism. Presumably, heavy drinking preceded most of the occasions when Swinburne lost consciousness. Yet, in his day as well as ours, the term *epileptic* implies a motor component to the attack; had he merely "passed out" quietly in an alcoholic stupor, the more appropriate term of his day would have been *cataleptic*. Perhaps like many other persons with brain damage, Swinburne might have been more sensitive to alcohol than a normal man. On many occasions he seems to have become quite drunk and behaved obstreperously after drinking only a small amount of brandy, and the pattern of his "fits" is consistent with a lowered threshold.

However, the fainting fits stopped after Theodore Watts removed him to Putney in 1879 and persuaded him to stop drinking to excess.

The usual locus for "atypical relations with the developmental environment" lies in the interpersonal relations within the family group, and Swinburne's large family connections furnish a rich lode for potential psychopathology.[25] His mother and father were second cousins, and his mother's younger sister married his father's first cousin, Sir Henry Gordon. Of this bilateral consanguinity Mrs. Leith (nee Mary Gordon) wrote: "Our mothers . . . were sisters; our fathers, first cousins—more alike in characters and tastes, more linked in closest friendship, than many brothers. Added to this, our paternal grandmothers—two sisters and co-heiresses—were first cousins to our common maternal grandmother; thus our fathers were also second cousins to their wives before marriage."[26] One is reminded of the old aphorism that in England "fornication is the vice of the lower classes; adultery, of the middle class; incest, of the upper class." Like many old adages it need not be taken literally, but intermarriage among the English gentry and nobility reached considerable proportions and was of dynastic, social, and occasionally genetic importance. In any event, the Swinburne and Gordon families lived in close proximity in the privacy afforded the wellborn and well-to-do on the Isle of Wight. Swinburne's parents had six children—Algernon, four daughters, and then another son. The Gordons had only one daughter, Mary, and the children grew up as one sibship, separated only by the Swinburnes' summer visits to the captain's father, Sir John Swinburne, in Northumberland while the Gordons were visiting Sir Henry's family in Scotland.

Three of Swinburne's sisters lived to adulthood; but with such philoprogenitive parents it is striking that none of the surviving daughters ever married or even, so far as is known, seriously considered marriage. His brother Edward did marry a first cousin; but it was an unhappy match, and they were soon estranged—to such a point that when Edward returned to England in 1891 dying of heart failure, his wife's whereabouts were unknown to his family. With Algernon's incapacity, Edward's mésalliance, and the daughters' apparent rejection of marriage, one is left with the suspicion that their parents, by word or example or both, may not have inculated in their children a normal attitude toward marriage and reproduction. Although one cannot see behind the closed bedchamber door, the life cycle of the Swinburnes' children is both socially and statistically abnormal.

There is little documentary evidence about Swinburne's relationship with his father. Charles Swinburne was born in 1797 and had his days at sea behind him when he was promoted to the rank of captain in 1835 and married. He settled on the Isle of Wight with his bride, began to raise a family, and was in his fortieth year when his firstborn son arrived. He was conservative, dignified, and somewhat reticent in character; one doubts that he was prepared for a child like Algernon. Given the nature of the boy's neurological disabilities, it is easy to picture the father's difficulty in controlling a hyperkinetic child. It is reasonable to infer that Charles Swinburne, accustomed to having seamen flogged, may have had occasion to spank his son for breaches of discipline or decorum. But it is not reasonable to believe that corporal punishment was so frequent or so severe as that described in *Love's Cross-Currents* (1877)[27] or *Lesbia Brandon* (begun *circa* 1864).[28] At no time did Swinburne assert that his father had been unduly severe with him as a child, yet his flagellatory verse has as its predominant theme a schoolmaster, a father substitute, beating a refractory student. The overt content of these verses can be taken as an elaboration of actual events at Eton, and we have only slight clues about the nature of Swinburne's unconscious masochistic fantasies as a child.

Georges Lafourcade (1932) advances the view that "during most of his childhood and adolescence there existed a strong antagonism between the poet and his father."[29] This judgment is based partly on the strong letter of condemnation Captain Harewood wrote to his son Reginald in *Love's Cross-Currents* and partly upon a letter Swinburne wrote to William Rossetti in 1870. The necessity of developing the novel's story line seems to diminish the significance of Lafourcade's interpretation that Captain Harewood's letter reflects Swinburne's actual feelings about his father. The letter to Rossetti admits of an even less harsh valuation:

I think you are rather hard upon [Shelley] . . . as to the filial relation. I have no more doubt that it may be said for Sir Timothy that his son was what Carlyle calls 'an afflictive phenomenon' than that I was the same to my father before, during, and since my Oxford time; but I do not think you make allowance for the provocation given (as well as received) by a father, who may be kindly and generous, to a boy . . . with whom he has no deep or wide . . . sympathy beyond the animal relation or family tradition.[30]

That Swinburne should compare Shelley's relationship with his father with his own points up the difference between the two examples, and the facts were well known to Rossetti. When Shelley was sent down from Oxford in disgrace, his father, Sir Timothy, waxed melodramatically wroth and soon thereafter disinherited him and forbade him to return to the family home. On the other hand, Charles Swinburne hardly rejoiced at his son's academic debacle, but he tried to guide him toward a suitable vocation. Unlike Shelley's father, Swinburne's father was not an irascible, insentient boor. Admittedly, literature was not his first choice for his son's profession, but one cannot classify the Swinburnes as antiintellectual country gentry as were the Shelleys. For instance, Sir John Swinburne, the poet's grandfather, owned the largest library in Northumberland and in his youth had been an acquaintance of Mirabeau and Wilkes; he was an important influence on his grandson's avant garde literary tastes and political republicanism. Charles Swinburne, although not so affluent as his father, amassed a library of his own valued at £2,000 which he bequeathed to Algernon. In fact, when Algernon tried to have his first book published, his father paid the costs and later provided his son with a liberal allowance of £400 a year.

Swinburne writes of provocation given and received; Swinburne's abjuring the family's high church Anglican faith (two generations before they had been Roman Catholics) and flaunting his republicanism in the face of his parents' conservatism demonstrate that the "generation gap" existed a century before that term became fashionable. There was lack of common ground, even lack of sympathy, between father and son, but it was not expressed as an overt "strong antagonism." Probably Charles Swinburne was perplexed by his firstborn child; young Algernon was not what a naval officer with quiet tastes had bargained for when he set out to raise a family. Certainly he had every reason to be disappointed with his son as a grown man; one cannot expect him to have been proud of a son who was incompetent, alcoholic, and a sexual deviate. Yet when Algernon got into scrapes in London, when he was seriously ill after his alcoholic debauches, his father arranged for him to be brought home to be cared for. On balance, Charles Swinburne behaved with more kindness than many fathers of that era.

However, the above exculpation does not elucidate Charles Swinburne's role in his son's rearing or the extent to which his conduct may have influenced his son's psychosexual development. At no time did Swinburne ever complain that his father had mistreated him nor can we charge him with administering anything more than the conventional domestic discipline of the period. Most likely, the father remained aloof and a bit remote from the children when they were young, leaving the details of their rearing to his considerably younger wife and her staff. Apart from his father and uncle who were older and remote, Swinburne passed most of his formative years in a ménage of women. His only brother was not born until a year before he went off to

Eton; except for summer holidays in Northumberland, his only regular playmates were his four younger sisters and his cousin Mary Gordon. Was it because he was surrounded by females that his poems and plays have as a prominent theme the suffering and physical sacrifice of a young man for the love of a dominating, heartless woman? Does that choice of subject reflect any of his unconscious childhood fantasies? Was this why, when it came to the sticking point, he purchased flagellation from female prostitutes rather than from an older man or men, behavior grossly at variance with the content of his overtly flagellatory writings? Or was it merely a matter of convenience and the availability of female flagellants? The worst charge that can be made against Charles Swinburne is that he attempted to raise an unusual child by the formulae and to the standards of his class—a common blunder. What can be stated as a numerical datum is that only two letters from Swinburne to his father are preserved, none from father to son.

By constrast, Swinburne carried on a voluminous correspondence with his mother; all biographical sources affirm her solicitude and devotion to him and his reciprocal affection for her. She was intelligent, well read, cultivated, and accomplished. Her eldest brother was the fourth earl of Ashburnham, that testy Hamilton who collected a vast library of early manuscripts and incunabula. From Lady Jane, young Swinburne, a precocious boy, learned to read and write French and Italian—languages that shaped his literary tastes and political orientation as an adult. He was one of Victor Hugo's early enthusiasts; he was the first English critic to approach Baudelaire with intellectual and emotional insight; he adulated Mazzini and championed the cause of a united Italy. These matters were central in his life, and the direction given his mind by his mother should not be underestimated. It was she who sent him off to Eton with a copy of Shakespeare (Bowdler's version) at a time when Shakespeare was "not taught" in public schools.

But Lady Jane was a conventional and extremely pious woman. Her son's defection from and outward hostility toward any organized religion pained her deeply. So did the frank sensuality of his poems and plays, but she was not alone in this distress; they scandalized almost the entire "establishment." Undoubtedly, such topics as sexual behavior and genitalia were unmentionable in the Swinburne household. One cannot resist speculating what effect such taboos might have had in inhibiting the normal sexual curiosity and psychosexual development of her son and in ensuring that her daughters remained in a state of perpetual virginity.

It is currently fashionable to designate parental influence, usually maternal, as the principal or determining factor in the evolution of sexual deviation; but a cause and effect relationship is by no means invariable, let alone predictable or reproducible. Indeed, the parents of most masochists and other deviants seem to have raised other children in the same household according to similar principles without abnormal sequelae. It is more difficult to pervert a child's sexual instinct than is generally conceded. Much depends upon one's definition of deviant behavior. Was Swinburne any more deviant because he was a masochist than his sisters who remained chaste? Complete frustration and inhibition of the sexual instinct may be as abnormal as its misdirection. Can Lady Jane be cast in the role of the "castrating mother," or is that overworked stereotype inapplicable? Can a reader equate Lady Jane with Lady Midhurst in *Love's Cross-Currents,* the character who cynically manipulates the lives and loves of the younger generation? The question remains partly open, but the resemblance is not close. Thousands of boys have had mothers and fathers much like Swinburne's, have been raised among sisters who never married, have even had their juvenescent sexuality stimulated by a young kinswoman (as did Swinburne), yet have developed normally. However, they did not have Swinburne's neuropathology as a substrate upon which such a situation might react.

Most of Swinburne's childhood memories seem banal, but one of them may be of significance, perhaps a clue to later events. In a letter to Stedman, written in 1875, he wrote: "As for the sea, its salt must have been in my blood before I was born. I can remember no earlier enjoyment than being held up naked in my father's arms and brandished between his hands, then shot like a stone from a sling through the air, shouting and laughing with delight, head foremost into the coming wave."[31] It is easy to attach too much importance to a single recollection from childhood or indeed any single item in the fabric of memory—witness the pitfalls of interpretation surrounding Leonardo's dream. Swinburne's account of being tossed into the waves suggests a "screen memory," that is, an event that happened many times but is condensed and recollected as a single, dramatic episode. The game of holding a youngster aloft, then tossing him into the waves at a shallow spot is common enough, just the sort of activity a father engages in with a lively, active child. In such games adults almost invariably misinterpret the child's yelps and squeals as a sign of pleasure, and indeed Swinburne as an adult recollected it so. What he suppressed was the moment of terror he experienced when he was tossed in the air without physical support, a terror he learned to anticipate with each repetition of the game. The terror was followed by a stinging cutaneous sensation as the breaking wave lashed his naked body, a sequence of stimuli that found later recapitulation in the boy on the flogging block awaiting the first stroke of the birch. Swinburne's introduction to the flagellatory action of the sea, which later became a punitive mother image, was at his father's hands.

Perhaps Swinburne's imperfect motor coordination was improved when he went swimming. Twentieth-century readers may be able to draw a parallel with the case of the late President Roosevelt who, though crippled by poliomyelitis, was able to swim with considerable strength and founded the familiar institution at Warm Springs, Georgia, for just that purpose. Swinburne's love for the sea amounted to thalassophilia, and he became an accomplished swimmer when he was a young boy, which gave him an opportunity to compensate, possibly overcompensate, for his awkwardness on dry land. Hence such lines as: "as a boy/That leaps up light to wrestle with the sea" (*Tristram of Lyonesse*, 1882). But like so many emblems that Swinburne held dear, the sea was also overlaid with masochistic distortions:

> I will go back to the great sweet mother,
>   Mother and lover of men, the sea.
> I will go down to her, I and none other,
>   Close with her, kiss her and mix her with me. . . .
>
> O fair green-girdled mother of mine,
>   Sea, that art clothed with the sun and the rain,
> Thy sweet hard kisses are strong like wine,
>   Thy large embraces are keen like pain. . . .
>
> Fair mother, fed with the lives of men,
>   Thou art subtle and cruel of heart, men say.
> Thou has taken, and shalt not render again;
>   Thou art full of thy dead, and as cold as they.
>   (*The Triumph of Time*, 1865)

From the sea as the cruel, punitive mother it is only a step to the sea as flagellatrix. In *Lesbia Brandon* Swinburne describes the boy Herbert Seyton, his alter ego, going for a swim in the middle of a storm: "the scourging of the surf made him red from the shoulders to the knees, and sent him on shore whipped by the sea into a single blush of the whole skin."[32] Seyton is depicted as a boy who is unmercifully flogged by his tutor and who has a quasi-incestuous love for his sister. Earlier in the text of this unfinished novel Swinburne wrote: "All cruelties and treacheries, all subtle appetites and violent secrets of the sea, were part of her divine nature, adorable and acceptable to her lovers."[33] Given such an attitude, it is not surprising to find that one of the pivotal episodes in *Lesbia Brandon* describes Herbert Seyton receiving a severe flogging after he has rescued another lad from the rough sea.

Combining the evidence of neurological damage with Swinburne's pleasure in being stung by surf and breakers, one may question whether he had lesions involving the sensory as well as the motor functions of the central nervous system. Did he sense pain as normal persons do, or was his threshold higher? Could a strategically placed lesion in the thalamus or thalamoparietal radiation have modified his perception of cutaneous stimuli? In the absence of specific information or a postmortem examination of his brain, such lesions are an *ignis fatuus,* and speculation easily outruns data.

But psychodynamic implications are present as well as simple mechanistic ones. We can easily construe the "screen image" of being tossed into the sea as Swinburne's unconscious masochistic fantasy involving his father, and we can then consider his subsequent identification of the sea with a punitive mother as the next and conscious phase of the fantasy. Given this episode and the fertile soil of anoxic brain damage, his childhood experiences at the Isle of Wight in the bosom of what externally seemed a conventionally happy family constellation were the sowing and first growth of the seeds of psychopathology. In this locus the impact of environmental factors determined the form and content of his later abnormal behavior—a specific example of how a damaged soma leads to a disturbed psyche.

Unlike Swinburne's sisters, his cousin Mary Gordon did marry and have children. In 1865, at the age of twenty-five, she married Col. Disney Leith, a man twenty-one years her senior, and went to live on his estate near Aberdeen, a considerable distance from the Isle of Wight. Swinburne was then twenty-eight (over four years since he had been sent down from Oxford). Mary Gordon, as Lang first pointed out, was Swinburne's Dolores, the Lady of Pain. The recent publication of her letters to him as "Cy merest dozen" (i.e., my dearest cousin) by Jean Overton Fuller reinforces the evidence that she is a central figure in his masochistic fantasies.[34] Their relationship, it is clear, was the raw material for many of the poems in *Poems and Ballads* (1866), but it is another matter to define the limits of that relationship.

Her own account, written eight years after Swinburne's death when she was seventy-seven, is a self-serving declaration and cannot be taken at face value. In 1917, Mrs. Leith assures us that their relationship up to 1865 was like that of an affectionate brother and sister, and doubtless that is the way she chose to remember it more than fifty years later. But no one aware of recent biographical revelations can doubt that Mary

Gordon was the original for *Dolores* and *Faustine* (1862), that she was the model for the incestuously desired woman in both *Love's Cross-Currents* and *Lesbia Brandon*, for whose sake Reginald Harewood and Herbert Seyton are whipped, or that *The Triumph of Time* (1865) describes Swinburne's reaction to her marriage. She was the confidante to whom he related his experiences on the flogging block at Eton when he came home on holiday; and as late as 1864, ten years after he had been withdrawn, he wrote reminding her how he had been birched for attempting to imitate the galliambics of Catullus's *Atys*.[35]

There is little doubt that Swinburne, who had just begun to make a name for himself in London literary circles, began to consider seriously in 1863–64 the idea of proposing marriage to Mary. But what was her reaction to him as a potential husband, and what could have transpired in their youth that made him feel she might accept him? Recalling innumerable similar cases, the prurient mind of the psychobiographer can speculate whether they, while still prepubescent, had indulged in mutual genital exhibition and exploration, whether or not they were caught at it, and whether young Algernon (the elder, the boy, hence the guilty one) was spanked for it. It is a plausible anecdote, but it remains an unsupported fancy. Likewise, it is possible that during adolescence or early maturity they had exchanged passionate kisses and embraces, hence the lines in *Dolores*:

> By the ravenous teeth that have smitten
>   Through the kisses that blossom and bud,
> By the lips intertwisted and bitten
>   Till the foam has a savour of blood,
> By the pulse as it rises and falters,
>   By the hands as they slacken and strain.

Intense youthful lust followed by a little fumbling, a little sweating, and then satiety: Swinburne was impotent with women.

Fond as Mary Gordon may have been of her cousin, possibly because he had been the first to stir her adolescent sexuality, and protective as she was of his memory in later years, there is no evidence that she thought seriously of marrying him. She was alert, articulate, and had a mind of her own. Consanguinity might not have been a decisive impediment, but it was understood in the family circle that Swinburne was not a normal young man, though Mary alone may have had an approximate idea of the extent of his disturbance. F. A. C. Wilson directs our attention to characters in Mrs. Leith's novels who resemble Swinburne and to a recurrent plot in which a somewhat boyish girl (which she was) has to choose between a younger and an older suitor, settling on the latter for reasons of security.[36] The closest she came to suggesting what might have happened between herself and Swinburne was in her novel *Rufus* (1886), in which the heroine envisages the young Swinburne-like hero as a brother, ineligible for marriage, but who forcibly embraces her, to which she responds by slapping his face. But this incident, of course, is fiction written many years after the hypothetical act.

Slender support for the actual occurrence of such an incident is suggested by Swinburne's lines in *Satia te Sanguine* (1866), written at about the same time as *The Triumph of Time:*

> You thrill as his pulses dwindle,
>   Your brighten and warm as he bleeds,
> With insatiable eyes that kindle
>   And insatiable mouth that feeds
>
> Your hands nailed love to the tree,
>   You stript him, and scourged him with rods,
> And drowned him deep in the sea
>   That hides the dead and their gods.

But the reference to any specific incident is far from clear.

Undoubtedly, Mary's marriage and move to Aberdeen deprived Swinburne of the woman he felt closest to, and he reacted to it strongly, casting her in the role of the cruel sadistic female. But this occasion did not prompt his first use of that image; the pattern for it had been set several years earlier in his youthful poetic dramas. There is no evidence that he and Mary acted out his masochistic fantasies. She may have shared a vicarious sexual excitement when they discussed them, but in all probability their relation was that of *diseur* to *auditeur,* the flavor of which can be found in the passage in *Love's Cross-Currents* where Reginald describes his "swishings" at school to Frank who is two or three years younger. Since Swinburne's impotence made marriage in the usual sense impossible, he may have hoped that Mary would remain unmarried and that their quasi-erotic relationship would continue unchanged—anything beyond that would suggest his grasp of reality was impaired. I shall let Mary Gordon Leith have the next to the last word: "We met, not long after [my marriage], when both visiting at an uncle's (Lord Ashburnham's) house in the country; and though nothing of particular moment occurred, I chiefly remember lively and merry games in the evening with him and the large party of cousins, such games as 'consequences' and the like."[37] Of course, if nothing had happened before her marriage or if "nothing of particular moment occurred" except for " 'consequences' and the like" after her marriage, why is she so anxious to reassure her readers that it did not?

Probably Swinburne wished he were capable of possessing her, but he knew he was not. Possibly she would have preferred it if he were, but she knew it was beyond hope. A plausible conjecture is that after adolescence had passed, some of Swinburne's identification with his mother was displaced onto Mary Gordon, the important difference being that she could be imagined as a sexual partner. Such a fantasy carries with it a potential violation of the incest taboo, an easy defense against which is impotence.

The "consequences" of Mary Gordon's defection are plainly set out in *The Triumph of Time:*

> Before our lives divide for ever,
>   While time is with us and hands are free,
> (Time, swift to fasten and swift to sever
>   Hand from hand, as we stand by the sea)
> I will say no word that a man might say
> Whose whole life's love goes down in a day;
> For this could never have been; and never,
>   Though the gods and the years relent, shall be.

In later stanzas of this poem he refers to the sea *(vide supra)* as the "mother and lover of men" whose "large embraces are keen like pain" and who is "fed with the lives of men." Regardless of what his masochistic fantasies were, only after Mary Gordon's marriage did he begin to patronize a flagellation brothel. The dynamics of Swinburne's abortive love for his first cousin lend support to the Freudian maxim that masochistic practices are not only the punishment for the forbidden genital relation but also the regressive substitute for it.

The discussion of Mary Gordon has taken us ahead in chronology to 1865; let us return to Swinburne as a boy of twelve entering Eton in 1849. Whatever contribution cultural factors and the emotional polarities of intrafamilial relationships may have made to Swinburne's masochism, the pattern was reinforced and crystallized when he was exposed to the cultural context of institutionalized sadomasochism in the English public school system. Corporal punishment was not an invention of the Victorian era; schoolboys had been flogged long before Nicholas Udall, author of *Ralph Roister-Doister* (ca. 1541), had earned the reputation for being an exceptionally harsh headmaster at Eton during Henry VIII's reign. Histories of flagellation uniformly pay homage to the redoubtable right arms of Colet (Saint Paul's), Busby (Westminster), and Keate (Eton); even Arnold of Rugby was known to apply the birch with some frequency. Victorian society accepted this tradition without much question. It was simple, practical, and inexpensive to maintain discipline and decorum at school by flogging the students as they always had been.

When Swinburne entered Eton, he was short for his age, his frame was slight, and he looked frail even though he was rather tough and wiry. He did not present the appearance of being physically equal to his peers. Motivated by the same overcompensation that had made him a fearless but reckless horseback rider despite several spills, the same drive that later led him to climb Culver Cliff alone and without equipment, he probably approached the idea of being flogged as a test of manliness, courage, and the ability to endure pain. He succeeded all too well. Maladroit and uninterested in games, given to solitary reading, known for his ability to recite vast quantities of Elizabethan verse, he escaped becoming a butt for bullying by his bravado on the flogging block. At first, he probably accepted his floggings with stoicism; later, when he saw bigger and stronger boys blench at the birch, he began to enjoy them, partly because of the prestige his "heroism" conferred and partly, probably after puberty, because of the erotic sensations they produced.

The only preserved literary product of Swinburne's Eton days is a tragic verse drama, *The Unhappy Revenge* (ca. 1853–54) modeled freely upon Tourneur's *The Revenger's Tragedy* (1607). Even though immature, it shows some of the metrical skill he later developed to perfection, but one ought not emphasize its "blood and thunder" horrors as premonitory signs of masochistic tendencies. It was derived from literature, not from life. Before coming to Eton, while still a boy playing with his sisters and cousin at Bonchurch, he had shown facility for writing dramatic "scenes" in which the stage direction "stabs the king" was so frequent that it became a household phrase. In the absence of supporting evidence one ought not to conclude that this frequently used phrase was sublimation of juvenile death wishes toward his father. Such modes of expression would be natural for a precocious boy with a talent for verse who was steeped in Elizabethan and Gothic horror literature.

At Eton, Swinburne made excellent academic progress. He won prizes for his skill in modern languages (i.e., French and Italian) and in four years was within a few places of being in the headmaster's form. In later life he looked back fondly upon Eton; he had none of the dislike for it which he developed for Oxford. To be sure, in a letter written in 1867 to George Powell, who went to Eton after Swinburne had left, he explained just what he liked most about Eton: "I should like to see two things there again the river—and the block. Can you tell me any news of the latter institution or any of its present habitués among our successors? the topic is always most tenderly interesting—with an interest, I may say, based upon a common bottom of sympathy."[38] Powell was thoroughly aware of Swinburne's obsession with flagellation and sympathetic to it; he sent his friend a valued gift, a used birch, which Swinburne acknowledged: "A thousand thanks for your gift which is trebly valuable for interest and external belongings and as the seal of friendship. I long to thank you in person and to enjoy the sight and touch of the birch that has been used. I don't think I ever more dreaded the entrance of the swishing room than I now desire a sight of it. To assist unseen at the holy ceremony . . . I would give *any* of my poems."[39]

Less than two months later Powell procured a photograph of the flogging block for Swinburne, who replied: "Many thanks for the photograph, which is most interesting. I should like of all things to have a large one, but what a pity the scene is imperfect, a stage without actors. . . . I would give anything for a good photograph taken at the right minute—say the tenth cut or so—and doing justice to *all sides* of the question."[40] There is every justification for Fuller's comment that he was "psychologically domiciled in the flogging-room. The experience, with its pain, its humiliations, its terrors and its ecstasies, had dominated his entire existence, to the extent of making him incapable of a passional experience in which it played no part."[41]

Swinburne paid a somewhat more conventional tribute to his old school in *Eton: An Ode* (composed and presented in 1891, published in 1904) to honor the school's four hundred fiftieth anniversary. The wreath sent by Eton to the poet's funeral in 1909 contained an excerpt:

> Still the reaches of the river, still the light on field and hill,
> Still the memories held aloft as lamps for hope's young fire to fill.

But the official ode is counterbalanced by *Eton: Another Ode* which is part of the canon of his flagellatory verse.[42]

A veil of silence has been drawn over the circumstances leading to Swinburne's withdrawal from Eton in September 1853. He was certainly not dismissed for academic deficiencies; and had he been involved in sadomasochistic or sexual misconduct with another boy, he would have been expelled. The official version is that "following representations" his parents chose to withdraw him. In view of his later career, a plausible conjecture is that the masters at Eton recognized his erotic response to flagellation and were unwilling or unable to cope with it. Although schoolmasters were considered naive in the eyes of the world, they were no doubt able to recognize sexual psychopathology. No one knows in what terms the situation was put to Swinburne's father; but if it was a tactful approximation of the truth—and it is difficult to imagine on what other terms the suggestion to withdraw a good student could have been broached—it was the first time someone had drawn his attention to his son's condition, although he may have entertained unvoiced, possibly repressed, suspicions of his own.

After Eton, Swinburne was tutored privately to prepare him for the university, and he also traveled on the Continent with an uncle. At seventeen, he was a bit too old for birching, and there are no data about his psychosexual orientation or practices during his two-and-a-half year interlude. He entered Balliol in January 1856. Little relevant information exists about his undergraduate career, but two items of importance can be noted: He made the acquaintance of the Rossettis and their Pre-Raphaelite Brotherhood and he wrote *Laugh and Lie Down* (1859), a drama that evidences persistent sadomasochistic tendencies.[43] The leading character is Imperia, a famous courtesan of Milan, and the dramatic development centers around her relations with her twin pages, Frank and Frederick, who appear as potential transvestites wearing the costumes of either sex successively. Swinburne clearly identifies with Frank and Frederick:

> Imperia: Come, come, you are not old enough.
> Frank: I have bled for your sake some twenty times a month,
>   Some twenty drops each time; are these no services?
> Imperia: I tell you, if you use me lovingly,
>   I shall have you whipt again, most pitifully whipt,
>   You little piece of love.[44]

While at Oxford, Swinburne also began work on his verse drama *Rosamond* (1860); again, its chief character is a *femme fatale*. It was for the publication of *Rosamond* and *The Queen Mother* (1860), a work of comparable kidney (or should I say spleen?), that Adm. Charles Swinburne (promoted from captain in 1857) furnished subvention shortly after his son had been sent down from Oxford. His expulsion occurred under circumstances that remain obscure but to which the poet later affixed the adjective "scandalous," thereby suggesting his dismissal was no mere question of academic inadequacy or of the usual college peccadilloes. By this time Swinburne, now twenty-four, was a confirmed masochist in thought, though possibly not in deed; most of his fantasies remained unfulfilled. The denouement of his relationship with Mary Gordon lay almost five years ahead. He was determined to make a name for himself as a poet, dramatist, and man of letters. And in this aim he succeeded.

From 1860 to 1879 Swinburne lived in London in a succession of rented quarters. The details of his rise to literary fame and the controversy caused by *Poems and Ballads* have been thoroughly chronicled.[45] What concerns us during these years is his deviant behavior, not so much in shabby detail as in general outline, particularly his mental state and interpersonal relations. He was not reticent about his masochistic inclinations. They were clearly understood by his friends and acquaintances; some viewed them with Bohemian tolerance and others shared them in part or in whole. His acquaintanceship with the Rossettis, begun at Oxford, ripened into friendship. Beginning in 1862 Swinburne was a tenant of sorts at that curious communal establishment run by Dante Gabriel Rossetti at 16 Cheyne Walk, and his correspondence with both Dante Gabriel and William Michael Rossetti is filled with many references to flagellation. They tolerated his aberration sympathetically, but there is no evidence they had any particular interest in it. To be sure, Dante Gabriel had problems of his own and ultimately became addicted to chloral hydrate, and his friendship with Swinburne came to an end in 1872; but William Michael, the more stable brother, remained a friend for life.

In May 1861 Swinburne made the acquaintance of Richard Monckton Milnes (created Baron Houghton in August 1863). It was an ambivalent relationship; on the one hand, Milnes recognized Swinburne's gifts and was anxious to help promote them, but he also used Swinburne as a pawn in his social game, inviting him as a curiosity and bait for his salon, spreading elaborate breakfasts in Upper Brook Street, arranging visits to his country seat at Fryston in Yorkshire. Milnes was well known as a collector of pornography and he gave Swinburne access to his collection, including such of the Marquis de Sade's writings as were then available. Milnes did not collect "curiosa" for scholarly purposes; he just liked to read dirty books and took vicarious pleasure in reading about flagellation, though he never practiced it himself. It would be incorrect to claim that Milnes corrupted Swinburne by introducing him to de Sade's works; Swinburne was already "hooked." The sadomasochism in *Laugh and Lie Down* (1859), *Rosamond* (1860), and *The Queen Mother* (1860), written two or three years before they met, was a continuing element in Swinburne's poems and plays for the rest of his career. Even before he had the chance to read de Sade, he wrote a poem in French in 1861 titled *Charenton* (the name of the asylum in which *le bon marquis* had been confined), a rather poor poem but a paean of praise. However, more important is Swinburne's reaction to de Sade as a writer, an opinion based chiefly on *Justine* and expressed in a long letter of August 1862 to Milnes:

At first, I quite expected to add another to the gifted author's list of victims; I really thought I must have died or split open or choked with laughing. . . . it appears to me a most outrageous *fiasco.* I looked for some sharp and subtle analysis of lust—some keen dissection of pain and pleasure—'quelques tail-lades dans les chairs vives de la sensation': at least such an exquisite relish of the things anatomized as without explanation would suffice for a stimulant and be comprehensible at once even if unfit for sympathy. . . . De Sade is like a Hindoo mythologist; he takes *bulk* and *number* for greatness. . . . as if a number of pleasures piled one on another made up the value of a single great and perfect sensation of pleasure. You tear out wombs, smash in heads, and discharge into the orifice. Après? You scourge and abuse your mother and make dogs tear off her breasts, etc. Après? Suppose you take your grandmother next time and try wild cats by way of a change. . . . Shew me the point, the pleasure of all this, as a man of genius ought to do in a few touches.[46]

Here Swinburne has touched the reason why pornography is nonlit-erature: Usually it consists of little more than successive and monoto-nous repetitions of the same mechanical acts; the genitalia are larger than life; the sexual athleticism is more fanciful than the wildest ado-lescent fantasies come true; the number of orgasms is biologically impossible, but inexhaustible nonetheless; and in the case of Swin-burne's penchant for flogging, such works contain whippings of un-precedented severity and duration, the cries of the victim shrill and piercing beyond belief, and the flow of blood almost enough to pro-duce peripheral vascular collapse. The exaggerations and elaborations of pornography reveal nothing about human passions or lusts, save that they exist; the quantitative excess of the genre ultimately proves antierotic, leading rapidly to satiation. Politics may be the art of the possible, but pornography is the art of the impossible. Yet, despite his awareness of this fault in de Sade, when Swinburne wrote his own flagellatory verses, he fell into the same trap. His analysis of de Sade continues for some pages, describing them finally as "flat, flaccid, impotent, misshapen, hung awry," fit only to be "bound up with *Télé-maque* or *Paul et Virginie.*"[47] One might think that after so scathing a denunciation Swinburne would never have bothered to read another line by de Sade and that he was immune to the marquis's message. But no, he became a convert and disciple, and de Sade's writings became his "Book of Revelation." Though one cannot pretend that Milnes cor-rupted Swinburne's mind or body, de Sade's works surely corrupted his literary taste and judgment.

Swinburne's acquaintance with Milnes developed, and he pandered to the latter's tastes as *lecteur* by writing him accounts of fantasied swishings, addressing him as M. Rodin, the name of the sadistic schoolmaster in *Justine,* and signing his letters Redgie or Frank Fane, names that he gave to the flogged boys in *Love's Cross-Currents* and in the verses of *The Flogging-Block.* In a letter of April 1865[48] he developed the flagellatory metaphor to describe his feelings at the initial reviews of *Atalanta in Calydon* (1865), and in a letter of July 1865[49] he gently protested that Milnes (now Lord Houghton) would have been nearer the mark had he described him as "de Sade with a difference" rather than "Byron with a difference" when he reviewed that verse drama in the *Edinburgh Review.*

Flagellation was the unifying theme in Swinburne's letters to Milnes. In one of the gamier ones written in 1863 he reveals a certain *snobisme* about the birch, too good for the lower classes: "I am surprised that a man of refinement, whom I had taken to be an educational aristocrat of the purest water—and blood, should have mixed the bitter-sweet fountain of Heliconian brine, the pure salt Hippocrene of boys' tears and birchen pickle, with the obscene puddle of corduroy bourgeoisie. . . . Is a butcher's blood to tingle, a tailor's flesh to wince, from the discipline of nobles, the correction of a prince?"[50] A common attribute in deviant sexual behavior is the mystique of its exclusiveness, and Swinburne's attitude persisted. Thirteen years later we find him writing to Lord Houghton: "For centuries the birch had been the hereditary apanage of the young aristocrat—the heirloom of patrician adolescence—the feudal emblem of class divisions, the bloody badge of social exclusiveness, distinguishing by a crimson sign, even when his back was turned on them in scorn, the noble or gentle boy from his humbler fellows. . . . 'common humanity in peasant and in prince, in Howard and in Hodge, is not the same at bottom'!"[51] Spoken (or rather written) as one gentleman to another! Even before writing this letter, however, Swinburne saw through Lord Houghton's superficialities. In fact, in 1874 he wrote to John Morley that "I do shrink from the rancid unction of that man's adulation or patronage in criticism."[52] Yet his distaste was not so great that it prevented him from sending Houghton in 1880 the first copy of *Studies in Song* inscribed as "the maidenhead of my latest child."[53]

Another of Swinburne's friends was the rather sinister Charles Augustus Howell (1840–90), a man of dubious antecedents and a chequered career, who returned to London in 1864 claiming to have been involved in the Orsini conspiracy. He ingratiated himself with Rossetti and the Pre-Raphaelites; through them he met Swinburne. Even as he was happy to assist Rossetti form a collection of blue and white china, he was willing to lend a hand to Swinburne's fancy for flagellatory literature. Writing to him in 1865, shortly before Mary Gordon's marriage, Swinburne proposed: "I want you to compose for me a little dialogue (imaginary) between schoolmaster and boy—from the first summons 'Now Arthur (or Frank—or Harry) what does *this* mean, sir? Come here'—to the last *cut* and painful buttoning up—a rebuke or threat at every lash (and *plenty* of them) and a shriek of agonized appeal from the boy in reply. I want to see how like real life you will make it. Write me this—and you shall have more of my verses—a fair bargain."[54] From exchanging pornography with Swinburne, Howell soon became his man of affairs, helping him in the complicated dealings with his publisher at the time, the shady John Camden Hotten. Swinburne may even have been soliciting Howell's "imaginary dialogues" for flagellatory publications by Hotten. Soon they were close friends, as reflected in this letter of 1866 addressed to "My dear Charlie": "Come and see your affectionate pupil soon or what will become of my lessons? I shall never know them at this rate and shall be in rows with other idle boys."[55] Whether this note implies a physical component to their relationship is beyond conjecture. Howell continued to act for Swinburne with respect to Hotten until Andrew Chatto took over as Swinburne's publisher in 1873, after Hotten's death. But Howell's friendship with the Rossetti-Whistler circle proved to be less than unselfish. After his death a number of forged Rossetti drawings and surreptitious *tirages* of Whistler's etchings were found among his possessions. Before he died, he supposedly tried to blackmail Swinburne by threatening to sell his letters containing "flagellatory indecencies." Howell's reputation was so bad that an inaccurate account of his death easily gained credence, viz., that his body was found early one morning in a Soho street, his throat cut and a sovereign jammed between his teeth—a classical blackmailer's murder. The legend was accepted uncritically by many later writers but is refuted by Helen Rossetti-Angeli who informs us that he died in his own bed of natural causes.[56]

Swinburne's obsession with flagellation was so pervasive that even in the most inappropriate circumstances he would express himself by using a flagellatory metaphor. For example, in a letter to F. S. Ellis, who published a few of his works around 1871 and 1872, Swinburne corrected an error he had made in a Greek word used in an epigraph, commenting gratuitously that "it is a slip for which a schoolboy would be flogged."[57] Similar remarks are common coin in many others letters and probably adorned his everyday conversation as well.

But the *locus classicus* for Swinburne's epistolary obsession with flagellation is found in a letter to Dante Gabriel Rossetti written from his family's home where he was visiting over the Christmas holiday in 1869. Almost two years before, "In order to break him completely of his degrading and ignominious habit, D. G. Rossetti consulted one or two very intimate friends, who advised that he should be taken in hand by some sensible young woman who would 'make a man of him,' since he was known to have never had any physical connection, which, as Rossetti said, was ridiculous in the author of so many 'voluptuous' poems."[58] Therefore, Rossetti solicited the aid of Adah Isaacs Menken a stage performer, to seduce him. Needless to say, the attempt failed, and Miss Menken returned the £10 fee to Rossetti as unearned. Her comment. " 'I can't make him understand that biting's no use!' " has been recorded among other ludicrous Swinburneana.[59] Despite that fiasco, Swinburne was still on good terms with Rossetti, and doubtless finding time heavy on his hands at his family's home, he wrote his friend a long letter. It opens with several paragraphs commenting on some of Rossetti's recent poems, touches on Arthurian romance, then Dante, then Baudelaire, and finally, stimulated by Rossetti's allusion to Tennyson's *Pelleas,* Swinburne launches into the following prolix anecdote, which merits citation in full because of what it revals about his mental processes:

As for Tennyson's Pelleas, you flatter him by calling him a schoolboy who misses the birch—the generic schoolboy is precociously excitable "with all (such) *appliances* and means to boot"—but the very birch could hardly have drawn human blood—the blood of "a brother and a boy"—from that biped. Unlike a young cousin of mine (aetat. 15) to whom at his earnest prayer I gave a copy of my Poems (hoping they might be truly blessed to him through Jesus our Saviour and His redeeming Blood), but his tutor confiscated the book under penalties, and the boy of course cribbed it, and was (I am happy to say) caught, as he deserved, studying a most appropriately named and especially prohibited poem—and had what he calls "such a jolly good swishing" that his elder brother tells me he came out of his tutor's study with his clothes readjusted but the blood visibly soaking through his shirt and the seat of his breeches (these being, providentially, very light) in patches and stripes—to the wild delight of the junior male members of the household, who received him with acclamations. I wished *mon vieux* had been by to hear—it would have made him wriggle and bubble with enjoyment till his teeth came out—a sight profitable for admonition. . . . Well, I did think my poems had not much of ideal infamy to teach a public schoolboy of four or five years' standing, and he might have read them in holiday time "unwhipped of justice," saying to his tutor, "Hide thee, thou bloody hand" (in a double sense of the adjective). I must confess though he asked me one day lately to explain one or two points in Anactoria which perplexed his young intelligence; but I declined to coach him in Sapphics, and referred him to his tutor for a construe of Catullus "in Priapum"—but somehow he didn't seem to see it quite. I must say though I was sorry for him I was much tickled (otherwise tickled than he was, and elsewhere) at the idea of the blood of a young disciple having already watered the roots of the Church planted by me; and we know that "*Sanguis martyrum semen* (so to speak) *ecclesiae."* Not that I *enjoyed* it—for "Oh! monsieur—il est donc possible qu'on puisse prendre du plaisir à voir souffrir—à voir couler le sang?—Tu le vois, bougresse, lui répond cet homme immoral; oui, putain, tu le vois!" Vide the Marquis passim. Now if the boy had been reading the classic work of that immortal man there might have been some call for birch—if yet of any use. However I hope that like Justine he "offered his flogging to God"—though I'm sure I don't see what God could do with it; but that young woman you know always prayed thus after flagellation or other infliction—"Reçois, Etre Suprême, la triste offrande de mes souffrances!" So I suppose it is the right thing.[60]

The *"mon vieux"* Swinburne refers to is Lord Houghton who was in Egypt at the time attending the opening of the Suez Canal. Lang annotates the letter to indicate that the schoolboy who was flogged for reading his cousin's poems was Thomas Ashburnham (1855–1924), the son of Swinburne's uncle Bertram, the fourth earl. But in letters to Howell dating from September[61] and November 1870,[62] Swinburne relates a similar episode of a young Etonian cousin being birched, supporting it with a note he supposedly received from the cousin's older brother, who was also at Eton. Lang annotates the second letter, stating that he was unable to identify the Etonian cousins and is skeptical about their material existence. If so, the description of the flogging in the letter to Rossetti may also be a fantasy written down and embellished during an otherwise idle afternoon.

Once doubts arise about the historicity of one anecdote, others become suspect. Was Swinburne's account of his being flogged for imitating Catullus's galliambics in *Atys* a fiction? His imagination might have run as follows: "A boy who would read my poems is eating forbidden fruit and ought to be flogged. What if my cousin Thomas, now at Eton, were to be caught reading the copy of *Poems and Ballads* I gave him? Oh, I can see him now, like myself at that age, on the flogging block! And it reminds me of de Sade's *Justine* as well. As for the case of the galliambics: Any boy with the temerity to try his hand at such a difficult meter ought to be flogged. Didn't Joynes [i.e., James Leigh Jones, Swinburne's tutor at Eton] say that galliambics were no meter at all? Well, flogged I will be!" And so he duly recorded it as having actually taken place in letters to Mary Gordon long after the date of the supposed infraction and infliction.[63] In point of fact, Joynes had a reputation for mildness and was no enthusiast for flogging. His reaction to Swinburne's metrical *tour de force* might well have been amusement; schoolmasters do encourage some forms of preciosity but not others. Can there be any symbolic importance to the fact that Atys (Attis) was a self-castrated priest of Cybele? In both cases it is difficult to distinguish fantasy from fact, and we remind ourselves that the

Moebius strip is a twisted circle. But the incontrovertible evidence of the letter to Rossetti is that in the years following 1865 masochism in fantasy as well as in fact was the central idea around which Swinburne's psyche revolved and that it was ideas of flagellation that were its motive force. Considering his comments on the church, the blood of martyrs, and the offering of a flogging to God, one might say that Swinburne made a religion of his masochism.

The question whether Swinburne participated in homosexual acts has been raised repeatedly, but the evidence is elusive. The two leading candidates as coparticipants are his fellow Etonian, George Powell, and the painter Simeon Solomon. Both were overt homosexuals, and Swinburne's relations with them were long and close. Swinburne met Solomon no later than 1863, and their correspondence continued as late as 1872.[64] Swinburne's letters to Solomon have disappeared, but those by the painter to the poet have been preserved.[65] They contain extensive comments about flagellation, and Solomon executed a number of flagellatory drawings for Swinburne's delectation, some illustrating scenes in *Lesbia Brandon,* also a frontispiece for *The Whippingham Papers* (1887). Reviewing Solomon's *A Vision of Love Revealed in Sleep,* Swinburne labels him "a Hellenist of the Hebrews" in whom "Grecian form and beauty divide the allegiance of his Hebrew spirit with Hebraic shadow and majesty." However, this exchange does not constitute evidence of homosexual practices.

The most suspicious evidence is that on one occasion, possibly more, Swinburne and Solomon disported themselves naked in the house at 16 Cheyne Walk.[66] London is not conducive to nudism, and domiciliary exhibitionism is a bit unusual. If one accepts the story that a known masochist and a known homosexual were seen prancing together in the nude, the plausible inference is that some form of sexual activity was about to start, was under way, or had been completed. Perhaps Swinburne tried to introduce Solomon to the pleasures of the birch, and Solomon tried to show Swinburne that homosexual acts were gratifying. But even if such experiments were performed, neither party seems to have been convinced that the other man's meat was his perversion.[67]

Swinburne introduced Solomon to Lord Houghton, Richard Burton, and George Powell, as well as to other literary figures. Solomon had more in common with Powell than with Swinburne and visited Powell at Nant-Eos on several occasions. But in 1873 Solomon was arrested for indecent behavior, convicted, and sentenced. From that point he sank lower and lower, dying in a workhouse in 1905. Not long after his disgrace he tried to sell Swinburne's letters back to him, but details of this blackmail have been effectively hushed up. Later writers have chided Swinburne for his lack of sympathy and charitable understanding for his former friend, but it is difficult to imagine what he could have done for him short of providing him with money, which would have been tantamount to acquiescing to blackmail.

Swinburne's relations with Powell, who was his social equal, who had published some poems and some Icelandic legends, and who was presentable to Swinburne's family, were on a different plane. Their friendship was uninterrupted until Powell died in 1882; it was marked by many visits back and forth, and they exchanged gifts frequently. As a former Etonian, Powell was familiar with the birch and the block, the pain and the pleasure, and the Swinburne-Powell letters are full of allusions to flagellation. It was Powell who procured for Swinburne a used birch from Eton and a picture of the flogging block. Swinburne had no qualms about informing Powell in 1868 about his visits to a flagellation lupanar: "My life has been enlivened of late by a fair friend who keeps a maison de supplices à la Rodin—There is occasional balm in Gilead!"[68] To Powell he could indulge in amusing banter about their shared schoolboy experiences of being beaten. In 1873, when Powell was trying to straighten Swinburne's disordered financial affairs, the latter commented: "I was at first surprised at the apparently Sadique excess of discipline inflicted on the refractory carpet—8s. for a beating! Why, our own floggings came cheaper than that at Eton if I remember the charges aright."[69]

Swinburne and Powell passed a holiday together at Etretât in Normandy in the autumn of 1868. This visit was the occasion for Swinburne's daring swimming escapade from which he had to be rescued by fishermen quite far from land. De Maupassant happened to be in the neighborhood and met them; his impression that they were both English pederasts may have been colored by the conventional reaction of the French bourgeoisie to the comportment of the British upper classes, and perhaps he was judging Swinburne by Powell. However, the following spring, when Powell was planning a return visit and suggested that Swinburne join him, the poet was unable to but wrote "Give my remembrances to my sailors."[70] and a few months later "Remember me 'de coeur' to my sailors."[71] One speculates whether Swinburne had struck up a casual acquaintance with some sailors much as vacationers in search of local color are wont to do, or whether Powell, being more experienced in such negotiations, and Swinburne had picked them up for sexual purposes. If it had been a casual acquaintance over a drink or two in a café, why the remembrance "de coeur"? Or, did Swinburne persuade one or more of them to flog him? The evidence is incomplete and no verdict can be given.

Munby's diary cites an incident at the Arts Club in June 1869 when Charles Cameron, an ex-consular official, "and Swinburne both got drunk, made a scandalous noise in the diningroom and hall, and actually—incredible dictu—embraced one another in some indecent fashion."[72] Although asked to resign from the Arts Club, Swinburne was still a member when Munby had a long tête à tête with him before dinner some time later. Conversation about Shakespeare's sonnets "however led to worse talk; he expressed a horror of sodomy, yet *would* go on talking about it; and an actual admiration of lesbianism, being unable, as he confessed, to see that that is equally loathsome."[73]

Whether Swinburne actually took part in homosexual acts may not be a matter of primary importance. During this time, his masochism was operating at two levels—one, fantasy, the other, reality. The fantasy was the one held since Eton, that he was a schoolboy being birched by a schoolmaster—almost exclusively the subject of his flagellatory verse. Such a fantasy is a displacement of the desire to be used sexually by a father figure. The unconscious desire is unacceptable to consciousness and is transformed. If Swinburne had actually let himself be used passively by a man, it would probably have engendered feelings of guilt and shame. He had already accumulated a sufficient quantity of guilt: failure to live up to his family's expectations, failure to possess Mary Gordon, impotence with women. At the level of reality he was a patron of a flagellation brothel where he was beaten by either or both of "two golden-haired and rouge-cheeked ladies."[74] This form of masochism—suffering and punishment for the sake of or at the hands of a cruel, dominating female figure—is the recurrent theme of Swinburne's published dramas and many of his published poems.

The duality of Swinburne's masochism can be clarified by considering that congenital brain damage and its neurological sequelae led to a moderate degree of ego impairment. His many failures at school and in interpersonal relations reinforced the ego impairment and added a sense of guilt. The social and educational tradition of flogging in his segment of English culture provided a vehicle that fixated his reinforced sense of guilt and inadequacy in a passive position: To accept physical punishment was both compensatory and expiatory. He acted out the fusion of sexual and aggressive impulses by displacing them from his mother and cousin onto prostitutes, and the purchase of flagellation became a separate part of the transaction. In the scenes he enacted, the flogging block became the equivalent of the bed, the buttocks a substitute for the vagina, and the upraised hand or birch, a symbolic penis; the flagellee, having adopted a posture of passive reception, a feminine identification, was ready to become the victim of a symbolic homosexual attack. Swinburne seems to have oscillated between two of the stages of the mechanism described by Freud, being beaten by males in fantasy, by females in fact.

But such an attack would perforce have to remain symbolic, for at the same time Swinburne's masochism was a defense against unconscious homosexual wishes. On this side of the Moebius strip he visualized himself as passive to a dominating male figure. The same equivalents for block, buttocks, and birch remained, but the sense of anal penetration became displaced to the more diffuse gluteal erognous zone. By substituting a female figure in his actual practices, he made anatomically impossible the pederasty that might follow flagellation by a male. That Swinburne rejected homosexual impulses can be partly attributed to his Christian upbringing and the mores of Victorian society, under the canons of which he could only incur further guilt and shame, but in equal or greater part to his interest in the classics and his identification with Greco-Roman hedonism. Though pederasty was a sanctioned feature of that society, the adult passive pederast was a figure both comic and contemptible.

Returning from hypothetical psychodynamics to biographical fact, we have no information about a repressed incident or sequence of events in Swinburne's childhood that helped establish him as a passive flagellant. His reaction to the flogging block at Eton may have set the seal on his masochism, but the psychological background had been prepared before that, and the physical background had been set at birth. Once established, the pattern persisted until it became an obsession, permeating not only his literary productions but the fabric of his daily life. Like the young lovers in his dramas, he was proud to sacrifice himself to be birched by prostitutes who, like the heroines of his dramas, were either indifferent to their lovers' sufferings or else deliberately cruel—the transformation Swinburne's imagination made of Mary Gordon, a love that was never physically consummated.

During his years in London Swinburne became more and more addicted to alcohol. The legend is that Richard Burton, whom Swinburne met through Milnes (Lord Houghton), introduced him to brandy in the early 1860s and it became his favorite drink. Like any Oxford undergraduate Swinburne had had his experiences with the bottle, but until the fateful year 1865 his drinking habits caused no one any concern. In a letter dated November 1865, a few months after Mary Gordon became Mrs. Disney Leith, Swinburne's friend William

Bell Scott, the painter, wrote to Lady Trevelyan, who served as Swinburne's tutelary confidante until her death in 1866, that "you will do him the very kindest of actions if you can touch his sensibility on his vanity—a little sharply. Of late he has been very much excited, and certainly drinking. Gabriel and William Rossetti think he will not live if he goes on as lately without stopping."[75] He did not stop, and ten months later replied to a letter from William Rossetti:

As to your screed of friendly counsel concerning Bacchus. . . . I own the soft impeachment. . . . It's the fault of good conversation. . . . I will never trespass on your hospitality again, however, nor, certainly "ask for" any (like Oliver Twist) after such a warning. Du reste, permit me to recall to your mind the words of wisdom uttered after dinner and before torture by M. le comte de Gernande: "L'ivresse, mes amis, est un vice vraiment délicieux et dont le véritable philosophe ne saurait se passer. Apprends, Justine, que tous les vices s'entrelacent et que celui-ci conduit à tous les autres."[76]

The specious use of de Sade's argument to justify drinking was a clear indication that Swinburne would not stop, and the phrase "tous les vices s'entrelacent" was certainly applicable to his own case. But Rossetti's fear that he would speedily drink himself to death was not borne out; the decline was a much slower process.

Swinburne continued to drink heavily; Gosse's manuscript gives many details, and Munby cites no fewer than six occasions when he saw him drunk at the Arts Club in the early 1870s. That he was sensitive to small quantities of alcohol, consistent with brain damage, is shown on one occasion when he became intoxicated after only a pint of wine. During these years Swinburne's letters are filled with apologies for being unable to fulfill engagements because of a "bilious attack" or unable to write because of a "wretched influenza," transparent disguises for chronic gastritis and the malaise of a continuing hangover. He suffered many painful accidents when he would stumble and fall while drunk. By 1879, when Theodore Watts (later Watts-Dunton) rescued him from his filthy, disordered quarters on Guildford Street near Russell Square and moved him to The Pines, he was probably on the verge of delirium tremens. A plausible conjecture is that by that time alcoholism had deadened his sexual and masochistic impulses. There are only vague hints of such conduct after his father died in 1877.

Most men move to the suburbs and become alcoholics, but Swinburne, as usual, managed to reverse the pattern. The story of his removal to No. 2, The Pines, Putney, by Theodore Watts needs no retelling. From a medical point of view Watts's regimen was enormously successful. He restored Swinburne to health; his alcohol intake was reduced to a bottle of beer at luncheon, and there were no more visits to St. John's Wood. Watts took a grubby schoolboy of forty-two—that was Swinburne's *Selbstbildnis*—and turned him into a clean old man. Only a few items of psychopathological interest require clarification.

There is no reason to think that Watts was unaware of Swinburne's masochism. Their acquaintance began in 1872 when Watts, a qualified solicitor, helped Swinburne with the problems arising from his dealings with his publisher, John Camden Hotten. Writing from his parents' home in 1875, Swinburne refers to the manuscript of *Lesbia Brandon*, parts of which were then in Watts's possession, then continues: "I have been laid up . . . with a badly sprained foot . . . having hurt my left foot eleven days ago in jumping from a fence (N.B. it was 'the Sabbath morn')—rather a schoolboyish mishap for a man of my reverend time of life—but the chastisements of the Lord are heavier than those in use at Eton. (By the by have you seen the Etonian epistle in the July Macmillan? I have been exploding with laughter over it on my bed of pain—it refers *just* to my time, and I daresay I knew the writer)."[77] Was Swinburne drunk when he jumped from the fence? It is not likely that he would be intoxicated at his parents' home, let alone on a Sunday morning. Of course, this sort of accident could happen to anyone, but more likely to a man with poor neuromuscular coordination. The allusions to Eton indicate that Swinburne had taken Watts into his confidence to some extent. The epistle in Macmillan's was titled *Eton Thirty Years Ago* and signed "The Boy Who Was Flogged." Whatever Watts had not heard from Swinburne he could easily have learned from others. Swinburne's masochism was well known to his friends, and Watts was fully capable of conducting a discreet inquiry.

The most unexpected event in the placid Putney villa was Swinburne's attachment to Bertie Mason, the son of Watts's sister. The boy was only five when Swinburne moved in; always sentimental about babies, Swinburne was enchanted. Emotion reached its peak in May 1881 when Bertie, now seven, was taken away by his mother for a month's holiday. The separation led Swinburne to write *A Dark Month*, a series of thirty-one verses (apparently one for each day Bertie was away) with such inappropriate lines as: "I am only my love's/True lover" and "But I pine for the touch of a fetter,/The curb of a strong king's hand."

Swinburne never became the boy's true lover, and the boy did not grow up to be a strong king but a chartered surveyor. Quite revealing is Swinburne's reply to a letter from his mother in March 1881, two months before the boy left on holiday: "I quite understand how (as you say) 'a mother loves those words' which warn us against offending one of the little ones—but to me the divinest of all divine words and thoughts—is that 'of such is the kingdom of heaven.' I am very sure it is so here on earth—where nothing—except age in its brightest beauty . . . is so adorable as a little child is."[78] But two months later Lady Jane wrote to Watts: "His love for that little friend amounts to devotion and I often hope that it may lead to the faith of his youth in some hidden way—for the love of . . . innocent childhood is good and *wholesome*. You and no doubt his Parents will guard the little child from any harmful views on that subject that Algernon might inadvertently lead him into."[79] It sounds very much as if Lady Jane believed that her peccant son was capable of pedophilia with a seven-year-old boy. Upon what past anecdotal basis her suspicion may have rested remains unknown; but if such was its basis, it was surely an incident from Swinburne's own boyhood or youth.

Time passed slowly in Putney, and the household remained stable until 1905 when Watts (now Watts-Dunton) married for the first time at the age of seventy-two. Only then did he cease his opposition to the publication of *Love's Cross-Currents* with its themes of flagellation and incest. To be sure, it had been printed with the title *A Year's Letters* in 1877 as a serial in *The Tatler* under the pseudonym Mrs. Horace Manners, but it created no stir, and Swinburne's authorship was not generally known. Yet, its autobiographical content would have been evident to anyone who knew him, had the book been published under his own name. The 1905 publication won modest praise and, oddly enough for the post-Wildean era, it created no scandal.

There has been considerable speculation about the relationship of Swinburne and Watts. Recently a journalist wrote: "their joint household resembled, in all particulars but sex, a steady and successful homosexual union. Swinburne was the docile, stay-at-home 'wife'; Watts was the 'husband,' who managed all their business affairs, dictated the decisions, and doled out the pin money."[80] Not an inaccurate description, for Swinburne's burnt-out masochism made him a suitably passive "wife" for Watts, who gave up his work as a solicitor to manage Swinburne's affairs and to carve out a modest but agreeable literary career for himself. But there was another facet to the relationship, arising from Swinburne's need to be passive and managed. The clue is in a letter to Watts in 1894, written when Swinburne was visiting relatives at Chestal, one of his rare trips away from Putney without Watts. He described a ramble in the woods:

Your minor had (he must confess) broken bounds and played truant in very Etonian fashion, and came home so torn with brambles and stung with nettles that he felt rather as if he were returning from a subsequent and consequent interview with the Head Master (the birch itself could hardly have stung more, or lacerated the flesh quite so severely—I can feel, while I write, one long jagged cut or scratch on the fleshy hinder part of my right thigh: quite appropriate as the truant's doom, and vividly suggestive of vivid reminiscences).[81]

It was over forty years since Swinburne had been at Eton, and the letter is an example of "in memory only, reconsidered passion." But the key lies in Swinburne casting himself as "your minor" to Watts—the term used in English public schools to denote a younger brother, the same term Mary Gordon Leith used to describe her relation to Swinburne in the "Cy merest dozen" letters. The substitution of roles was complete.

English poetry has a long tradition of using flagellation as a subject. Examples can be found in the writings of, *inter alios*, Marlowe, Herrick, Shakespeare, Butler, Pope, and Shenstone. But in these loci, sado-masochism was not the major theme. An early example is an epigram derived from Ovid and ascribed to Christopher Marlowe but actually by John Davies:

> When Francus comes to solace with his whore,
> He sends for rods and strips himself stark naked;
> For his lust sleeps, and will not rise before
> By whipping of the wench if it be awaked.

Half a century later Robert Herrick, that master of the light love lyric, wrote *The Dream:*

> Me thought, (last night) love in an anger came,
> And brought a rod, so whipt me with the same:
> Mirtle the twigs were, meerly to imply:
> Love strikes, but 'tis with gentle crueltie.
> Patient I was: Love pitifull grew then,
> And stroak'd the stripes, and I was whole agen.
> Thus like a Bee, Love-gentle stil doth bring
> Hony to salve, where he before did sting.

Only a few decades separate Herrick from Samuel Butler whose *Hudibras* deals at length with an episode in which a lady offers to go surety for Hudibras and permit his release from prison if he will undergo a whipping, viz.:

> But if a beating seem so brave,
> What glories must a whipping have?
> Such great achievements cannot fail
> To cast salt on a woman's tail.

and half a canto later she repeats:

> If matrimony and hanging go
> By dest'ny, why not a whipping too?
> What medicine else can cure the fits
> Of lovers when they lose their wits?
> Love is a boy, by poets styled,
> Then spare the rod, and spoil the child.

But neither Marlowe, nor Herrick, nor Butler lost sight of "the right true end of love." Their whipping motifs were in the context of an otherwise usual sexual relation, not a substitute. A more recent echo is found in one of Leopold Bloom's transient fantasies in the Circe episode of *Ulysses*, "A warm tingling glow without effusion. Refined birching to stimulate the circulation."[82] Butler's suggestion that flagellation has educational value—"spare the rod, and spoil the child"—was taken from Proverbs (13:24), and the dictum had been common coin since the Middle Ages. One might go so far as to credit King Solomon with shaping educational practices up to, and in some areas including, the twentieth century. But in the eighteenth century, England could rely on William Shenstone's lengthy poem in imitation of Spenser titled *The School-Mistress:* she dwells "In every village marked with little spire," and is

> A matron old, whom we school-mistress name,
> Who boasts unruly brats with birch to tame . . .
> And in her hand for sceptre she does wield
> Tway birchen sprays.

Continuing the Spenserian vein and prefiguring Swinburne, Shenstone goes on:

> As erst the bard by Mulla's silver stream,
> Oft, as he told of deadly dolorous plight,
> Sighed as he sung, and did in tears indite.
> For brandishing the rod, she doth begin
> To loose the brogues, the stripling's late delight!
> And down they drop; appears his dainty skin,
> Fair as the furry-coat of whitest ermilin.

Shenstone was being coyly and bucolically descriptive, taking common everyday experience and couching it as a deliberate archaism. The only substantive point is that birching was a democratic process, one found in every dame school, not "the hereditary apanage of the young aristocrat," as Swinburne would have had it.

Alexander Pope was a more aristocratic poet and in keeping with his character satirized the procedure—but at an elitist level—in the *Dunciad:*

> Proceed great days! till learning fly the shore,
> Till Birch shall blush with noble blood no more,
> Till Thames see Eton's sons forever play,
> Till Westminster's whole year be holiday,
> Till Isis' Elders reel, their pupils' sport,
> And Alma Mater lie dissolved in Port!

Pope's acid touch found its continuation in *Don Leon,* a satire doubtfully ascribed to George Colman the Younger, who catalogued Lord Byron's variations on what was becoming an all-too-familiar theme. Along with incest and sodomy we are told:

> At college bred, and destined for the church,
> You turn a Busby, and you wield the birch.
> Think you there's no incentive in the sight
> Of sixth-form bottoms, naked, round, and white?
> Ask Drury, Butler, sleek-gilled Goodenough,
> How looks a kallipygic disk in buff?
> Ask him of Eton, who if fame speaks true,
> Made open boast he all his scholars knew
> By their posteriors better than their face,
> As most familiar with the nether place.
> Flog, lechers, flog, the measured strokes adjust:
> 'Tis well your cassocks hide your rising lust.

Not great verse, and Byron went to Harrow in any case, but Colman came uncomfortably nearer the truth about schoolboy flagellation than his predecessors. Understandably, the poem was suppressed. There is no reason to believe that Swinburne was acquainted with it, even though the tone is closer to his than any of his precursors.

Swinburne's direct inspiration was *The Rodiad,* a poem falsely ascribed to Colman the Younger, first published in 1871.[83] It extols and almost hallows flagellation in all walks of life and all levels of social relations, failing only to claim it as a patriotic duty or religious obligation, two virtues that no doubt slipped its author's mind. The author of *The Rodiad* tells us that flogging is

> Delightful sport! whose never failing charm
> Makes young blood tingle and keeps old blood warm.

Among Swinburne's own contributions to this subliterary genre are *Eton: Another Ode*, [84] *The Flogging-Block, The Whippingham Papers* (1887), *Charlie Collingwood's Flogging* (1879), and *Frank Fane—A Ballad* (1880). The first two remain in manuscript; just how the others attained underground publication is obscure. Perhaps the verses and sketches of *The Whippingham Papers* and the poems that appeared in *The Pearl* were items Swinburne had sent to Howell who, finding himself pressed for money, sold them to an enterprising publisher whose name was probably not "E. Avery," which appears on the title page of *The Whippingham Papers.* There can be no doubt regarding Swinburne's authorship of these unsigned pieces; they have his metrical thumbprint and include some of the cast of characters that appear in *The Flogging-Block.*

Using the watermarks on the manuscript pages, Fuller finds the earliest possible date for *The Flogging-Block* as 1869, the latest 1887. But the extant pages seem to be holograph fair copies rather than first or second drafts; and one can conjecture that Swinburne, now removed to Putney, his poetic imagination fallow, passed much of his time recopying the stanzas in which his flagellation fantasy, no longer realizable, took shape. The fourteen floggings are described in prolix detail and with relish, and even though penmanship was tiresome, it was his only erotic outlet. As Gosse put it, "he experienced an ecstatic pleasure in letting his mind rest on flagellation, and in conjuring up scenes of it." [85]

With respect to the content of the fantasy, Swinburne was a purist; it consists only of the block, the boy, the bottom, and the birch. At no point is there a description of genitalia, or even a hint of erotic reaction in the schoolmaster, the boy, or the witnesses. Nor does he mention associated fetish objects—no furs, high-heeled boots, leather or rubber garments, none of the paraphernalia which figure so prominently in other literature of the genre, especially that originating on the Continent. A few passages can illustrate what occupied Swinburne's mind; he announces his stance in *Arthur's Flogging*, a chapter in *The Whippingham Papers:*

> I sing of Arthur's Flogging: I, who heard
>   The boy himself sing out beneath the birch,
> Louder and shriller than a singing bird,
>   Or screaming parrot on its gilded perch.

His metrical skill is unimpaired. Swinburne adroitly matches his meter as a correlative to the insistent rhythm of the repeated strokes of the birch. In *Rufus's Flogging,* a chapter in *The Flogging-Block,* he provides an example of the sadistic sarcasm of Dr. Birkenshaw (*birk* is the Scottish word for birch), the schoolmaster:

> There's a score for the birch and your bottom to settle,
> And I've usually found you a lad of some mettle.
> Now no better match can be played in the field
> Where both sides are well-matched and unwilling to yield
> Than the match—an experience you often have had—
> Between a good rod and a mettlesome lad.
> The sight of a naked and smarting young dunce
> Is a sight to amuse and admonish at once,
> A sight to remember as well as enjoy:
> Go down for the hundredth time, Rufus, my boy.

Many of the imagined floggings were carried out in the presence of other boys whose comments of sympathy, amusement, or recollection of past suffering are interwoven as counterpoint in the dialogue between master and boy, punctuated by the sound of the birch, indicated as "Swish!" In the prologue to *The Flogging-Block* (subtitled "An Heroic Poem by Rufus Rodworthy, Esq., With Annotations by Barebum Birchingham, Esq."), Swinburne asks, "who is the bare-breeched Boy there kneeling?" And the reply comes back:

> With visionary eye reversed I see
> Myself in him, and gaze myself on me.
> I see the Shirt drawn up, the Bottom bared;
> The Bottom daily stripped and never spared.

The fantasy continues to develop:

> I see, tenacious of the lifted Skirt,
> My Brother and my Cousin holding up my Shirt:
> I see them smile and leer upon each other;
> A cruel Cousin! A more cruel Brother. . . .
> At each fresh Birchen Stroke they smile afresh
> To see "the young one" suffer in the Flesh.
> Each time the twigs bend round across my Bum
> Pain bids "Cry out," but Honour bids, "Be dumb."

The presence of a fictive older brother and cousin (can the latter be a transformation of Mary Gordon?) and the call by "Honour" to be stoical reinforce the idea that Swinburne approached his floggings at

Eton in an attitude of overcompensation *coram familia* for physical inferiority. For him the *rite de passage*, his initiation into the tribe of young English gentlemen, took place upon the flogging block at Eton with the schoolmaster as high priest. It is not the only instance in which a damaged brain has fused an erotic with a religious experience.

Swinburne's other masochistic fantasy—being subjugated, treated cruelly, even beaten by a woman—found its expression in his published poems and plays. The most penetrating analysis of this fantasy is in Praz's *The Romantic Agony* in the chapter titled "La Belle Dame sans Merci"; the literary antecedents of the theme are familiar. In Swinburne's underground, overtly sadomasochistic sketch titled "Hints on Flogging, Shewing How to Enjoy It in Perfection, in a Letter to a Lady," one of the pieces in *The Whippingham Papers* (1887), is the sentence so often quoted: "One of the great charms of birching lies in the sentiment that the floggee is the powerless victim of the furious rage of a beautiful woman." Almost never quoted from this same piece is his recipe for a satisfactory and satisfying *modus operandi:*

I propose that you shall keep a small book containing a series of birch scenes, written in dramatic form, which, when your visitor calls, you should put in his hands, and ask him which of them he would like to enact with you. . . . Previous to commencing the drama it should of course be arranged what number of strokes your visitor should receive, and that being settled it should be understood that no solicitations, or prayers, or entreaties for mercy or struggles on his part, which, of course, *to keep up the illusion* he will make, should influence you to reduce the number agreed on.

To this proposal Swinburne affixed a sample scene titled "The Enraged and Jealous Wife" in which the "husband" is flogged by his "wife" who had caught him in a compromising situation with a maid-servant. The plot may be banal, but when one reflects that Swinburne was impotent, yet fantasied being flogged for deceiving his nonexistent wife—that is, he aspired to potency with two women in fantasy while he had none in reality—the question remains open: To what extent was his desire to be flogged by a woman expiation for guilt feelings about sexual inadequacy? From one woman to two is a "double your pleasure" fantasy, one realizable and often realized by many men; but from zero to two is impossible to execute because the multiplier is infinity—beyond the limit of the hedonic calculus.

To Swinburne any sort of relationship with a woman was a martyrdom of love. Praz summarizes its archetypes: "The influence of the crime-stained Renaissance of the Elizabethan dramatists, of the gory Middle Ages of the Pre-Raphaelites . . . of Gautier's orgiastic antiquity and Baudelaire's grim Modernity; finally the Ate of Greek Tragedy, the implacable doctrine of the Old Testament, and the cruel nihilism of Sade—all these were sources which flowed easily into one single stream, and found a natural bed in such a mind as Swinburne's, which was predisposed to receive them."[86] Even in his Oxford days, a few years before the denouement of his relationship with Mary Gordon, the literary *belle dame* appears in *Rosamond* (1860):

> Yea, I am found the woman in all tales,
> The face caught always in the story's face:
> I Helen, holding Paris by the lips,
> Smote Hector through the head; I Cressida
> So kissed men's mouths that they went sick or mad,
> Stung right at the brain with me.

Swinburne's litany of cruel female idols includes Atalanta and Mary Stuart, Faustine and Lesbia Barndon, Dolores and Mary Gordon. He tried to deliver himself from them by submitting to the figures on the opposite side of the Moebius strip—if there is an opposite surface—the "two golden-haired and rouge-cheeked ladies" in St. John's Wood. For Swinburne, like other Romantics, life and art were symbiotic. They sucked all the *Angst* and excesses of their art back into their life styles; behavior was another metaphor.

Excluding sadomasochistic and sexual content, the purely sensual features of Swinburne's poetry when coupled with his extravagant manner of speech and excesses of life-style, the façade he showed society, led many of his contemporaries, self-styled "responsible" critics, to rush to judgment on moral grounds. In their defense, the general tone of intellectual Victorian life emphasized morality (the term is not used pejoratively) with little sense of possible fallacies in judgments made from that base. The critic Meredith contented himself with a mild assertion that he could find no deep moral center in Swinburne's poems; the remark was made *en passant* about some early poems, and Meredith did not reaffirm it or develop the point. Lesser figures took up the cudgels. *Poems and Ballads* was too "hot" for some publishers to touch. Lord Lytton gave Polonius-like advice to his son that Swinburne was "a dangerous companion to another poet. . . . wholly without moral sense."[87] Bayard Taylor referred to his "colossal wilfulness" and called him "a great but utterly unbalanced poet,"[88] with a "weak moral sense" and a "disorganizing element in his nature."[89] Fair comment—even Swinburne's apologists would concede he was willful and unbalanced. That his life-style was disorganized is evident; but given his premises, were his poems and plays disorganized? No twentieth-century reader can view with other than amused tolerance Taylor's unenlightened comment that "a clear headed and hearted woman could cure . . . his morbid relish for the atrocious forms of passion."[90] By 1867 it was much too late for that.

There was a moral center in Swinburne and his work. One cannot credit him with being a profound thinker; as e. e. cummings put it, "Punished bottoms interrupt philosophy." But in early life Swinburne chose the political ideals of republicanism in a society that considered it radical, and he rejected the received theology of his class and vocation. Perhaps Swinburne's hatred of Louis Napoleon and the Second Empire was juvenile and naively expressed. The coup d'état of 1851 occurred when Swinburne was at Eton, and its political chicanery and double dealing would naturally offend a British schoolboy's sense of fair play. What young Swinburne did not recognize was that the coup's success depended on the consent of a majority of the French people who at that time did not want a republican form of government. Nonetheless, the coup was an apostasy from the stated principles, the moral basis, upon which Louis Napoleon had been elected following civil disorder in 1848. Historians disagree whether Louis Napoleon ever had a moral center in either public or private life; one cannot charge Swinburne with abandoning his moral center.

By the same token, Swinburne's unswerving devotion to the cause of Italian liberation as well as to Mazzini, a man of high moral purpose, was not the choice of an opportunist looking for a cause. One recalls Boswell's attachment to Paoli and the struggle for Corsican independence. The success of the Italian risorgimento was based on its true reflection of the will of the Italian people to shake off French and Austrian hegemony. Again, Swinburne's allegiance stemmed from a moral center. He was not motivated by a desire for public recognition; in fact, he wisely declined to stand for Parliament when that bizarre notion was broached by members of the Reform League. Not even Swinburne could visualize himself in Hansard's pages.

A comparable sense of personal moral choice lay beneath his decision to withdraw from communion with the Church of England. It was a private choice carried out with no fanfare, no public declamation like Shelley's defense of atheism. In a letter to Stedman in 1875 he supplied his explanation: "I always felt by instinct and perceived by reason that no man could conceive of a *personal* God except by brute Calibanic superstition or else by true supernatural revelation; that a natural God was the absurdest of all human figments; *because* no man could by other than apocalyptic means . . . *conceive* of any other sort of divine person than man with a difference . . . man with the good in him exaggerated and the evil excised. . . . Men give him the qualities they prefer in themselves or about them."[91]

Profound theology it is not, but in rejecting superstition and revelation Swinburne would have earned support from the respectable school of philosophy called pragmatism which opted for reason over animal faith. One need not subscribe to his views on religion to concede that they represent a moral choice based on principle, and one may ask whether persons who accept uncritically a received faith merely because it was their fathers' hold it because of a personal moral center.

Perhaps the clearest insight into Swinburne's moral base is in his role as the first English critic to comprehend and transmit the importance of Baudelaire's poetry. Literary affinities between the two have been explicated in detail by Praz, but the biographical parallels are less familiar. After commenting on the "open-air" normalcy of Swinburne's childhood in contrast to the "boudoir" atmosphere of Baudelaire's, Harold Nicolson makes a Plutarchean comparison:

The school careers of both were marred by failure. . . . They both began with exemplary docility and ended them in an atmosphere of rebellion and disgrace. . . . They both succumbed to the temptations of inebriation—Swinburne to brandy, Baudelaire to drugs. They both refused to work at the professions prescribed for them by their parents. Each received a strong impulse, not from the literature of his own country, but from a foreign author, . . . Hugo was no less important to Swinburne than was Poe to Baudelaire. They both began composing verses at about the same state of their development . . . both postponed publication for several years . . . both, on publication, were faced with a prosecution for obscenity. They were neither of them perverted in the accepted meaning of that term. But for both of them the sexual impulse was deformed by partial impotence forcing them to derive from cerebral excitation that relief which they were physically denied. . . . The love affairs of both these poets were a source of acid disappointment, humiliation, and shame.[92]

The antepenultimate sentence was written before Swinburne's masochism and impotence became public knowledge, but that does not invalidate the generalization that follows.

Both Baudelaire and Swinburne recognized their mutual affinity. Reviewing *Les Fleurs du Mal* in 1862, Swinburne wrote:

Throughout the chief part of this book, he has chosen to dwell mainly upon sad and strange things—the weariness of pain and the bitterness of pleasure—the perverse happiness and wayward sorrows of exceptional people. . . . Failure and sorrow, next to physical beauty and perfection of sound or scent, seem to have an infinite attraction for him. . . . Not the luxuries of pleasure in their simple first form, but the sharp and cruel enjoyments of pain, the acrid relish of suffering felt or inflicted, the sides on which nature looks unnatural, go to make up the stuff and substance of this poetry.[93]

Comparable analyses have since appeared; but the time the review was written is important—after Swinburne had read de Sade but before the crisis with Mary Gordon. In the context of what we know about Swinburne's psyche, it is not surprising that his perception should be more on target than any of Baudelaire's other contemporary critics. Nor is it unexpected that Swinburne should single out *Litanies de Satan* with its refrain, "O Satan, prends pitié de ma longue misère!" as the keynote in which "all failure and sorrow on earth and all the cast-out things of this world—ruined bodies and souls diseased—made their appeal, in default of help, to Him in whom all sorrow and all failure were incarnate."[94] But such a judgment was well in advance of its time and depended for its special plea upon the insight of a codefendant: "there is no one poem of the *Fleurs du Mal* which has not a distinct and vivid background of morality to it. . . . It is not his or any artist's business to warn against evil; but certainly he does not exhort to it, knowing well enough that the one fault is as great as the other."[95] To a culture that valued poetry for its didactic or homiletic stance, its pot of message, this view was a challenge, a gauntlet no one picked up, a controversy no critic chose to join. The question was not proper for debate in England in the 1860's. If it can be granted the accolade of being a minority opinion, it was a minority of one. Yet, half a century later this idea of "the artist's business" was an orthodoxy of the avant garde, and a century later a truism.

"For to be a Satanist . . . one must also be a Godist" is Aldous Huxley's epigram to describe Baudelaire's polarity, and he continues: ". . . the present age is singularly Godless. Debauchery was a tragical affair in Baudelaire's [and Swinburne's] day; it is now a merely medical one. We feel scientifically about our sins, not satanically."[96] For this reason a medical view of Swinburne's masochism and its consequences has a justification. In a generation notable for its public violence, when private violence has become commonplace, incidental, or anecdotal, cases like Swinburne's require evaluation, not only for the unique insight into the subject itself but for its more general application. In discussing Marlowe's *Edward II*, the drama of a king whose *modus moriendi* was prescribed as appropriate to his deviation, Harry Levin commented: "the moral advantage of masochism over sadism is, to say the least, a delicate question. But it marks a psychological advance, from terror to pity, when the protagonist experiences genuine agony; while, in philosophical terms, it replaces the values of Epicureanism with those of Stoicism."[97]

CHAPTER 3

Lady Chatterley's What?

Confronted by a novel written during its author's last illness, the physician-reader should be alert for the effects of disease upon literary production. Almost all prose fiction contains a clue to biography, however deeply hidden or remote. Implicit in the concept of psychosomatic medicine—one of our own generation's approaches to the mind-body problem—is the idea that a patient's symptoms, or literary productions, if he is a writer, will reflect something of his intrapsychic conflicts. Such revelations, we believe, are more likely to be enhanced by a chronic, disabling, even life-threatening illness. That the patient's or writer's reactions will depend on his psychologic status before he became physically ill is almost axiomatic.

Medical interest in D. H. Lawrence centers around two elements: his pulmonary tuberculosis, an organic disorder, and his psychosexual problems, a complex set of functional disorders. His last novel, *Lady Chatterley's Lover,* was written between 1926 and 1928 while he was suffering from the advancing pulmonary tuberculosis which finally killed him in 1930 at the age of forty-five. Now that the novel has been officially and legally declared not to be obscene—was it really obscene in 1928, or does obscenity vary with time?—we can examine it as we would any other novel, taking it as a "symptom" and its writer as our patient.

Lawrence was the fourth child and youngest of three sons in the family of a collier in the Midlands. Noah Fabricant's essay summarizes the anamnestic data.[1] His first illness was "bronchitis" at the age of two weeks. He was a "delicate" child who had frequent respiratory infections and a nervous hacking cough. Present-day sophistication suggests the possibility of juvenile bronchiectasis or hypogammaglobulinemia, but neither of these two rare conditions could have been diagnosed in Lawrence's youth. Bronchiectasis was not well described until the 1930s, and hypogammaglobulinemia is a nosologic entity unknown until the late 1950s. It is idle to speculate along these lines; neither possibility can be substantiated in the absence of suitable tissue or serum for laboratory diagnosis. It is far more likely that Lawrence's childhood respiratory illnesses were the banal infections so common among children in the lower economic levels: the result of faulty diet, naive concepts of hygiene, lack of central heating (not exclusively the misfortune of the lower classes in England), and living in close quarters in a wretched climate. There is no firm medical evidence denoting Lawrence's primary infection with the tubercle bacillus. Any one of his youthful respiratory infections might have been juvenile tuberculosis followed by healing and a Ghon complex.

In his seventeenth year Lawrence had a severe attack of pneumonia which, according to him, damaged his health for life. It is doubtful that so well defined a pneumonitis could have been related to tuberculosis either as a primary acid-fast infection or as a bacterial infection predilectively superimposed upon a lung already severely damaged by tubercle. If Lawrence had had a primary juvenile tuberculosis complex previously, it was probably quiescent in 1901–2.

Lawrence's next illness is less precisely defined. He refers to 1911 as his "sick year," but it is difficult to tell whether he, then twenty-six years old, was suffering from recurrent pulmonary problems or an emotional reaction to his mother's death from cancer at the end of 1910. He had already completed his collegiate education and had begun his brief career as an English teacher in the suburbs of London. During his "sick year" he was well enough to write most of the first draft of *Sons and Lovers*, his overtly autobiographical novel. He did have a severe bout of pneumonia in the autumn of 1911 following exposure to cold and rain on a railway platform. This may very well have reactivated an arrested juvenile tuberculous infection. Emile Delavenay reports that David Garnett, whose country place Lawrence visited frequently, found a bloodstained handkerchief left behind in 1913.[2] If this is taken as the first evidence of hemoptysis, Lawrence had a well-established pulmonary infection by that time. By late 1915 such close friends as Philip Heseltine, Robert Nichols, and Cynthia Asquith spoke of him as consumptive. Lawrence was rejected for military service as physically unfit in 1915–16; the reason may not have been told him, or, if so he may have suppressed it. His tuberculosis was not improved by the hardships

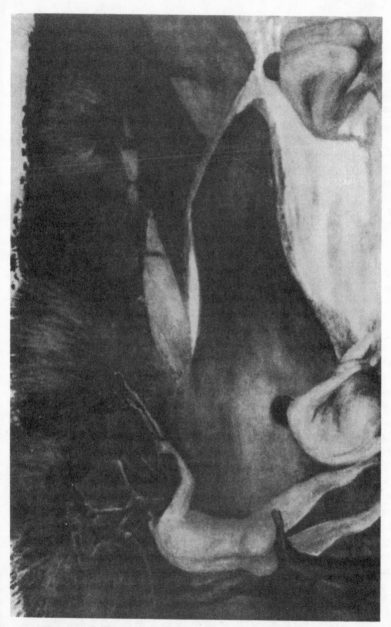

The Willow Tree, by D. H. Lawrence. Courtesy of Harry T. Moore

he and his wife Frieda underwent during the war when they lived under primitive conditions in Cornwall, often without adequate food or heat.

Lawrence continued to have episodes of poor health which he characterized as "beastly flu" or "bronchitis" until his first pulmonary hemorrhage in 1925. There is no telling how long he had had tuberculosis before this date, but from then on his course was progressively downhill. Lawrence's emotional adaptation to chronic pulmonary infection was an attitude of *denial.* At no time in his life would he admit that he had tuberculosis; the word was taboo. He employed the usual euphemisms such as "bronchitis," "my bronchials," or "flu." He habitually "forgot" what his doctors told him and followed their recommendations haphazardly or not at all. According to Fabricant, "In Mexico City during February 1925, Lawrence suffered a violent attack of what he was told was tuberculosis. Although he was not yet forty, he knew, despite his refusal to acknowledge it to the world, that he had not much longer to live." It is not necessary to describe the downhill course of his disease, the recurrent pulmonary hemorrhages, the fever, weakness, weight loss, and debility. The course of the disease from 1925 followed the textbook pattern, and the biographies by Harry T. Moore and Richard Aldington supply the necessary details.[3]

At this point I should state my position about D. H. Lawrence lest readers construe the grave reservations I shall express about the value of *Lady Chatterley's Lover* as an attack on Lawrence as a person and as a novelist. Put simply, I have much admiration and a moderate degree of sympathy with Lawrence as a man. I have no doubts that *Sons and Lovers* is one of the most important novels of this century; parts of it never fail to move me no matter how often I reread them. *The Rainbow* and *Women in Love* are both fine novels; few writers approach Lawrence in his grasp of female psychology. Many of his short stories are splendid, though I think he is at his best in larger forms. I must confess that his poetry does not touch me, though many passages can be described as beautiful without debasing that word. I am somewhat wary of Lawrence as a literary critic; far too many of his statements seem to be self-serving declarations; as a critic, he is long on feeling and short on reason. Lawrence's life on this earth was difficult and complex. His range of personal associations was wide, and his friends and associates have not been shy about publishing their recollections. Regardless of his intellectual limitations, he must have been a compelling figure, albeit socially difficult, if not impossible. The view I have chosen to adopt is that of the physician who, though involved with his patient, must retain some objectivity. Like any physician, I want my "patient" to do well. What concerns me most is to determine, so far as I can, what psychological problems Lawrence had which prevented him from being so successful as his talents would entitle him to be, to determine, insofar as legitimate inference will permit, what role the combination of his progressive pulmonary tuberculosis and psychosexual conflicts played in shaping the failure which I think his last novel is.

That *Lady Chatterley's Lover* is generally available for reading in un-expurgated form is the result of two legal trials, one in the United States, the other in England. Charles Rembar describes in detail the Post Office Department hearing (not a trial by jury) in 1959 at which he successfully appealed an administrative decision barring the Grove Press edition from the mails.[4] His two literary experts, Malcolm Cowley and Alfred Kazin, cogently stated their views why the book was not "obscene" and testified to its literary values. The trial in England, *Regina v. Penguin Books Ltd.*, was a public trial by jury in 1960, and the defense consisted chiefly of the testimony of some three dozen distinguished figures in British letters and public life who testified that the novel had literary merit and that the "four-letter words" describing the sexual organs and act were not obscene, that their use was integral to Lawrence's artistic purposes.

A summary of that trial has been published, but we need not re-capitulate most of the testimony.[5] Lawrence's stated purpose in writing the book was so that men and women would "be able to think sex, fully, completely, honestly, and cleanly. . . . Sex lashes out against counter-feit emotion, and is ruthless, devastating against false love."[6] Judge Bryan's decision in New York, a year before the trial in England, had taken this view into account: "The book is almost as much a polemic as a novel."[7] The trial in England hinged almost exclusively upon the question of vocabulary. Over a quarter of a century previously, Allen Walker Read had examined this problem: "[The words] are not cant or slang or dialect, but belong to the oldest and best established element in the English vocabulary. They are not even sub-standard, for they form part of the linguistic equipment of speakers of standard English. . . . Surely, no sensible person would maintain that sex in itself is obscene. . . . The determinant of obscenity lies not in words or things, but in the attitudes that people have toward these words and things."[8]

Professor Read went on to make an important distinction, an argument which seems to have been lost sight of in the smoke of literary battle: "A distinction must be made . . . between a taboo of *concept* and a taboo of *word*. The taboo of concept is the relatively simple avoidance of a subject that is felt to be not suitable to the occasion. The enigmatic problem arises over the taboo of *word:* when a subject is admissible at all, why should not the plain, outspoken terms be the best ones to use?" With specific reference to *Lady Chatterley's Lover,* Professor Read comments: "A courageous attempt to ignore the taboo was made by D. H. Lawrence. . . . His use of the word in sincere simplicity differs strikingly from the inverted taboo of those who trade upon sex as a dirty secret. However, with most people of the present day, his experiment, admirable in aim, is a failure, for the lurid words stand out with all their smirched associations and cannot be accepted at their innocent face value."

A whole generation of novel writers and their readers have passed since that was written, and the taboo words have appeared in print with greater and greater frequency. Sir Allen Lane, the founder of Penguin Books, testified that he was taking a calculated risk in the cause of literary freedom. Ever a pragmatist, he discounted the importance of the testimony of literary experts: "Either I'll go to prison or I won't. I don't expect to. The only features of the book that anybody could possibly object to are the four-letter words, and there is not one of them that has not appeared in print in this country before."[9]

In a sense *Lady Chatterley's Lover* is a rather old-fashioned novel. It is the story of a married woman who falls in love with another man, the "triangle" which is as old as classical mythology and as new as the latest bedroom farce. Lady Chatterley is merely one of a fictional sisterhood which includes at its best such characters as Hester Prynne, Emma Bovary, and Mollie Bloom, as well as thousands of less important, less interesting adulteresses. The story is related in a conventional manner; the novel has a beginning, a middle, and an end. Its style and structure are not unlike those of dozens of novels in the late Victorian and Edwardian period. Lawrence's prose approximates the tradition of Thomas Hardy and George Meredith; he was not strongly influenced by the stylistic innovations of his avant-garde contemporaries such as Joyce, Proust, Henry James, or the young André Gide. Lawrence's only new contribution in *Lady Chatterley's Lover* was the explicit description of scenes of sexual activity and the use of the demotic vocabulary.

Lawrence's thesis in *Lady Chatterley's Lover* is two-fold: First, that a fully satisfactory relationship for both partners is an essential ingredient for a happy marriage, that marriage is a sacred institution, the highest expression of intimacy which man and woman can share. Second, that the progressive industrialization of England (or any other country) is not only a blot on the landscape but robs men of their virility and women of the femininity, especially insofar as it leads them to pursue false values and materialistic goals. It is difficult to believe that anyone would seriously quarrel with this position, not in 1928 any more than today. The theses are neither original nor daring. Victorian novelists had recognized the importance of the sexual element in marriage; they called it "love," a four-letter Anglo-Saxon word one rarely finds chalked up as a *graffito*. Other writers, too numerous to mention, had dealt with the dangers of an industrial society, how man's soul is warped by pursuit of wealth, possessions, and power. Lawrence himself had promulgated these same ideas in his previous novels, *Sons and Lovers, The Rainbow,* and *Women in Love,* as well as in some short stories. The only unflattering remark one might make about the subject matter of *Lady Chatterley's Lover* is that Lawrence was repeating himself. One may well ask why Lawrence, no stranger to official censorship, knowing that he had advancing tuberculosis and not too long to live, chose to make his novel a restatement, albeit more explicit in vocabulary, of a position he had already established.

Lawrence did his own cause no good in the literary world. In a letter to Aldous Huxley, dated August 15, 1928, he referred to James Joyce's *Ulysses* as "deliberate journalistic dirty-mindedness."[10] Charity toward his contemporary novelists was not one of Lawrence's virtues, and one may question whether it was poetic or pornographic justice that *Ulysses* was declared not obscene vis-à-vis the United States mails by Judge Woolsey in 1933, over a quarter of a century before the public purification of *Lady Chatterley.* Even among his friends Lawrence had a reputation for anti-intellectualism and lack of logical reasoning. Richard Aldington has commented: "This absurdity of self-contradiction as well as denying the plainest reality, so valuable to an imaginative artist, infuriated prosaic and pedantic persons into writing angry books of refutation. . . . If a fact displeased, hindered, or contradicted him, he denied the fact; and he denied the reality of other people's feelings to suit his own convenience."[11]

Esther Andrews, a close friend of both Lawrence and Frieda, who had stood by them loyally when they were having trouble with the police in Cornwall during World War I, comments on his tactics in debate: "But at the slightest touch of adverse criticism or hostility, Lawrence becomes violent. His vituperation is magnificent. He spares none. He has quarrelled with everyone. . . . [He] is a Puritan, really, and his intellectual reaction against it is so violent that he hurls himself against it with all of himself, destroying himself as he does it.[12]

Even his friend and admirer, Aldous Huxley, presents a similar portrait of Lawrence, disguised as Kingham in *Two or Three Graces:* "it was always difficult arguing with Kingham. You might think you had him cornered; you raised your logical cudgel to smash him. But while you were bringing it down, he darted out from beneath the stroke through some little trap door of his own discovery, clean out of the argument. It was impossible to prove him in the wrong, for the simple reason that he never remained long enough in any one intellectual position to be proved anything."[13]

Apart from its being exasperating in the daily accommodations of interpersonal relationships, logical inconsistency to this degree and the inability to tolerate disagreement are dangerous qualities in a writer, particularly a writer of polemical fiction. Such a mind is capable of constructing any fiction to suit the needs of its own fantasies. That type of mental process need not be deleterious to literary imagination and productivity; it is the next step which makes them dangerous. When the mind which constructs such fictions begins to insist that they are real (sometimes more real than real), that they have a validity outside of satisfying the writer's unconscious needs and wishes, that these fictions can be applied to the lives, motives and conduct of other people, then the writer is at the mercy of unconscious forces which he cannot control. In his last decade Lawrence all too often fell into this trap.

The emotional response to chronic illness colors the patient's attitude toward the disease (sometimes for better, sometimes for worse); it colors his relationship to his family, his friends, his work, even the minutiae of his daily living. All these revolve in part about the fact that he is ill and in part about the nature of his illness. From 1925 on, Lawrence was seriously ill, sick more often than well. His literary powers during the last five years of his life declined as noticeably as his physical strength. To maintain the integrity of his own ego he often adopted, as already noted, the defense of denial, not an uncommon defense, but one which makes for a patient who will not follow his doctors' advice. It is one defense of a *mens sana* against a diseased *corpus;* yet at the same time the patient "knows" that he is seriously ill. Given a patient like Lawrence, a man with powerful emotions and great imaginative facility, one can even predict that the patterns of his reaction to illness may be unpredictable. But his emotional responses will depend in large measure upon his previous psychological history and his emotional status before his illness became established.

As we have seen, the precise date of onset of Lawrence's tuberculosis cannot be fixed, but as the "sick year" of 1911 progressed, he found himself increasingly less able to attend to his teaching duties and he finally resigned his post in 1912. The next eighteen years were marked by periods of remission and exacerbation of his pulmonary disease, and one cannot doubt that so sharp an observer as Lawrence, raised in a Midlands coaling village, was unfamiliar with the prognostic implications of a chronic lung infection. The poverty and deprivation he suffered during the war years and the difficulties he encountered in getting his work published during the next few years did nothing to help his disease. The warm and sunny climate in such places as Arizona, Mexico, and Italy may have been beneficial, but by 1925 it was apparent that the remissions were getting shorter and the exacerbations longer and more debilitating.

Never blessed with a reposeful temperament, Lawrence became increasingly "difficult." His mind was always alive and brimming with ideas, some splendid, others hopelessly wrongheaded. Like any man of strong will he hated the idea of being sick. He disliked and distrusted most of his doctors, not without reason, as there was all too little they could do for him. His hostilities toward the world he knew he would soon leave became intensified; his most frequent emotional response to situations was anger, and he became adept at finding things to become angry about. Moore has developed the medical evidence that his outbursts of anger may have released adrenocorticoid hormones which gave him added strength and may even have prolonged his life.[14] But, if so, these benefits were transient. Current medical evidence is that tuberculosis can be activated (or, if latent, reactivated) by adrenocorticoids which suppress the inflammatory tissue response that restrains the tubercle bacillus. Lawrence began writing *Lady Chatterley's Lover* in 1926; the novel was conceived under the prevailing mood of anger, bitterness, and hostility. It was Lawrence's last defiant indictment of those elements in man's soul and in the world around him which he despised the most. His targets were well selected to suit his emotional needs, but his aim was often faulty. Some of his thrusts went wide of the mark because they were poorly planned; others missed because his execution was at fault.

One's first question might well arise in connection with the book's title. Lawrence had originally planned to call the novel *Tenderness,* and in retrospect he seems well advised to have changed it. (His second proposed title was *John Thomas and Lady Jane!*) It is difficult for any reader to reconcile such passages as, "he took her, short and sharp and finished, like an animal,"[15] and "sensuality sharp and searing as fire, burning the soul to tinder"[16] with any sort of physical tenderness, not even Lawrence's own "phallic tenderness." The actual plot of the novel could, of course, be entitled *The Sexual Awakening (or Enlightenment) of Lady Chatterley* without doing violence to the facts; it is that feature which gives the novel continuity, and much of the *res gestae* deal with Constance Chatterley's sexual responses. By shifting the titular emphasis to the *Lover,* Lawrence directs the reader's attention to Mellors. Yet Mellors is the only one of the three principal characters whose personality does not change or develop in the course of the action. At the close of the book he is just what he was when he makes his first appearance in Chapter 6, the man close to nature, untrammeled by society's conventions and deceits, the instrument of Lady Chatterley's sexual release. He is Lawrence's spokesman or mouthpiece, and to a large extent Lawrence identifies himself with Mellors.

Mellors was not Lawrence's first gamekeeper. Annable in *The White Peacock* (1910), Lawrence's first novel, is also the vehicle through which Lawrence expresses his own ideas. Like Mellors' first wife, Annable's first wife is also equated with the destructive type of woman. Precisely why Lawrence should endow both his gamekeepers with unfortunate first marriages is not clear, but his predilection for that calling can be explained. A gamekeeper is, by virtue of his occupation, kept in close communion with feral, unspoiled nature. He is a self-taught expert on the reproductive habits of animals; the pheasants Mellors is breeding represent the avian counterfoil to himself and Constance Chatterley; it is significant that they are caged. However appealing this symbolism may be, a moment's reflection will lead one to the conclusion that expertise in animal copulation and reproduction does not necessarily confer expertise in human sexual relations. Or, are we to infer that for all his high-sounding phrases about the ennobling aspects of sexual fulfillment that Lawrence *au fond* really believed that man couples like the beast? Lawrence's choice of an occupation for Mellors is not entirely a happy one. Can we justify it in terms of a desire on Lawrence's part to upset the social order: viz., a gamekeeper is hired to prevent poaching on his master's preserves; ergo, by poaching on his master's wife, usurping his property, Mellors is a symbol of social revolution, the triumph of the Jacquerie *per coitum?* At best this is a sophistic interpretation, quite alien to Lawrence's usual way of using fictional characters as symbols, though not inconsistent with the general tenor of his thought. But Lawrence was afraid to make Mellors an ordinary countryman; he endows him with some intellect and education. If Lawrence had to adopt this device in order to make Lady Chatterley attracted to him or so that he would serve as a convincing mouthpiece for Lawrence's ideas, he has compromised his thesis to some extent: without some redeeming quality of cerebration and articulacy the purely elemental, naturalistic life is not sufficient.

Apart from the question of vocabulary and the "four-letter words," the literary evidence in *Regina v. Penguin Books Ltd.* did elicit two useful observations. Graham Hough cites Yeats as having said that, "Only one of the lovers uses coarse language, the other merely accepts it . . . the lady listens, but never once answers in kind . . . if she had, the gamekeeper would no doubt have been deeply scandalized."[17] It would be easy to defend Lawrence's failure to put the "four-letter words" into Lady Chatterley's mouth as being "out of character," but his failure does lay him open to the point that even though she had experienced complete sexual release and fulfillment, she was still bound by the taboo of the word.

Lady Chatterley does not respond to Mellors's paean about her cunt and her arse with similar laudatory remarks about his cock and his balls. Parenthetically, though Mellors is eloquent about Lady Chatterley's genitalia, he never once comments on her tits. Possibly Lawrence himself was not free from inhibition about hearing a lady use coarse language or putting "four-letter words" in the mouth of a woman he had created in fiction. Possibly the female mammary gland was too closely bound up with his own affective relationship to his mother for him to use the "plain, outspoken term" in reference to it. Sometimes it is as important to notice what a writer does *not* say as what he does say.

A decisive point made at the trial about Lawrence's attitudes was by Richard Hoggart that *Lady Chatterley's Lover* is "highly virtuous and, if anything, puritanical."[18] As one might anticipate, the last word came under considerable attack, some of it sarcastic, by the prosecutor. Hoggart's masterful definition of "puritanical" under cross-examination leaves no room for doubt as to what he meant and what Lawrence's philosophy was: "Many people do live their lives under a misapprehension of the meaning of the word 'puritanical.' This is the way in which language decays. In England today and for a long time the word 'puritanical' has been extended to mean somebody who is against anything which is pleasurable, particularly sex. The proper meaning of it, to a literary man or to a linguist, is somebody who belongs to the tradition of British puritanism generally, and the distinguishing feature of that is an intense sense of responsibility for one's conscience. In this sense the book is puritanical."[19] Conceding to Lawrence all virtue of intent, a refinement of conscience which led him to write the novel in the way he did, we must ask ourselves: Why did it fail?

It is easy enough to assert in retrospect that *Lady Chatterley's Lover* failed in 1928 because the shock value of the vocabulary far outweighed any literary relevance, and in 1934, Professor Read did advance this view.[20] Until that time, even though the words were often used in speech, their appearance in print was restricted to frank pornography. They were not part of the working vocabulary of a serious novelist, regardless of how frankly he might treat sexual matters. Writing three decades later, Richard Aldington expressed a somewhat different view in a letter to Professor Harry T. Moore, dated April 13,

1959: "The thought is perhaps unworthy, but from the beginning I have wondered if DHL were not a little hopeful to cash in on the pornographic market of *Ulysses*, especially as his royalties were declining rapidly. . . . No doubt the 'words' are basic Saxon and were used innocently in the Middle Ages, but they have unluckily been encrusted with nastiness, and they cannot in this age be used with the purity DHL claimed. The author is not a dictator of language—he must take into account the use of it by the people."[21] Even discounting Aldington's imputation of literary opportunism, one can always rebut by suggesting that he was still viewing the book in 1959 with the eye and mind of a 1928 reader. The same words Lawrence used appear now with noticeable frequency in prose fiction and in speech on the contemporary stage. Much of their shock value has been dissipated, yet their point seems lost.

Two related reasons may be assigned for the failure of the "four-letter" vocabulary. Lawrence's initial draft of the novel, titled *The First Lady Chatterley*, told much the same story, but the "words" were not used. He added them only in the third and final draft. This may lend some weight to Aldington's charge of "trying to cash in on the pornographic market of *Ulysses*," but to a reader four decades later the words seem to be something appliquéd, a deliberate encrustation of language to suit a special purpose of the author. To that extent they are inappropriate and out of place, even unnecessary. One is reminded of the minister who tells off-color stories to show that he is "one of the boys"; he never quite manages to tell them effectively; it is a strain. The reader senses that he is being manipulated. That the "four-letter" words appear only in the final draft raises the question whether their use is so integral to the writer's intention as he and his apologists claim. The second reason is that the use of this special vocabulary serves a non-literary rather than a literary purpose; Lawrence was deliberately beating a drum for his own cause. One can only speculate whether he himself in moments of intimacy actually used such language; my guess is that he did not. Like every other Englishman or American he was familiar with the words from childhood, but the maternal taboo would probably have been too strong for him to use them naturally, without feeling self-conscious, even slightly guilty. Frieda's memoirs are singularly silent on this point.

A collateral but tangentially related failure in vocabulary lies in the context of their *usage*, not the context of the action, specifically the sexual action, but the context of Mellors's speech. Throughout the novel most of Mellors's discourse is in the "broad" Derbyshire dialect, a device Lawrence employs to underscore Mellors's contempt for and

rejection of middle- and upper-class values, an attitude which Lawrence shared. Mellors is not restricted to speaking "broad"; he has had
some degree of education and can speak proper English when he
chooses. Dialect, as a device in prose fiction, is to be used with caution,
particularly if it necessitates modified orthography. For many readers
to find a simple statement or phrase spelled out in an approximation of
phonetic dialect is visually disturbing; if the idiosyncratic spelling is
carried on for some length, this feature can become irritating. An
occasional word or phrase may lend local color, but continued exploita-
tion of the dialect becomes monotonous. At first Mellors's resort to
Derbyshire idiom lends him individuality and distinction, as Lawrence
had planned, but after a few chapters it becomes insistent and ludicrous. Once Mellors has established his rejection of values outside his
own class, it is not necessary to direct the reader's attention to it at every
opportunity. Inevitably, as page succeeds page, one is reminded of
one's juvenile experiences in reading the *Br'er Rabbit Tales* by Joel
Chandler Harris, and one is tempted to speculate how, were the scene
of the novel shifted to Manhattan, Mellors's counterpart might sound
if his native idiom were Yiddish. A device which might have been
effective becomes low comedy because Lawrence failed to use it judici-
ously.

A novelist who sets about deliberately to use his novel as a pulpit
from which to preach a sermon on society and its discontents assumes
an obligation not shared by a mere teller of tales. He must present a
convincing argument and he must make his point seem reasonable. If
he fails, the reader may legitimately conclude that the novelist's ideas
and values are personal idiosyncrasies—to which he may be perfectly
well entitled, but restricted to himself and a small coterie of friends who
share them. In theory there are no restrictions on the writer: he can
create characters as he pleases; he can move them around the map; he
can invent situations to suit them; they can spout his ideas at length; the
range of literary latitude is almost unbounded. But in practice there
are limits; certain devices are inadmissible, not because they are wrong
in and of themselves, but because they fail to persuade the reader. It
requires little experience or insight to detect when a writer is manipu-
lating a character to suit his own fancy; in ordinary parlance this is
called setting up a straw man.

If Lawrence is to convince us of the truth and worth of his ideas, we
must accept the relationship between Constance Chatterley and Oliver
Mellors as a proper solution to their problems and we must reject
Clifford Chatterley's way of life as empty and meaningless, even self-
destructive. One may concede the former without giving way on the

latter. Quite early in the novel, the reader is put on guard that Sir Clifford is Lawrence's straw man, and as one reads on, one is disappointed at the naïveté with which the marionette is made to dance as Lawrence pulls the strings.

As the novel begins, Clifford Chatterley is presented as an amiable young man of good family with an estate in the Midlands and extensive holdings in coal mines. Within a few weeks of his marriage to Constance Reid, the daughter of an R.A., he is shipped off to Flanders in 1917 and returns from the war a paraplegic. Confined to a wheelchair, he embarks on a career as a writer. Pirandello may have allowed his characters a life of their own, but not Lawrence. Clifford Chatterley's literary talents are limited by his creator: "He had taken to writing stories; curious, very personal stories about people he had known. Clever, rather spiteful, and yet, in some mysterious way, meaningless. The observation was extraordinary and peculiar. But there was no touch, no actual contact. It was as if the whole thing took place in a vacuum. And since the field of life is largely an artificially-lighted stage today, the stories were curiously true to modern life, to the modern psychology, that is."[22] Lawrence reinforces his opinion of Chatterley's writing through the mouth of Sir Malcolm Reid, Constance's father, who tells her that Clifford's writing is "smart, but there's nothing to it. It won't last!"

It seems that Sir Clifford had been poaching on Lawrence's own preserves by writing stories about people he had known—clever, rather spiteful stories. Lawrence was adept at this genre, and the history of his literary feuds is too, too extensive to recount. Clearly he was not going to tolerate any competiton from a character of his own devising; hence the stories Clifford wrote were "in some mysterious way, meaningless." There is no mystery at all; they were meaningless to Lawrence because he was unwilling to create a character who had any real literary talent. But Lawrence's foot slips; we are given a glimpse of Clifford Chatterley's literary skills. Late in the novel he writes a lengthy letter to Connie when she is in Venice; its style is lively and amusing; he has a knack for recounting incidents; the letter is one of the best-written passages in the whole novel.[23] Oddly enough, it reads a bit like some of Lawrence's own letters. We cannot accept at face value Lawrence's critical judgment on Clifford Chatterley. Besides, when did Lawrence ever have a kind word for a contemporary novelist, a competitor?

Midway through the novel Clifford decides to take an interest in improving the efficiency of the coal mines in which he has a serious financial stake. When the war broke out, he "hurried home from Bonn where he had been studying the technicalities of coal mining."[24] The Chatterley's moved into Wragby in 1920. At first Clifford devoted himself to writing. Even as Connie's affair with Mellors was building up, Clifford's renewed interest in coal mining developed and flourished. This, of course, was anathema to Lawrence. The coal mines symbolized everything that was wrong with English society—ugly, brutal, destructive of nature, destructive of man. For Lawrence every person connected with the collieries was base and degraded; the workers were the victims of an inexorable and oppressive economic system, and the owners were the epitome of the usually frigid, sometimes patronizing indifference of the propertied classes toward the lower classes upon whose daily toil they parasitically survived. Lawrence's position is quite tenable; it does not differ materially from that found in the proletarian literature which became popular in the wake of socialism, Fabianism, and other reform movements. One can even sympathize with Lawrence, who had been born the son of a collier; he had every reason to hate and fear the coal mines. However keenly he may have felt this, it is not sufficient to convince a disinterested reader that all the people connected with the coal mines were inherently despicable and pursuing evil ends. One may or may not be enthusiastic about coal mining, but most people would concede that Sir Clifford was more to be commended than censured for improving the efficiency of the mines and seeking out ways to sell their by-products.

To the average reader, insentient as Clifford Chatterley may be, he is not an unsympathetic character. On balance, he has done a good job. Despite his paraplegia he has been successful as a writer and as an industrialist. To be sure, he was "successful" in these fields in a manner which Lawrence considered meaningless, if not downright destructive. But we are not obliged to accept Lawrence's valuation merely because it is his. Indeed, as the novel continues, it is possible to think of Clifford Chatterley as a man much imposed on by his creator. Certainly he was emotionally dependent; most men are to some extent, and a man confined to a wheelchair is likely to be even more so. The reader is supposed to feel contempt for Clifford Chatterley when he breaks down after receiving Connie's letter telling him of her decision to terminate their marriage; my subjective reaction was one of pity, not contempt, and I am not so vain as to think my emotional responses unique. Likewise, we are supposed to find something shameful, even unnatural in Sir Clifford's relationship with Mrs. Bolton—her furtive kisses and his squeezing her breasts. Granted such pseudosexual substitutes are not pleasant, one may well ask what other outlets did the man in the wheelchair have? Having stacked the deck, Lawrence deals out the hand; the bidding is predictable and so is the outcome of the contract.

Let us not forget that Clifford Chatterley's impotence is organic, physically caused, the result of war injuries. Lawrence could have strengthened his case that industrialization was despoiling Englishmen of their manhood by having Clifford return from war sound in body, then, over a period of time, become *psychologically* impotent as the price for pursuing false values. This was an opportunity Lawrence missed, a lapse of judgment, as we shall later see, determined by his own life situation at the time he wrote the novel. But an alternative reading is possible: Lawrence's attitude toward the war was well known. The shabby story of his harassment by police, the emphasis on the fact that Frieda was German and her cousin a German air hero, all this and even more disgusted Lawrence with the war, with military ideas, with soldiers, with "war literature," and presumably with the idea of a military hero. He may have even deliberately created Clifford Chatterley as the object of his pitiless indignation and scorn, using his impotence to emphasize that *not even* paraplegic war veterans, natural objects for our sympathy, merited any special consideration. Surely, Mellors's remark, "It's not for a man i' the shape you're in, Sir Clifford, to twit me for havin' a cod atween my legs,"[25] is spiteful, venomous, and sadistic. It is a statement which goes beyond the bounds of what one man may decently say to another, more especially if the man to whom the remark is addressed is not aware that he has been cuckolded by the man who made it. It is at this point that one loses whatever sympathy one might have had with Mellors. And we must remember that in this scene Mellors *is* Lawrence.

Much of *Lady Chatterley's Lover* deals with a sexual problem, and one cannot come to grips with Lawrence's solution of it without taking into account his own psychosexual development. To any reader of the present generation it is self-evident that Lawrence had a strongly developed Oedipus complex and that *Sons and Lovers* is the eloquent exposition of his struggle with it. A generation ago, when psychoanalysis was not so firmly established as a scientific discipline, it might have been more acceptable to write that "Lawrence had a strong emotional attachment to his mother and disliked his father." What seems so clear to us today was not always accepted in literary circles, despite Lawrence's own interest, ambivalent though it was, in psychoanalysis (see his *Psychoanalysis and the Unconscious*, 1921). The preface to the early Modern Library edition of *Sons and Lovers* by John Macy contains the comment: "No, it is not an Oedipus-Jocasta 'complex' nor a Hamlet-Gertrude 'complex,' though you may assimilate this touching story to those complexes if you enjoy translating human life in such terms."[26] (This preface has been replaced in a newer Modern Library edition by one more sympathetic to the vocabulary of psychoanalysis.) Commenting on the interplay between language and emotion, Jean Starobinski writes that "An emotion can attach itself to a word (especially a word in fashion), but this does not occur without some rather important consequences. . . . As soon as the name of the emotion is brought to light, the word, through its very efficacy, helps to fix, to propagate, to generalize the emotion with it represents. . . . Nowadays, the language of psychoanalysis presents us with a *model,* permitting us to understand the significance of our emotions; it proposes a form for them."[27]

Lest there be any lingering doubt as to the nature of Lawrence's Oedipal attachment as depicted in the character of Paul Morel, lest there be any reluctance to call this emotion by its proper name in today's usage, one passage will suffice: "Paul loved to sleep with his mother. Sleep is still the most perfect, in spite of hygienists, when it is shared with a beloved. The warmth, the security, the peace of soul, the utter comfort from the touch of the other, knits the sleep, so that it takes the body and soul completely in its healing."[28] This striking insight was written as long ago as 1912, even before Lawrence was introduced to Freud's ideas by Dr. David Eder.[29]

In *Sons and Lovers* Paul Morel falls in love with Miriam Lievers, and the rise and fall of their relationship parallels very closely (with minor deviations *gratia artis*) Lawrence's own youthful romance with Jessie Chambers. Paul and Miriam struggle against their inhibitions much as did Lawrence and Jessie: "They were both late in coming to maturity, and psychical ripeness was much behind even the physical. . . . Perhaps, because of the continual business of birth and of begetting which goes on upon every farm, Miriam was the more hypersensitive to the matter, and her blood was chastened almost to disgust of the faintest suggestion of such intercourse. Paul took his pitch from her, and their intimacy went on in an utterly blanched and chaste fashion. It could never be mentioned that the mare was in foal."[30] Like Lawrence, Paul Morel tried to resolve his Oedipal attachment; he compared himself with other men and their own solutions:

A good many of the nicest men he knew were like himself, bound in by their own virginity, which they could not break out of. They were so sensitive to their women that they would go without them forever rather than do them a hurt, an injustice. Being the sons of mothers whose husbands had blundered rather brutally through their feminine sanctities, they were themselves too diffident and shy. They could easier deny themselves than incur any reproach from a woman; for a woman was like their mother, and they were full of the sense of their mother. They preferred themselves to suffer the misery of celibacy, rather than risk the other person.[31]

Returning from fiction to real life, Lawrence and Jessie Chambers appear to have consummated a sexual act fewer than five times. It was a "failure," which Jessie later attributed to Lawrence's "forced" attitude.

Lawrence's relationship with Jessie began to deteriorate even before his mother died in 1910. By this time he was living and teaching in South London; his first novel had been published and his second was nearing completion. He was no longer the inept virginal youth from Eastwood. He had been initiated, probably in 1908, into the physical mysteries of sex by Alice Dax, who lived in Eastwood. (Cf. Paul Morel's sexual initiation when he too was twenty-three.) Alice Dax was the wife of Henry Dax, a local pharmacist who later became an oculist. It is probably significant, in view of later events, that she was a married woman, experienced and safe. Once in London, Lawrence's sexual horizons broadened considerably. He became seriously interested in a succession of young ladies and was "engaged" seriatim to Louise Burrows, a girl from the Midlands, then Alice Holt, also a schoolteacher, in South London. He became friendly with Helen Corke, another schoolteacher, who had run off with a married man who had committed suicide. (Her experience served as the basis for his second novel, *The Trespasser*, 1912; and she wrote her own version of that disastrous love affair in *Neutral Ground*, 1933 which was written chiefly in 1918.) There is little point in cataloging Lawrence's sexual successes and failures; memoirs by participants and onlookers are conflicting and unreliable. The important point is that by 1912 Lawrence had established himself as heterosexually competent and active.

The story of Lawrence's affair with Frieda has been told too often to require extensive documentation. For our purposes a brief outline will serve. Frieda von Richthofen, the daughter of a German baron, had married Ernest Weekley, a man fifteen years older than herself, who became Professor of French at Nottingham. Lawrence had been one of his students between 1906 and 1908. In March, 1912, when he resigned from schoolteaching because of ill health, he apparently felt sufficiently close to Professor Weekley to visit him to seek advice about a position in Germany; he had never met Frieda Weekley before. When he arrived chez Weekley, the professor was not at home but Frieda was. They were drawn to each other almost immediately and irresistibly. Frieda was bored with her life in Nottingham. Her husband was no longer a satisfactory sexual partner; he was forty-seven, she thirty-two, and they had had three children. She had had at least one, possibly more, extramarital affairs of dubious satisfaction and was ready for more. Lawrence was twenty-six and "available." Their passions blazed, and after a mere six weeks Frieda went off to Germany, leaving her three children, ostensibly to visit her family, but accompanied by Lawrence as her lover. A curiously revealing incident occurred during their courtship. Frieda invited Lawrence to spend the night with her on an occasion when her husband was away. Lawrence declined; he felt constrained about carrying on a sexual affair beneath the roof of a man who stood in *loco parentis* to him. It need scarcely be pointed out that to run off with the wife of one's professor, a father figure, with a woman older than himself, the mother of three children, is the consummation of the Oedipal act. Lawrence attempted to resolve his Oedipus complex by embracing it.

Any number of questions arise about the emotional nature of Lawrence's relationship with Frieda. Neither his own comments nor her hysterical memoirs can be taken at face value; the bias and need for self-justification are obvious. It will not be considered an injustice if one notes that in addition to her wifely functions Frieda also served as his mother-substitute. There is abundant evidence in the recollections of their friends, literary and otherwise, that despite their interminable quarrels she could both scold him and cajole him, that she put up with his outbursts of petulant infantilism, that she nursed him and protected him, and gave him physical love as well. There is no reason to doubt that their sexual relations were mutually satisfactory at the start; in fact this was the primary basis for their being together. Regarding the later years, there are a few unreliable stories by paraliterary gossips that Lawrence may have dallied with one or another woman on occasion. Mabel Dodge Luhan hints that Lawrence may have had a brief affair with an American woman named Esther Andrews. Another gossip reports that when Lawrence was in Taos he was "always running off into the bushes with Indian women." There is little merit in retailing such trivia or magnifying them out of proportion. All too often they are the products of spite from a woman who offered herself but was ignored or rejected. If such episodes occurred, and it is by no means certain that any did, they probably had no great emotional significance for Lawrence, despite his protestations about the sacred nature of the sexual relation; at most they represented a casual moment of lust, easily satisfied, easily forgotten. However, Frieda's sexual eclecticism may have added to his anxieties about his manhood.

More significance is to be attached to the report by Richard Aldington that, "in the last five years of Lawrence's life (1925–30), Frieda used to go about complaining that he had become impotent."[32] Whether the alleged reduction of potentia was due to decreased libido, inability to achieve erection, or ejaculatio praecox, is not stated. It is not unreasonable to infer that a man suffering from far advanced pulmonary tuberculosis would be sufficiently debilitated to be unable to respond to sexual stimuli and unable to perform as satisfactorily or as frequently as before. If so, we must add that *Lady Chatterley's Lover* was written not only in a mood of anger against the world, but one of impotence and frustration. Considerable strength is given to Aldington's assertion of Frieda's complaint by John Middleton Murry whose wife, Katherine Mansfield, had died of tuberculosis in 1923. The Lawrences and the Murrys were good friends and had shared living quarters during the war. The love affair between Murry and Katherine Mansfield was not without its unconventional elements and more than tinged with psychopathology. Yet, if we can rely on Murry's assertion, some time between 1927 and 1928, Frieda broached to him the idea that she and he might have a love affair. Frieda's taste in men, was to put it kindly, idiosyncratic, and I am tempted to take Aldington and Murry at their word.

It is regrettable that we do not have a dossier on the complete sexual experiences of our patient, Mr. Lawrence. Apart from what he chooses to reveal in his novels, anecdotal details of his own psychosexual development are lacking. As an adult he wrote disapprovingly of masturbation; he considered it unproductive and unfulfilling. But we have no historical data regarding his own masturbatory practices. We can reject as unlikely the hypotheses that he never masturbated or was a compulsive masturbator; the first is statistically improbable, the second out of keeping with his character. It is more than probable that at puberty and during adolescence he did masturbate on occasion, and we can infer from the prudish religious attitudes in his home that he experienced a certain amount of guilt feelings. He almost certainly masturbated when returning home after his unsatisfactory assignations with Jessie Chambers. But we cannot gauge the depth of such inferred guilt feelings, and the question remains an empty speculation.

Lawrence is not unduly self-dramatizing when he depicts his own developing heterosexual needs in the guise of Paul Morel in *Sons and Lovers*. But one must note that in none of his novels or short stories up to the time of *Lady Chatterley's Lover* does he create a character who suffered from failure of the libido or inability to perform sexually. Though he was realistic enough to know that sexual behavior is learned behavior, that trial and error are part of the process, he never describes the failure of the male to achieve orgasm. Even Michaelis, Constance

Chatterley's first extramarital adventure, has his ejaculation; it satisfies him, though not Constance. The idea of male impotence is anxiety-producing, and Lawrence defends himself against both impotence and anxiety by displacing the former onto Clifford Chatterley towards whom he maintains a relentlessly hostile attitude. By contrast, Mellors (i.e., Lawrence) is always "at the ready."

Aldington, as well as others, has written that Lawrence was a latent homosexual. The literary basis for the assertion is in a passage from *The White Peacock* (1910) in which two young men bathe in a mill pond:

[George] knew how much I admired the noble, white fruitfulness of his form. He saw I had forgotten to continue my rubbing, and laughing he took hold of me and began to rub me briskly, as if I were a child, or rather, a woman he loved and did not fear. I left myself quite limply in his hands, and, to get a better grip of me, he put his arms around me and pressed me against him, and the sweetness of the touch of our naked bodies one against the other was superb. It satisfied in some measure the vague, indecipherable yearning of my soul; and it was the same with him. When he had rubbed me all warm, he let me go, and we looked at each other with eyes of still laughter, and our love was perfect for a moment, more perfect than any love I have known since, either for man or woman.[33]

George was the fictionalized character of Jessie Chamber's brother; it had been through friendship with him that Lawrence, still a young adolescent, had been introduced to the Chambers family. There is no evidence that their friendship eventuated into overt homosexual activity; it seems to have gone no farther than the permissible bounds of adolescent affection. In a letter dated March 16, 1960, Aldington wrote that Lawrence was "85 percent hetero and 15 percent homo;" precisely how such a numerical value is calculated remains obscure.[34] An interview with Helen Corke, who was on close terms of friendship with Lawrence around 1912, elicited a reply to the question whether Lawrence was "a normally sexed man": "Only in the sense that he was near what I would call the middle of the spectrum relating to sex, with the extreme masculine at one end, the extreme feminine at the other, and the intermediate position which has been, I believe, the position of some of our finest artists."[35] Little attention seems to have been paid to *Women in Love* in this regard, but the relationship between Rupert Birkin and Gerald Crich is clearly one of latent homosexuality, and in the "Prologue" Lawrence describes Birkin as a typical latent homosexual, though he does not use the term as such. Lawrence may very well have been aware of and much troubled by his own latent homosexual impulses as early as 1916. At this time Lawrence was much influenced by Edward Carpenter's ideas on "homogenic love." Carpenter, who had read mathematics at Cambridge and was ordained a curate, became a farmer in Derbyshire in 1882. He had published a number of books and pamphlets promoting libertarian ideas about sexual conduct. He was an overt homosexual in the tradition of Whitman whom he had visited in 1877. Lawrence's revision of his essay on Whitman and destruction of its first draft as well as his withdrawal of the "Prologue" to *Women in Love* were consciously planned, perhaps at Frieda's instigation, to suppress further damage to his reputation should his interest in sexual inversion become public knowledge. Whatever Lawrence's latent homosexual feelings were, it is very doubtful that they were ever transmuted into sexual acitivity. Certainly as an adult, his defenses would have made participation in an overt homosexual act unlikely, if not impossible.

Prior to 1925, Lawrence displayed considerable insight into homosexual behavior. The lesbian relationship in *The Rainbow* between Ursula Brangwen and her schoolmistress was written with both sympathy and sufficient accuracy of detail to help get the book banned. Nor did homosexuals in real life pose so much of a threat to his heterosexual integration that he was unable to be kind and helpful to the unfortunate Maurice Magnus, much kinder than Magnus's overtly homosexual friends proved to be. Yet when he came to write *Lady Chatterley's Lover,* he has Mellors say, "When I'm with a woman who's really a lesbian, I fairly howl in my soul, wanting to kill her."[36] The entire digression about lesbian women in this scene seems gratuitous, irrelevant to the events which precede and follow it. Possibly the vehemence of Mellors's diatribe can be traced to a streak of latent homosexuality within himself. Mellors's description of the colonel he served under in India tells us: "He had risen from the ranks. He loved the army. And he had never married. He was 20 years older than me. He was a very intelligent man: and alone in the army, as such a man is: a passionate man in his way: and a very clever officer. I lived under his spell while I was with him. I sort of let him run my life. And I never regret it."[37] There is no hint of an overt homosexual relationship but there is a strong scent of a latent one, as with master and schoolboy. Again, we must remember that Mellors is Lawrence. Writing now in 1926–28, debilitated by tuberculosis, sexually impotent, Lawrence may have felt that homosexuality, especially female homosexuality, was a threat to his masculine defenses, hence the words he put in Mellors' mouth.

At the risk of seeming trivial, I should like to point out that Lawrence grew his beard in 1914, after his marriage to Frieda. This is the physiognomy we remember; it is the face he presented to the world.

We know from his own writings that Lawrence's adjustment to adult heterosexuality was difficult. We may even say that it was incomplete or imperfect; his marriage fused his Oedipal strivings into the marriage bed, never a comfortable or stable solution. He may have had many deep-seated reasons to be anxious about his masculinity. Could not the beard have been adopted as an outward mark, a public demonstration, of a virility of which he was uncertain?

A less fortunate victim of an unresolved Oedipus complex and latent homosexual impulses was James M. Barrie. His affection for Margaret Ogilvy, his mother, parallels that of Lawrence for his mother, and she too encouraged her talented son to pursue a literary career. Barrie's "kailyard" is not materially different from the colliery at Eastwood, but Barrie had the advantage of a father who rose from a weaver's trade to become a school inspector, a good step above Lawrence's father who remained a collier all his life. Barrie's marriage at the age of thirty-four was a failure; he and his wife soon separated. Under the veil of late Victorian delicacy it is not difficult to sense his sexual inadequacy. His subsequent avuncular attachment to the five Davies boys marked a rigorously repressed homosexual tendency. Unlike Lawrence, Barrie never attempted to solve his sexual problems. His idealization of "the boy who never grew up" is a literary transformation of paedophilia; to grow up and assume adult (sexual) responsibilities was not only a loss of innocence but a loss of the fantasy.

Peter Coveney has analyzed the story of Barrie's *The Boy David* in the following terms:

The main and eccentric dramatic point of the whole play (resides) in David's obsession with acquiring Goliath's spear. After the battle the boy trails the stage disconsolately because he cannot raise the treasured possession on to his shoulder. In the final scene he confides to Jonathan that he can at last raise it, and the final curtain finds the boy on the highest rock on the stage with the spear shaft as wide as a "weaver's beam" mounted on his shoulder. From anyone who would deny the phallic character of the symbol (it is to be remembered that Barrie's father was in fact a weaver) it would be interesting to have an explanation of the dramatic point.[38]

Disguises for paedophilia are almost transparent in *Peter Pan*. The boy's name alone is one of the most phallic names given any character in literature, combining a slang term for the penis with that of the Greek god of sexual sport. What distinguishes Peter from other little boys is that he can *fly*, and he teaches his little playmates how to master that skill. That flying is a symbolic transformation of sexual activity is so well accepted a canon in psychology requires no further explanation of

the book's fascination for children. Captain Hook, of course, represents the paternal castration threat. By convention, the audience
applauds when Peter asks them, "Do you believe in fairies?" I think
they believe in them, but they prefer them to be latent. Barrie's fantasy
posed no challenge to the established values of society, and in his old
age he was rewarded with the rectorship of Glasgow University.

Like Barrie, Lawrence repressed his homosexual impulses, but as is
so often the case, they appeared in his art. John Sparrow has advanced
the claim that in *Lady Chatterley's Lover* Lawrence deliberately "planted"
hints that one form which the intercourse between Mellors and Constance Chatterley took was *coitus per anum,* or, to use its English name as
Sparrow does, buggery.[39] Sparrow combines his precise legal mind
with his flair for literary insight to construct a convincing case. Some of
the key points in his argument involve such passages as "folded in the
secret warmth, the secret entrances!"[40] and "Burning out the shames,
the deepest, oldest shames, in the most secret places."[41] The use of the
plural would be unnecessary were not the anus used in addition to the
vagina. In a letter to Connie at Venice, Clifford Chatterley's comments
on the scandal created by Bertha Coutts, Mellors's first wife, include
the sentence, "Humanity has always had a strange avidity for unusual
sexual postures, and if a man likes to use his wife, as Benvenuto Cellini
says, 'in the Italian way,' as well, that is a matter of taste."[42] There is
other evidence to support Sparrow's claim, but his essay is better read
than paraphrased. As a former Cantabrigian, I can only remark how
felicitous it is that the Warden of an Oxford College should be the first
to detect a hint of buggery in the proceedings.

It is not difficult to relate Lawrence's advocacy of buggery to his
latent homosexuality. The formulation, "I would like to bugger a man"
is unacceptable to consciousness, and the object is displaced; the cognitive field is restructured into "I want to bugger a woman," a course of
action more readily reconciled with Lawrence's ideas of sexual freedom. Writers who preach sexual libertarianism attract a wide audience,
and their doctrine is always popular with the young in heart (and
body). It is a necessary corrective to establish the unconscious motivation underlying such teachings lest the young in mind accept such ideas
uncritically. One man's meat is another man's perversion. One may or
may not opt for buggery—it seems an acquired taste—but the decision
requires a rational basis as well as an instinctual one.

In Lawrence's case the issue is complicated by his physical illness. His
reduced potentia was not only an added blow to his physical integrity,
including his patterns of sexual adjustment, but to his sense of power,
of mastery and control. By endowing Mellors, a projection of himself,

in literary fantasy, with a taste for anal intercourse, he adds the element of domination over a submissive partner. In such situations the sexual element in the genital act may be more apparent than real, and the fictional buggery may be pseudohomosexual in background. The motive for Mellors's sexual patterns with his wife and his conquest of Lady Chatterley may have been as much a question of power as of his omnipresent gonadal urges. William Niederland suggests that the idea of *coitus per anum* might be suggested to Mellors who, by virtue of his duties as a gamekeeper, observed the coital position of animals.[43] A corollary might be that Lawrence, writing this novel in a state of impotent rage, could have had the motive to degrade womanhood, which he could no longer satisfy sexually, to the level of the passive female animal.

Many commentators have noted that Lawrence did not practice what he preached. Ostensibly advancing the notion of "a more perfect union" by mutual fulfillment, "he manages to mask and muff, if not conceal entirely his essential message . . . that the male in order to reach fulfillment must assert himself utterly, wilfully, perversely, *using* the female 'like a slave' in sex."[44] So astute an observer as Bertrand Russell attributes this to his egotism: "in sex alone he was compelled to admit that he was not the only human being in the universe. But it was because this admission was so painful that he conceived of sex relations as a perpetual fight in which each is attempting to destroy the other."[45] To the noble philosopher-mathematician one can reply *tu quoque* and also charge him with oversimplification. Lawrence's need to dominate women and degrade them in sexual intercourse sprang not only from his egotism but from his latent homosexuality and the anxiety engendered by his loss of potency, and these in turn stemmed from the sequential pattern of his psychosexual development.

Lawrence proclaimed loudly and publicly that *Lady Chatterley's Lover* was a novel which dealt with sex openly and frankly, without concealment or reservation: no holds barred! Certainly he knew that the overt sexual subject matter would create a storm of furious protest, that a novel which condoned adultery and described sexual activity in explicit terms would be unacceptable to the public at large. To write it was an act of fearless, open defiance of all conventions of his day, both literary and social. The importance of the novel lay as much in the intensity and fervor of his belief that his ideas of sexual freedom were correct, healthy, and liberating as in the ideas themselves; he set himself up as an apostle, not only by his writings but by his life. In retrospect, it is even fair to say that he gave up the last years of his life to the cause of sexual freedom and enlightenment. Given that cause and the platform of *Lady Chatterley's Lover* to argue from, it was no occasion to insert cryptic hints about the practice and value of a form of sexual intercourse which was not only a felony at law but usually classified as a perversion. It took four decades before the penetrating mind of a critic with legal training exposed these surreptitious allusions to buggery. It is not so much the advocacy of buggery but his concealment of that advocacy which damages Lawrence's cause. It is "this failure of integrity, this fundamental dishonesty" which is largely responsible for the failure of *Lady Chatterley's Lover* as a work of art.[46]

Aldington tells us that "Lawrence always argued for victory, never to discover truth."[47] The pugnacious anti-intellectualism he adopted made it possible for him to argue that upper-class women should leave their husbands and run away with lower-class lovers at the same time he was vehemently insisting that marriage is for life and inviolable. Aldington cautions the reader: "Do not ask how he reconciled such contradictions—he never bothered to try."[48] It was this unlimited capacity for self-deception which enabled him to insist that *Lady Chatterley's Lover* was completely open and frank while at the same time he knew he had included material that was "covert and oblique instead of being open and direct . . . relying on clues and suggestions instead of describing in plain forthright language."[49] We must ask ourselves whether, to use his own phrase, he "did dirt" upon his own sexual creed.

It is one thing to advocate buggery, another to practice it. If we accept Sparrow's claim that Mellors practiced buggery on Bertha Coutts and Constance Chatterley (and I do accept this argument), it is only proper to inquire whether Lawrence, a latent homosexual, practiced it himself. Was he speaking from theory or experience? A meager hint is furnished in *Sons and Lovers;* describing the evolution of Paul Morel's affair with Clara Dawes, Lawrence writes, "Their loving grew more mechanical, without the marvelous glamour. Gradually they began to induce novelties, to get back some of the feeling of satisfaction."[50] That was written in 1912, and we shall never know what "novelties" Lawrence had in his imagination. There does not seem to be any evidence whether or not Lawrence and Frieda practiced anal intercourse. If they did, he was acting out his latent homosexual impulses. If he wanted to but did not try, he did not have the courage of his erections; he obtained this form of gratification vicariously through Mellors.

If we conceive of Mellors as the creation of a latent or pseudo-homosexual writer whose heterosexual libido was waning to the point of impotence, it is not difficult to plot a rough guide to Lawrence's unconscious psychodynamics. The homosexual impulses, having been firmly repressed during his period of active heterosexual achievement, now, under the stress and anxiety engendered by impotence (partial or complete), and activated also by his chronic physical illness, began to emerge upward in the unconscious, approaching the preconscious level. These impulses were still unacceptable to Lawrence's cognition, and their threatened encroachment upon it, the feeling that they might burst into consciousness (or even into action) only served to increase Lawrence's general tension and anxiety—hence the increasing hostility toward others, toward society, toward the world, during his last few years. Nonetheless, these impulses required that they be dealt with; their presence near consciousness was intolerable. Having more anxiety that he could handle by his usual mechanisms of defense, Lawrence unconsciously resolved his pseudohomosexual conflict by substituting a female for a male object—hence the innuendos about buggery. To compensate for his impotence he displaced his loss of potentia onto Clifford Chatterley and created the character of Mellors, the always potent, sexually agile male, the vehicle through which he enunciated his ideas about sex. Identifying himself with Mellors, he was able to initiate Lady Chatterley into the full sexual life as he conceived it, to satisfy her, as he was now unable to do with Frieda, and to fertilize her. Significantly, Lawrence and Frieda were childless, though she was a woman of proven fertility in her previous marriage. There are many possible medical reasons why a given couple may be infertile, and one can only speculate why this marriage was barren. However, it is difficult to believe that Lawrence, an exponent of "natural" sex, used contraceptives. Through Mellors at least he was able to share in the creation of a new life. He also endowed Mellors with the desire, means, and opportunity to practice buggery, his own displaced, unconscious wish. In sum, Mellors was Lawrence's concept of the complete sexual man, and he used Mellors's virile sexuality as a defense against the threat which tuberculosis was to his life and physical integrity as well as to his potency. Mellors was not only Lady Chatterley's lover but Lawrence's image of himself, not as he was but as he would have liked to be. Between the wish and the reality falls the shadow, and it is the shadow of artistic failure as well as personal defeat.

Lawrence's claim to importance as a novelist who presents a personal emotion and morality has been called into question in very simple words, and these, I think, summarize the case against him. W. W. Robson writes that "It is easy to discover that Lawrence as a moralist is thoroughly incoherent. . . . [He] is too obviously generalizing improperly, and at times erroneously, from his own case. This is especially clear in the matter of sex."[51] Whatever relationship Lawrence bore in his own imagination to Lady Chatterley, he was not her lover. Probably the most pithy comment on the novel was made by C. S. Lewis shortly after the trial: *"Lady Chatterley* has made short work of a prosecution by the Crown. It still has to face more formidable judges. Nine of them and all goddesses."[52] As a physician, I should like to point out that these goddesses were the daughters of Apollo and siblings to Aesculapius.

The preceding view of Lawrence and *Lady Chatterley's Lover* is not the only view one can take. Many important critics disregard the element of psychopathology and focus attention on other values. Alfred Kazin speaks of "Lawrence's romantic-religious, antinomian, ecstatic faith that sex is holy" and places him

in the great tradition of English and American literary radicals, with Emerson and Thoreau and Whitman as surely as with Blake and the young Wordsworth and Shelley, in his belief that "the holiness of the heart's affections" can revolutionize society, can transform the "dark Satanic mills," the hated cities, the industrial reek and blackness which Lawrence saw as the enemy of the free human spirit... Lawrence's novel was an effort to give religious values to relations between the sexes . . . [his] supreme subject is love, not sex. . . . Our belief in psychology as determinism [militates against Lawrence], since to us love is helpless and compulsive. So does the sheer lack in America of the rural mystery, the old English wood in which the lovers make love. Lawrence's exultant, almost unbearably sensitive descriptions of the countryside can mean little to Americans for whom the neighborhood of love must be the bathroom and the bedroom, both the last word in sophisticated privacy. Lawrence's description of the naked lovers gamboling in the rain, his ability to describe a woman's sensation and a man's body with feminine sureness—all this belongs to another world.[53]

It might seem irrelevant to counter Mr. Kazin's praise by pointing out that *civis Americanus sum,* but that it was a group of English critics who first called attention to the concealed innuendos about buggery. One grants that bathrooms have improved somewhat since classical antiquity, but the bedchamber *(thalamos)* was where the ancient Greeks and Trojans mingled their flesh. There is nothing sophisticated about the desire for privacy during copulation. Shakespeare might have been able to bring Birnam Wood to high Dunsinane hill, but I confess my inability to bring the English wood to the American landscape; nonetheless, there is abundant space in America for coitus al fresco as the abundance of condoms in brooks and rivers can testify. If Americans are not sylvan cohabitors, they are at least riparian. Last, I would raise an eyebrow at Lawrence's ability "to describe . . . a man's body with feminine sureness"; this is a skill which might well be greater in latent homosexuals than any other group. But Mr. Kazin's major premises are correct: Lawrence *is* romantic-religious, and he is certainly antinomian, and men who write from such a position are not likely to find sympathetic ears among readers who do believe in psychology as determinism.

R. H. Welker takes up the point that Lawrence's subject is love, not sex. He tells us that,

Lady Chatterley's Lover is a love story . . . a novel offering heterosexual love as the way to salvation for humankind, and condemning all that prevents and denies and inhibits such love as the means of our damnation. . . . To be intellectually satisfied by Lawrence's lovers is one thing, but to be emotionally convinced is another. If Connie's spontaneous weeping over the pheasant chick and Mellors' blindly passionate reaction, and their first physical union do not intimately involve the reader, he is in danger of rejecting the rest of the book. . . . If he is indifferent to Lawrence's powerful description of nature, if he finds incomprehensible the idea of love-making in the rain, if he sniggers at the twining of flowers in pubic hair, the book has failed him, or he the book. . . . If the reader cannot accept Lawrence's version of love, or at least entertain it as a hope or a possibility, he must find *Lady Chatterley's Lover* a dullish diatribe against a provincial and dated capitalist society, with ludicrous or even pornographic sex interludes.[54]

One does not have to "snigger" at the twining of flowers in pubic hair to reject it as a generally applicable mode of conduct *post coitum,* nor does one have to find the idea of lovemaking in the rain "incomprehensible" to reject it as a form of personal recreation. As Mr. Welker aptly puts it: *If the reader cannot accept Lawrence's version of love.* Most readers would agree with Lawrence's version in part, but when the reading reveals a taste for sexual perversion, a touch of sadism, and a whiff of latent homosexuality, I think most readers will opt out. If this means that the book has failed them or they the book, so be it. As with any other book, one can either agree with the author or not; in the old maxim, "You pays your money and you takes your choice." But is it not the obligation of the critic to describe accurately the writer's position? I would be much more persuaded by Messrs. Kazin, Welker, and others who share their opinions, if they would come to grips with the issue of sexual psychopathology and then accept it as a "version of love, or at least entertain it as a hope."

CHAPTER 4

Drowsed with the Fume of Poppies: Opium and John Keats

Current interest in hallucinogenic drugs prompts reappraisal of the effects of older drugs, as the narcotic experience of each new generation recapitulates that of past generations. Although such ancient physicians as Dioscorides, Avicenna, Caelius Aurelianus, Paulus Aegineta, and Isidore of Seville were familiar with the toxic and narcotic effects of "poppy and mandragora," they were not acquainted with hallucinogenic effects. It is not beyond conjecture that addiction and drug-induced hallucinations may be culturally determined and of relatively recent origin. The first accounts by physicians of the effects of an hallucinogenic drug on imagery and ideation were by S. Weir Mitchell[1] and Havelock Ellis[2] who, at the turn of the century, reported their sensations after ingesting crude extracts of mescal buttons. However, medical reporting was preceded by literary reportage by almost a century. Meyer Abrams has analyzed the effects of opium, taken as laudanum, on the writings of Samuel Taylor Coleridge, Thomas De-Quincey, George Crabbe, and Francis Thompson.[3] Significantly, the title of Abrams's illuminating thesis, *The Milk of Paradise*, is a phrase taken from the last line of Coleridge's *Kubla Khan*, a poem composed under the direct influence of opium. The received legend is that a fortuitous caller interrupted the poet while he was writing; his drug-induced trance vanished, and he was never able to recapture the mood.

In the middle of the nineteenth century Théophile Gautier[4] and Charles Baudelaire[5] related their hallucinatory experiences with hashish, and Baudelaire's *Les Paradis Artificiels* came to occupy a position in French letters analogous to DeQuincey's *Confessions of an English*

Opium-Eater as the *locus classicus* of the narcotic experience. In our own century Jean Cocteau[6] and Aldous Huxley[7] have reported their reactions following the use of purified opium extract and mescaline, respectively. The 1960s witnessed a proliferation of reports of the effects of such hallucinogens as psilocybin, *d*-lysergic acid diethylamide (LSD), and dimethyl-tryptamine (DMT) by laymen, litterateurs, social scientists, as well as by psychiatrists and other physicians.

It is of interest that three British poets who used opium also had medical training: George Crabbe, Francis Thompson, and John Keats. None of them attempted a systematic, objective account of his drug experiences; it is revealed in their poetry. Abrams's analysis of the effects of opium on the imagery of Crabbe and Thompson make it unnecessary to add more than a few additional comments to a synoptic view of their problems, but Keats's occasional use of opium and its effect on his poems are not well known and will occupy the major portion of this study.

Within a permissible latitude of individual differences in response, drug-induced hallucinations have many features in common, regardless of the specific drug used. The intensity and duration of the hallucinations seem to vary roughly with the dosage and the frequency with which the drug is taken. Disorientation in space and time is common to most of these hallucinations; conception of both space and time becomes distorted, usually expanded, and apparently infinite. Roger Dupouy[8] writes *"Le temps n'existe plus, l'espace est illimité,"* a curious echo of DeQuincey's observation that "Space swelled, and was amplified to an extent of unutterable and self-repeating infinity. This disturbed me very much less than the vast expanse of time." Visual hallucinations are frequent, ranging from a simple intensification of perception to perceptions of scintillating bright lights, from strange, unidentifiable objects with glowing, gemlike coloration to recognizable images of fountains, streams, castles, and exotic, brightly colored landscapes. Even Huxley, who describes himself as a "poor visualizer," possibly the result of his iritis, states: "mescaline raises all colors to a higher power and makes the percipient aware of innumerable fine shades of difference, to which, at ordinary times, he is completely blind."[9] Auditory and olfactory hallucinations are less frequent and less striking, but Gautier heard identifiable musical selections, and Ellis felt himself to be in a garden with strange flowers and surrounded by a mysterious, unidentifiable scent. Synesthesia of images is not infrequent; colored visions may assume a tactile quality; sounds may be perceived as colors. The visual, auditory, and olfactory images change rapidly. Ellis speaks of "a constant succession of self-evolving visual imagery," which he compares to images produced by a kaleidoscope.[10]

Ideational content may be seriously affected. With mild to moderate dosage of opium, especially if not taken regularly, there is blunting of the sensorium, often accompanied by a sense of depersonalization and deanimation of hallucinated objects. Individuals with strong religious interests may have mystical experiences; typical of this effect are Huxley's "beatific vision . . . being-awareness-bliss," the religious poems of Francis Thompson, and the emphasis on certain Oriental religious practices by persons who use LSD. High doses and addiction may elicit dreams of terror, as in the examples of Crabbe, DeQuincey, and Thompson; such dreams usually contain ideas of persecution and flight. Addiction rarely occurs in individuals with a strong, well-structured personality but is common in those with poorly socialized, dependent personalities. Currently, the occurrence of psychoses marked by hallucinations and aggressive or self-destructive behavior in those who use LSD is reported with increasing frequency in the public as well as in the medical press. However, even single, isolated doses within the therapeutic range may produce transient dreamlike states with mild to moderate hallucinatory effects.

George Crabbe (1754–1832) first came to public notice in 1783 when he published his poem, *The Village*, a work of social realism written as a corrective to Goldsmith's roseate view of rural life in *The Deserted Village*. Crabbe had been born in poverty in Aldeburgh, a small coastal town in Suffolk. In 1770 his father had apprenticed him to an apothecary-surgeon who used him chiefly as an errand boy and farm laborer and made him sleep with the stableboy. In 1775 he set out for London "to acquire a little surgical knowledge as cheaply as possible." He then returned to Aldeburgh, where he became the ill-paid assistant to the local surgeon. When the latter moved away, Crabbe attempted to take over the practice but failed miserably. Uniable to earn even a subsistence wage as a surgeon-apothecary, he set out in 1780 for London and a literary career. After some struggles he obtained patronage from Charles Manners, duke of Rutland, through the intercession of Edmund Burke, who recognized his merits and introduced him to the leading figures in London's literary world. At Burke's instigation, Crabbe applied for holy orders, was ordained deacon in 1781, and priest in 1782. He became chaplain to the duke of Rutland and was awarded an LL.B. degree by John Moore, archbishop of Canterbury, to qualify him for further preferments. After the duke's untimely death in 1787 he was presented to a suitable rural curacy.

Crabbe did not begin to use opium until 1790, a decade after he had

Facsimile of the manuscript of Keats's *Ode to a Nightingale*. Courtesy of the Fitzwilliam Museum

stopped practicing medicine. The drug was prescribed by a physician whose diagnosis of a fit of vertigo and syncope was that of a digestive disturbance. The respectable rural clergyman-poet continued to take laudanum daily, probably in moderate doses, without apparent ill effect on his constitution for forty-two years. His mental powers remained unimpaired and his interpersonal relations did not suffer. In fact, it was his wife, not he, who developed a profound mental depression after the successive death of five of their seven children in the 1790s; her depressive psychosis lasted until her death in 1813. Crabbe's literary gifts did not lie fallow between 1785 and 1807, but during this period he published nothing. Periodically, he would hold an "incremation" at which he and his two surviving children would burn his manuscripts.

In 1807 Crabbe returned to poetry with the publication of a volume titled *Poems,* which includes among others a dramatic scena, "Sir Eustace Grey." Abrams has analyzed this poem as well as another (of uncertain date) titled *The World of Dreams* and has demonstrated their hallucinatory content. However, even more revealing is additional information about Crabbe's dream life and its relation to his somewhat better known poems *Peter Grimes* and *Ellen Orford* (1810). Benjamin Britten's opera, *Peter Grimes,* incorporates material from both these narratives, and their substance is currently familiar. René Huchon quotes the evidence from Edward Fitzgerald of *Rubáiyát* fame, a close friend of Crabbe's son and a frequent visitor, about one of Crabbe's recurrent dreams: "He was troubled with strange dreams: in one of them he thought he was followed and hooted at by a set of boys, whom he tried to beat off with a stick, but to no purpose, because they were made of leather! He would sometimes reply, when he was asked whether he had slept well, 'The leatherlads have been at me again.' "[11] While we have no information about Crabbe's psychosexual development other than that he was made to sleep with the stable boy, the implications of this dream content are undeniable. Only in recent years have we come to recognize the nature of leather as a fetish object in homosexuality and sadomasochism. The symbol of being pursued by a gang of boys dressed in leather and trying vainly to beat them off with a stick suggests a rather complex but distinctly abnormal set of sexual desires released into dream content under the influence of a narcotic, yet sufficiently under control of the dream censor to be modified.

Ellen Orford features incest and the seduction of a feeble-minded girl, but *Peter Grimes* is a sordid and tragic tale of overt sadism with latent homosexuality. Grimes is depicted as an unmarried fisherman who leads a solitary life, who has broken off relations with his family and is somewhat alienated from the society in which he lives. After his father's death he hires a series of young apprentices, whom he beats and starves. The first apprentice dies of starvation; the second, Grimes insists, fell from the main mast into the hold; the third was a boy "of manners soft and mild" of whom Crabbe says:

> Passive he labour'd, till his slender frame
> Bent with his loads, and he at length was lame;
> Strange that a frame so weak could bear so long
> The grossest insult and the foulest wrong.

Although Grimes is acquitted of criminal charges, he goes mad and is haunted by hallucinations and dreams of terror. He sees the specter of his father rise from the waters, holding "a thin pale boy in either hand." They glide on top of the salt water without touching it and vanish when Grimes brandishes an oar at them. At a second manifestation the vision is enriched by an act of retribution from the father, an image of blood-guilt, and opium-induced synesthesia:

> He, with his hand, the old man, scoop'd the flood,
> And there came flame about him mix'd with blood;
> He bade me stoop and look upon the place,
> Then flung the hot-red liquor in my face.

Relentless, the spectral vision recurs and continues to haunt Grimes until his dying day, much as the leather lads haunted Crabbe's dreams. It would seem that Crabbe was astute enough to keep his opium usage within reasonable bounds; the price he paid for his habituation was a recurrent dream of terror and pursuit, and some of his poems do reflect elements of hallucinated imagery as well as narrative elements traceable to intrapsychic conflicts.

In contrast to Crabbe's quiet life and moderate habituation, the life of Francis Thompson (1859–1907) was that of an overt psychopath and known addict. Like Coleridge, DeQuincey, and Crabbe, Thompson's first use of opium was by medical prescription. In 1879, then almost twenty-one years old and ostensibly a medical student at Manchester, he had an attack of "lung fever" for which laudanum was prescribed. Finding it pleasant, he continued taking it and, within a few months, by the time of his mother's death in 1880, was habituated. There is abundant evidence of his unstable, withdrawn, schizoid personality prior to this period.

Born the son of converts to Roman Catholicism, his father a successful homeopathic physician in Ashton-under-Lyme, Thompson was brought up with his sisters in a "hot-house atmosphere of provincial piety."[12] Debarred by his religion from having friends among his peers, Thompson developed a rich fantasy life, and came to accept his interior fantasies as reality. Unable to relate to the give and take of the boys' college at Ushaw, where he was sent at the age of eleven, he took refuge in writing poetry "as a means of escape and self-dramatization . . . a repository of dreams and a confessional."[13] His parents had sent him to Ushaw to see if he could qualify for the priesthood, but the fathers decided that his inadequate personality disqualified him from attempting pastoral duties. At the age of eighteen, in 1877, Thompson returned home with a doubtfully sound classical background but no purpose in life.

Young Thompson supinely offered no objection when his father sent him to medical school in Manchester. He commuted there daily from Ashton, but having no interest in medicine soon stopped attending classes and demonstrations; he spent his day loitering around Manchester. He failed his examinations after two years; not surprisingly, he failed after another two years, but by this time he was addicted to laudanum. He failed a third time in 1885 after "attending" medical school for six years. Some form of personality deterioration must have been evident, for his father accused him of drinking. The "failed medico" denied it, but there must have been a scene and an ultimatum, for he left home the following day, procured a liberal supply of laudanum in Manchester, then set off for London.

It is reasonable to conjecture that addiction to opium helped him bridge the gap between ambition and accomplishment. Though his father would not have opposed a literary career, Thompson was afraid to admit his literary ambitions to his father or anyone else, lest he be encouraged in them and fail, even as he had at his trial for the priesthood. Alone and rudderless in London, Thompson became a derelict until he was "discovered" by Wilfred and Alice Meynell in 1888. The Meynells arranged for him to enter a hospital, take the "cure" and then, through their connections with the hierarchy, for Thompson to stay at a monastery as a "guest." For the next decade, his most productive years, he lived at one monastery or another, interspersing his visits with sporadic journeys to London. When in London for any time, he would revert to laudanum. In this manner he wrote *Poems* (1893) and *New Poems* (1897). Most of his poems were written while he was at these monasteries and not taking opium daily; technically, Alice Meynell was correct when she claimed they were not written under the influence of drugs. Thompson's fantasies were elaborated by opium rather than produced by it; he was a natural dreamer. The hallucinatory imagery and religious ideation were committed to paper some time after they had been experienced. Reid says bluntly that Thompson turned to poetry as a substitute for opium; however, the opium liberated his consciousness for poetry.

Thompson developed a friendship with Coventry Patmore, and the older poet, well established and secure, served as a father-substitute for him. Unfortunately, Patmore died suddenly in 1896, as did Thompson's real father later that year. In 1897 Thompson left the monastery in Wales, where he had been sheltered for several years, and returned to London and to opium. His poetic output declined sharply; he supported himself and his addiction by writing articles, reviews, and hack books. He returned to monastic walls in 1906, wasted and dying. On his deathbed he confessed to Meynell, "I am dying of opium poisoning!"[14] But, like most of his attempts at self-dramatization, the statement was false; he died of tuberculosis.

Like Coleridge, DeQuincey, and Crabbe, Thompson suffered from nightmares. In a letter to Everard Meynell, the son of his editor and his later biographer, Thompson wrote: "a most miserable fortnight of torpid, despondent days, and affrightful nights, dreams having been in part the worst realities of my life."[15] Abrams has described the hallucinatory content of Thompson's prose fantasy, *Finis Coronat Opus,* in which the guilt-ridden hero, like Crabbe's Sir Eustace Grey, is tormented by dreams of horror and terror, including visual and auditory hallucinations. His use of the words "illimitable" and "boundless" suggest the effect of opium on his perception of space; in another poem he alludes to God as the "King of infinite space."

A striking example of synesthesia is seen in his *Ode to the Setting Sun,* written in 1889 shortly after his first refuge in a monastery, coincident with his first real withdrawal from opium for several years:

> Thy visible music-blasts make deaf the sky,
> Thy cymbals clang to fire the Occident,
> Thou dost thy dying so triumphantly:
> I *see* the crimson blaring of the shawms!

Another poem rich in narcotic fantasy is *The Poppy,* a lyric dedicated to Monica Meynell, one of his editor's children. The gaudy hallucinatory palette describes the opium-giving flower as leaving its "flushed print" on the earth like a "yawn of fire" which the wind puffs to "flapping flame." The poppy with its "burnt mouth, red as a lion's" is called "this withering flower of dreams," and the poem closes with a precognition of his fate; the poppy signifies both the instrument of his release and his destruction.

However, a wider response to the effects of opium is seen in *The Hound of Heaven,* probably his best-known work. The familiar opening lines depict the poet being pursued by his God:

> I fled Him, down the nights and down the days;
> I fled Him, down the arches of the years;
> I fled Him, down the labyrinthine ways
>   *Of my own mind.* (Italics added)

Thompson leaves no doubt that the pursuit and flight are products of his own ideation. He fancies himself chased by a dog, and after many lines of disordered imagery and neologisms, the poem reveals his posture in relation to his God as: "Naked I wait Thy love's uplifted stroke?" This is an expression of the most masochistic attitude ever adopted by any poet who has written in English, even beyond the customary limits of self-flagellation or martyrdom.

Despite Thompson's ability to create unusually vivid descriptions of both natural and imagined objects, the Hound itself is never clearly depicted; it is a presence. Not only the selection of a dog as God's image, but the fact that he could not bring himself to supply a shred of physical imagery about this symbol, is revealing. In real life Thompson was deathly afraid of dogs. Patmore's son wrote in later years: "Francis Thompson often stayed with us. Great poet though he was, I fear I had but a poor idea of him, a weakly little man . . . he had a peculiar dread of dogs, and as he could not hide his terror of our retriever Nelson, I regret to say that my only feeling for him was unmixed contempt."[16] The only item lacking to reify the paraphernalia of Gothic fantasy is a voice from the wings saying, "Mr. Holmes, they were the footprints of a gigantic hound!"

One reason why Thompson's poetry has declined in reputation in recent years is that his long and profound addiction to opium released into his writing not only the vivid imagery of hallucination but also the ill-formed, distorted attitudes of a weak, indecisive, withdrawn personality which was, by virtue of upbringing and later environment, obsessed with religion to the point of religiosity. His talent was more profoundly damaged by narcotic addiction than that of any other English poet.

It will come as a surprise to most readers to find John Keats (1795–1821) included among the opium eaters. Keats was not an addict, and his use of laudanum was only occasional. However, he was trained and licensed as an apothecary (the equivalent of a general practitioner of today); there is documentary evidence of possession from one source and usage from another. The effects of opium on his poetry can be found in the imagery and ideational content of his *Ode to a Nightingale* as well as in a few other poems to a lesser degree. It is not likely that Keats was influenced to take laudanum by Coleridge, whom he met but once, nor is there any reason to think he was acquainted with DeQuincey, whose *Confessions of an English Opium-Eater* were not published until late in 1821, months after Keats's death.

Keats's short, unhappy life is too familiar to require detailed restatement. His father died in 1804 and his mother in 1810; the orphaned lad was apprenticed to a surgeon at Edmonton in 1811 when he was sixteen. In 1814 he broke his apprenticeship and went to London to study medicine at Guy's and St. Thomas's Hospitals, which were then combined for teaching purposes. He received his certificate as an apothecary in July 1816, and continued intermittent attendance as a dresser at Guy's until well in 1817, when he decided to abandon medicine and devote himself to literature. Although his medical notes in anatomy and physiology have been preserved and published, there is no documentary evidence of what he studied in materia medica. We must infer that he was acquainted with the clinical use of opiates and their effects, as the drug was then freely prescribed for all manner of ills, and he must surely have spoken with patients who had received it.

In 1818 Keats's younger brother Tom developed pulmonary tuberculosis; Keats nursed him devotedly, living in the same small room with him until the boy died in December of that year. There is no doubt that Keats himself contracted tuberculosis from this prolonged and intimate contact. Although the dramatic episode of his sudden hemoptysis on February 3, 1820, provides us with a date for the definite establishment of pulmonary infection, Keats's letters indicate that he had preclinical symptoms well before that time. As early as the autumn of 1818, while Tom was still alive, he complained of a persistent sore throat, which progressed with only transient remissions through the winter, spring, summer, and autumn of 1819. The sore throat by itself is a nonspecific symptom, and it certainly cannot suggest tuberculosis laryngitis, which would be a late complication, but it became associated with progressive malaise, a low-grade intermittent fever, and tightness in the chest, which are more suggestive. There is no documentary evidence that Keats took opiates at this time for relief, nor is there any documentation regarding the medications prescribed for Tom.

Although Keats tried to present a brave face to his friends after Tom's death, he was emotionally depressed and poetically unproductive during January, February, and March of 1819. He moved into the house owned by his friend Charles Armitage Brown. In an effort to relieve his low spirits, he went out on March 18, 1819, with some friends to play cricket and was hit in the eye by a cricket ball. Walter Jackson Bate informs us that Brown "had a little opium and gave him some of it that evening as a palliative."[17] However, in a letter to his elder brother George, then seeking his fortune in America, Keats wrote: "Yesterday I got a black eye—the first time I took a Cricket bat—Brown who is always one's friend in a disaster applied a leech to the eyelid and there is no inflammation this morning."[18] A few lines further in this journal letter, dated March 19, Keats records a feeling of lassitude on the morning after:

This morning I am in a sort of temper indolent and supremely careless—I long after a stanza or two of Thomson's *Castle of Indolence*—my passions are all asleep from my having slumbered till nearly eleven and weakened the animal fibre all over me to a delightful sensation about three degrees this side of faintness—if I had teeth of pearl and the breath of lillies I should call it langour—but as I am[19] I must call it laziness—in this state of effeminacy the fibres of the brain are relaxed in common with the rest of the body, and to such a happy degree that pleasure has no show of enticement and pain no unbearable frown. Neither Poetry, nor Ambition, nor Love have any alertness of countenance as they pass by me: they seem rather like the figures on a Greek vase—a Man and two women—whom no one but myself could distinguish in their disguisement.[20]

It is unusual to sleep late after a painful injury to the eye, and the feeling of relaxation and indifference to the usual stimuli for pain or pleasure are certainly consistent with the aftereffects of a single dose of laudanum; one would scarcely expect them from a leech. The allusion to figures on a Greek vase might bear some relationship to the *Ode to a Grecian Urn* written in May, about two months later. However, the entire passage seems more directly related to the *Ode on Indolence*, probably written at about this time:

> One morn before me were three figures seen, ...
> They pass'd, like figures on a marble urn, ...
>   Ripe was the drowsy hour;
> The blissful cloud of summer-indolence
> Benumb'd my eyes; my pulse grew less and less;
> Pain had no sting, and pleasure's wreath no flower.

The figures pass by Keats's eye as the urn seems to revolve slowly, and there is a sense of slowed motion and time in addition to the diminution of the pulse and the abolition of pain and pleasure which are more specifically similar to the known effects of opium.

By contrast, the phrase "Drowsed with the fume of poppies" in the *Ode to Autumn* composed in October 1819 bears only a tenuous relation to opium usage, as the metaphor is not pursued nor related to any of the other known effects of the drug. It is the sort of image which might occur to any Romantic poet, especially one trained as an apothecary. If any of Keats's poems shows the effects of opium usage, it is the *Ode to a Nightingale,* written in late April or early May of 1819, about six weeks after the incident of the cricket ball.

Yet even a month after Keats received the black eye and its treatment by leech or opium (or both), his journal-letter to his brother George records on April 16, a dream which bears a striking similarity to those reported after opium, mescaline, psilocybin, and LSD:

The fifth canto of Dante pleases me more and more—it is the one in which he meets Paolo and Francesca—I had passed many days in a rather low state of mind and in the midst of them I dreamt of being in that region of Hell—I floated about the whirling atmosphere as it is described with a beautiful figure to whose lips mine were join'd as it seem'd for an age—and in the midst of all this cold and darkness I was warm—even flowery tree tops sprung up and we rested on them sometimes with the lightness of a cloud till the wind blew us away again—I tried a Sonnet upon it—there are fourteen lines but nothing of what I felt in it—O that I could dream it every night.[21]

The sonnet was the one beginning "As Hermes once took to his feathers light." It contains no internal evidence of the effect of drugs, but Keats himself wrote that it contained nothing of the sensations he experienced in the dream. Inability to communicate in words the nature of the narcotic experience, the *indicible* nature of the images and ideas, is a constant theme in the literature on drug effects. In the dream Keats says he felt warm despite the cold and darkness around him; this may be construed as a disorder of the sensorium, but that would be stretching a point. Likewise, one may dream of floating in space and being blown by the wind without having recourse to opiates. The evidence furnished by the dream content is suggestive but not specific.

George Keats returned to England for a brief visit in January 1820. He was under considerable financial pressure, and it was rather a tense time for his family and friends. Keats was living in Brown's house during most of this period, and Brown's memoir, written about 1840 to 1841, alludes specifically to Keats's use of laudanum. Though Brown's dating leaves much to be desired, the context indicates that the events occurred at about the time of George's visit, i.e., shortly before the first hemoptysis on February 3, 1820. Brown records that: "he began to be reckless of health. Among other proofs of recklessness, he was secretly taking, at times, a few drops of laudanum to keep up his spirits. It was discovered by accident, and, without delay, revealed to me. He needed not be warned of the danger of such a habit; but I rejoiced at his promise never to take another drop without my knowledge; for nothing could induce him to break his word, when once given."[22] By January 1820 Keats certainly had symptoms which in retrospect presaged the overt development of pulmonary tuberculosis, and he may have been taking the laudanum not only to keep up his spirits but as self-medication for his symptoms. Regrettably, Brown's memoir is silent regarding the incident of the cricket ball and the possibility of his having given Keats a single dose of opium as a palliative in the preceding March.

The only other documentary evidence linking Keats with opium is supplied in a letter from Rome dated January 25 and 26, 1821, written by Joseph Severn, the young artist who had accompanied Keats there when he left England in September 1820. Apparently Keats had procured a bottle of opium, probably as tincture of laudanum, shortly before sailing. In his letter addressed to Joseph Taylor, Keats's publisher, Severn writes:

> The hardest point between us is that cursed bottle of Opium—he had determined on taking this the instant his recovery should stop—he says to save him the extended misery of a long illness—in his own mind he saw this fatal prospect—the dismal night—the impossibility of receiving any sort of comfort—and above all the wasting of his body and helplessness—these he had determined on escaping—and but for me—he would have swallowed this draught 3 months since—in the ship—he says 3 wretched months have I kept him alive.[23]

The letter establishes possession, hints at a suicidal gesture in September, but confirms the fact that Keats was not an addict, for even though he suffered all the misery he sought to avoid, he could not bring himself to use the bottle which was at hand. Keats died a month after Severn's letter was written.

Having established possession and use of opium in 1820, and having a strong suggestion of at least a single therapeutic dose in March 1819, one more speculative comment may be added. A person who uses opium tends to conceal his practice. Brown states that Keats's use of laudanum was secret. Also, in none of the seventy letters written *after* his first hemoptysis, from February through November 1820, when he became too weak to write, does Keats mention any specific medication by name, though his letters are filled with reports of visits from his physicians, accounts of his symptoms, and the advice his physicians gave him. In a man with medical training such reticence hints that he may have had something to conceal.

Like Coleridge's *Kubla Khan*, the *Ode to a Nightingale* was written in a single burst of inspiration. Brown's memoir recounts the circumstances:

> In the spring of 1819 a nightingale had built her nest near my house. Keats felt a tranquil and continual joy in her song; and one morning he took his chair from the breakfast-table to the grass-plot under a plum-tree, where he sat for two or three hours. When he came into the house, I perceived he had some scraps of paper in his hand, and these he was quietly thrusting behind the books. On inquiry, I found those scraps, four or five in number, contained his poetic feeling on the song of our nightingale.[24]

We must accept the poem as the expression of a unified frame of mind and emotional attitude. There is every reason to believe that the final form does not differ greatly from the first inspired draft. The opening four lines of the poem are pharmacologically explicit:

> My heart aches, and a drowsy numbness pains[25]
>   My sense, as though of hemlock I had drunk,
> Or emptied some dull opiate to the drains
>   One minute past, and Lethe-wards had sunk.

Cruel as it is to paraphrase, Keats tells us that he feels depressed, that his sensorium is obtunded as if he had just taken a drug. He mentions hemlock, which does not produce this effect, despite its association with Socrates, and opiates which do so. Sinking "Lethe-wards" implies that he has entered an amnesic, trancelike state. In this trance he hears, or thinks he hears, the nightingale, the "light-winged Dryad of the trees," singing of the approaching summer in "full-throated ease." Whether or not the nightingale's song is an auditory hallucination is a question Keats never fully resolves. Brown's account does inform us that there was, at least, a real nightingale. But there is no room for doubt that Keats does compare his mood and state of sensory apperception to a drug-induced trance.

Unlike the nightingale in medieval lyrics, which sang of unfulfilled desire, Keats's nightingale sang of spontaneous and unremitting joy. Though somewhat recovered from the depression and work inhibition which developed after his brother's death, Keats still had some feelings of alienation when he wrote the *Ode,* and he contrasts his concern with sickness, pain, and death, the inevitable human lot, with the bird's immortal song. He presents this contrast *after* he has indicated the failure of three routes of escape, each with its own distinctive liberation: opiates, wine, and the exercise of the poetic imagination—"the fancy cannot cheat so well." In point of biographical as well as poetical fact, Keats never did resolve this conflict.

In the next stanza the poet seeks to escape from a world of stern reality: "That I might drink and leave this world unseen," the constant motive and plea of escapists from time immemorial. Keats does not specify precisely what he wishes to escape; biographically, it could have been any number of problems or the concerted impact of many. Opiates having served their initial purpose in the poem, the induction of the trance, the quick and ready route for escape is alcohol, specifically wine:

> O for a draught of vintage. . . .
> O for a beaker full of the warm South,
>   Full of the true, the blushful Hippocrene,
>   With beaded bubbles winking at the brim,
> And purple-stainèd mouth.

At this point one begins to question the accuracy of his visual imagery. The allusion to Hippocrene is to a spring on Mount Helicon from which the Muses drank and received inspiration. A very apposite allusion indeed, but surely the waters of Hippocrene[26] are crystal clear, not "purple-stainèd." Has not the poet added, while in an opium trance, an hallucinated color? R. H. Fogle considers this stanza to contain the finest example of synesthesia in all of Keats's poems.[27]

The plea for escape, amnesia, and depersonalization continues in the third stanza, but this time Keats specifies some memories he would like to escape:

> Fade far away, dissolve, and quite forget
>   What thou amongst the leaves hast never known,
> The weariness, the fever, and the fret
>   Here, where men sit and hear each other groan;
> Where palsy shakes a few, sad, last gray hairs,
>   Where youth grows pale, and spectre-thin, and dies.

This image recalls Keats's own experiences in hospitals and fuses them with recollections of the recent death of his brother. His wish to forget such depressing scenes is not unreasonable, but he does manage to telescope the hospital images of 1816 with the more recent illness and death of his brother late in 1818, not unlike the distortion of time which occurs in drug-induced trances.

In the fourth stanza Keats banishes such melancholy ideas and gives voice to a desire to join the nightingale and be identified with her:

> Not charioted by Bacchus and his pards,
>   But on the viewless wings of Poesy
> Though the dull brain perplexes and retards.

Now abjuring the fruit of the vine as a source of inspiration, he affirms his poetic gift and seeks escape on the invisible wings of the poetic imagination. In this endeavor he is partly hindered by a "dull brain," which one may equate with the "drowsy numbness" induced by the opiate. Even as sensory perception is somewhat obtunded by drugs, so mental processes may be also retarded. It is a comment on a mind partially drugged, yet not so deeply as to be unaware of the effects on its higher mental processes.

Although the poem was written in the clear daylight of a spring morning, Keats now develops the idea of darkness—"But here there is no light," a phrase which might be consistent with sinking more deeply into the trance. He dimly senses a garden of flowers and an undefinable scent in the atmosphere around him: "I cannot see what flowers are at my feet, / Nor what soft incense hangs upon the boughs." Havelock Ellis described similar visions of flowers and a "vague perfume" after taking mescal extract, but Keats goes beyond that level of perception when he describes the soft tactile quality of the incense and pictures it hanging physically on a bough, a striking example of synesthesia. The fantasy continues, and Keats has thoughts of death, death as an escape from both his vision and from reality: "Now more than ever seems it rich to die, / To cease upon the midnight with no pain." It is scarcely necessary to point out that the primary medicinal purpose of taking opium is to alleviate pain.

In the penultimate stanza Keats declares the nightingale to be immortal; "the self-same song" that Ruth heard "amid the alien corn" is the same song Keats hears in his trancelike state. This auditory hallucination, telescoped in time, opens his eyes through "charmed magic casements" to additional visions of "perilous seas, in faery lands forlorn." The notion of perilous seas is not sufficiently definite to be equated with the visions of infinite space and boundless, bourneless bodies of water so common in narcotic hallucinations. Possibly stronger and more frequent dosage is necessary to evoke a more evident hallucination of spatial distortion. However, the "faery lands" do anticipate Baudelaire's artificial paradises. Keats came closer to the typical vision of limitless space in the "whirling atmosphere" of the Dante-inspired dream of April 15 and 16. The visual correlative for Keats with his lips joined to those of the diaphanous creature of the dream would resemble one of Blake's illustrations for the *Divine Comedy*. The girl of Keats's dream seems to bear no relation to Fanny Brawne, whose very name suggests something solid and earthbound rather than an ethereal, freely floating maiden with linear flowing drapery envisioned by Blake. Keats does suggest a vision of infinite space in *The Fall of*

Hyperion written at the end of 1819 in which he takes a draught of an unspecified potion and falls into a "cloudy swoon." On this occasion he states that the hallucinogen is "no Asian poppy or elixir fine," but its effect seems much the same. In this trance he dreams he is in sort of Levantine or quasi-Egyptian sanctuary of incredibly vast proportions: "Builded so high, it seem'd that filmed clouds / Might spread beneath, as o'er the stars of heaven." As he surveys his surroundings, he raises his eyes

> to fathom the space every way;
> The embossed roof, the silent massy range
> Of columns north and south, ending in mist
> Of nothing,

undeniably a drug-induced vision of expanded space. Weir Mitchell describes a similar vision of a Gothic castle after taking extract of mescal buttons, and common to both visions is the imagery of a collection of specifically mentioned bright objects within the hallucinated building. Keats describes: "Robes, golden tongs, censer, and chafing-dish, / Girdles, and chains, and holy jewelries."

Returning from this "perilous sea" and "faery land" of magic and enchantment, we encounter the word *forlorn*. This word has a particular valence for Keats, and he echoes it for emphasis in the next line which opens the final stanza: "Forlorn! the very word is like a bell / To toll me back from thee to my sole self!" Here we have for the first time an explicit statement of the poet's alienation or, to use a more homely, less fashionable word, his loneliness. The word recalls the poet from listening dreamily to the nightingale's song to his *sole self*. Both the word and the recall are put in the form of exclamations. As the nightingale's "plaintive anthem fades," Keats is brought back from his trance to solipsism and narcissism, two of the most prominent traits in the oversimplified psyche of a person who uses drugs. (The addict tries to solve his diverse, complex problems by reducing them to only one problem, namely getting his daily fix.) In much the same fashion Keats tried to reduce all the complex problems in his life—his illness, his unfulfilled love for Fanny Brawne, his economic uncertainties, his manifold relations with his friends—into one existential act, the writing of poetry as a way of escape—"for I will fly to thee . . . on the viewless wings of Poesy." Though Keats did not habitually use drugs, his mechanism of escape is comparable, and he projects this into consciousness in the *Ode to a Nightingale;* the poem takes its departure from the frame of mind and affect induced by "some dull opiate."

In this respect Keats shows features in common with contemporary users of psychedelic drugs. Even as early as the first book of *Endymion,* which he began writing in the spring of 1817, a year before his brother's illness, we find him writing

> Wherein lies happiness? In that which becks
> Our ready minds to fellowship divine,
> A fellowship with essence; till we shine,
> Full alchemiz'd, and free of space. Behold
> The clear religion of heaven!

Contemporary readers will not find this entirely alien to the nirvana described by individuals who go on "trips" together by using LSD. Surely, persons who use LSD have been "full alchemiz'd" and are "free of space." Keats was able to conceive of such a state even without the use of drugs.

As the effect of the drug begins to wear off, the poet comes out of his trance. Keats then asks what can be taken as a perfectly reasonable question, the sort of question any patient might ask on recovering from an anesthetic, a hypnotic, or a narcotic: "Was it a vision or a waking dream? / Fled is that music:—do I wake or sleep?" It is precisely at this point, the recovery phase, that the perception of reality is likely to be confused. There are no longer any visions or hallucinations, but there is disorientation as to time, place, and the real nature of one's surroundings. The patient is not quite sure that he is fully conscious. A hint of similar sensory confusion can be found in one of George Crabbe's newly discovered poems: "Where am I now? I slept to wake again, / And to forget."[28] Crabbe was addicted to opium in moderate dosage for many years and paid the price for it by having recurrent dreams of persecution and flight. He probably had more to forget or repress than Keats, but Keats, the better poet by far, has phrased the sensation of the trance more tellingly.

The *Ode to a Nightingale* is, then, a poem which, among other matters, describes a trancelike state containing several of the experiences that are known to follow the ingestion of opium. Keats was medically trained and cognizant of the effects of opium. There is evidence that he may have been given or had taken a single dose of opium for medicinal purposes prior to the date of the poem's composition. There is no evidence that the poem was a conscious attempt to recreate a narcotic experience, but its content suggests that Keats had had such an experience and drew upon it. There is documentary evidence that Keats had possession of and used opium in the form of laudanum after the *Ode to a Nightingale* was written; there are passages in other poems which tend to support this view. There is no evidence for, and every evidence in contradiction of, any notion that Keats was an addict or used opiates with any frequency, even in the terminal stages of his illness.

CHAPTER 5

Madness and Poetry: A Note on Collins, Cowper, and Smart

Precision in textual criticism is no guarantee of profundity in poetic analysis. In his Leslie Stephen lecture of 1933, *The Name and Nature of Poetry*, A. E. Housman wrote:

Meaning is of the intellect, poetry is not. If it were, the eighteenth century would have been able to write it better. As matters actually stand, who are the English poets of that age in whom pre-eminently one can hear and recognize the true poetic accent emerging clearly from the contemporary dialect? These four: Collins, Christopher Smart, Cowper and Blake. And what other characteristic had these four in common? They were mad. Remember Plato: "He who without the Muses' madness in his soul comes knocking at the door of poesy and thinks that art will make him anything fit to be called a poet, finds that the poetry which he indites in his sober senses is beaten hollow by the poetry of madmen!"[1]

Not every reader would concur in the dogma of the first sentence, and the judgment of the second sentence is rhadamanthine; the anathema seems to be personal rather than professorial. But Housman's selection of William Collins, Christopher Smart, and William Cowper with respect to their poetic language is the shrewd comment of a professional philologist and requires examination. For the purpose of this chapter I shall exclude William Blake, partly because of the chronology, partly because his may be a special case.

The passage from Plato is taken from the *Phaedrus,* and the text as rendered seems to be Housman's own paraphrase. The key word is "madness," and shortly after the Stephens lecture was published Ezra Pound took issue with Housman in a polemic titled "Mr. Housman at

Little Bethel": "If the Greek word there translated means 'madness' in the sense of Smart's and Collins' and Willie Blake's being occasionally sent off to do a week-end in an asylum; if it means anything more than a certain tenseness of emotion, a mental excess, no more insane than the kind of physical excess . . . that enables the sabre ant to cup a spider . . . Mr. Housman can pack that sentimental drool in his squiffer, and turn his skill to throwing the dart in the pub next adjacent."[2] Pound's tone is so ill-mannered and inappropriate that one does not hesitate to recall that a few years later his comeuppance was somewhat longer than a mere weekend in the "happy house." But his point about the word "madness" is well taken, albeit not made with the usual precision of *il miglior fabbro*.

Plato's word for the muses' madness is μανικη (mania), which he contrasts in the passage preceding Housman's excerpt with μαντικη the "madness" of prophecy (cf. the suffix "—mancy" as in necromancy). Plato distinguished clearly between prophetic insights and intuitive insights into the nature of reality. He distrusted the latter as being nonrational, but his use of the term mania does not necessarily imply irrationality or psychosis. Even today, in English usage, mania encompasses a wide range of attitudes and behavior, from folly through uncontrollable impulses to overt psychosis; it is not a restrictive term. Housman, who should have known better, chose to disregard the continuum of rational-nonrational-irrational in favor of the oversimplified dichotomy between madness and sanity. (Later in the Stephens lecture Housman describes his sympathomimetic correlative for his own poetic inspirations. His muse, it appears, would draw nigh when he was shaving and induce a dermatopathic response, his arrector pili muscles contracting to produce something akin to gooseflesh.) It is bad enough to be hoist by one's own autonomic nervous system, but for the professor of classics at Cambridge to be taxed with misconstruing a simple Greek word out of a familiar context implies that there is more to the relation between madness and poetry than "allusions to profound emotions rigidly controlled." Mania in the classical sense can imply that the mind has been taken over by a god or by the muses.

Pound, too, oversimplifies; there is more to the muses' madness than a certain tenseness of emotion and a mental excess. The sterilized vocabulary of latter-day psychology uses such phrases as "rapid restructuration of the cognitive field" to describe the intuitive perceptions which Plato held suspect. Shakespeare assigns the image (but not the seat) of poetic inspiration to the poet's eye "in a fine frenzy rolling," and we are fortunate that in his day the anatomy of the inner ear had

Caius Cibber's figure of *Melancholy Madness* from the entrance gate of Bethlem Hospital

not yet been unraveled, else we might have had "the poet's ear, its cochlea in a fine frenzy spiralling." There seems to be no dearth of psychopathology among poets past (*praetereo* poets present), and we cannot doubt that poetic frenzy does involve some disturbance of the sensorium.

But no reader is so naïve as to imagine that Collins, Cowper, or Smart wrote poetry because they were mad or that they went mad because they wrote poetry. Rather, we are concerned with the idea that they wrote the kind of poetry they did and used the language of poetry in a particular fashion because their mental condition enabled them to perceive reality in a fashion different from the ordinary run of men (alternatively, *dis*abled them from perceiving reality as most men do). To apply rational analysis to a nonrational (not *ir*rational, but beside or beyond reason) perception of the world is fraught with danger. Our concern is with the *use of language* to describe such perceptions and what such usage tells us about the poetic process; at a further remove we may be able to discover what the practice of poetry tells us about mental disease.

Certain precautions have to be taken: "instruments / To take the measure of all queer events." It is reasonable to interpret the life and works of poets in the light of what has happened to poetry since their time and even with the illumination of modern psychology. But it is not proper to credit them with prescience; the term "preromantic" is dangerous. Neither Collins, Cowper, and Smart, nor Thomas Gray, Mark Akenside, and others knew in the 1740s and 1750s that William Wordsworth would publish *Lyrical Ballads* in 1798 and that the romantic movement in English poetry would dawn with a thunderclap. Nor can one safely attribute to them a deliberate disavowal of Plato's distrust of mania. One of the central themes of romanticism is its acceptance of the irrational, its interest in the unnatural as contrasted with the natural, be it in attitude, vision, or behavior. None of the poets who flourished between the death of Alexander Pope in 1744 and the revolution of 1798 tried to solve his personal and poetic problems by adopting a romantic stance: "Unluckily they were their situation." That Collins, Cowper, and Smart went mad was not the result of their choosing an incorrect solution; madness does not stem from failing a multiple-choice examination.

Another precaution is to delimit the field. Poets who were not mad need not apply. Richard Savage (1697–1743) occupies a problematic position in the poetic demimonde. Samuel Johnson liked him and gave credence to his story of being the rejected illegitimate son of the unchaste countess of Macclesfield by Earl Rivers; Johnson's *Life of*

Savage is disproportionately long by comparison with Savage's poetic gifts and our sympathies are earnestly solicited. In retrospect, there are three possible solutions: 1) Savage's account of his birth and rejection is true, and his bizarre conduct is explained by his quest to establish his correct identity. 2) Savage's account is false and he knew it. If so, we must account him a scheming rogue. A rogue may be a good poet, and a good poet may be a rogue, but Savage was not a good poet. 3) Savage's account is false but he was convinced of its truth. If so, it was a well-systematized paranoid delusion but, as is often the case in true paranoia (monomania), his intellectual powers were not impaired. Documentary evidence fails to establish any of these three possibilities beyond doubt. The record of Savage's life—his murder of James Sinclair in a tavern brawl, presumably in self-defense, his vituperative quarrel with Lord Tyrconnel, his irregular habits, viz., roaming the streets at night and consorting with low company, his continuous alienation of his would-be friends by petulant letters—all these point to what we should now classify as a personality that was psychopathic but not psychotic. Savage's personality may have been "assumed," but there is no evidence of disturbed reason or perception in his pedestrian poetry or his language.

Clarence Tracy construes Savage's notion of the poet as bard in *The Wanderer*—"He takes his gifted Quill from Hands divine, / Around his Temples Rays refulgent shine!"—to indicate the stereotype of the mad poet receiving revelations from heaven and being transformed at his death into a seraph complete with flowing vestments and halo, a concept of the poet "we have grown accustomed to call romantic."[3] The point is open to rebuttal: that poets were divinely inspired and elevated to demigod status post-mortem is well within the canon of orphic verse; only the nimbus is an accretion of the Christian era, and a purely decorative one at that. This study is confined to three poets who had overt psychoses and who had to be institutionalized. To be sure, many poets are queer and have been known to behave in extraordinary ways, but we are on safer ground if we stick to those who, in the judgment of their peers, were certifiably insane.

A final precaution is to maintain a position of clinical detachment and not to inflict subjective or doctrinaire interpretations upon a twentieth-century readership. To gauge at a remove of two centuries the intent and meaning of the words chosen by "a mind unhing'd" invites speculation. Exuberance of a poet's metaphor is to be expected; exuberance of a reader's interpretation all too often defeats its own aim. One must avoid the pitfall of the archer whose accuracy was achieved by shooting his arrows, then drawing a circle around the place they hit. I have taken one liberty with chronology: because of the nature of their psychiatric problems the sequence of Collins, Cowper, and Smart provides a more coherent pattern than the sequence by birth dates of Collins, Smart, and Cowper.

Biographical materials about Collins are scanty and are likely to remain so; his sister Anne Sempill burned his papers after his death. What we know of Collins comes to us from a few public records, recollections by friends, memoirs by literary annotators, a few passing comments in miscellaneous writings of the period, two manuscript letters of little importance, and a few *Drafts and Fragments*[4] of verse preserved by chance among the Warton papers at Trinity College, Oxford. There is, however, enough information for us to trace the outline of his life and arrive at reasonable inferences about his mental status.

Collins's father was a successful hatter who had risen twice to become mayor of Chichester before Collins was born in 1721. His only siblings were two sisters, seventeen and sixteen years older. We have no data on the obstetrical history of Collins *mère* to explain the sixteen-year interval between her second and third children; one may conjecture a series of miscarriages, a period of infertility, the successful practice of contraception followed by a "menopause baby"—but it remains a matter of conjecture. The only established fact is that Collins's two sisters were almost grown women when he was an infant and he grew up in a household of adults. Whether his having "three mothers" played any role in the subsequent development of his mental disease is pure speculation. We do know that Collins gave early promise of intellectual talent; precocity is not uncommon in children living almost exclusively among adults. After preliminary education at Chichester he was sent in 1733 to public school at Winchester. Among his fellow Wykehamists was Joseph Warton,[5] and the close friendship between them was a decisive element in Collins's development. It is not difficult to imagine the hatter's son being impressed by the greater intellectual sophistication of the ex-professor's son. Together they shared an interest in poetry; Collins appears to have had the greater poetic gift, but Warton, one infers, was superior in critical analysis and dialectic. Presumably the two boys debated the aims and methods of poetry, and Warton's ability to articulate his ideas in a coherent, logical argument helped shape Collins's poetic aspirations. Collins's first published poem dates from 1739; he, Warton, and a schoolfellow named Tomkins each sent a poem to the *Gentleman's Magazine* in a single packet. Collins's contribution was the charming lyric *When Phoebe Form'd a Wanton Smile*, published over the signature "Delicatulus." The conceit of Venus rising from a lover's teardrops is pleasant and fully realized. Confirmation of Collins's intellectual promise was seen when he stood first on the list of successful candidates for New College in 1740; Warton was second to him. There was no vacancy at New College, and Collins had to settle for admission to Queen's College as a commoner. This, Samuel Johnson tells us, was "the original misfortune of his life." Joseph Warton entered Oriel, but the friendship between the two budding poets continued unabated. The following year Collins was elected to a demyship at Magdalen.

At Oxford, Collins first footsteps conformed to Johnson's description of the young scholar:

> When first the college rolls receive his name,
> The young enthusiast quits his ease for fame;
> Through all his veins the fever of renown
> Burns from the strong contagion of the gown.

Collins applied himself industriously to poetry; in 1742 he published anonymously his *Persian Eclogues* (republished as *Oriental Eclogues* in 1757). The following year saw the publication of his *Verses Humbly Address'd to Sir Thomas Hanmer on his Edition of Shakespear's Works* by "a Gentleman of Oxford." He revised the poem for its second edition in 1744 and subjoined to it the agreeable *Song from Cymbeline*. Despite these successes, Collins was unhappy at Oxford. Whether this can be attributed to his disappointment over failing to be placed at New College or the unfulfilled vague hope for patronage from Hanmer, who had retired from his political career, is uncertain, even doubtful. In any case he was dissatisfied with the undergraduate curriculum of those days and, despite his brilliance, soon acquired the reputation for indolence. This may be the first hint of his later mental depression. According to a few contemporary hints he indulged in occasional dissipations. Graduating as B.A. near the end of 1743, Collins went to London to embark on a literary career and enjoy the pleasures which the metropolis had to offer. He rejected the Aristotelian rigidities of the academic life

> Where Science, prank'd in tissued Vest
> By Reason, Pride, and Fancy drest,
> Comes like a Bride so trim array'd,
> To wed with Doubt in Plato's shade!

in favor of "that ampler Range, / Where Life's wide Prospects round thee change" and "To learn, where Science sure is found, / From

Nature as she lives around." Collins's attitude is not unlike that of the
undergraduates in the 1930s who were "fed up and going down."

Collins managed to follow Nature's example and "live around" in
London. We catch glimpses of him leading the life of a young man
about town, enjoying the pleasures of Ranelagh and Vauxhall, listening to music, indulging in a few casual love affairs. His father had died
in 1734; his mother died in 1744 and left him a modest legacy. His gay
life in London soon disposed of his financial resources. In the meantime he had not neglected his literary ambitions entirely. He had made
the acquaintance of many of the figures on the literary scene; these
included James Thomson and Samuel Johnson, and in 1746 he proposed a plan to bring out a volume of odes in conjunction with Joseph
Warton. The joint project seems to have foundered when Collins, who
was in financial straits, asked for ten guineas as his solatium. The two
volumes of odes appeared separately, under different publishers' im-
prints, in December 1746. Warton's seventeen *Odes on Various Subjects*
received favorable notice and reached a second edition. Collins's twelve
Odes on Several Descriptive and Allegoric Subjects went unnoticed. Bitterly
disappointed, he had to account them a failure. This failure marks a
decisive point in Collins's career. Though he subsequently projected
several other literary schemes, none of them ever came to fruition. In
fact, he completed only two major poems thereafter: the touching *Ode
on the Death of Mr. Thomson* and the somewhat overrated *Ode on the
Popular Superstitions of the Highlands of Scotland,* both dating from 1749.
Collins had never been a *Vielschreiber,* but the sharp decline in his
output after 1746 coincides with the disaster of the *Odes,* and from this
date we can trace the decline in his mental powers and energies which
culminated in his psychosis.

Information about Collins's life and movements between 1747 and
1750 is fragmentary and sometimes contradictory. Collins was able to
solve his financial problems, but whether it was from the estate of his
uncle Colonel Edmund Martin who died in 1749 or that of his uncle
Charles Collins who had died in 1745 remains debatable. A legend has
developed that when he came into his inheritance he purchased the
unsold copies of his *Odes* from A. Millar, the publisher, and burnt
them. The onset of his mental disorder seems to have been gradual,
and at first his associates were probably unaware of the serious nature
of his illness. Johnson tells us that after his melancholia began he
"snatched that temporary relief with which the table and the bottle
flatter and seduce." No stranger himself to melancholy, Johnson recognized the inadequacy of such psychotherapy. He also reports that
Collins tried to dispel his unhappiness by a trip to France, the well-

known "change of scene" which affords little benefit to patients who carry their mental disease within themselves. It seems likely that after 1749 Collins retired to Chichester and lived under the care of his sister Anne, now married to Captain Hugh Sempill. There is evidence that he collected a considerable library there, and one infers from the *Drafts and Fragments* that he tried to write poetry on occasions when he felt well enough but gradually sank into a depressive psychosis from which he never emerged.

Writing in his *Lives of the Poets* some three decades later, Johnson describes his symptoms as "not alienation of mind, but general laxity and feebleness, a deficiency rather of his vital than his intellectual powers. What he spoke wanted neither judgment nor spirit; but a few minutes exhausted him, so that he was forced to rest upon the couch, till a short cessation restored his powers, and he was again able to talk with his former vigour."[6] Johnson was probably drawing upon his memory of Collins in the early stages of an uncomplicated depressive psychosis; he was not aware of the occasional manic episodes. In 1754 Collins visited Oxford to be near his friends, Joseph and Thomas Warton. He is described as lacking the energy to drag himself from his lodging in St. Aldate's to Warton's rooms in Trinity, but a few days later Gilbert White of Selborne writes of seeing him "in a very affecting situation, struggling and conveyed by force, in the arms of two or three men, toward the parish of St. Clement's, where there was a house which took in such unhappy objects."[7] This was Collins's last public appearance away from the seclusion of Chichester where he spent his last few clouded years, visited occasionally by the Wartons and by a few other friends. A letter to Thomas Warton from the vicar of Saint Andrews at Chichester, who buried Collins in 1758, tells us that in the last stages agitated depression had supervened: "Walking in my vicarial garden one Sunday evening, during Collins' last illness, I heard a female (the servant, I suppose) reading the Bible in his Chamber. Mr. Collins had been accustomed to rave much, and make great moanings; but while she was reading, or rather attempting to read, he was not only silent but attentive likewise, correcting her mistakes, which indeed were very frequent, through the whole of the twenty-seventh chapter of Genesis."[8] Our own skeptical age will readily accept the vicar's evidence of raving and moaning, but there is a suggestion of self-serving religiosity which makes suspect the vicar's image of Collins on his deathbed correcting the servant's mistakes in the Holy Writ.

Edmund Blunden's *Study of William Collins*, which introduces the handsomely printed 1929 edition of Collins's poems, preserves one important anecdote from Collins's last year. About 1756 William

Smith, treasurer of the ordnance, who had shared chambers with Collins at Winchester, came to visit him at Chichester. Collins was asleep when Smith arrived, and the visitor's entrance aroused the poet

whose first remark was, "Smith, do you remember my dream?" Smith remembered it well. His schoolfellow had been seen one morning "particularly depressed and melancholy. Being pressed to disclose the cause, he at last said it was in consequence of a dream: for this he was laughed at, but desired to tell what it was; he said, he dreamed that he was walking in the fields where there was a lofty tree; that he climbed it, and when he had nearly reached the top, a great branch, upon which he had got, failed with him, and let him fall to the ground. This account caused more ridicule; and he was asked how he could possibly be affected by this common consequence of a schoolboy adventure, when he did not pretend, even in imagination and sleep, to have received any hurt; he replied that the Tree was the Tree of Poetry."[9]

We must eschew the easy interpretation that climbing a tree is a dream equivalent for the sexual act and that to fall out of it before reaching the top signifies premature ejaculation, a common source of worry among schoolboys. We have no information about Collins's psychosexual development nor his sexual activities when mature; in the absence of any objective events to which this dream can be related, such an interpretation cannot be affirmed. We are on safer, though less imaginative, ground to interpret the dream as reflecting Collins's youthful anxieties about whether his abilities would match his aspirations. In point of fact, they did not; and in this sense the dream is prophetic.

The antistrophe of the *Ode on the Poetical Character* reinforces Collins's image of himself as failing to attain the poetic height to which he aspired. After alluding to Milton as an oak and paying honor to Waller's myrtle shades, Collins closes with

> My trembling Feet his guiding steps pursue
> In Vain—Such Bliss to One Alone,
> Of all the Sons of God was known.

that is, to Milton, whom Collins admired more than any poet other than Shakespeare. To the extent that poetic expression of such autobiographical emotion lies beyond the classic Augustan canon, Collins is taking a small step in the direction which romanticism was later to explore at length and in some depth.

Given the known facts, it seems reasonable to assign Collins's feelings of inadequacy as a major cause of his depression. Whether this emotional state was superimposed on some unknown (at this date unknowable) constitutional predisposition or organic factor is a matter of idle speculation. If Collins was haunted by a sense of inadequacy as a schoolboy, it is quite plausible that when confronted by real failure as an adult—the lack of favorable notice toward the *Odes* of 1746—a reactive depression should develop. Failure to bring any subsequent major literary projects to completion can be seen as both the result of the initial depression and the mechanism whereby the depression was intensified and persisted. To have produced only two odes between 1747 and 1749 must have been a certain sign to Collins that his powers as a poet were not great and that the top of the tree would continue to elude him.

An undated fragment of a poem by Collins recovered among Warton's papers includes the line: "No more, sweet Maid, th' enfeebling dreams prolong!" It is tempting to assign this fragment to the period of his melancholia, implying as it does an invocation to the muse to relieve him of the cause of his depression, but actually it is more likely part of a rejected stanza in an ode of 1746 *To Simplicity*. We may ask ourselves if Collins's schoolboy dream was recurrent, but there is no evidence that this was the case.

What evidence of poetic mania can we find in Collins's poems? In what respect is his "true poetic accent" related to his mental state? The *Persian Eclogues* cast no light on these questions. They were written before any mental disturbance was evident. Pleasant though they are, their substance is little more than that of a gifted undergraduate experimenting in an established form. The *Odes* of 1746 furnish a few modest clues to Collins's mental state, but before examining these clues it may be helpful to consider Joseph Warton's *Odes on Various Subjects* which were coeval with Collins's. Collins sent his *Odes* naked into the world, but Warton prefaced his with an essay setting forth their *raison d'être*, a preface which might well have served for the odes of both of them had the original plan of a joint publication been carried out. Like other young men of their generation Warton and Collins chafed at the restraints of the neoclassic heritage of Dryden and Pope. Feeling that the moral and didactic poetry of their predecessors had exhausted that vein, they wished to enlarge their experience and free their language. Imagination was in the air; two years previously Akenside's *The Pleasures of Imagination* had stirred the literary world, and the emphasis of the rising generation was on "fancy." The year before, Akenside had revived the Pindaric ode in a somewhat different form from Cowley in order to have a vehicle in which to express more personal emotions. Warton warned his readers against identifying the true subject matter of poetry with the moral and didactic themes to which writers at the time had confined their efforts.

Historically, there is a convention of revolt in English poetry. Each new generation tries to replace the values of the generation just past with material based on its own values and interests. Sometimes the revolution is real, vide *Lyrical Ballads* in 1798, but more often it is merely a shift in tone, a slight change in the direction of the poetic compass. Rupert Brooke did not revolt effectively against the tradition of Byron; Wilfred Owen did. Neither Collins nor Warton had sufficient intellectual strength or poetic energy to mount a full scale revolution. There is some justice in H. W. Garrod's comment that "There was . . . a change of taste, not a change of heart."[10] Joseph Warton was very explicit about his aims, and there is no reason to believe that Collins was not in substantial agreement. "The Advertisement" to Warton's *Odes on Various Subjects* states his position bluntly:

The Public has been so much accustomed of late to didactic Poetry alone, and Essays on moral Subjects, that any work where the imagination is much indulged, will perhaps not be relished or regarded. The author therefore of these pieces is in some pain lest certain austere critics should think them too fanciful and descriptive. But as he is convinced that the fashion of moralizing in verse has been carried too far, and as he looks upon Invention and Imagination to be the chief faculties of a Poet, so he will be happy if the following Odes may be look'd upon as an attempt to bring back Poetry into its right channel.[11]

But the language of the *Odes* of 1746, whether one reads Collins's or Warton's, is much the same. Thomas Gray thought he could distinguish between the two. In a letter dated December 27, 1746, he wrote: "Each is half of a considerable man, and one the counterpart of the other. The first [i.e., Warton] has but little invention, very poetical choice of expression, and a good ear. The second [i.e., Collins] a fine fancy, modelled upon the antique, a bad ear, great variety of words, and images with no choice at all."[12] Posterity has reversed Gray's judgment, but the rhetoric of personification, prosopopoeia, and language of generality is common to both Collins and Warton, and one might add Akenside and Gray himself to the list. However, Collins went mad and Warton did not. Given random passages in a "blindfold test," one would be hard put to decide whether Collins or Warton was the author of a given passage.

The personified lyric was a form characteristic of the eighteenth century, and personification was the figure of speech used to give structural unity to the poem, as in Collins's *Ode to Peace*. The device can be traced back, if necessary, to Greek and Latin lyrics, but the immediate source for the use of personification in English poetry was Milton, who found it irresistible and whom Collins much admired.

Collins, Warton, and Gray tended to use personification in an allegorical sense; other poets tended to use it more metaphorically. But no diagnostic inference can be made from Collins's frequent use of personification; it was common coin among all poets of the age, didactic or nondidactic as they might choose their odes to be. Poets with so varied neurotic syndromes as Pope, Johnson, and Gray—not to mention a host of lesser talents—all used personification. In this respect Collins's use of language is the product of chronology; it represents no advance, nor the "true poetic accent emerging," nor a result of his disordered mind, nor even a liberation of his thought and feeling.

Yet even before the *Odes* of 1746 Collins had indicated his espousal of the cause of "poetic imagination." Speaking of Shakespeare's works in the *Verses to Hanmer* (1743) he had written

> Where'er we turn, by Fancy charm'd, we find
> Some sweet Illusion of the cheated Mind.

Much as Collins admired Shakespeare's inventive genius and imagination, when he came to use his own, he found it deficient, stored with furniture from the lumber room of a "classical" education, filled with abstractions which led him to write odes *To Pity, To Fear,* etc. His imagination, even *en rêve,* could lead him only so far up the tree of poetry.

An occasional line in the odes can be taken to indicate that Collins had some insight into his deficiency of affect. Alluding again to Shakespeare at the end of the ode *To Fear,* he exclaims "Teach me but once like Him to feel"; and near the close of *The Manners,* he apostrophizes Nature,

> If but from Thee I hope to feel,
> On all my heart imprint thy Seal.

But Collins's hope for rich personal emotions was never to be realized. His emotional experiences did not expand; they contracted as his melancholia progressed. It is, possibly, noteworthy that in *The Passions* he never once refers to love, and in his *Ode on the Poetical Character* he devotes most of his language to the magic girdle whose possessor becomes endowed with the gift of poetic speech. The lack of references to love in these poems may bear some obscure relation to the idea that the cestus (magic girdle) which endows its wearer with fancy in the *Ode on the Poetical Character* is the girdle which, as Collins states at the poem's opening, was the test of chastity in the *Faerie Queene.* One might speculate whether in Collins's mind Fancy depended upon chastity, a virtue he had lost, hence a possible cause for feelings of guilt and unworthiness. Collins may have experienced deep emotional upheavals, but he was either unable or unwilling to express them in his poetry. To that extent he was a poet manqué.

The modified Pindaric elements in his odes enabled Collins to liberate his feelings and his language to a limited extent. A hint of the depressive psychosis which was to develop three years later can be found in *The Passions:*

> With Eyes up-rais'd as one inspir'd
> Pale *Melancholy* sate retir'd,
> And from her wild sequester'd Seat,
> In Notes by Distance made more sweet,
> Pour'd thro' the mellow *Horn* her pensive Soul:
>   And dashing soft from Rocks around,
>   Bubbling Runnels join'd the Sound;
> Thro' Glades and Glooms that mingled Measure stole,
> Or o'er some haunted Stream with fond Delay,
>   Round an holy Calm diffusing,
>   Love of Peace, and lonely Musing,
> In hollow Murmurs died away.

The variable number of feet in the lines is quite suitable for verses to be set to music, as indeed the poem was, but the landscape is pedestrian Gothic with Pale Melancholy appearing as an abstract personification. The same limitation applies to the anxieties, so common in the content of the psychopathology of depression, described in the ode *To Fear:*

> Ah *Fear!* Ah frantic Fear!
>   I see, I see Thee near,
> I know thy hurried Step, thy haggard Eye!
> Like Thee I start, like Thee disorder'd fly.
> For lo! what *Monsters* in thy Train appear!
> Danger! whose limbs of Giant Mold
> What mortal Eye can fix'd behold?
> Who stalks his Round, and hideous form
> Howling amidst the Midnight Storm,
> Or throws him on the ridgy Steep
> Of some loose hanging Rock to sleep:
> And with him thousand Phantoms join'd,
> Who prompt to Deeds accurs'd the Mind:
> And those, the Fiends, who near allied,
> O'er Nature's wounds, and Wrecks preside;
> While *Vengeance*, in the lurid Air,
> Lifts her red Arm, expos'd and bare:
> On whom the rav'ning Brood of Fate,

> Who lap the Blood of Sorrow, wait;
> Who, *Fear*, this ghastly Train can see
> And look not madly wild, like Thee?

This is as close as Collins came to expressing "the grandeur of wildness and the novelty of extravagance," and the lines coincide with his personal experiences. The final line of *To Fear* indicates Collins's recognition that his fears and anxieties would abide with him, but it is doubtful that he could foresee a psychotic breakdown: "And, I, O *Fear*, will dwell with *Thee!*" In the next century poets who avowed their romanticism were to place a high value on the validity of such subjective experiences. These are "the terrible dreams that shake us nightly," and Collins was somewhat in advance of the poetic content and diction of his day when he wrote them. It was as far as he could bring himself to express his mania in poetry. We read the lines, sense his disturbance, but are stopped from closer inspection of its content by Collins's lack of specific, denotative imagery.

But there is no evidence in such passages to indicate that Collins's perception of reality was disordered nor that the images he created were nonrational or irrational. The Monster and his ghastly train are not Goyaesque hallucinations; they are spirits summoned from the vasty deep for rhetorical effect. Their personifications are abstract and the emotion they denote is generalized rather than personal. That the arm of Vengeance should be red is wholly reasonable, even pedestrian, the the Blood of Sorrow is its natural result. Collins's prosopopeia might safely be illuminated by the linear outlines of neoclassic figures in the mode of John Flaxman. The midnight storm with the Monster's victim lying on a ridge of loose-hanging rocks is a stage set waiting for thunder; the blood follows the thunder a few lines later. In an epoch during which one of the prime functions of poetry was supposed to be to elicit visual responses from its readers (cf. Lord Kames's axiom, "the eye is the best avenue to the heart")—Collins's visual imagery was conventional. If, in fact, he was seeking for visual novelty, his efforts fell wide of the mark. Collins may have had visions or been a visionary poet, but he was not a visual one. Whatever mania he had was not manifest in unusual perceptions which he could communicate; if anything, his perceptual range was limited and inhibited.

The two odes of 1749 furnish no further evidence of the content of Collins's anxieties and fears. The *Ode on the Death of Mr. Thomson* compares the late poet to a druid, but Collins injects none of his own personality. Collins's failure to express a more personal involvement in the grief at James Thomson's death may be ascribed to a sense of classic reticence, but it may equally be symptomatic of a blunting of his own affect and power to be affected by the death of a friend. The *Superstitions Ode*, though incomplete, is Collins's last poem, and it contains the ominous line in which the poet, referring to a "luckless swain," asks: "What now remains but tears and hopeless sighs?" A number of biographers have suggested that Collins may have been thwarted in love by a young lady who did not reciprocate his feelings. Documentary evidence of this is lacking, and the argument is based on one or two of the lyric poems and this passage in the *Superstitions Ode*. Was the posture of being disappointed in love based on real events or was it a stance within the poetic convention? Did Collins identify himself with the "luckless swain"? But the verse quoted seems to describe, if not predict, the last nine years of Collins's life.

The *Superstitions Ode* is likewise one of the clearest examples of Collins's use of an adjectival vocabulary in which participial forms are strikingly frequent. Patricia Spacks has commented that although Collins used individual adjectives with sensitivity and precision, there are simply too many of them, particulary at the expense of verb forms in the active voice.[13] And the verbs which Collins does use tend to describe appearances rather than suggest action. This type of diction is consistent with, though not necessarily diagnostic of, an attitude of passivity and withdrawal. To predict that any poet who uses adjectives to excess and active verbs too little is destined to develop a depressive psychosis would be an exaggerated claim. Gerard Manley Hopkins comes immediately to mind as an adjectival poet who was withdrawn from this world but not psychotic. Diction alone does not establish the diagnosis of a prepsychotic personality. The tabulations by Josephine Miles demonstrate that Collins's proportionate use of adjectives, nouns, and verbs was average for his decade;[14] both Joseph and Thomas Warton as well as James Thomson used a higher proportion of adjective-noun combinations and fewer verbs, yet none of them went mad. Miles's further tabulation of majority and minority vocabulary as well as individual word usage does show that Collins used such words as "joy," "life," and "love" less frequently than most poets of his time, but again he shares this characteristic with nonpsychotic poets. His excessively frequent use of the word "*maid*" might be consistent with a preoccupation with frustrated love, but this solitary idiosyncrasy is susceptible to a variety of interpretations.

Possibly more significant than vocabulary or diction is Collins's "repeated unconcern for syntactical logic or consistency."[15] A striking example is the entire strophe of the *Ode on the Poetical Character*, a single twenty-two-line sentence which has been described as grammatically impenetrable. Another syntactical flaw is Collins's knack for separating a relative pronoun an unconscionable distance from its antecedent. If we add to a passive, withdrawn diction the disjunctive, incoherent syntax and both of these to a poetic content expressing fear and anxiety as well as an inadequacy of affect, it is possible to outline a constellation of effects which, taken together, suggest depressive psychosis as that form of mental disturbance most likely to develop. To this extent Collins's mania was expressed and can be detected post hoc in his poems. Whether this constitutes a poetic accent which is "true" in Housman's sense is a question best decided by readers who can conceive of a poetic accent in true-false terms. But such interpretations are subject to the caution that many poets wrote on melancholy, on thwarted love, on their fears and anxieties, and only a few developed clinical psychosis. It would be unwise to apply the argument in reverse, that one can predict from the diction, syntax, and content of a group of poems that the poet is doomed to madness. Nor do the life and work of Collins lend credence that poetry written by a man "in his sober senses is beaten hollow by the poetry of madmen," that is, provided the man of sober sense is a poet of equal gift.

How many examination papers have put the question "Compare and contrast Cowper with Collins"? A fair question, and the alliteration makes it a pretty one: every man his own Plutarch. Unlike Collins, William Cowper has been the subject of extensive biographical study. Without difficulty one can find over twenty full length biographies; Lord David Cecil's *The Stricken Deer* [16] is the most readable, and Charles Ryskamp's *William Cowper of the Inner Temple, Esq.* [17] provides as much information about his formative years as we are likely to have. Cowper's letters occupied four volumes when edited by Thomas Wright in 1904; by 1925 Wright had collected enough additional letters for a fifth volume, and there are papers yet unsifted. We do not lack for information about Cowper, nor do we lack for opinion; the scholarly literature contains more than three hundred articles and special studies. Collins's literary career lasted for only a decade (1739–49), aet. sua eighteen to twenty-eight, and his literary remains comprise four eclogues, a verse essay, sixteen odes, and a handful of short lyrics. Cowper's first extant poem dates from 1748, when he was a lad of seventeen, and he continued writing for more than half a century; the Oxford Standard Authors' edition runs to six hundred-odd pages with two appendices. Such riches embarrass the short essayist; he can barely touch the peaks.

Most schoolboys first encounter Cowper through his ever-popular recitation piece, *John Gilpin's Ride*, and it is difficult to reconcile its good humor with the later knowledge that Cowper described himself as the "stricken deer that left the herd . . . to seek a tranquil death in distant shades." But for all his productivity and outward geniality, Cowper was a psychotic who suffered from mental depression with suicidal tendencies. His madness was colored strongly by religious delusions centering about his own damnation. To his friends and physicians Cowper was a man of sorrow and acquainted with grief. Yet when placed in the shelter of a well-structured environment, when protected from the stress of making decisions, Cowper's psyche and its disorders were kept in a reasonable state of compensation. In such a milieu he was able to write a considerable body of poetry which is effective and durable.

It is not difficult to sketch the biographical background against which Cowper's madness developed, but despite the wealth of factual data, many important questions remain open for lack of evidence, evidence which is no longer retrievable. Cowper's family was of some consequence. His father, John Cowper, the rector of Berkhamsted, was a son of Spencer Cowper the judge, and a nephew of William, first Earl Cowper, twice lord chancellor. His mother was Ann Donne, a collateral descendant of John Donne, a member of a family which proudly traced its ancestry back to Henry III and was distantly related to the great families of Boleyn, Mowbray, Carey, and Howard. The poet's father became rector of Berkhamsted in 1722, married Anne Donne in 1728, and proceeded to get his wife with child six times in the nine years of their marriage. Their home was no stranger to the high infant mortality of the age. The birth of William Cowper, who survived, had been preceded by the neonatal deaths of a firstborn son in 1729 and twins in 1730. Following William's birth a daughter was born in 1733 who died at the age of two, then a son in 1734 who lived for only two weeks and, finally, in 1737, the birth of William's younger brother John, who survived to become a fellow of Corpus Christi College, Cambridge. Ann Cowper died six days after the birth of this last child; William lacked but two days of his sixth birthday. Knowledge of death and grief must have surrounded him almost from the cradle.

More than fifty years later, when his cousin, Ann Boham, sent him a copy of his mother's picture, Cowper wrote:

> Oh that those lips had language! Life has passed
> With me but roughly since I heard thee last . . .
> Voice only fails, else, how distinct they say
> "Grieve not, my child, chase all thy fears away!". . .
> And, while that face renews my filial grief,
> Fancy shall weave a charm for my relief—

Cowper's fancy enabled him to recollect his nursery, his being escorted to school by the gardener, his mother's tenderness:

> Thy nightly visits to my chamber made,
> That thou might's known me safe and warmly laid;
> Thy morning bounties ere I left my home,
> The biscuit, or confectionary plum; . . .
> All this, and more endearing still than all
> Thy constant flow of love, that knew no fall.

His visual memory in 1790, aided by fancy, was so keen that he even remembered his mother's funeral:

> I heard the bell toll'd on thy burial day,
> I saw the hearse that bore thee slow away,
> And, turning from my nurs'ry window, drew
> A long, long sigh, and wept a last adieu!

Surely Cowper missed the constant flow of mother love and quite possible these were real memories; the lines have often been quoted by others to indicate the sharpness and persistence of Cowper's grief. Without minimizing the trauma of losing a mother at the age of six, one can question whether Cowper actually remembered the scenes and incidents he described or whether he seized the occasion to discharge an emotion by using conventional poetic imagery and speech. The Cowper household was an upper-middle-class ménage with several servants, and his mother had her share of social obligations attendant upon her being the rector's wife as well as being pregnant three times during William's infancy. At that time parent-child relations were more formal than today; it is reasonable to think that most of the boy's waking hours were superintended by servants and that he saw his mother and father at appointed hours. Without impeaching the credibility of the nightly good-night kiss, one notes that Cowper, by 1790 more deeply religious than either parent, fails to mention whether his mother heard his nightly prayers. Though there is sufficient evidence from Cowper's later relations with women that part of his psychological problems involved a quest for a lost mother or a mother-substitute, one must leave unanswered the question why he went mad while his infant brother John, who never knew a mother, did not.

A few weeks after his mother died Cowper was sent to the Reverend William Pittman's boarding school at a village some seven miles away; the nearby school at Berkhamsted had fallen on evil days. This marked the last time he lived continuously under his father's roof. The remainder of his childhood and youth was largely spent away at school or visiting relatives. One cannot tax Cowper's father with being indifferent to his son's welfare, nor is there any but inferential evidence that young Cowper interpreted his being sent away to school so soon after his mother's death as a form of rejection. But the Reverend John Cowper seems to have been a dutiful rather than an affectionate father. Certainly he was occupied with running the affairs of his parish, and possibly he was preoccupied with his own grief. Nonetheless, he provided for his older son's material needs and saw to it that he had a proper education. The eighteenth century was not a period notable for its attention to the emotional needs and sensitivities of young children. John Cowper's relation with his son was consistent with the standards of his class in his day. Cowper never reproached his father; he dutifully respected him. But it seems to have been a formal relation without warmth.

Had Cowper been happy in the Reverend Pittman's school, his separation from the parental home might not have proved so disastrous. But Cowper soon became the victim of a school bully. His autobiographical *Memoir* written in 1766, three years after his first major depression, recalls that

> my chief affliction consisted in my being singled out from all the other boys by a lad about fifteen years of age as a proper object upon whom he might let loose the cruelty of his temper. I choose to forbear a particular recital of the many acts of barbarity with which he made it his business continually to persecute me; it will be sufficient to say that he had by his savage treatment of me impressed such a dread of his figure upon my mind that I well remember being afraid to lift up my eyes upon him higher than his knees, and that I knew him by his shoe-buckles better than any other part of his dress.[18]

It is a clear enough statement of juvenile sadism with Cowper as victim, but we shall never know whether there was a sexual element in the bullying which Cowper's modesty and the literary standards of his age made it impossible for him to commit to writing. Concomitantly, he had his first brush with using religion and religious texts as a way of solving his personal problems. The *Memoir* continues:

> One day as I was sitting alone on a bench in the school, melancholy and almost ready to weep at the recollection of what I had already suffered . . . these words of the Psalmist came into my mind, "I will not be afraid of what man can do unto me." I applied this to my own case with a degree of trust and confidence in God that would have been no disgrace to a more experienced Christian.[19]

Again, much like the poem on his mother's picture, one questions whether the event occurred as stated or whether Cowper was creating the literary expression of a religious emotion suitable for the occasion. But the oppression by the adolescent bully was real, all too real.

At this moment it may be profitable to consider another open, unanswered question about Cowper. Since 1834 there has been an undercurrent of rumor in literary circles that Cowper suffered from some form of genital malformation. The rumor is based on letters from the Reverend John Newton, Cowper's friend, to John Thornton, an Evangelical philanthropist. These letters were transmitted thirty-four years after Cowper's death to Robert Southey, who was then writing a biography of Cowper. Southey suppressed this particular anatomic detail, and the datum was first published in Charles Greville's memoirs in 1874, which hinted at "some defect" in Cowper's "physical conformation." To a pathologic anatomist this may mean any number of things, but according to Ryskamp, the most recent and authoritative edition of the text (1938) reads: " He was an Hermaphrodite; somebody knew his secret, and probably threatened its exposure."[20] That Cowper was an hermaphrodite as we now define the term is most unlikely; that he had a hypospadias is possible; that the genital deformity was a delusion founded a sense of sexual guilt overlaid by a depressive's preoccupation with his own anatomy and physiology is just as possible. The presence of an anatomic abnormality might account for Cowper's being considered an unsuitable suitor for his cousin Theodora's hand, for the peculiar relation he later had with Mary Unwin, and for the generally asexual nature of his life and poetry. But the answer to the question lies beyond proof. There is no extant report of an examination performed. Like Byron's clubfoot, Cowper's penis remains an object for idle speculation.

We are on surer ground if we stick to the chronologic record. Cowper's experience at the Reverend Pittman's school was damaging. The bully was found out and expelled; Cowper was withdrawn. But two traumatic years had passed, and Cowper at the age of eight developed what may well have been his first psychosomatic ailment; he complained of what is reported as "specks of the eyes." Cowper underwent no surgical correction nor in later life did he wear eyeglasses. According to unimpeachable biographic sources he passed the next two years in the home of a Mrs. Disney, described as "an eminent oculist." We may take as fact that young Cowper did have an ocular or visual disturbance, but it does not seem to have been an error in refraction, a cataract, or a tumor. Iritis or uveitis would not produce such a symptom. It might have been due to a chronic conjunctivitis which resolved slowly, but more likely his symptom was *muscae vol-*

itantes. That the symptom disappeared and did not recur permits us to raise the question whether it might not have been a reaction to the emotional strains of the two years preceding its onset. Again, this is speculation.

In 1742 Cowper, then ten and one-half years old, was entered at Westminster, where his father, grandfather, and other Cowpers had gone before him. It was a training and proving ground for future leaders of the Whig establishment, and Cowper's father had hopes that his intelligent but timid son might enter a career in law and politics, as many other members of the family had. In retrospect we can see that this was not Cowper's métier. In later years he satirized such parental ambitions in *Tirocinium, or a Review of Schools* (1784):

> They dream of little Charles or William grac'd
> With wig prolix, down-flowing on his waist;
> They see th' attentive crowds his talents draw,
> They hear him speak—the oracle of law!
> The father, who designs his babe a priest,
> Dreams him episcopally such at least.
> (Lines 360–65)

Despite his later reservations Cowper was happy and well adjusted at Westminster. He made friends easily, enjoyed living in London and visiting the homes of his many relations there. At Westminster he acquired his taste for literature and his skill at translation; here he began to compose verses, juvenilia which have not survived.

It was only after his mental breakdown and religious conversion that he assailed the quality of instruction in public schools:

> There shall he learn, ere sixteen winters old,
> That authors are most useful pawn'd or sold;
> That pedantry is all that schools impart,
> But taverns teach the knowledge of the heart.
> (Ibid, lines 210–13)

and that the curriculum contained

> No nourishment to feed his growing mind,
> But conjugated verbs and nouns declined,
> Nor such is all the mental food purvey'd
> By public hacknies in the schooling trade.
> (Ibid., lines 618–21)

to say nothing of the droll comment:

> The management of tiros of eighteen
> Is difficult, their punishment obscene.
> (Ibid., lines 220–21)

One can only speculate whether he had his father's image in mind when he, having become intensely religious, indicted the conventional non-Evangelical clergyman trained at England's public schools:

> Let rev'rend churls his ignorance rebuke,
> Who starve upon a dog's-ear'd Pentateuch,
> The parson knows enough who knows a duke.
> (Ibid. lines 401–3)

and, at a somewhat great eminence:

> Behold your bishop! well he plays his part—
> Christian in name, and infidel in heart,
> Ghostly in office, earthly in his plan,
> A slave at court, elsewhere a lady's man!
> Dumb as a senator, and, as a priest,
> A piece of mere church-furniture at best.
> (Ibid. lines 420–25)

Regardless of how his view shifted, it was at Westminster that Cowper became acquainted with the poetry which served as a model for his own—"Butler's wit, Pope's numbers, Prior's ease."[21] Successful though his poems may have been, Cowper was not gifted with great originality in devising poetic forms. He was content to express his ideas in the stanzas and meters of the century of English poetry which had preceded him: "He lisped the numbers he'd been taught at school." Converts to religious enthusiasm rarely acknowledge their indebtedness to the previous intellectual training which has equipped them to marshall their arguments, debate, exhort, and proselytize.

From Westminster Cowper readily acceded to his family's design for a career in law and public life. Articled to Mr. Chapman, a solicitor, from 1749 to 1752, he then entered the Middle Temple and was called to the bar in 1754. He finally bought chambers in the Inner Temple in 1759 and about this time was appointed a commissioner in bankruptcy. His interest in the law was superficial and he soon fell in with the convivial bonhomie of a group of old Westminsters of good family, the so-called Nonsense Club, comprising such poetasters and *bon vivants* as Charles Churchill, Bonnell Thornton, George Colman, Robert Lloyd, and others. Cowper's father died in 1756, but no elegiac verses from his son's pen are preserved. A few premonitions of impending mental disaster can be traced in extant verses of this period.

The lines written to Lloyd in 1754 tell us that he composed light verse as a means of escaping from depressing thoughts:

> To divert a fierce banditti
> (Sworn foes to anything that's witty),
> That, with a black infernal train,
> Make cruel inroads in my brain,
> And daily threaten to drive thence
> My little garrison of sense:
>   The fierce banditti which I mean
>   Are gloomy thoughts led on by spleen.

Cowper suffered a recurrent attack of spleen about three years later, but this can be traced to adequate external causes: his father's death, the loss by drowning of William Russell, his "favourite friend," and his uncle Ashley's permanent interdiction of his courtship of Theodora. Now in 1757 he wrote:

> Doom'd as I am in solitude to waste
> The present moments and regret the past;
> Depriv'd of ev'ry joy I valued most,
> My friend torn from me, and my mistress lost:
> Call not this gloom I wear, this anxious mien,
> The dull effect of humor, or of spleen!

Fits of melancholy were not unknown to eighteenth-century English psychiatry, and much has been made of the influence of George Cheyne's *The English Malady* (1733), but his views of mental depression had been largely anticipated by Nicholas Robinson in *A New System of the Spleen, Vapours, and Hypochondriack Melancholy . . . to which is subjoin'd, a Discourse upon the Nature, Cause, and Cure of Melancholy* (1729) as well as by Sir Richard Blackmore, F.R.C.P., a poet himself in his *Treatise of the Spleen and Vapours: or Hypochondriacal and Hysterical Affections* (1725). Blackmore was among the first to distinguish severe (or psychotic) depression from mild (or neurotic) ones, as some do today; he also wrote the first reasoned account for and against the prolonged use of "pacifick Medecines." Robinson's text was one of the most advanced of its century; he stressed the unity of mind and body; for him psychological processes were expressions of physical events in nerves, a view which was not to find laboratory validation for over a century. Cheyne's *The English Malady* served to popularize interest in melancholia among the reading public, then a select few, and his catchy title gave the dubious blessing of chauvinism to a malady which is universal.

Nonetheless, as Quinlan points out, "the mental depression of Johnson, Boswell, and Cowper was largely the result of religious doubts, scruples, and conflicts. Many, it would appear, suffered from a fear of ultimate damnation. While this prospect has harassed Christians at all times, it may have been stronger in an age when Calvinism, though no longer the positive force it had once been, still cast a lingering shadow of doubt and despair over the minds and hearts of men."[22] To such names of Johnson, Boswell, and Cowper, Quinlan might well have added numberless inarticulate souls of various denominations and national origins who took literally the doctrine of eternal damnation and whose lives were permanently discolored by this form of theological masochism, lacking the compensatory satisfaction of the flagellant's orgasm. For the time being, Cowper's versifying had helped him "to keep the silence at bay and cage/His pacing manias in a worldly smile."

He managed to find an antidote for his low spirits by translating part of Voltaire's *Henriade*, a joint project with his brother John, and he turned for further comfort to the poems of George Herbert. Without dispraise for Herbert's religious verses, their sadomasochistic images, viz.:

> Ah! how they scourge me! yet my tenderness
> Doubles each lash: and yet their bitterness
> Windes up my grief to a mysteriousness:
>   Was ever grief like mine?

or "Love is that liquor sweet and most divine / Which my God feels as blood; but I, as wine," to say nothing of the lines

> That when sinne spies so many foes,
> Thy whips, thy nails, thy wounds, thy woes
> All come to lodge there, sinne may say
> No roome for me, and flie away.

These are scarcely likely to restore balance to a mind already disturbed by religious guilt. Shortly after dissuading him from perusing Herbert's poems, Cowper's friends took him to Southampton for a change of scene. It was there (ca. 1758) that he developed the not uncommon delusion that he had committed the unpardonable sin.

The precise nature of the unpardonable or unforgivable sin seems to vary somewhat with the psyche of the person who claims to have committed it. Clearly, it cannot be defined as a simple physical act; the variety of possible misfeasances is too various and too idiosyncratic to permit a simplistic description. Rather, the unpardonable sin must consist of a voluntary mental act, perhaps that state of mind which denies that a sin, real or imagined, can be forgiven. For to deny forgiveness of sin is to deny the omnipotence of God or the all-merciful gift and sacrifice of our Savior. Such denial serves to place the minuscule mortal sinner *praeter salvationem*. If a rational man believes he has committed an unpardonable sin, he is guilty of hubris; if an irrational man believes this, it is merely a symptom of his loss of reason, and God will forgive him, though literary critics may not.

Cowper's fragile psyche could not long endure the strain of maintaining the façade of the well-adjusted Inner Templar. The crisis struck in 1763 when Cowper, whose finances were dwindling, was offered patronage by his cousin, Major Cowper, as either "reading clerk and clerk of the committees" or to the less valuable post of "clerk of the journals of the House of Lords." Political opposition to his proposed appointment to either of these sinecures developed, and Cowper was informed that he would have to stand examination for his qualifications. He manfully attempted to familiarize himself with the duties of these offices, but the thought unnerved him. His *Memoir* offers the clearest picture of his mental state: "I now began to look upon madness as the only chance remaining. I had a strong kind of foreboding that it would one day fare with me, and I had wished for it earnestly and looked forward to it with impatient expectation. My chief fear was that my senses would not fail me in time enough to excuse my appearance at the bar of the House of Lords.[23]

In October 1763 he made three maladroit suicidal gestures, first by drinking laudanum, then an attempted drowning in the Thames, and finally by suspending himself by his scarlet garters, which broke. Were these gestures not cries for help from a sorely troubled soul they might have their comic value; at least his competence as a suicidal actor is called into question. But Cowper was too far gone in psychosis; the content of his disordered mind hinged on fantasies of religious persecution, his own guilt and unworthiness. After failing to take his own life he tried to say the Creed, but had mysteriously forgotten the words: "I laid myself down, howling with horror, while my knees smote against the other. In this condition my brother found me, and the first words I spoke to him were, "Oh, Brother, I am damned!' "[24] His brother, according to the pious custom, sent for their cousin Martin Madan, who attempted to impress on Cowper his utter sinfulness for attempting suicide. Not surprisingly, he awoke the next morning with a sense of terror and depression even stronger than before. His brother and Madan arranged for his care in the private asylum of Dr. Nathaniel Cotton at St. Albans. "One should not give a poisoner medicine . . . nor a rifle to a melancholic bore."

Cowper remained in Dr. Cotton's Collegium Insanorum from December 1763 through June 1765. At first his improvement was slow and "Satan still plied (me) closely with horrible visions and more horrible voices." But Dr. Cotton was a man of sympathetic understanding with minor poetic gifts himself; his works may be found in Anderson's and Chalmer's collections. He proved a wise choice as a psychotherapist for Cowper. Denis Leigh comments that "to the eighteenth century physician the role of emotion in disease was all too evident. He moved in the same small social group as his patients, dined with them, heard their confidences, dealt with their excesses, their jealousies, their ambitions, and their weaknesses. No laboratory stood in the way of this human, personal relationship; no recondite theory of a personal or collective unconscious as yet obscured his clear and simple vision."[25] Cowper paid eloquent tribute to Nathaniel Cotton as a physician:

I was not only treated with kindness by him when I was ill, and attended with the utmost diligence; but when my reason was restored to me, and I had so much need of a religious friend to converse with, to whom I could open my mind upon the subject without reserve, I could hardly have found a fitter person for the purpose. The doctor was as ready to administer relief to me in this article likewise, and as well qualified to do it, as in that which was more immediately in his province.[26]

Cowper dates his restoration of reason to a sudden revelation from a text in the New Testament: "Whom God hath set forth to be a propitiation through faith in his blood to declare his righteousness for the remission of sins that are past through the forbearance of God" (Rom. 3:25). To this revealed truth he prefixed the comment: "Thus may the terror of the Lord make a Pharisee, but only the sweet voice of mercy in the gospel can make a Christian."

His spirit now exalted, possibly hypomanic, Cowper felt "unspeakable delight in the discovery and was impatient to communicate a pleasure to others that I found so superior to everything that bears the name. This eagerness of spirit ... made me imprudent, and, I doubt not, troublesome to many."[27] His relations arranged for a brief visit to Cambridge, then saw to it that he was comfortably installed at Huntingdon in the home of the Reverend Morley Unwin and his pious wife, Mary. When Morley Unwin was killed by a fall from his horse in July 1767, Cowper continued to live with Mary Unwin, whose relation to him was that of a mother. By this time he was a passionate advocate of the Evangelical movement, and in September 1767 Cowper and Mary

Unwin moved to Olney, an unattractive town on the Ouse where lacemaking was the principal industry.

At Olney Cowper came under the influence of the Reverend John Newton, a zealous convert to Evangelicism, who had passed his earlier days as captain of a slave ship. Cowper served Newton as a lay assistant; he visited the sick, conducted prayer meetings, and even organized parish affairs. Whether Newton's driving religious zeal—"he could preach men mad"—or Cowper's engagement to marry Mary Unwin was the responsible factor, by 1773 he was again suffering from religious hallucinations, was convinced he was irrevocably damned, and attempted to hang himself. Again, he was a suicide *manqué*. The net effect of this attempt at suicide was to convince Cowper that he had forfeited God's grace and mercy and was forever damned. He never again attended public worship; when grace was said at the table, he would remain seated, his knife and fork in hand, to show that grace was denied to him alone.

However, it was at Olney, chiefly between 1771 and 1773, that Cowper made his first significant attempt at poetry. His juvenilia and later *vers d'occasion* would scarcely entitle him to a footnote, but the *Olney Hymns* published in 1779 by Cowper—282 by John Newton—are one of the great glories of English hymnology. It may be true that some of Cowper's contributions are more of a personal devotion than a public choral chant, but this detracts neither from their fervor nor their grace. Taking for an example the famous hymn, *Oh! For a Closer Walk with God,* Norman Nicholson comments that it is "a private devotional poem rather than a congregational hymn" and that "the second and third stanzas refer to Cowper's own life and have a delicacy of sentiment which could hardly be shared by the ordinary hot-gospelling convert of the time." But Nicholson justly adds the observation that "the lines are astonishingly good for congregational singing, for the imagery is so simple, so clear and glowing, that everyone can recognize its truth. An intensely personal experience has become the expression of a universal longing."[28] Such other familiar hymns as *God moves in a mysterious way—His wonders to perform,* and *The Contrite Heart* succeed in breathing personal life and conviction into a form which was all too often stereotyped, devoid of substance, and stamped with the mediocrity of the *routinier*.

Considerable attention has been directed toward Cowper's *Olney Hymns* with respect to their prosody, their theologic content, their relation to the credo of Evangelicism, and there is little need to recapitulate the pieties and impieties of past commentators. It will not be considered out of place, however, if a morbid anatomist takes notice of their conspicuously sanguinary imagery. Cowper's hymns have a hemoglobin level somewhat in excess of normal values. Added to this rich measure of blood is a strong affinity for Old Testament sadomasochism; biblical Judaism was not an unbloodthirsty culture. The point is readily clarified by a few citations:

Hymn II reminds us that "This Abraham found, he rais'd the knife," and Hymn V tells us that Jesus's blood "so freely streamed to satisfy the law's demand," a thought which leads us directly into Hymn VIII in which "Comfortable thoughts arise/From the bleeding sacrifice."[29] Such comfort was ambivalent and found its expression in *The Contrite Heart* (Hymn IX) in an image not devoid of its metaphysical wit:

> I hear, but seem to hear in vain,
>   Insensible as steel;
> If aught is felt, 'tis only pain,
>   To find I cannot feel.

Finding himself a failed masochist, unable to take pleasure in his spiritual pain, Cowper turns to God in the final stanza and asks him to arbitrate upon what can only be a subjective judgment based on afferent neural pathways:

> Oh make this heart rejoice, or ache;
>   Decide this doubt for me;
> And if it be not broken, break,
>   And heal it, if it be.

Fortunately, despite his religious trauma, Cowper had had the saving grace of a public school education in the classics and some experience with the conventional modes of the Church of England. In Hymn XI he recognizes his standing in the form at Westminster; likening God to a headmaster and himself to a boy receiving instruction prior to confirmation, he writes:

> My God, how perfect are thy ways!
>   But mine polluted are;
> Sin twines itself about my praise,
>   And slides into my pray'r
> When I would speak what thou hast done
>   To save me from my sin,
> I cannot make thy mercies known
>   But self-applause creeps in.

Like Eton in the mid-nineteenth century, Westminster in the late seventeenth and early eighteenth centuries had a singular reputation

for its floggings. In Thomas Shadwell's *The Virtuoso* (1676) the hypo-
critical Snarl solicits flagellation from his mistress, Mrs. Figgup, saying
"I was so us'd to't at Westminster School I could never leave it off
since. . . . Do not spare thy pains. I love castigation mightily."[30] Schoolboy masochism recurs in the image of the first line of the following
Hymn XII: "My God! till I receiv'd thy stroke, / How like a beast was I!"
But the whippings of clever schoolboys with a gift for versification
leads inevitably to fantasies of blood (cf. Swinburne et al.), and in
Hymn XIV Cowper speaks of Jerusalem, informing us that "Jehovah
founded it in blood, / The blood of his incarnate Son." There is
considerable biblical as well as archeological evidence to the contrary,
and the blood shed in and near Jerusalem seems to be fairly evenly
distributed among Christians, Jews, Moslems, and even disbelievers.
One may pardon Cowper's Evangelical fervor, but images so palpably
lacking in historicity indicate that their writer's grasp of reality might
have profited from further psychotherapy. It may be the victor's pre-
rogative to rewrite history to favor the justice of his own cause, but such
a position is untenable for a hymnodist committed to Truth.

The *locus classicus* for Cowper's morbid affection for blood in his
hymns is found in the familiar Hymn XV, "There is a fountain fill'd
with blood / Drawn from Emmanuel's veins" The image is extended to
sinners who, "plung'd beneath that flood" are redeemed and made
virtuous, to the penitent thief as he lay gasping his last on the cross, and
to other situations in which the hemoglobin-rich fluid is endowed with
special virtues exceeding the claims of the most optimistic latter-day
hematologists. Remembering from laboratory experience that blood
becomes sticky before it coagulates, we learn that Cowper has washed
all his sins away in blood, that the Lamb's blood never loses its redemp-
tive (curative) powers, and that Cowper has purchased his celestial
harp with an offering of blood. Nicholson has commented that "the
combination of sacramental and anatomic imagery . . . is of immense
interest both to the antropologist and the psychologist, for in it we are
aware of rituals even older than the Old Testament: of the dying gods
of the fertility cults and of primitive symbols that probe deeply into the
subconscious mind."[31] That fertility cults loomed large on Cowper's
impuissant horizon is doubtful; he was both insular and pre-Frazerian.
His morbid interest in blood seems more of a schoolboy's attraction to
Count Dracula and Bela Lugosi with overtones of the eighteenth-
century classroom, as in Hymn XIX where

> In vain by reason and by rule,
> We try to bend the will;

> For none but in the Saviour's school,
>   Can learn thy heav'nly skill . . .
> How light thy troubles here, if weigh'd
>   With everlasting pain!

Pain and bloodshed seem to have been the key elements in Cowper's psychopathology. But if we seek a visual correlative for Cowper's agony of blood, we do not see the tortured souls of Bosch's purgatory nor Michelangelo's *Last Judgement*. Rather we see the style of painting depicted in a crucifixion at Pommersfelden in Franconia. An angel collects the bleeding drops from Christ's wounds after the blood has run through an elaborate system of gutters and drainpipes which discharge it through a large gilt spout several feet below where the Savior stands.

In Hymn XX Cowper deals in a sanguinary fashion with the Old Testament legend commenting on the paschal sacrifice and the blood-besprinkled door, the Lamb and the Dove whose blood of matchless worth serves as the soul's defense, and the idea of salvation *per sanguinem:* "Dipt in his fellow's blood, / The living bird went free." All this bloody imagery was written before the public execution by guillotine in the French Revolution became commonplace, though England had not been without its share of public decapitations.

Hymn XXIX is titled *Prayer for Children* and alludes with happy relish to the Lord's angel who

> Slew with an avenging hand,
> All the first-born of the land,
> Then thy people's doors he pass'd
> Where the bloody sign was plac'd;
> Hear us now upon our knees
> Plead the blood of Christ for these!

In a country where primogeniture was a pillar of the social structure this hymn could not have failed to be a stirring example of Christian virtue applied to an Old Testament legend.

In Hymn XXVIII we learn that Jesus himself was excited by the prospect of bloodshed, in this case, his own; Cowper tells us that as He entered Jerusalem, "He longs to be baptiz'd with blood, / He pants to reach the cross." The received legend is, of course, that Jesus was baptized not in blood but in running water by John the Baptist who later was decapitated by Herod's order at the behest of Salome. Perusal of the Gospels of Matthew, Mark, Luke, and John fails to reveal authority for Christ's desire to be rebaptized by his own blood.

Masochism without overt bloodshed returns in Hymn XXXVII:

> Long unafflicted, undismay'd,
>   In pleasure's path secure I stray'd;
> Thou mad'st me feel thy chast'ning rod,
>   And strait I turn'd unto my God.
> What though it pierc'd my fainting heart,
>   I bless thine hand that caus'd the smart;
> It taught my tears awhile to flow
>   But sav'd me from eternal woe.

The image most readily conjured to one's mind is the flogging block at Eton, but doubtless a similar apparatus was in use at Westminster in Cowper's youth. Many a lad was whipped for straying into pleasure's path and being late for chapel. e. e. cummings has told us that "punished bottoms interrupt philosophy," but the different tradition of the English public school is best exemplified, not so much in the pathologic verses of Swinburne (ca. 1869–88) but in the more contemporary lines addressed by Lytton Strachey to Roger Senhouse in 1929:

> How odd the fate of pretty boys!
> Who, if they dare to taste the joys
> That so enchanted Classic minds,
> Get whipped upon their neat behinds;
> Yet should they fail to construe well
> The lines that of those raptures tell
> —It's very odd, you must confess—
> Their neat behinds get whipped no less.[32]

But it is possible that the element of sadomasochism shown in the preceding examples can be overemphasized. Cowper may have intended little more than the literary conventions common to the poetry of Christianity tinged with Evangelical passion. Christ's sacrifice is central to all Christian sects. As in many other religions there is a strong, almost mystical, use of blood, either symbolic or transubstantiated in Christian rituals. Even in the application of Christian principles to politics, so gentle a man as Thomas Jefferson wrote that "The tree of liberty must be refreshed from time to time with the blood of patriots and tyrants. It is its natural manure." To say nothing of the constant allusions to the blood of martyrs and the blood of the lamb. That Jesus' blood "so freely streamed" in Hymn V may merely echo Faustus's last speech in Marlowe's *Doctor Faustus:* "See, see where Christ's blood streams in the firmament." And the image of the aching heart broken by God finds its correlative in "Batter my heart. . . ." in

Holy Sonnet XIV by John Donne, Cowper's collateral maternal ances-
tor. Cowper's Jerusalem in Hymn XIV is "not historical but typological: Jehovah's Old Jersalem will be reincarnate as the New Jerusalem
through Christ's sacrifice." But it is evident, regardless of the conventions of Christian poetics, that Cowper had a heightened sensibility
toward blood and that his general posture was that of a sufferer on this
earth. Both his attitude toward the Evangelical creed and the hymns
which it inspired satisfied whatever masochistic elements were represented in his psychopathology.

Like most boys educated in the upper-middle-class tradition,
Cowper was not unmindful of his duty to the poor. In Hymn LIII,
titled *For the Poor,* he reminds us that

> When Hagar found the bottle spent . . .
> A message from the Lord was sent
> To guide her to a well.

One is a bit surprised that she did not send Ishmael round to the corner
grocer for a liter of blood, but gin was the drink of the lower classes in
the 1770s, and Cowper was too conscious of his own class and that of his
readers to invoke an image which would lower the tone of his hymn.
But, best of all, Cowper found incredible therapeutic powers in blood
of religious origin. Hymn LXV informs us that

> Of all the gifts thine hand bestows,
>   Thou giver of all good!
> Not heav'n itself a richer knows
>   Than my Redeemer's blood.
> Faith too, the blood-receiving grace,
>   From the same hand we gain . . .
> Yet fly that hand, from which alone
>   We could expect a cure.

It is not difficult to conjecture that Cowper's propensity for images
of masochism, punishment by the rod, and the shedding of blood as a
means of redemption from guilt all stem from his juvenile exposure to
the unnamed bully at Dr. Pittman's school. Leslie Stephen's remark
that "Cowper is an instance of a thinker too far apart from the great
world to apply the lash effectually" is a clue to our understanding that
even in his satires such as *Tirocinium* he fell short of the corrective aim
of satire because he was the victim of a lash, specifically his own sense of
guilt and failure in the public world. Biographic details about other
disciplinary practices are lacking but were in all probability no differ-

ent from those prevailing in other English schools of the time. That the emotion engendered by these experiences was intensified during his period of preclinical depression (ca. 1754–63) and that his final release from the bonds of overt psychosis through Romans 3:25 with its emphasis on remission of sin *per fidem in sanguine Dei* were the decisive landmarks. Many of the interstices cannot be filled in for lack of documentation, but excessive proliferation of anamnestic data might serve only to muddy the outline.

Spacks speaks of Cowper's lack of control of his images, citing examples from the *Olney Hymns*. But his occasional imperfect control of language is not due to mania but rather maladresse. Cowper was far more concerned with the substance of his poems than with technique. After mildly disparaging stylistic refinement,

> Manner is all in all, whate'er is writ
> The substitute for genius, sense, and wit.
> (*Table Talk*, lines 542–43)

Cowper goes on to demonstrate that his chief interest lies in the poet's message:

> To dally much with subjects mean and low
> Proves the mind is weak, or makes it so . . .
> Else, summoning the muse to such a theme,
> The fruit of all her labour is whipt-cream.
> (Ibid., lines 544–45, 550–51)

This attitude is not uncommon among poets with a religious or social message, but it is not a symptom of mania. It would not be unfair to compare Cowper's poems written under the impulse of eighteenth-century Evangelicism with Herbert's written under the influence of seventeenth-century Anglicanism. Cowper, like other poets of his time, viewed in the historical perspective as falling between Augustan self-confidence and romantic energy, looked backward and forward at the same time, adrift on a current of slow change which neither he nor they could govern nor understand.

Following Newton's departure for the pulpit of Saint Mary Woolnoth in London, Cowper's overt, public involvement in the Evangelical movement became less intense. His later poems, inspired or instigated by Mary Unwin, Lady Hesketh (formerly Harriet Cowper, Theodora's sister), and Lady Austen dealt with more secular moral subjects and conspicuously avoided the self-revelation of the *Olney Hymns* and other poems of the 1770s. Much of his newer poetry was rurally pictorial, and he combined the two strains in the oft-quoted aphorism: "God made the country, and man made the town." Less intensely Evangelical, his poetry was more in harmony with the popular ethos of his day.

His moral essays and agreeable social verses interspersed with an occasional mock-heroic made him the most widely read and influential poet in England of his day. *Table Talk* (1782), *The Task* (1785), and *Tirocinium* (1785) served to establish his preeminence. The popular success of *John Gilpin's Ride*, published anonymously in 1782 and under Cowper's own name in 1785, put his name on everyone's tongue; its only rival in that light-hearted genre is *The Colubriad*, written in 1782 but not published until 1806. Cowper also contributed many topical poems to magazines of the day. Apart from a recurrent episode of depression and attempted suicide in 1784 he remained in his customary spirits and functioned efficiently. Except for the personal revelations in the *Olney Hymns*, Cowper at this time seems to have deliberately avoided poetry in which either form, content, or use of language might expose the carefully constructed defenses in his persona. Norman Nicholson has summarized this aspect of his career with insight:

He was at times a madman, and he was always one whose mental powers were unstable, yet his poetry is essentially the poetry of the sane. . . . The good common sense of the average intelligent man. . . . Living a life of extreme oddity, [he] became by far the most popular poet of his time . . . the spokesman for the conscience of the middle classes. . . . Though he lived in an out-of-the-way village, though he met scarcely anyone but a few selected friends, he was able to exercise a tremendous influence over a large section of society . . . his verse had more direct effect on politics than that of almost any other poet in English literature. Dryden, Pope, and Wordsworth no doubt made a deeper impact on their readers, but these belonged in each case to a small group: Cowper, on the other hand, influenced an enormous public, many of whom gave little attention to any other literature but the Bible and, maybe, *The Pilgrim's Progress* . . . because, through the Evangelical Revival, he was able to join in a great movement of popular thought.[33]

In addition to the *Olney Hymns* three of Cowper's poetical projects have psychobiographic interest, one for its design and purpose, the others for their content. In 1784 Cowper, then fifty-three years old, began to translate Homer at the instigation of Lady Austen. Despite an interruption by a serious recurrence of melancholia in 1787, Cowper continued this laborious task for more than seven years until it was completed and published. Eschewing Pope's example of heroic couplets, Cowper translated the *Iliad* and the *Odyssey* into blank verse. Richard Bentley, the great classical scholar, had said of Pope's translation, "It is a very pretty poem, but you must not call it Homer."

Cowper's translation has the virtue of accuracy, and Bentley might have praised it on that score, but it lacks the Homeric vigor; it fails to recreate the atmosphere of primitive myth. Though many passages may be singled out for their beauty, on the whole it fails to catch the fire of the original. Nonetheless an accurate translation of Homer by a man aged fifty-three to sixty-one whose history is marked by depressive psychosis can be taken as evidence that dementia was not present.

Somewhat more revealing are the five stanzas entitled *Lines Written During a Period of Insanity*. If they were written 1774 (cf. H.S. Milford, ed., *Cowper: Poetical Works*, 4th ed. Oxford Standard Authors, 1934), they refer to his episode of depression and attempted suicide in 1773 but if, as Ryskamp claims, they were written in 1763, they refer to his first major breakdown. The regular stanza form and use of language is too controlled for the lines to have been written during Cowper's acute madness, but he may well have jotted down notes and polished his verses later. The reader is scarcely surprised to find that they again relate to Cowper's conviction of his own damnation—"Hatred and vengeance, my eternal portion, / Scarce can endure delay of execution." After proclaiming that God has disowned him and that he is encompassed with a thousand terrors, Cowper finally develops an image in the last stanza which combines his masochism with the ideas of a unique funerary monument:

> *Him* the vindictive rod of angry justice
> Sent quick and howling to the centre headlong:
> *I*, fed with judgment, in a fleshly tomb, am
>   Buried above ground.

By contrasting himself with Abiram (Num. 16), who had placed his holiness on a level with Moses and was punished by being swallowed alive with his kith, kin, and substance into a bottomless pit, Cowper presented the image of his life on earth as a living tomb. In Nicholson's terms "The earth, in fact, was a knife-edge on which Cowper walked between the heaven he thought he had lost and the hell he feared would gain him."[34] It is not a position which lends itself to equipoise, but Cowper was able to state his dilemma, both spiritual and intellectual, in a language which did not betray mania, but rather explained it with lucidity.

Several reasons combined to keep Cowper's poetry within the usual bounds of sanity. To some extent he used the act of composition as a form of occupational therapy, and in *The Progress of Error* (1780–81), written after Newton had left for London, he was able to give voice to the relation between the mind-body problem;

> Faults in the life breed errors in the brain;
> And these, reciprocally, those again
> The mind and conduct mutually imprint
> And stamp their image in each other's mint.
> (Lines 564–67)

At the same time the public intensity of his Evangelical fervor subsided; Newton was no longer at Olney to serve as a goad, Cowper did not obtain his beliefs; he merely kept them private, for himself and a small circle of friends. This limitation is the point of the closing lines of *The Progress of Error:*

> I am no preacher, let this hint suffice—
> The cross, once seen, is death to ev'ry vice:
> Else he that hung there suffer'd all his pain,
> Bled, groan'd, and agoniz'd, and died, in vain.
> (Lines 621–24)

In such lines Cowper recognized the individual, subjective nature of neurotic ecstasy, a feeling which may combine both suffering and despair. Kenneth MacLean presents one aspect of this view when he says that "in time Cowper discovered that the poetic creation of language was very helpful in drowning out inner voices of despair: 'There is a pleasure in poetic pains / Which only poets know. . . .' as he wrote to save his own soul, he developed . . . an aesthetic which had something to do with saving the soul of poetry in his day. . . . The sense of terror . . . is most skillfully transferred into the symbols of those excellent poems frequently enclosed in a [private] letter. In some of these Cowper has drawn upon his beloved sea imagery as in *The Castaway,* his last poem and an ultimate image in lonely terror."[35]

The last few years of Cowper's life were those of slow decline. In 1791, the year his translation of Homer was published, Mary Unwin suffered the first of a succession of paralytic strokes which progressively crippled her body and mind until she died in 1796. By 1793–94 Cowper himself had entered his last phase of melancholy; at this remove it is difficult to decide whether it was a recurrence of his former depressive psychoses, the slow onset of senility, or a combination of both. One last poem, *The Castaway,* written in March 1799, barely more than a year before his death, is Cowper's most self-revealing poem since the *Olney Hymns* and *Tirocinium.* It is, as MacLean labels it, "an ultimate image in lonely terror," but it is more than that. It is based on an incident described in Richard Walter's *A Voyage Round the World* by George Anson (1748) and deals with the death of a sailor fallen overboard whose shipmates are unable to rescue him. Cowper compares his own fate with that of the gallant sailor on life's voyage. "No poet wept him," but Cowper describes the brave man's death agony and the helplessness of his friends, concluding with a comparison to his own unhappy lot:

> I therefore purpose not, or dream,
>   Descanting on his fate,
> To give the melancholy theme
>   A more enduring date:
> But misery still delights to trace
> Its 'semblance in another's case.
>
> No voice divine the storm allay'd,
>   No light propitious shone;
> When, snatch'd from all effectual aid,
>   We perished, each alone:
> But I beneath a rougher sea,
> And whelm'd in deeper gulphs than he.

The image of the soul lost in a tempest at sea is not unique to *The Castaway* of 1799. Cowper had used it before in verses *To Mr. Newton on his Return from Ramsgate,* "I, tempest-toss'd and wrecked at last, / Come home to port no more," and also in the lines *On the Receipt of My Mother's Picture,* "Always from port withheld, always distress'd— / Me howling winds drive devious, tempest-toss'd." For Cowper this must have been a very personal image, suggesting perhaps the need for a mother or father figure to guide him through what he interpreted as life's perils. It is without doubt a subjective image of an emotion deeply felt, but the actual language in which the image is expressed is metaphorically coherent. The mere fact that Cowper used metaphor rather than personification does not indicate poetic mania, but merely a shift in the poetic practices of the latter half of the century. Surely Housman could not have intended us to believe that the use of one form of figure of speech in preference to another was the "true poetic accent emerging from contemporary dialect."

Cowper shared an interest in natural science with other poets of his day, and many of his observations on the natural—especially botanical—aspects of the English countryside exceed the powers of observations granted to his contemporaries. But when he witnessed the growing atheism of his contemporary scientists, he rebelled with traces of his old Evangelical passion. It is in this sense that his use of language reveals the paradox of his conflict. Reared in a classic or Augustan school in which metaphor was a condensed simile or had a commonsense basis in likeness, he slowly turned his metaphor inward. In this sense Northrop Frye has focused attention on the central problem of the transition in poetic language: "where metaphor is conceived as part of an oracular and half-ecstatic process, there is a direct identification in which the poet himself is involved. . . . In the age of sensibility some of the identifications involving the poet seem manic, like Blake's with druidic bards, (cf. also Collins' druids in the ode on Thomson's death), or Smart's with Hebrew prophets, or *depressive, like Cowper's with a scapegoat figure, a stricken deer or castaway.*"[36] It was in this last poem, *The Castaway,* that Cowper most surely used the old language to express the new personal metaphor. His "deeper gulph" was not merely the physical and spiritual fact that each man dies alone, but a gulf of language which in his last utterance he successfully bridged.

Literary stereotypes die hard, and we are all familiar with Dr. Johnson's famous dictum that Smart ought never to have been confined: "His infirmities were not noxious to society. He insisted on people praying with him, and I'd as lief pray with Kit Smart as with anyone else. Another charge was that he did not love clean linen; and I have no passion for it."[37] Less familiar and less charitable is Thomas Gray's comment in a letter to Thomas Warton, written in 1747 when Smart was getting into difficulties at Pembroke College: "As to Smart he must necessarily be *abimé* in a short time. His debts daily increase. . . . Addison, I know, wrote smartly to him last week; . . . [as] for his Vanity and Faculty of Lying, they are come to their full maturity. All this, you see, must come to a Jayl, or Bedlam, and that without any help, almost without pity."[38] Both statements reveal as much about their authors as they do about Smart. Johnson was a man of broad sympathy and human understanding; Gray was too preoccupied with his own neuroses to develop insight into the problems of a fellow member of his college. Yet there are more important ways of leaving one's mark on history, and neither Johnson nor Gray tells us more than a fragment of Smart's story and nothing of his poems. Arthur Sherbo's biography makes it unnecessary to recite in detail the facts of Smart's unhappy life, wasted gifts, madness and confinement and, finally, death in a debtor's prison.[39] But a few salient features must be outlined if only to frame the picture in historical perspective.

Smart's father, who died when the boy was only eleven, was the steward for the large estates of the Vane family in Kent. We are told that Christopher, his first child and only son, was a sickly boy, and there are many comments about his small stature. We are also told that he developed an adolescent "crush" on Anne Vane, even carrying it to the extent of a juvenile "elopement"! After his father's death in 1733, his impecunious mother was enabled to educate Christopher, whose intellect gave promise, through the kind assistance of the Vane family, and the lad was sent to Durham School, many miles northwest of his native Kent. Any one of these particular items might have contributed to his later mental instability, and they have all been duly noted by his psychobiographers. But for the fifteen years after his father's death he led a straightforward, successful life, well adapted to his gifts as a student and scholar.

In 1739 he was admitted as sizar to Pembroke College, Cambridge, was graduated A.B. in 1742, and elected fellow in 1745. He had shown a happy facility for writing verse and was adept at translating from English into Latin. An omnivorous reader, he was truly a "scholar of the university," and many considered him "the pride of Cambridge and the chief poetical ornament of the university."[40] He was elected praelector in philosophy, then in rhetoric, and received his M.A. degree in 1747. But the signs of disaster were at hand, as Gray noted. Popular with both fellows and students, Smart could not resist living beyond his means, standing his share for rounds of drinks in local taverns, dressing expensively, and leading "the good life" in mid-eighteenth-century Cambridge.

Smart's chief motive for leaving Cambridge in 1748 or 1749 was to establish a financially successful career in London literary circles. He had some acquaintance with literary figures of the day, including a letter of praise from Alexander Pope of recent memory, and he was known to several publishers. At one time he developed an attachment for Anna Maria Carnan, the daugher of a printer and publisher. He married her in 1752, which made it necessary for him to give up his fellowship at Pembroke which the college authorities had kindly let him maintain in absentia. Christopher Devlin has developed a case that Smart's bride was a practicing Roman Catholic, that his guilt about the education of his two daughters in that faith may have played a precipitating role in his madness, and that Smart was actually committed at the instigation of his wife's father and brother, lest his religious mania lead to an official investigation of her religious practices and subject her to civil penalties.[41] The question remains open, but the significant events in Smart's life between 1749 and 1755 were not his hack work in Grub Street but his labors on the Seatonian Prize poems.

The Seaton Prize was awarded annually with its stipend of £30 for a poem written on "the attributes of the Supreme Being." Smart won it for four consecutive years (1750–53), did not enter in 1754, and won it again in 1755. One reason advanced for his being kept on the rolls of Pembroke even though he was in some disfavor was his success in the

Seatonian competition, and he was even allowed to enter and win after his fellowship had been revoked. More important than the external circumstances and even the welcome stipend was that the Seatonian poems were the only meaningful contact Smart had with his former academic life during his lean years in Grub Street. His victories were his badge of belonging to the intellectual community, albeit indirectly and at a distance. His earlier poems had dealt with more mundane and conventional topics. *The Hop-Garden* (1752) was a successful Georgic which recalled the landscape of his native Kent, and he had a felicitous turn of phrase in some occasional verses, for instance, the lines *To my Worthy Friend, Mr. T. B.* (1752):

> Where Light and Shade in varied Scenes display
> A Contrast sweet, like friendly *yea* and *nay*.
> My Hand, the Secretary of my Mind,
> Left thee these lines upon the poplar's Rind.

But on occasion he descended to passages worthy of *The Stuffed Owl*, as in the epilogue spoken by Desdemona in a 1751 revival of *Othello:*

> True Woman to the last—my *peroration*
> I come to speak in spite of Suffocation.

Like other poets of the post-*Dunciad* era, Smart tried his hand at literary satire in the Martinus Scriblerus tradition. In 1753 he wrote *The Hilliad,* poking fun at one Dr. John Hill, a notorious but versatile scientist and writer. It is accompanied by *Notes Variorum* which attempt to explain obscure points in the text but which add nothing but academic mirth. *The Hilliad* contains such gems as:

> Sweet boy, who seem'st for glorious deeds design'd
> O come and leave that clyster pipe behind.

It would be idle to pretend that Smart's odes, addresses, epigrams, and occasional pieces, even *The Hop-Garden* and *The Hilliad,* had any great poetic merit or substance. They are the pleasing effusions of a well-educated man who made his living by his pen. There is no hint of madness or incipient mania. The substance and language are well within the conventional canon of the time.

The first clue we find to Smart's later problems in reconciling mid-eighteenth-century science with religion is in one of his earliest preserved poems, the *Secular Ode on the Jubilee at Pembroke College, Cambridge, in 1743.* For a recent A.B. to have been chosen to write such an important poem in a high academic festivity was indeed an honor, and Smart began with an invocation appropriate to the occasion, but it contains the germ of the Seatonian odes, from which one can trace the origins of his religious mania.

> God of science, light divine,
> O'er all the world of learning shine;
>   Shine fav'ring from th' etherial way:
> But here with tenfold influence dwell,
> Here all thy various rays compell
>   To dignify this joyful day.

There is nothing, however, in the poem which foreshadows his anti-Newtonianism so evident in *Jubilate Agno*, the poem of his "madness."[42]

Unlike some religious-obsessives Smart has not left a day-by-day record of his spiritual grapplings with faith and reason, but we can trace his growing concern with religious questions in the Seatonian odes of 1750 and 1755. They represent a way station in his spiritual growth and reveal some of his conflicts. The first of the group, *On the Eternity of the Supreme Being* (1750), deals with the problem of creation and the last judgment. Smart asks the question which has baffled geologists and paleologists for the past three centuries:

> Thou art—all glorious, all beneficent
> All Wisdom and Omnipotence thou art,
>   But is the Era of Creation fix'd
> At when these Worlds began?

He does nothing more than pose the question, almost as an aside, but he makes it plain that mid-eighteenth-century natural science had taught him to look for scientific answers, or at least to ask questions which could be answered in the language of science. There is no need to revive the old controversies about fossils, e.g., Arbuthnot vs. Woodward, but Smart was of a generation of university men who could not accept explanations of nature on the basis of revealed truth alone, at least not in 1750. The remainder of the ode is given over to conventional rhetoric about the "flaming sword's intolerable blaze" and "forms Seraphic with their silver trump," culminating in a climax to the effect that

> for Thou art holy,
> For thou art One, th' Eternal, who alone
> Exerts all goodness, and transcends all praise.

Apart from the single question whether the time of creation is "fix'd," Smart presents no unconventional ideas about the eternity of God, and the poem's language is decorous enough to merit the prize it won.

The second Seatonian ode, *On the Immensity of the Supreme Being* (1751), employs the same iambic pentameter form, but William Jones points out that a decisive element is Smart's notion that "The mind loses its way in searching out the immensity of God, whether in the sky where the planets go harmoniously around the sun . . . or in the sea with its coral gardens and whales, or inside the earth with its rich jewels and hidden streams, or on [the surface of] the earth with its varied beauty that defies human art."[43] Here we find Smart's first admission that the human mind, specifically his own, can be overwhelmed by the Newtonian concept of a mechanical universe. Until this time, the scientific essay or scientific poem, of which Pope's *Essay on Man* is the best-known example, had usually illustrated and amplified the idea that God's wisdom, goodness, and power were the saving grace. True, in 1746 Collins and Joseph Warton had begun an abortive revolt against the moral poem, but they had met with little success. For Smart to admit that the mind was not equal to the strain was a novel idea. It surely opened a chink in his intellectual armor.

The third of the series, *On the Omniscience of the Supreme Being* (1752), threw down the gauntlet to science. Smart glorifies both man's powers of reason and the animal's instincts, but then takes to task that "proud reasoner, philosophic man" for failing to perceive through his reason that which the animals know by instinct. He casts doubt on the values of some types of scientific investigation:

> The venerable sage, that nightly trims
> The learned lamp, t' investigate the pow'rs
> Of Plants medicinal, the earth, the air,
> And the dark regions of the fossil world
> Grows old in following what he ne'er shall find;
> Studious in vain! till haply, at the last
> He spires a mist, then shapes it into mountains,
> And baseless fabric from conjecture brings.

One does not nowadays consider the work of Robert Boyle, Robert Hooke, James Tyson, Newton, or even Harvey's successors in medical physiology, to have constructed a "baseless fabric," but for Smart, who could not foresee the purpose and direction of natural science, the appeal to God's omniscience was a more satisfying alternative. Greene summarizes the anti-intellectual attitude: "Newton was very clever, but we must not forget that God is even cleverer." By 1752 Smart's position was close to Berkeley's anti-Newtonianism, and from this unsafe ground he never retreated.

The fourth poem, *On the Power of the Supreme Being* (1753), shows no change in Smart's moral or intellectual position. Smart deals chiefly with God's power to perform miracles and with some of the more terrifying aspects of nature: earthquakes, hurricanes, and electrical storms—and he implies that these are supernatural phenomena which will not yield their mystery to rational analysis. Magnetism and electricity come in for their share of disparagement on theological grounds:

> Survey the magnet's sympathetic love,
> That woos the yielding needle; contemplate
> Th' attractive amber's power, invisible
> Ev'n to the mental eye' or when the blow
> Sent from th' electric sphere assaults thy frame,
> Shew me the hand that dealt it!—baffled here
> By his omnipotence, Philosophy
> Slowly her thoughts inadequate revolves,
> And stands, with all His circling wonders round her,
> Like heavy Saturn in th' etherial space
> Begirt with an inexplicable ring.

It is supererogatory to point out that the next century provided explanations for what Smart felt was inexplicable. The point in his mind was that science had failed to furnish the explanations he sought, and he preferred to place his trust in God's powers and a supernatural interpretation of the cosmos.

The fifth and last Seatonian ode, *On the Goodness of the Supreme Being* (1755), eschews the conflict between faith and reason. It is a paean praising God's goodness for the plenitude of Nature, exhibiting "in an imperceptible point, as well as in an unbounded sphere, the perfections and attributes of an infinite God."[44] The net effect of the Seatonian poems was to deepen the channel of Smart's thought and cause him to be more preoccupied than ever with the relation of the human soul to God. They prepare the way for Smart's three most revealing religious poems, the *Hymn to the Supreme Being* (1756), *Jubilate Agno* (1759–63), and *A Song to David* (1763). By 1755 Smart's mind, not exactly at peace, somewhat beset by external problems, had committed itself to a religious outlook on life, and the last fifteen years of his life were devoted to the literary expression of that faith, even at the expense of mania.

The precise date of onset of mental illness is always a biographical problem, and after two centuries the details of psychopathology tend to become blurred. Sherbo cites constant financial pressures as a precipitating factor and minimizes the role of Smart's drinking. It seems reasonable to believe that he drank to excess only when troubled, and that it was a symptom of ill-directed self-therapy rather than a cause. Devlin emphasizes Smart's concern about his wife's Roman Catholicism and his doubts about his daughters' religious education as a major event in the development of his mental disease. Some writers have taken an allusion in the *Hymn to the Supreme Being* (1756) as denoting Smart's recovery from his first bout of madness. Support for this theory has been found in the comparison with Saul, king of the Israelites, in the opening stanzas and in the later lines:

> When Reason left me in the time of need,
>   And sense was lost in terror or in trance,
> My sick'ning soul was with my blood inflam'd,
>   And the celestial image sunk, defac'd, and maim'd.

Smart records his recovery from this illness by writing "The lamp of life renew'd with vigour burns, / And exil'd reason takes her seat again." Sherbo argues with some force that Smart's illness in 1756 was not a mental breakdown but more probably an acute infectious disease, now undiagnosable, but accompanied by high fever and toxic delirium. That the delirium was colored by hallucinations reflecting Smart's predilective religious bent satisfies both possibilities, organic and functional. There seems to be no cause to doubt from the sense of the poem that Smart's contact with reality during his illness was abnormal and that on recovery he recognized it as such. It is clear that his friends and associates did not consider him non compos mentis at the time, for between this illness and his confinement publishers were willing to enter into contractual relations with him, advancing monies with reasonable expectation that marketable literary wares would be delivered.

The "official" onset of Smart's overt madness is revealed in a letter written many years later by his eldest daughter. The pathetic text informs us that

Previous to my father's showing any symptom of insanity, my sister, a child of three years old, awoke one night screaming and saying that her *papa had lost his head*. This singular presentiment . . . was soon after verified, and it was found necessary to confine him. He was committed . . . to the care of a Mr. Potter who kept a private house at Bethnal Green. There I remember to have been taken to see him by my mother, and I retain a faint recollection of a small neat parlour in which we were received. He grew better . . . He never recovered the clearness of his intellect, though he continued to write and publish.[45]

This letter was written in 1831, and it is possible that Smart's daughter was confusing his second confinement with his first. The records at St. Luke's Hospital in its *Curable Patients' Book* show that Smart was confined there from May 6, 1757 through May 11, 1758. He did not become a patient at Mr. Potter's until an unspecified date in 1759 and he left there in 1763. Smart was discharged from St. Luke's as incurable, and the interval between May 1758 and his admission at Bethnal Green was largely occupied by petitions from his friends to have him admitted to the Incurable Ward at St. Luke's.

Parenthetically, there is no record of Smart's having been a patient at Bethlem. The literary anecdotes about friends visiting him there and finding his health improved by gardening are to be taken with caution. Sherbo informs us that his treatment at Mr. Potter's was humane and enlightened: "Provided with pen and ink and paper, allowed visitors, digging in the garden, playing with and talking to his cat, reading books and periodicals, possibly even allowed a few hours, accompanied freedom ... Smart spent almost exactly four years in the private madhouse at Bethnal Green. Part of each day ... was ritually devoted to the composition of one, two, or three pairs of lines that were then written down neatly in the document he entitled *Jubilate Agno*."[46] This effectively disposes of the romantic myth of Smart laboriously scratching his verses on the wall of his cell with a pin. No doubt some of his time at Bethnal Green was spent writing *A Song to David*, which appeared in print on April 8, 1763, nine weeks after Smart's discharge. He must also have written some of his *Translations of the Psalms of David*, for on the last pages of the *Song* he solicited subscriptions for them, stating that copy was already in the hands of the printer, but the Psalms were not published until 1765.

Two contemporary comments, each by a redoubtable raconteur, give us a clue to the nature of Smart's aberrant behavior. First, Dr. Johnson writes: "Madness frequently discovers itself merely by unnecessary deviation from the usual modes of the world. My poor friend Smart showed the disturbance of his mind, by falling on his knees, and saying his prayers in the street, or in any other unusual place. Now although, rationally speaking, it is greater madness not to pray at all, than to pray as Smart did, I am afraid there are so many who do not pray, that their understanding is not called in question."[47]

This is the authentic voice of the Great Cham making a general proposition and supporting it with the ideals of a staunch and regular communicant of the established church. It provides little insight regarding the cause and nature of Smart's madness and merely attempts to rationalize his conduct. A more penetrating comment comes from Hester Thrale Piozzi:

The famous Christopher Smart . . . would never have had a commission of
Lunacy taken out against him, had he managed with equal ingenuity (that is,
kept his eccentricities private)—for Smart's melancholy showed itself only in a
preternatural excitement to prayer . . . taking *au pied de la lettre* our blessed
Saviour's injunction *to pray without ceasing.* So that beginning by regular addresses at stated times to the Almighty, he went on to call his friends from their
dinners, or beds, or places of recreation, whenever the impulse towards prayer
pressed upon his mind. In every other transaction of life no man's wits could be
more regular than those of Smart's for this prevalence of one idea pertina-
ciously keeping the first place in his head, had in no sense except what
immediately related to itself perverted his judgment at all. . . . Now had this
eminently unhappy patient been equally seized by the precept of *praying in
secret,* as no one would have been disturbed by his irregularities, it would have
been to no one's interest . . . and the absurdity would possibly have consumed
itself in private . . . for mean observers suppose all *Madness* to be *Phrenzy,* and
think a person *Insane* in proportion as he is wild, and disposed to throw things
about—whereas experience shows that such temporary suspensions of the
mental faculties are oftener connected with delirium than with *mania,* and, if
not encouraged and stimulated by drunkenness, are seldom of long duration.[48]

Mrs. Piozzi is garrulous to a fault, but her social and clinical acumen
are sound and to the point. Had Smart been content with private
devotions, however elaborate, he would have come to little harm. But
when his public praying disturbed more than the small community of
literary London, it became necessary to confine him for the convenience of others. Smart may have suffered from hallucinations and his
public conduct was often aggravated by inebriety, but in essence his
disease was religious monomania. Unfortunately, it became a community scandal.

From *Jubilate Agno* we know that he created public disturbances by
praying in St. James's Park and in Pall Mall.

> Let Shobi rejoice with the Kastrel blessed be the name of JESUS in falconry
>   and in the MALL.
> For I blessed God in St. James's Park till I routed all the company . . .
> For the officers of peace are at variance with me and the watchman smites
>   me with his staff.

He prayed on the rooftops, the flat leads of the neatly porticoed,
commonsense, eighteen-century houses:

> For a man should put no obstacle between his head and the blessing of
>   Almighty God . . .
> For the ceiling of the house is an obstacle and therefore we pray on the
>   house-top.

There was very little need for such a muezzin in Georgian London, but Smart also committed the solecism of praying naked in the rain which gave him a sense of added purity: "For to worship naked in the Rain is the bravest thing for refreshing and purifying the body." Creating a public disturbance and praying "in the Emperor's clothes" are likely to come to judicial notice, and magistrates often commit persons to psychiatric institutions despite their protestations of sanity simply because their behavior is at variance with accepted norms.

But Smart never considered himself insane, regardless of the opinion of his family, friends, neighbors, and of the fact of his confinement. In this sense his estimate is not wholly false; society confines many persons because their beliefs and the manner in which they exercise them constitute "disorderly conduct." There is no evidence that Smart developed intellectual deterioration or dementia; he was not a depressive like Collins, nor did his religious mania lead to guilt feelings and attempts at suicide as in the case of Cowper. Smart's religion was one of exaltation and ecstasy. Curiously, he derived his religious notions not from the use of drugs nor from an exotic, Oriental cult but from such mundane sources as the King James Bible and the *Book of Common Prayer*. He was a Tory and an Anglican; he believed in the Apostles' Creed and the Thirty-nine Articles. His offense was that he enjoyed them. He even took them seriously. In the age of reason this was sufficient cause to be put away.

The test of Smart's mental status in relation to his poetry rests chiefly on *Jubilate Agno,* written during his confinement at Mr. Potter's between 1759 and 1763, and *A Song to David,* surely conceived, probably drafted, and possibly corrected in 1763 toward the end of his confinement. The literary history of *Jubilate Agno* is well known and requires only brief mention. The manuscript came into the possession of the Cawardine-Probert family which generously permitted William F Stead to publish it in 1939.[49] It was not known to Housman when he delivered the Leslie Stephen lecture in 1933, and Housman's estimate of Smart's madness can be based only on *A Song to David*. In evaluating *Jubilate Agno* we must always remember that the manuscript represents a mutilated original of the poem with a subtitle of Stead's own devising, "A Song from Bedlam," indicating he felt it was the product of a deranged mind. Stead described it as a "strange composition . . . the fundamental brainwork was broken down, the walls, as it were are cracked . . . frequent intrusions of the meaningless and grotesque." His introduction and notes show that he did not credit Smart as having anything more preserved in his mental faculties than a good memory.

Smart's reputation was more fortunate in his next editor. In 1954

William H. Bond revised Stead's order and fundamental plan of the fragments. He described *Jubilate Agno* as a "discarded experiment . . . an attempt to adapt to English verse some of the principles of Hebrew verse as expounded by Bishop Robert Lowth in his pioneering study, *De Sacra Poesi Hebraeorum*, first published in 1753 . . . Smart was on familiar terms with Lowth Himself."[50] Bond emphasizes the antiphonal nature of the "Let" and "For" sections and their origin in both Hebrew and early Christian liturgy. He advances the claim that Smart's experience in the asylum permitted him to "contemplate his past life and present condition, [in which] he worked out a poetic theory and a personal philosophy, and he experimented with form and style in a manner wholly original and unconventional. He was forced to give up the world, and in so doing he found himself."[51] This may be idiosyncrasy, but it is not madness, at least in any medical sense of the term. That Smart was able to conceive a complex aesthetic theory and compose a highly organized poem, albeit incomplete, is substantive evidence of the soundness of his ratiocination. His use of language and personal allusions are other questions whose consideration for the moment can be deferred.

More recently A. D. Hope has developed the idea that *Jubilate Agno* is an apocalyptic vision, a poem cast as a *Magnificat*, written to glorify and praise a systematic cosmology, a theory of the universe based on Smart's extensive scholarly reading—"a single fairly coherent theory of the universe which must have been elaborated before his confinement and which he probably continued to hold after his cure—or, should one say, his release?"[52] Citing in detail Smart's reading lists when he was praelector in philosophy at Pembroke, a literary experience which ranged from Sir Isaac Newton's theological speculations to Patrick Delaney's *An Historical Account of the Life and Reign of David, King of Israel, in Four Books . . . by the Author of Revelations examined with Candour* (1740–42) and included Thomas Burnet's *Sacred Theory of the Earth*, William Whiston's *The Accomplishment of Scripture Prophecies*, and Richard Burthogge's *Of the Soul of the World and of Particular Souls*, Hope points out that "such theories, however wild they may look today, were held by learned and rational men."[53] In Smart's era this was a legitimate effort to replace a materialistic cosmology with a spiritual and animistic one, an attempt to reconcile imagination with reason. Smart viewed himself as the bearer of the Lord's cross, the heir to the tradition of the Old Testament psalmists, writing under divine inspiration in praise of that view of God's creation and creatures which he had excogitated.

One reason advanced for Smart's abandonment of *Jubilate Agno* is that he was able to rephrase and crystallize his personal philosophy in *A Song to David* toward the end of his confinement. Hope tells us:

To the later eighteenth century [it] seemed an insane poem, demonstrating that though the author had been discharged from the asylum, he was as mad as ever. To the nineteenth century it seemed a glorious extravaganza displaying a wild and unusual imagination, but not insane. Only in the last forty or fifty years has it become apparent that it is . . . a highly organized poem, extremely complex in its design and as intellectual as it is ecstatic. Admittedly, it conceals a system of ideas which no one has quite succeeded in making explicit and a mysterious symbolism of numbers and correspondences which still eludes complete explication. But it is neither an insane poem in itself nor does it suggest an insane mind.[54]

It is not difficult to recognize that the Seatonian odes were the precursors for *Jubilate Agno* and *A Song to David*. This accounts for the point of view, prevalent until recent years, that *A Song to David* was a unique poem, an outpouring of deeply felt personal religious emotion quite startling in a man like Smart whose only other known poems were conventional, even dull. It was even thought that the poem was "a lucid interval" in the life of a madman. It remained for Raymond D. Havens to demonstrate that *A Song to David* with its eighty-six-line stanzas follows a careful plan, the stanzas being arranged in groups of three or seven, or multiples of these mystical numbers.[55] In one sense *A Song to David* is the finished product from the blueprint of *Jubilate Agno;* it was the one poem of Smart's to achieve any reputation for a century and a half after his death. Not long before the manuscript of *Jubilate Agno* came to light, Laurence Binyon achieved a remarkable insight:

Obsession with a fixed idea is a common form of insanity. But such obsessions are a mental imprisonment; whereas the *Song to David* is unmistakably the expression of a great release. I speak as a mere layman in these matters, but it seems to me that, while there is nothing in the poem to betray an insane mind—no confusion of the real with the unreal—the mental disturbance must have indirectly affected Smart by shaking him out of his normal self, so that *for the time he was freed from the inhibitions which had dominated till then his creative impulses.*[56] (Italics added)

If this is true of *A Song to David*, it is equally true of *Jubilate Agno*.

But even in his obsession Smart was orthodox. Unlike Blake, who was a visionary and a rebel from his youth, Smart's education and mental outlook were conventional. Binyon asks the same question as Housman: "Does poetry need a kind of madness for its liberation?" His reply was that Smart was exploiting his unconscious but, to his advantage, was unaware of it. "No effort of intellect will ever produce . . . the propitious state. One cannot tap the unconscious at will." But Binyon and Housman, writing before *Jubilate Agno* was published, estimated the liberating effects of Smart's religious monomania on *A Song to David,* and Binyon asked whether, if we knew nothing, should we say that this poem was the work of a madman. The net effect of Smart's mental disturbance was, according to Binyon, "an estrangement of his mind from his century, a liberation of the vein of true and impassioned poetry that was in him but so long disguised and hidden." In that sense *A Song to David* is a Dionysiac poem, a religious poem of an intensity rarely found in England, except for such poets as Thomas Traherne and in occasional passages in Richard Crashaw and George Herbert. Smart's "estrangement"—or alienation, to use a term now in fashion —merely took him back a century in terms of religious feeling, and in *Jubilate Agno* to a Hebraic rather than an English rhetoric.

That the language of *Jubilate Agno* is idiosyncratic, even eccentric, no one can deny. But the text contains accurate references to classical and contemporary literature, the new science, philosophy, religious and theologic controversies then current, as well as to astrology, occultism, and numerology. As Stead demonstrated, Smart retained unimpaired the wide range of knowledge he had acquired while a scholar at Pembroke and from his reading assignments necessary to fulfill his work as a Grub Street hack. The many scattered strokes of imagination, arresting images, gnomic utterances, flashes of wit and insight enable us to put in perspective the occasional passages of self-justification, e.g.: "For I have abstained from the blood of the grape, and that even at the Lord's table—" a bit at variance with the known fact of Smart's intermittent trips to the local tavern from which he had to be carried back. Contrasted with trivia of that sort are lines rich in magical incantation: "For in my nature I quested for beauty, but God, / God hath sent me to sea for pearls—" an image so autobiographical that it echoes forever. Nor can one even mention Smart's freedom of vision without recalling the famous passage about his cat Jeoffry:

> For at the first glance of the glory of God in the East he worships in his way.
> For this is done by wreathing his body seven times round with elegant
>   quickness.

The famous comments about Sir Isaac Newton—"For Newton nevertheless is more of error than of the truth, but I am the Word of God" and with specific reference to Newtonian optics, "For Newton's notion of colours is ἀλόγος unphilosophical, for colours are spiritual"—are to be taken in the sense of an attempt to refute the mechanistic theory of the universe which developed from Newton's theories; they are not an attempt to refute him at the level of experiments in physical science.

Spacks traces Smart's verbal freedom to Lowth's lectures *De Sacri Poesi Hebraeorum,* where the claim is made that "The origin and first use of poetical language are undoubtedly to be traced in the vehement affections of the mind. For what is meant by that singular frenzy of poets, which the Greeks, ascribing to divine inspiration, distinguished by the appellatión of *enthusiasm,* a style and expression directly prompted by nature itself, and exhibiting the true and express image of a mind violently agitated."[57] This is not far removed from Laurence Binyon's "shaking him out of his normal self." The idea of enthusiasm was scarcely new to poetics, either in classical theory and practice or in English poetry, but Smart was par excellence the poet moved to enthusiasm by religious ideas. Because of the circumstances of his life, especially conduct which led to his confinement in an asylum, his enthusiasm was confused with mania.

In *Jubliate Agno* the experiment with enthusiasm and the Hebraic antiphonal mode was uncontrolled, and it is not to Smart's discredit that he abandoned the experiment. We, of a later generation, can only admire its fragmentary successes. Conversely, *A Song to David* was a controlled expression of his enthusiasm. Its recent exegesis by Sophia Blaydes has served, in her own words, to "justify Smart's sanity, his adherence to the codes of his age, and his particular genius which transformed many dicta into brilliant poetry."[58]

The physiognomy of the poem is not disturbing. The six-line rhyming stanza in *aabccb* pattern with *aa* and *cc* in iambic *tetrameter* and the *bb* lines in iambic trimeter was not unusual for the century. It recalls many of the strophic odes set by Handel, William Boyce, William Felton, and lesser composers, and the musical analogy is surely apposite for the century's psalmist. The vocabulary is well within the canon of eighteenth-century usage. Take, for example, stanza XVIII in which Smart describes David as a psalmist praising God:

> He sung of God—the mighty source
> Of all things—the stupendous force
>   On which all strength depends;
> From whose right arm, beneath whose eyes,
> All period, pow'r, and enterprise
>   Commences, reigns, and ends.

There is nothing in these lines which could cause even the most conservative Anglican divine to raise an eyebrow, nor is the general thrust of the poem with its emphasis on adoration and glorification of God outside the tradition of religious poetry at any time, except perhaps in its fervor and the vigor of its expression.

A Song to David is notable for the richness and variety of its images, the number of objects Smart conjures up to fit into his hierarchial scheme of the universe for which he lauds God. This is surely enthusiasm rather than mania, and Norman Callan describes Smart as "a poet with the eye of a painter developed to an unusually high degree. He has the stereoscopic vision which makes the object leap to the eye, the painter's sense of physical texture, and his skill in 'composing' a picture."[59] Similar comments can be made about Blake, who actually was a painter and illustrator, but with respect to Smart one can select such examples of painterly vision as:

> The pheasant shows his pompous neck;
> And ermine, jealous of a speck,
>   With fear eludes offence:
> The sable, with his glossy pride,
> For ADORATION is described,
>   Where frosts the wave condense.

It is a striking fusion of natural imagery set down with almost scientific accuracy to illuminate the adoration by the animal kingdom. For this sort of writing Smart was rejected by his own age and almost sanctified by the Victorians. Is it too much to expect that the twentieth century, which prides itself on enlightened insight into psychopathology, should achieve a more balanced view? One test of the value of a religious poem, not necessarily the best, is whether the poem will have enduring interest, even excitement, in a nonreligious age, and this much we can claim for Smart and his language.

Smart lived for eight years after his release from the asylum. He did not return to his wife and children but took lodgings, first near St. James's Park, later in Chelsea. Not wishing to be returned to custody, he was careful to avoid associations or involvements which might lead to a public profession of his enthusiasm. There is no reason to believe that he modified his idea of a hierarchical universe; his personal cosmology remained unaltered. It is erroneous to believe, as some critics have, that his writings reverted to the conventional level of his early work; once begun, the transformation continued. But the critical response was discouraging. *A Song to David,* published in 1763, elicited a lukewarm response: "his friends were too ready to be saddened, and his enemies too eager to be pleased, by discovering signs of madness in everything he did."[60] Admittedly, his two oratorio texts, *Hannah* (1764) and *Abimelech* (1768), set to music by John Worgan and Samuel Arnold respectively, are not memorable achievements, but his four-volume verse translation of Horace (1767) is a vigorous and felicitous rendition, redeeming his hackwork, prose translation that dated from his Grub Street days.

Smart's most important works during his last few years were his metrical translation of the *Psalms of David,* published in 1765, including with it a cycle of hymns for the Christian year, followed by the versification of the *Parables of Our Lord and Saviour Jesus Christ* (1768), and finally the *Hymns for the Amusement of Children* (1770). These works were consonant with his image of himself as the man chosen to carry on the psalmist tradition. Unconscious of any incongruity, he infused Christian imagery and ideas into his translation of the *Psalms.* Though he translated each verse, the rendering was "free," to say the least. Two examples will suffice to exhibit the limitations:

The passage in Psalm 98:3, which in the King James version reads, "He hath remembered his mercy and his truth toward the house of Israel; all the ends of the earth have seen the salvation of our God," in Smart's hands becomes

> Christ Jesus has declar'd
> That sinners shall be spar'd.
>   And that through him salvation came;
> The world could not convince
> Of sin the righteous prince,
>   So manifest his spotless fame.

And Psalm 95:6—"O come, let us worship and bow down: let us kneel before the Lord our maker"—is transformed into

> Come, O come with Christian union
>   Let us these our frames abase.
> And approach to his communion
>   Kneeling, falling on our face.

Disregarding their intrinsic lack of poetic merit, they are not so much translations as propaganda at the level of a religious tract, far beneath the attainments one might expect from a one-time praelector in philosophy at Pembroke. They indicate not madness but Anglican insularity. But Smart's later religious poems lie beyond the scope of this essay.

His last years were not easy. His daily life was one of continual financial harassment. He could not make a living from his writing and he had no other trade. In 1770 he was arrested for debt, confined to the King's Bench Prison, where he died in 1771, ending as Thomas Gray unkindly predicted "in Jayl . . . almost without Pity."

When we apply medical psychology to the cases of Collins, Cowper, and Smart, we fail to find any unifying principle, any common denominator in their clinical states. Collins was a case of simple depression or melancholia. As his emotional status deteriorated, his poetic output declined. If there is any effect of his depression to be seen in his poetry, it lies in the absence of any strong emotional expression. Whatever syntactical incoherence is present is more likely the result of technical maladresse than disordered cerebration. The account of his dream of falling from a tree before he reached the topmost branches has its psychodynamic and symbolic implications, but there is too little factual data about his life and personal relations to permit further exploration. Insofar as Collins's own poetical intentions are concerned, we learn them not from him but from his friend Warton's "Advertisement," a modest desire to expand the ode form into the area of invention and imagination, replacing thereby the "moralizing in verse" which till then had been in fashion. Only a handful of poems followed the odes of 1746. By 1749 he was sufficiently depressed to have to retire to Chichester, and his career as a poet was finished.

Cowper's psychopathology was more complex, and clues to its pathogenesis was better documented. The major episodes are best described as agitated depression with attempts at suicide. The traumas of his childhood, loss of his mother at six, and sadistic treatment at school may have sensitized his impressionable mind. Whether a congenital organic defect, specifically a penile malformation, was a contributing factor must remain an open question in the absence of clear anatomic evidence. But the precipitating factors in Cowper's episodes of agitated depression can be traced to a set of religious beliefs: guilt-ridden, he believed himself eternally damned. He deliberately adopted the writing of poetry as a form of occupational therapy, and only occasionally can the reader gain a glimpse into his conflicts. Most notable are the blood motif in the Olney hymns and passages in *Tirocinium* which reflect a latent sadomasochistic component, and his last poem, *The Castaway,* which brings into the open his fear of loneliness and his sense of alienation. It would be difficult to make a case for Cowper as an imaginative poet, but it is the subject matter of selected poems rather than the language in which he clothes the subject that reveals his mental state. Theory would outrun data were one to claim that his psychological state freed his language in advance of the idiom of his day.

Collins and Cowper were both overtly psychotic; whether Smart was psychotic is debatable. In retrospect, the most suitable diagnosis is religious monomania without intellectual deterioration. Both Cowper and Smart shared the element of intense religious feeling at the centers of their mental disturbances, but the operation of religious sentiment was completely different in each. In Cowper it led to a sense of guilt, depression, and attempted suicide. In Smart it led to a sense of exaltation and enthusiasm; his conviction of his sense of divine mission, rather than mental deterioration, led to the conduct which precipitated his confinement. Yet the two poems to which "madness" has been imputed were written when he was in the asylum, and even critics who defend his sanity agree that his psychological experience was a "release" or that it freed him from inhibitions. Even though one judges an incomplete manuscript, *Jubilate Agno* is different from and possibly more freely expressive than any poem therefore written in English. Whatever the form may owe to an imitation of Hebrew antiphonal verse, the language is not that commonly used by English poets to that time. Tightly as *A Song to David* may be constructed, impeccable as its private logic may be, the work is unusual among English devotional or adorational poems and a departure from those written before it; both its form and language may be more controlled than *Jubilate Agno*, but apart from Blake and Gerard Manley Hopkins, who came later, it achieved an intensity of language which was new.

Returning to the opening theme, the only evidence of Plato's divine mania in these three "mad" poets can be found in Smart's *Jubilate Agno*, which does transcend the rational, physical world into a spirit of nonrationality, but not to the point of irrationality. Whether his insights are prophetic rather than intuitive lies beyond the purview of a twentieth century antinomian and skeptical reader. But the use of poetic language by Collins and Cowper is generally that of men in their "sober senses," and whatever insights they achieved were more anamnestic in light of their personal intrapsychic problems than prophetic. In none of the three cases can we claim that an "assumed personality" freed their language. The poems of Collins and Cowper all stemmed from the previous tradition of English verse and were a logical outgrowth from it. The same stricture applies to most of Smart's poems; only in *Jubilate Agno* did he seek a different tradition of poetical rhetoric, and indeed he was not able to complete that poem.

CHAPTER 6

Chekhov among the Doctors: The Doctor's Dilemma

Gifted with more psychological insight than his biographers and critics, Chekhov appraised his human condition and stated it with his usual concision:

Self-made intellectuals buy at the price of their youth what gently born writers are endowed with by nature. Go, write a story about a young man, the [grand]son of a serf, the son of shopkeeper, a choirboy, brought up to respect rank, to kiss the priest's hand, to defer to others' opinions, to offer thanks for every slice of bread, flogged repeatedly, fond of dining with rich relatives, playing the hypocrite before God and man with no other cause than the accepted consciousness of his own unimportance—then tell how this young man presses the slave out of himself one drop at a time, waking up one fine morning to feel that real human blood flows in his veins, not the blood of a slave.[1]

Writing this in his twenty-ninth year, Chekhov interpreted his quest for identity as an emancipation. His wretched childhood and inferior education are formulaic, but his march to independence began when his father's small retail shop went bankrupt and the family moved to Moscow, leaving the sixteen-year-old boy to complete his education at the gymnasium at Taganrog, a grubby port on the Sea of Azov. He began to write short sketches, many wryly humorous, for the school paper. By the time he rejoined his family in 1879 to enter the medical school at Moscow, he had mastered the rudiments of the journeyman writer: brevity and speed. His next step toward independence developed when he became the effective head of the household, supporting his mother and younger siblings by writing innumerable sketches and squibs for the lower stratum of the Moscow press. He wrote them at top speed, and his unrevised first drafts were "printable."

Chekhov received his medical degree in 1884 and was posted to a *zemstvo* hospital in the country some thirty miles outside of Moscow. He worked there for a year, trying in the meantime to establish a general practice in Moscow and, pressed by circumstances, continued to write in order to make ends meet for his family. All of Chekhov's early pieces were published under the pseudonym of Antosha Chekhonte. It requires little insight to recognize that this was a form of denial; he did not wish his medical colleagues to form an image of him as a writer. But his real name is only thinly veiled, and to it be affixed *"honte,"* the French word for shame, whether knowingly or not remaining unknown. However, Chekhov's acquaintances and friends were chiefly drawn from literary and artistic circles. Most of them were struggling or merely scraping by; they were delighted to secure free of charge the services of their young friend, now a qualified physician. Paying patients did not flock to Chekhov, nor did he ever feel his income from medical practice was enough to warrant setting up an office. But his warm, generous nature made it impossible for him to refuse a call, and he continued to live off his literary output. Also, in 1884 he had his first hemoptysis. In retrospect, we know it was tuberculosis, but a single hemoptysis does not make a diagnosis, and Chekhov was quite willing to assume a posture of anosognosia. Repeated episodes of hemoptysis coupled with cough and constitutional symptoms slowly developed and, certainly after 1889, when his brother Nicholas died of tuberculosis, Chekhov was unable to maintain the façade of denial, at least to himself, though he avoided mentioning the disease by name to his family. The inroads of tuberculosis were slow and almost imperceptible; he suffered more conscious pain from hemorrhoids, often aggravated by alternating attacks of diarrhea and constipation. His letters contain more frequent allusions to his rectal problems than to his pulmonary disease, using one level of symptomatic reality to minimize the anxiety engendered by another.

A decisive event in Chekhov's literary career was a letter of praise he received in 1886 from Dmitri Grigorovich, then a man of importance in Russian letters. Comments such as "You have a *real* talent, one which places you in the front rank of the coming generation"[2] were coupled with advice to write less prolifically and to concentrate his energies. It was not easy to cut down production, particularly when money was badly needed, but Chekhov, who had published 129 pieces in 1885 and 112 in 1886, retrenched to 66 in 1887 and only 12 in 1888. Numbers

Anton Chekhov in his garden at Yalta, ca. 1900

tell only part of the story; Chekhov was able to follow Grigorovich's sound advice because he had established relations with Alexis Suvorin, editor of *Novoe Vremia*, a magazine which not only had prestige but paid high rates. That the magazine's policies were right-wing, antilibertarian, antiegalitarian and, of course, anti-Semitic did not bother Chekhov at the time; he was apolitical. His later breach with Suvorin belongs to another chapter; by that time Chekhov had been exposed to repeated reviews admonishing him for keeping his art separate from life and holding as an example for him Tolstoy's commitment to social causes.

Chekhov's own view of his double life as physician and writer during the period 1886 to 1897, when he finally collapsed with a severe attack of tuberculosis, can be epitomized by two excerpts from his correspondence:

You advise me not to pursue two hares at a time and to abandon the practice of medicine . . . I feel more contented and more satisfied when I realize that I have two professions, not one. Medicine is my lawful wife and literature my mistress. When I grow weary of one, I pass the night with the other. This may seem disorderly, but it is not dull, and besides, neither of them suffers because of my infidelity. If I did not have my medical work, it would be hard to give my thought and liberty of spirit to literature.[3]

It was scarcely two years since Grigorovich's letter had set him to writing seriously. The self-criticism inherent in rewriting first drafts, "rejecting his own thoughts," had shown him explicitly the value of "liberty of spirit," and he had a new sense of his own importance, having adopted a new (and double) persona. The following year he sent an autobiographical sketch for publication in a class album to his classmate, Grigory Rossolimo, one of the few physicians with whom he maintained acquaintanceship:

My work in medical sciences has undoubtedly had a serious influence on my literary development; it significantly extended the area of my observations, enriched my knowledge, and only one who is himself a physician can understand the true value of this for me as a writer; this training has also been a guide, and probably because of my closeness to medicine, I have managed to avoid many mistakes. Familiarity with the natural sciences and scientific method has always kept me on my guard. . . . I do not belong to those literary men who adopt a negative attitude toward science, and I would not want to belong to those who achieve everything by cleverness.[4]

An added dimension can be given this position statement from a comment of Chekhov's quoted by Ivan Leontiev-Scheglov: "A simple person looks at the moon and is moved as before something terribly mysterious and unattainable. But an astronomer looks at it with entirely different eyes . . . with him there cannot be any fine illusion! With me, a physician, there are also few illusions. Of course, I'm sorry for this—it somehow desiccates life."[5]

Chekhov's success as a writer stemmed from his ability to adopt a detached clinical attitude, to observe people's conduct, their mixed motives, their compromises with reality—much as a sensible doctor looks at a patient. His ability to detach himself from his immediate environment and transform experience into literature stems at least in part from his adolescent experience of being left on his own in Taganrog to complete his education. Living in part off hand outs from relatives, in part from casual earnings, he developed a streak of self-sufficiency and alienation, an ability to disengage himself from close relationships. Perhaps this helps explain his many romances with women that never came to fruition and his late marriage when ill health reduced his desire for complete independence. Consciously, he tried to create artistic unity out of life's disorder by assimilating his view of human behavior into literary expression. His eye was sharp for telling detail, his ear keen for the cadence of everyday speech, even the speech which partly conceals and partly reveals motive, and he had an almost intuitive grasp of character. His biographer Simmons writes, "In his infinite concern to avoid the superfluous . . . he achieved by artistic measure and economy of means a refinement of expression that was truly classical, and an illusion of reality—based on his favorite touchstones of objectivity, truthfulness, originality, boldness, brevity, and simplicity—that seemed quite complete."[6] But, as is usually the case in fiction or drama, it is the *illusion* of reality which is created, and the *seeming* completeness, though it begins with the writer's work, depends in part upon the reader's ability (or willingness) to follow him in his desire and pursuit of the whole.

Literary success and public acclaim—he was awarded the Pushkin Prize in 1889—did not make Chekhov's life complete. Such phrases as "There is a sort of stagnation in my soul" and "For the lonely man, the desert is everywhere" can be lifted from his letters. He had a semiconscious desire to expand his horizons of action, a motive which, coupled with his frustration and loneliness, led to his famous trip to Sakhalin in 1890–91. For a man who had half-admitted to himself that he had pulmonary tuberculosis, such a trip across the Siberian wastes before the days of the Trans-Siberian railroad was, objectively speaking, sheer folly. And to what end? Chekhov proposed a census of that remote dismal penal colony north of Japan which would be tantamount to a sociological survey (the term had not then been coined) of the life of the exiled felons. Moreover, he proposed to carry out the study without assistants. He prepared for it by reading everything about Sakhalin on which he could lay his hands. He sought help from official quarters but received almost none; the czar's government was not interested in having the facts of life on its Devil's Island exposed to public view. It took Chekhov three months to get there, and he spent almost four months taking notes, interviewing as many convicts as he could, but it was a period during which he saw nothing but misery and human degradation. Any reasonable fool could have told him he was risking his health, wasting his energy, squandering his talents on a lost cause.

Chekhov's interest in Sakhalin was not a sudden fancy. He had read Ivan Goncharov's *Frigate Pallada* as a schoolboy, and Vladimir Korolenko's *Sokolinets* [Escape from Sakhalin], which describes in grim and gory detail the escape of a group of convicts, had been published in 1888, firing Chekhov's imagination further. Chekhov's correspondence during the period of preparation assigns a mixture of motives for the hazardous journey; to different friends he told different stories. Probably a skein of intertwined motives—"literary, scientific, humanitarian, and personal"[7]—impelled him. In some respects the journey to Sakhalin can be likened to the quest in a *Bildungsroman* of middle life, related at many removes of time, place, and culture to Dante's "Nel mezzo del cammin di nostra vita / Mi ritrovai per un selva oscura, / Che la diritta via era smarrita." In many ways Chekhov's life had its perplexities and ambivalences, and certainly the literary milieu of Moscow and St. Petersburgh of the 1890s can be described as a "selva oscura." It does not diminish Chekhov's stature to suggest that at this stage in his life he was groping for resolutions. The perilous journey was a respite and a catharsis, his private bell for inexplicable needs; possibly he finally resolved his quest for emancipation by comparing his "liberation of spirit" as a physician and writer with the lot of the dead souls on Sakhalin. Some sins are not crimes against the state.

On his return he wrote *The Island of Sakhalin,* which was published in 1892, a straightforward piece of reportage describing conditions as he saw them. He had no conviction that such a free-lance study would persuade the government to modify its policies, nor did he ever mount a public campaign for reform, though he continued to correspond with individual convicts whose plight had touched him. Predictably, the book had no effect on penological policy. Viewed in context, Chekhov's mission seems almost a gratuitous act by a man who felt himself superfluous. And, having digested that slice of life, he was satisfied by converting it to a literary experience.

He made one futile gesture to find an audience for his ideas. In 1893 he conceived the notion of submitting *The Island of Sakhalin* as a thesis for the degree of Doctor of Medical Sciences which would have qualified him as a *Privatdozent,* permitting him to lecture at the medical school. He enlisted the aid of Rossolimo, then well on his way to distinction as a neuropathologist, writing: "If I were a teacher, I would try to draw my audience as deeply as possible into the area of the subjective feelings of patients, for I think that would prove really useful to the students."[8]

Chekhov's desire to have a foot in academic medicine may have developed from his experiences the previous year when he had returned to active medical work by helping control a cholera epidemic near Melikhovo where he lived, but that could have been only an immediate precipitating cause. A deeper reason was his sensitivity to the emotions he saw being acted out by the people he knew, as well as the implicit recognition, known so well to any man with first hand medical experience, that these emotions are intensified, even uncovered, in the sickbed. Of course, the dean disregarded the petition for the degree, but it can be construed as an example of Chekhov's partly formed ideas on medical psychology (as distinct from clinical psychiatry, which then dealt chiefly with major organic and functional psychoses). It was half a century before the term "psychosomatic medicine" came into vogue, but we can credit Chekhov with having such an idea in embryo and for having derived it himself.

Chekhov's fascination with human conduct and motivation was deep-seated, and upon it depended his ability to create fictional characters who seemed "real" or "natural." Every critic has commented on the vast number of characters from all walks of life who populate Chekhov's pages. Yet Chekhov was not merely attracted to people as a passing parade; he presented their surfaces in order to illuminate their interiors, hence his famous dictum on the style of naturalism in the Russian Art Theatre with which he was closely identified from 1897 to his death in 1904:

After all, in real life people don't spend every minute shooting at each other, hanging themselves and making confessions of love. They don't spend all their time saying clever things. They're more occupied with eating, drinking, flirting and talking stupidities—and these are the things which ought to be shown on the stage. A play should be written in which people arrive, go away, have dinner, talk about the weather and play cards. Life must be exactly as it is, and people as they are—not on stilts. . . . Let everything on the stage be just as complicated, and at the same time just as simple as it is in life. People eat their dinner, just eat their dinner, and all the time their happiness is being established or their lives are being broken up.[9]

Chekhov projected onto his own characters his personal mode of assimilating experience and reacting to it; the perception of reality from inner needs, regardless of external circumstances. Both in his own life and in his fictions the outlook and self-definition of individuals are informed by and result from an internalization of reality.

But one must exercise caution in pursuing Chekhov's psychological insights and analyzing particular stories as if they were designed to illuminate psychological principles. Chekhov's psychology was based on the ideas current in his time, those of the late nineteenth century. He had no crystal ball to tell him that twentieth century psychodynamics would emphasize the unconscious as a motive force, that its *res gestae* would be the ontogeny of individual cases, tracing current problems back to events in childhood and reconstructing elaborations from such starting points. Using the short story and the stage drama as his chosen media, Chekhov limited himself to presenting the "here and now," the situation as it existed in a small segment of time. On at least one occasion he tried to write a novel but found that the extended form was alien to him. Sharp as were his *aperçus* into an immediate situation, he usually lacked the ability to depict its evolution from initiating causes into florid symptoms.

Nor did Chekhov attempt to systematize or develop a set of generalizations from his insights. On many occasions he disavowed the idea that he, as a writer, should either teach or preach. Although, his early years excepted, he was not a miniaturist, he was a particularist. Much like a pointillist painter, he placed his sentences and short paragraphs on paper as if they were small, discrete spots of color on a canvas, creating a picture which became organized as a cognitive entity only when the reader held it at arm's length and examined it from a middle distance. With too close a view his images do not take shape, nor is the relation of one to another decisive; from too great a distance the particularity of the experience being rendered lacks substance, and even its color pales.

In some of Chekhov's short stories the psychological element is typological, for example: Gromov's break with reality in *Ward 6* (1892) is readily diagnosable as paranoid schizophrenia with transient, ill-structured ideas of persecution, solipsistic withdrawal, and mental deterioration; in *The Black Monk*, Kovrin experiences visual hallucinations with religious content; in *Grief*, the cab driver Potapov displays the need for catharsis when overwhelmed by the death of his son. But some of the most illuminating examples of psychopathology are to be found among the fictive physicians whom Chekhov created. It is in these, the literary counterparts of members of his chosen profession, that Chekhov most clearly shows his hand. The open question is: To what extent did Chekhov's own limited success in medicine contribute to the projection of doctors in his fictions? How did he internalize the reality of his own status? How did he transform life into letters? Let us examine a few of his doctors and see what light they shed on his dilemma.

Dr. Startsev, the hero of *Ionych* (1898), enters as the rural district medical officer stationed outside a small provincial town. He makes the acquaintance of the Turkin family, the pretentious leaders of the bourgeois intelligentsia, who seem to believe they are running a salon. He falls in love with their daughter Katerina, but she has her heart set on studying the pianoforte at the conservatory, and she trifles with him. Soon after she leaves town, Startsev opens his practice; despite his distaste for the narrow-minded provincial types, he prospers. Katerina returns, having found that her musical talent is inadequate for a career. She would now like to marry Startsev, but his interest in her has flickered out. Chekhov leaves him as a greedy, choleric bachelor whose original ideals have been corroded.

Doubtless Chekhov drew upon his own experiences in provincial towns for the setting, upon his own observations of more than one fellow physician who succumbed to materialism, and upon any number of pseudointellectuals for the other characters. It is much the same ambience that Sinclair Lewis described in great detail in *Main Street* and *Babbitt;* both Chekhov and Lewis knew the stifling effect of small towns and hated them. Chekhov's tale is a slice of life, but the picture he draws is too close to the real to be a complete fiction, and his figures are not heroic enough to support the idea of a myth. Underlying the denouement is a theme common to many of Chekhov's stories: namely, that men and women who attempt to develop an intimate relation, whether consummated or not, wind up lonely, frustrated, unhappy, alienated, and defeated. This tells us more about Chekhov than he might wish us to know, but precisely why his Dr. Startsev lacks either the ability to perceive his plight or is unable to escape from it remains uncharted.

A more complex failure is Dr. Ragin in *Ward 6*, the director of a hospital in a small provincial town who gradually withdraws from the task of properly managing his understaffed, poorly equipped hospital, taking refuge in reading philosophy and history, drinking vodka, and eating cucumbers. This doctor rationalizes his maladresse by developing the idea that men must seek peace and satisfaction in themselves, not in the world around them. Though he maintains his internal equipoise, his stance is of little help to the psychotic patients in Ward 6, who are at the mercy of the brutal guard Nikita, who beats them frequently and cheats them of even their few kopecks. Dr. Ragin establishes a quasi friendship with Gromov, a mildly paranoid schizophrenic on the ward, who contrives to be a philosopher of sorts. Dr. Ragin's inadequacy makes it easy for Dr. Khobotov, his scheming assistant, to force his resignation. Ultimately, after a financially ruinous trip to Moscow with a friend, Dr. Ragin is committed to Ward 6, where Nikita beats him and he dies of a stroke, having lost the comfort of his quietist philosophy, finally aware of the years of physical pain and moral suffering which his withdrawn way of life had inflicted on his defenseless patients.

As Chekhov's fiction goes, it is a long story, even a novella, and here he does have space and scope. Step by step, he shows the gradual nature of Dr. Ragin's withdrawal and his increasingly tenuous grasp of reality. The secondary characters are fleshed out; tension is increased by having first a patient, then a fellow physician alternate as deuteragonist to the central character. Even as Chekhov leads the reader slowly into the unreal pseudophilosophical world of Dr. Ragin's prolix dialogues with Gromov, he returns him to the level of reality in the scenes with Dr. Khobotov and the intercalated episode of Dr. Ragin's financial ruin. One passage prefigures the existential mode; Dr. Ragin remarks: "My illness is only that in twenty years I've found only one intelligent person in the whole town, and he's a lunatic. There's no illness whatsoever; I simply fell into a bewitched circle from which there's no exit."[10] As the proverb tells us: Life? One can never get out of it alive.

Shorter than *Ward 6* and narrower in scope is *A Dreary Story* (1889), relating the case of Dr. Stepanovich, a professor of medicine, who describes in the third person his failing mental and physical powers. Insomnia is his chief complaint, but he cannot find a satisfactory cause. The reader is not surprised when the aging professor unwittingly reveals that he is in love with his young ward Katya. Lust and illicit passion are alien to his self-controlled, rational persona; consequently he represses his feelings. The anxiety so engendered manifests itself as insomnia, fear of imminent death, and a congeries of minor psychosomatic symptoms. Much of this story's success depends upon the relatively simple nature of the protagonist's intrapsychic conflict which enables Chekhov to maintain the narrative flow at a single level.

Chekhov's doctors share a lack of self-confidence and purpose; he presents them as incomplete men in an advanced state of copelessness. To generalize that they are projections of himself is a simplistic notion which will not stand under close scrutiny. But Dr. Lvov in *Ivanov* (1888) is young, unmarried, idealistic, and the moral conscience of the play; to that extent he bears a superficial resemblance to his author. However, Lvov stands aghast but impotent as Ivanov cruelly deceives and manipulates his wife, who is dying of tuberculosis. Lvov has a passionate desire to cure humanity's ills but he cannot prevail against Ivanov's cupidity and lechery. Ivanov's wife's distress is made more poignant by Chekhov's casting her as a Jewess who has been rejected by her family for marrying outside her faith and has no recourse. One may speculate that Chekhov was attracted to the theme of intermarriage because in 1886 he was sufficiently in love with a Jewish girl to consider marriage, a scheme which foundered when she would not apostatize and he would not consider civil marriage.

Equally impotent is Dr. Dorn in *The Sea Gull* (1896), an aging bachelor of fifty-five, an engaged bystander to Treplev's love affair with Masha but even more fascinated by Treplev's play. He regrets his limitations: "You know, I've led a varied and discriminating life. I'm satisfied, but if it had ever been my lot to experience the exaltation that comes to artists in their moments of creation, I should have despised this earthly shell ... and I'd have soared to the heights, leaving the world behind."[11] Alas for his lofty *Anspruchsniveau:* when Treplev commits suicide, the doctor and would-be artist is immobilized; confronted by the suffering of his friends, he can say only, "What can I do, what can I do?"[12]

Another aging, disillusioned doctor is Dr. Astrov in *Uncle Vanya* (written 1890, produced 1898). More interested in forestry than medicine, he comments, "Only God knows what our real vocation is": a fair statement of Chekhov's own plight.[13] Astrov imagines that his reforestation scheme—even the 1890s had their ecological problems—is the plan of a scientist-artist-creator-savior whose change in nature can effect a change in man, a romantic notion which is insufficient to conceal that he is a burnt-out case. Although he is able to talk Uncle Vanya out of a suicidal gesture, he is not able to convince Elena (or himself) that his affection for her is substantial enough to be considered love. Nothing happens, nothing is consummated. Astrov is reduced to the vague hope "that when we are sleeping in our graves we may be attended by visions, perhaps even pleasant ones."[14]

The last of Chekhov's stage doctors is the incompetent Ivan Chebutykin in *Three Sisters* (1900–1901). The play deals with the blighted hopes of the principal characters, and Chebutykin's contribution to the general attitude of despair is to add further negative values. Depersonalized and with a schizoid attitude toward reality, he is mildly alcoholic, unlettered, and socially gauche, and little more than a stock fool. In reply to Irina's question about an incident on the boulevard he replies: "What happened? Nothing. Nothing worth talking about. It doesn't matter." The schoolteacher Kulygin attempts to draw the incident out of him, but he replies again: "I don't know. It's all nonsense." To which Kulygin responds: "In a certain seminary a teacher wrote 'nonsense' on a composition, but the pupil, thinking it was Latin, read 'consensus.' "[15] Chebutykin is a grotesque caricature of a man. Instead of marrying the widowed mother of the three sisters (are we supposed to think of them as Fates?), he breaks the woman's clock, a symbolic defloration where none would be required, thereby foreclosing a successful resolution. He abdicates his responsibilities, even pretending ignorance about the arrangements for the duel in which Tuzenbach is fated to die and leave Irina bereft. Pretending to know nothing, he becomes nothing, and is even willing to acknowledge his nonexistence: "Perhaps we imagine that we exist, but we don't really exist at all. . . . Perhaps I'm not even a man at all, but just imagine I've got hands and feet and a head. Perhaps I don't exist at all and only imagine that I walk and eat and sleep. . . . Oh, if only I didn't exist."[16] Finally, Chekhov has managed to reduce one of his doctors to existential nothingness.

There is no doctor in Chekhov's last play, *The Cherry Orchard* (1903-4). Following his severe recrudescence of tuberculosis in 1897, Chekhov gave up any semblance of practicing medicine and confined his waning energies to writing. His chief interest lay in the Moscow Art Theatre, which produced his plays, and through it he met the actress Olga Knipper, who became his wife in 1901. Having disposed of the archetype in Chebutykin, he no longer had any need to create lonely, hollow men out of his fictive physicians.

The most frequent comment about Chekhov's plays is that "Nothing happens." That is, "people just eat their dinner." At the same time the drama of life continues, and the course of these people's lives is being decided at the same time, but they are unable to influence events by insight or will. Even as Chekhov wrote his plays and stories, enjoyed the company of his friends, wrote letters, helped build schools and libraries, courted his wife, and ate his dinner, the tubercle bacillus continued its unremitting work of destruction. The germ which attacked him when he was a young man learning to heal the sick shortened his life, and there is no reason to doubt that for the last seven years of it he knew his time was short. In one sense, the "nothing happens" posture is a defense which implies "nothing is happening to me."

Chekhov died in Germany in 1904. When his doctor wanted to apply an ice bag to his chest, he looked up and said, "One does not put ice upon an empty heart." He then asked for a glass of champagne, drank it, and died. His body was returned to Moscow in a train marked

"Oysters." Had he been alive to witness it, the *bon vivant* in him would have commented on the felicity of the final marriage between champagne and oysters, but as it was, "nothing happened," and, as in Werther's sorrows, Charlotte, like a well-bred girl, went on cutting bread and butter.

CHAPTER 7

William Carlos Williams, M.D.: Physician as Poet

Men of letters and physicians have an interest in those who pursued careers in letters along with their medical work. One of the time-honored technics of medicine is known as the case method, a summary of a patient's medical biography arranged more or less in historical sequence; in fact, we call it taking a history. It will not be out of place, therefore, if an account of William Carlos Williams, M.D., is prefaced by a brief description of the circumstances of his life.

The most convenient source is his own autobiography, published in 1951, a dozen years before he died. Autobiography can be as revealing for its omissions and distortions as for what it states, and Dr. Williams wrote his autobiography with the ear of a litterateur rather than that of a literary historian. The book succeeds in presenting an attractive picture of a vital man, what he thought, and how he felt. It is anecdotal in method, and one sees the image of Dr. Williams diffracted through a multifaceted prism of short sketches, a flash of light here, a dab of local color there. The autobiography will earn no praise from pedants nor from the feuilletonists of the minutiae of literary history. Its chronology is haphazard; certain events are not precisely defined in time and space; unidentified people appear and disappear. Yet the outline of Dr. Williams's life is clear.

He was born in 1883 in Rutherford, New Jersey, then a small town on the Erie Railroad, some eight miles southeast of Paterson, the county seat of Passaic County. His entire life centered around Rutherford; he grew up there, went to public school there, married a Rutherford girl, practiced medicine, reared his children, wrote his poems, plays, and novels, all in Rutherford. In an age of great social mobility William Carlos Williams remained fixed and stable. We associate his name with a single town more than any American poet since the Concord school. His father was an Englishman who never became an American citizen. He was employed as an executive by a New York mercantile house and occasionally had to take prolonged business trips to South America. However, he established himself and his family in Rutherford, serving as the superintendent of the local Unitarian Sunday School for almost twenty years. His wife, the physician-poet's mother, was a Hurrard from Martinique, of mixed French and Spanish descent; her native tongue was Spanish, and she gave her first-born son the middle name Carlos in honor of her eldest brother. The Williamses were not affluent but able to live in comfort; they had enough to educate their two boys and for a certain amount of foreign travel.

Dr. Williams describes what seems to be, or seemed to him, a normal, healthy boyhood in a small American town at the end of the nineteenth century: the bandstand in the park, the streetcar running along the main street, the boys in corduroy knickerbockers, and the girls with braided hair in gingham shirtwaists. Yet he describes incidents which would make a psychiatrist's nose twitch: Williams persisted in drinking milk from his bottle until he was six; his mother had a peculiar seizure disorder during which she claimed to have second sight; she would also "whale hell out of us with anything she could lay her hands on"; his father's half brother suffered from a form of religious paranoia and once frightened him deeply by attacking one of his playmates. Williams had no sisters or female cousins and was plagued by an intense curiosity about female genitalia. Oddly enough, these traumas which he recounts so guilelessly never seem to have bothered him very much. It was all part of a normal boyhood in a small American town, just as normal as blueberry pie.

In 1897, when his father had to go to Buenos Aires for a business trip lasting over a year, Williams's mother took him and his younger brother to Europe. The boys went first to the Château de Lancy school near Geneva, then spent several months in Paris. When they returned in 1899, they were sent to the Horace Mann School, then on Morningside Heights at 120th Street. He went directly from prep school into medical school, sans college. This lacuna may account for his nonintellectualism. Who among us could write, or would if it were true, as Williams did in his seventh decade: "Only yesterday . . . did I realize for the first time that the derivation of the adjective venereal is from Venus! And I a physician practicing medicine for the past forty years."[1]

Whether his preparatory schooling was well rounded or not, Williams matriculated at the University of Pennsylvania School of Medicine in 1902 and received his M.D. degree there in 1906.

The years in Philadelphia proved to be decisive. Here Williams made friends with Ezra Pound, a dominant influence, and with Hilda Doolittle (the poet H.D.), whose father was professor of astronomy at the University. It was under their encouragement and influence that he first began to write. Until this time he had had only a conventional, alert schoolboy's approach to literature. He enjoyed reading, but most of it was "on assignment" and very little of it was spontaneous. He certainly had not previously set himself to writing as a deliberate vocation. Also, while in medical school, he made friends with Charles Demuth, the first of many contemporary painters whom he was to number among his intimates. In addition, he met John Wilson, an older man, who was also a painter. On occasion he would visit Wilson's studio, be given an easel, a canvas, some paint, and brushes, and then try his hand at painting. He became interested in the theater and participated in campus theatricals. Up to this time neither Williams nor anyone else believed he had the talent to become a creative artist. Yet by his last year in medical school he had begun work on what he describes as "an Endymion-like long romantic poem."[2] Mercifully, and with good judgment, he burnt it a couple of years later, but it was a start.

Following medical school, Williams returned to New York for his hospital training. He spent a year at French Hospital, then at Thirty-fourth Street between Ninth and Tenth Avenues, followed by a year at the Nursery and Child's Hospital at Sixty-first Street and Tenth Avenue, just above Hell's Kitchen. Traditionally, the life of a house officer in a hospital in a big city is filled with lurid anecdotes, and the West Side of Manhattan need take a back seat to no other area for the rich variety of tabloid type human drama which Williams encountered and recounts with such gusto. Even as he learned the art of medical practice and the rudiments of surgery, how to deliver women, and take care of their babies, he continued to write poems. Toward the end of his houseship he became betrothed to Florence Herman whom he married three years later. Between his hospital appointments and the time he set up practice he went on an extended trip to Europe, visiting Ezra Pound in London, meeting Yeats and other figures on the London literary scene, as well as seeing his brother Ed, who was studying architecture in Rome, and the glories of Italian Renaissance painting, sculpture, and architecture. He does not tell us whether he showed any of his poems to Pound or, if so, what Pound thought of them.

Williams decided to go into general practice in Rutherford, believing

William Carlos Williams's home at 9 Ridge Road, Rutherford, New Jersey. Photograph by Walter F. Goddard

The Great Falls of the Passaic River at Paterson, New Jersey. Photograph by Walter F. Goddard

that the demands of a city practice would take time from writing. This proved to be a wise decision, as general practice in Passaic County is no great tax on the intellect and does provide one with a certain amount of raw human material. In 1910 his first office was the old kitchen pantry of his parents' house; the front hall served as a waiting room. Before beginning practice he had had a local printer publish his first volume of verse, a paperbound pamphlet titled *Poems*. It appeared in 1909, and four copies were sold at twenty-five cents each. His practice increased; by the end of 1912 he was able to marry and set up light housekeeping next door to his parents. The next year, when his wife was already seven months pregnant, they bought the commodious house at 9 Ridge Road in Rutherford which was to serve as their home and his office for the next fifty years. Williams's interest in pediatrics had been stimulated by his year at the Nursery and Child's Hospital, and he continued to enrich his skills in that field, then in its infancy, by working as a volunteer at Babies' Hospital in New York three afternoons a week, then at the Post-Graduate Medical School and Hospital. In later years, although his practice was general, it always had a higher proportion of obstetric and pediatric patients than was usual. He retired from active practice in 1951 following his first cerebrovascular accident. Although his health gradually failed over the next twelve years, he continued to write poetry, and his work of this time included some of his finest pieces, in some aspects his richest vintage.

The period before World War I was marked in literature by the rise of free verse and the imagist school in poetry and in visual art by the impact of the Armory show of French impressionist, postimpressionist, fauve, and cubist paintings (1913). These two movements complemented each other. Williams had close friends in both fields, and his poetry exhibits these influences. He became a frequent visitor at Alfred Stieglitz's studio in New York. He met Walter Arensberg, that sympathetic patron of both modern poetry and painting. Among his painter friends were Charles Sheeler, Marsden Hartley, William Zorach, and, to a lesser degree, Marcel Duchamp and Man Ray. In Greenwich Village he was on close terms with Maxwell Bodenheim, Lola Ridge, Louise Bogan, Marianne Moore, and Alfred Kreymborg. He even played the male lead in Kreymborg's play, *Mushrooms,* when it was put on by the Provincetown Players in MacDougal Street. Other friends included Malcolm Cowley and Kenneth Burke, whom Williams visited many times in later years at his home in rural New Jersey. His poems were printed in a variety of half-forgotten little magazines of the decade. Through the influence of Ezra Pound, Williams's second book of poems, *The Tempers,* was published in London in 1913. Somehow, during the war years he managed to write enough poems for three books, *Al que quiere, Sour Grapes,* and *Kora in Hell,* for each of which he paid the Four Seas Company of Boston something in the neighborhood of $250 to print. Some of his better poems appeared in *The Dial,* in *Others,* and in Harriet Monroe's *Poetry.* Yet poetry and the literary-artistic swim was only part of his life. He always returned from New York refreshed, ready to take up the daily round of medical practice in Rutherford, delivering babies, diagnosing childhood diseases, and taking care of the sick, the wounded, and the depraved.

With complete candor Williams lets us into the secrets of his workshop. He explains the advantage of having his roots in Rutherford and his friends in New York: "There is a great virtue in such an isolation. It permits a fair interval for thought. That is, what I call thinking, which is mainly scribbling. It has always been during the act of scribbling that I have gotten most of my satisfactions."[3] For example, he describes afternoon visits to Kenneth Burke forty miles west of Rutherford in Andover, New Jersey:

All afternoon would be spent in argument, we hugging our glasses of applejack. Reactivated, I'd go home to the eternally rewarding game of scribbling. Thought was never an isolated thing with me; it was a game of tests and balances, to be proved by the written word. Then would come the trial. The poem would be submitted to some random editor, or otherwise meet its fate in the world. . . .

When and where, after such forays, did I or could I write? Time meant nothing to me. I might be in the middle of some flu epidemic, the phone ringing day and night, madly, not a moment free. That made no difference. If the fit was on me . . . I would be like a woman at term; no matter what else was up, that demand had to be met.

Five minutes, ten minutes, can always be found. I had my typewriter in my office desk. All I needed was to pull up the leaf to which it was fastened and I was ready to go. I worked at top speed. If a patient came in at the door while I was in the middle of a sentence, bang would go the machine—I was a physician. When the patient left, up would come the machine. My head developed a technic . . . Finally, after eleven at night, when the last patient had been put to bed, I could always find the time to bang out ten or twelve pages. In fact, I couldn't rest until I had freed my mind from the obsessions which had been tormenting me all day. Cleansed of that torment, having scribbled, I could rest.[4]

One gets no scent here of "profound emotion recollected in tranquility." One is even left with the uneasy feeling that a goodly number of such poems, or scribblings, were sent off in the following morning's mail to that hypothetic random editor "to meet their fate in the world." It is evident that Williams wrote on impulse, and it is fortunate that he was a man of good, warm, humanitarian impulses. One can even construct hypothetic jacket blurbs: "Written at white heat, Dr. Williams' poems lay bare the human soul as surely as with a scalpel," or "Untrammeled by convention, Dr. Williams' sure sense of poetic imagery captures those rare moments of insight." Somehow, such words as "incisive," "well-disciplined," and "poetic scrutiny of both the cosmos and this world" do not occur to one. It is a happy coincidence in time that Williams's "method" or work habits happened to flourish in that period in literary and artistic history when freedom of forms, of expression, and of experimentation were all highly valued. In terms of the aspirations of his times and the requirements of his contemporaries we must account him a successful poet. If Williams did not take the time or make the effort to revise and rewrite, there is a class of reader which does not feel obliged or even stimulated to reread.

One can readily see how the exigencies of medical practice determined his work habits. Thus, his most frequent form of literary utterance would be the short lyric poem, the result of the inspiration of the moment. His friend Kenneth Burke describes him as "master of the glimpse."[5] It is somewhat less obvious that there is an element in the nature of general medical practice which has something in common with the sort of lyric that Williams excelled in. The general practitioner does not have much time for reflection. He is confronted at any hour of the day or night with a medical problem in medias res. He deals with the here and the now, the visible, tangible, audible, percussible, smellable, and even tastable. There is no time for a lengthy prologue; he has to make full use of his five senses, come to a decision about the nature of the problem, and plan a course of action. This is what Williams did as a doctor and what he did as a poet. His visual images are in the form of adroit linear sketches; almost never do we find a finished landscape. His ear is attuned to the main melody; rarely do we encounter subtle verbal harmonies, rarely any counterpoint of ideas matched against the main theme. His poetic vocabulary is based on simple words and short phrases; this was the style in which he communicated to his patients; this was the style in which he communicated to his readers. In many respects one can draw an analogy between Williams and Chekhov, who was also a general practitioner of medicine. Chekhov, too, opens his stories in medias res; the incident itself is often the entire story. Chekhov, too, communicates in simple language, by a direct gesture, a short phrase; the action on the surface is designed to reveal the character beneath. Yet in all fairness it must be pointed out that Chekhov was incomparably the greater artist, a writer with a much wider range; but Chekhov finally gave up medical practice and devoted his full time to writing.

Chekhov was ahead of his times, won few honors, and died young. Williams was attuned to his times, won many honors, and lived to a ripe old age; during his last years he could have posed as the Sage of Rutherford, a Grand Old Man of avant-garde American literature. The record shows that he won the Guarantor's award from *Poetry* in 1924 and the Dial prize in 1926. His long poem, *Paterson,* won the National Book award for poetry in 1950. He was given the Gold Medal for poetry by the National Institute of Arts and Letters in 1963 and, also posthumously, the Pulitzer Prize. By the time he died he had published about forty books of poetry, short stories, and plays.

What Williams claimed for himself in his *Autobiography* was a special advantage accruing to a physician-poet, the unique insight of the humane, practicing physician who also has a literary gift:

> My "medicine" was the thing that gained me entrance to ... (the) secret gardens of the self. It lay there, another world, in the self. I was permitted by my medical badge to follow the poor, defeated body into those gulfs and grottoes. And the astonishing thing is that at such times and in such places— foul as they may be with the stinking ischiorectal abscesses of our comings and goings—just there, the thing, in all its greatest beauty, may for a moment be freed to fly for a moment guiltily about the room. In illness, in the permission I as a physician have had to be present at deaths and births, at the tormented battles between daughter and diabolic mother, shattered by a gone brain—just there—for a split second—from one side or the other, it has fluttered before me for a moment.[6]

It is possibly for his sometimes less than articulate feeling for human values that we consider Williams as a source of inspiration. It would be empty rhetoric to ask what "the thing" is, but it is a sensation of presence which many people have experienced.

The selection of points of merit in Williams's poetry is bound to be subjective and arbitrary. I have always been struck by the strong influence on Williams of styles in the visual arts. One can document this by noting his close friendship with many painters, his frequent allusions to specific pictures in his poems (*Pictures from Breughel*), but possibly best in his own lines:

> I, a writer, at one time hipped on
> painting, did not consider
> the effects, painting.[7]

It is not unusual for poetry to influence painting; thousands of pictures have been turned out to illustrate a literary theme. But the reverse situation is uncommon. Painting, by the inherent limit of canvas and frame and by the fact that the entire work is exposed at one view, tends to be static; poetry and prose extend in time and have a sense of movement. Cubism managed to eliminate the spatially fixed viewpoint, examining a subject from many angles, even seeing around corners. The technic involved reducing the subject to its essentials of profile, form, and volume, then reorganizing them into a meaningful configuration. Even as cubism succeeded in creating static images from a shifting eyepoint, futurism and vorticism created the illusion of movement within a fixed frame. The best example of the latter is Duchamp's *Nude Descending a Staircase,* the most publicized item in the Armory show, a picture Williams cites by name on more than one occasion. Williams continues his poem, *Raindrops on a Briar:*

> painting,
> for that reason, static, on
>
> the contrary the stillness of
> the objects—the flowers, the gloves—
> freed them precisely by that
> from a necessity merely to move
>
> in space as if they had been—
> not children! but the thinking male
> or the charged and deliver-
> ing female frantic with ecstasies;
>
> served rather to present, for me,
> a more pregnant motion.[8]

Williams has a close affinity with Chagall whom, so far as I recall, he does not mention in any of his poems. Chagall's chosen milieu is based on his recollections of his youth in Vitebsk, much as Williams's frame of reference is the Rutherford-Paterson area of his boyhood and young manhood. In addition to the "how dear to my heart are the scenes of my childhood" motif, both Chagall and Williams share a sentimental-imaginative treatment of the mundane objects associated with it.

A stock example of the impact of analytic cubism on poetry is Wallace Stevens's *Thirteen Ways of Looking at a Blackbird;* the title alone is a dead giveaway. Williams has an even greater number of poems than Stevens which would qualify as notes for a painting. Some are influenced by his early imagist experiments, but it would be rash to classify any given poem as impressionist, cubist, vorticist, or other form. The frequently anthologized poem, *The Yachts,* is intensely visual, combining a shifting eyepoint with a sense of movement. Part of its beginning suggests a seascape in the pictorial tradition extending from Turner through Boudin to Dufy:

> Mothlike in mists, scintillant in the minute
> brilliance of cloudless days, with broad
> bellying sails
> they glide to the wind tossing the
> green water
> from their sharp prows while over them
> the new crew crawls
> and like, solicitously grooming them,
> releasing,
> making fast as they turn, lean far
> over and having
> caught the wind again, side by side,
> head for the mark.[9]

Another type of canvas is seen in Williams's pictorial skill in depicting the muted landscape of *Spring Strains;* the palette is softer and the brush strokes delineate the subject more precisely:

> In a tissue-thin monotone of blue-grey buds
> crowded erect with desire against the sky—
>   tense blue-grey twigs
> slenderly anchoring them down, drawing
> them in—
>   two blue-grey birds chasing
> a third in circles, angles,
> swift convergings to a point that bursts
> instantly!
>   Vibrant bowing limbs
> pull downward, sucking in the sky
> that bulges from behind, plastering itself
> against them in packet rifts, rock blue
> and dirty orange!
>   But—
> (Hold hard, rigid jointed trees!)
> the blinding and red-edged sun-blue—
> creeping energy, concentrated
> counterforce—welds sky, buds, trees,
> rivets them in one puckering hold![10]

This passage is imagism at its trivial best, but Williams is more incisive when he gives us the direct, undeveloped image in *Paterson: The Falls*— "The Falls, combed into straight lines / from that rafter of a rock's lip."[11]

Yet curiously, the poems taken directly from famous paintings seem stiff and unconvincing. *The Dance,* modeled after Breughel's *Kermesse,* is merely a short description, all on the surface, and the ten poems which comprise the *Pictures from Breughel* rarely transcend the literal. We learn something about Williams's *character* when we find that the pictures he chooses from Breughel are chiefly the scenes of peasant life and the children's games; apparently he was not attracted by the other side of Breughel, the bitter, satiric illustrations of biblical and classical maxims, nor by the Bosch-like imagery of his private inferno. Williams seems to have chosen the "wholesome" pictures over those which might have given a hint about Breughel's morbid introspection.

Music also inspired Williams to poetic outbursts. He recorded his reactions to Brahms's First Piano Concerto and to the bells of the local Catholic church. The campanile sounds a cheerful note:

> Tho' I'm no Catholic
> I listen hard when the bells
> in the yellow-brick tower
> of their new church
>
> ring down the leaves
> ring in the frost upon them
> and the death of flowers
> ring out the grackle . . .
>
> . . . Let them ring
> for the eyes and ring for
> the hands and ring for
> the children of my friend
>
> who no longer hears
> them ring.[12]

One does not doubt that the bells are ringing for Williams as he drives by the church on his way to the hospital. It even suggests tinnitus. By contrast, *The Desert Music* is a long and more ambitious poem concerning a trip to Mexico when he was old and ailing, in the mood to be restored by warmth, sunshine, and colorful native music and dances. Parts of the poem are awkward and musically naïve, unintentionally; but the concluding quatrain affirms a sound biologic attitude:

> And I could not help thinking
> of the wonders of the brain that
> hears the music and of our
> skill sometimes to record it.[13]

I do not think a poet who was neither a biologist nor a physician would have stated his conclusion in quite that way.

His poem, *The Orchestra*, is probably the most characteristic of his style in the years between 1939 and his death. It employs the triadic stanza with the measured line and the variable foot. A profitable subject for a doctoral thesis done with the aid of a computer might be a statistical analysis of the norm and deviation from this formal and metrical device. Williams began experimenting with it in the mid-1920s in *Paterson*, for free verse was by then as dead as Queen Anne. Over the years he perfected his personal use of this rhetorical device, and in his hands it proved to be an effective way of making those statements about man and the world which he chose to make. One may profitably compare his broken line with the brush strokes of Van Gogh or the pointillisms of Seurat. I would not go so far as to say, as one critic has, that Williams's "poetic line is organically welded to American speech as muscle to bone," inasmuch as American speech is quite variegated in its rhythms and patterns, so varied as to defy ready classification. In all fairness to Williams, I do not think he ever came out and said that his triadic stanza with its measured line and variable foot was distinctively American. Maybe he was too polite to come out and say that otherwise well-intentioned critics were talking nonsense. What Williams actually did say in his lecture, "An Approach to the Poem," before the English Institute in 1947 was:

> We must break down
>   the line
>   the sentence
> to get at the unit of the measure in order to
>   build again.[14]

This was the nature of his break with traditional verse forms and conventional prosody. He amplified his idea of "measure" as follows:

> What we today, I believe, are trying to do is not only to disengage the elements of the measure but also to seek what we believe is there: a new measure or a new way of measuring . . . a poem that will be commensurate with the social, economic world in which we are living as contrasted with the past that will return to us our sense of reality in the poem. It is in many ways a different world from the past calling for different "signs," "terms" of different scope, if we are to make that which was recognizable also to us today. We are nosing along a mysterious coast line and have not yet broached the continent. An attitude toward it is all I am proposing.[15]

At about the same time as this statement, he wrote the following lines in
The Desert Music:

> Only the counted poem, to an exact measure:
> to imitate, not to copy nature . . .
>   Only the poem
> only the made poem, to get said what must
> be said, not to copy nature, sticks
> in our throats.[16]

A few years later he wrote nine short exercises titled "Some Simple
Measures in the American Idiom and the Variable Foot," but they can
scarcely be counted among his triumphs. Williams was a man of his
times and he varied his metrical practices freely. Perhaps his last
explicit comment occurs as the closing lines of his *Tribute to Neruda the
Collector of Seashells* where he speaks of "the variable pitch / which
modern verse requires."[17] He makes no hard and fast rule about the
triadic stanza, the measured line, and the variable foot.

Let us return to *The Orchestra* with its triadic stanza. It is not a perfect
poem by any means, but after seven introductory triads Williams
sounds his theme:

> Ah, ah, and ah!
>   together, unattuned
>   seeking a common tone.
> Love is that common tone
>   shall raise his fiery head
>   and sound his note.

Then Williams develops the theme.

> The purpose of an orchestra
>   is to organize those sounds
>   and hold them
> to an assembled order
>   in spite of the
>   "wrong note." Well, shall we
> think or listen? Is there a sound addressed
>   not wholly to the ear?

And after a few more stanzas of musical development, he states his
coda:

> Now is the time
>   in spite of the "wrong note"

        I love you. My heart is
innocent.
        And this the first
        (and last) day of the world
The birds twitter now anew
        but a design
        surmounts their twittering.
It is a design of a man
        that makes them twitter.
        It is a design.[18]

Surely this is an ennobling sentiment. One listens to an orchestra and thinks of love as the motive force of art, that love and art are in some way welded to the order imposed on sound by music written for an orchestra, that this love with art and with order creates a cosmos broad enough to encompass a few "wrong notes." One is not quite certain what the "wrong note" implies; is it like Whitman's "barbaric yawp," does it imply human error and fallibility, or does it indicate that in even the best-ordered cosmos there is some unresolved discordant element? However, despite the "wrong note" we learn that Williams loves someone (a previously unspecified "you" appears at line 76), and his heart is innocent. This great love affair takes place on the first and last day of the world ("But our beginnings never know our ends / Why have we not developed into friends?") whenever that day is, and then the birds twitter, one gathers in appreciation of this man-made cosmos, and one hopes in tune with the music of the orchestra with love and with order. It is all very nice, and I am sure there are a great many people who can derive meaning and pleasure from it. I find the thought at once simplistic, stated in an unnecessarily confused manner, and marred by such flat-toned phrases as "The purpose of an orchestra is to organize those sounds and hold them to an assembled order" which sounds like a poorly written definition in a pretentious textbook.

Williams is best enjoyed as an imagist-impressionist poet. His much quoted short poem, *The Red Wheelbarrow,* is typical of this purely denotative vein:

                So much depends
                upon
                a red wheel
                barrow
                glazed with rain
                water
                beside the white
                chickens[19]

I can hear the reedy voice of one poet and critic asking, "And sir, precisely what depends on the red wheelbarrow?"

Unfortunately, Williams does not choose to tell us what precisely depends on the red wheelbarrow, and the reader is left to supply his own conclusion, whether rightly or wrongly. I am reminded of Gerard Manley Hopkins's comment on poems by R. W. Dixon, "He is faulty by a certain vagueness of form, some unpleasing rhymes, and most by an obscurity—partly of thought, partly of expression—suggesting a deeper meaning behind the text, without leaving the reader any decisive clue to find it." Williams is not obscure because of his vocabulary or syntax. His images, like the red wheelbarrow, are optically precise, but the associations he has with it are neither explicit nor clearly formulated in his own mind. Granted that some poets may be excessively rational, even to the point of being unfeeling, but Williams often goes to the other extreme, an excess of feeling or sympathy with the subject of his poem at the expense of adequate reasoning about it. There is a considerable body of readers who do not find that very much of importance depends on the red wheelbarrow. In such instances Williams fails to convince us of the value of his predicate.

Williams wrote a number of poems to prominent figures of the day. The list is quite revealing: one to Ezra Pound, an *Elegy for D. H. Lawrence,* another elegy *To Ford Madox Ford in Heaven;* these make an oddly assorted set of literary bedfellows. The one to Pound is weak and the elegy for Lawrence, though deeply felt, cannot be rated a success. However, *To Ford Madox Ford in Heaven* must be ranked as one of Williams's more attractive pieces; it shows one of his rare flashes of good humor in poetry. Although in his private life he was usually an amusing conversationalist, he took pains to conceal his charming wit and humor when he wrote poetry. I never cease to be amazed at the masks some people will don when they wear their "public face." It begins with the lines "Is it any better in Heaven, my friend Ford, / than you found it in Provence?" and closes with

> Provence! the fat assed Ford will never
>   again strain the chairs of your cafés,
> pull and pare for his dish your sacred garlic,
>   grunt and sweat and lick
> his lips. Gross as the world he has left to
>   us he has become
> a part of that of which you were the known
>   part, Provence, he loved so well.[20]

The elegy on Ford was written in 1940 at the request of the editors of *Furioso* in which it first appeared. It is not written in Williams's habitual broken rhythms but has a more conventionally elegiac flow. One may question whether Williams did not, on this occasion, drop his self-conscious stance of creating his own verse rhythms, whether traditional speech patterns were more deeply built into his auditory imagination than he would care to confess, or, conversely, whether he deliberately adopted a new posture for the occasion. As an elegy it is free from the customary pompous nonsense, and the reader can be grateful that medical training does enable a poet to consider the body of a dead friend with some objectivity. Doctors see too much of death to mourn in the usual way.

Other personages to whom Williams addressed poems were Sibelius in a poem titled *Tapiola*, Albert Einstein in a poem titled *St. Francis Einstein of the Daffodils*—the comparison eludes me—and, curiously, one *To the Ghost of Marjorie Kinnan Rawlings*. The gallery is small and rather selective, especially when one considers all the prominent people Williams knew. I am a bit surprised not to find one on Albert Schweitzer, the only man in Africa in the 1960s who could wear a pith helmet and get away with it; but Schweitzer did outlive Williams, and possibly Dr. Williams thought it improper to pass poetic comment on a fellow practitioner while he was still alive and in active practice. *The Crimson Cyclamen* is Williams's tribute in fawn colors to the memory of his friend Charles Demuth, an able American painter who died of diabetes before the discovery of insulin.

There are some items one does not find in Williams's poems, at least not to any conspicuous degree. One does not find satire. An occasional flash of good humor, an occasional use of irony, not usually adroitly managed, as found in the reiterated refrain "Beautiful Thing" in *Episode* from Book III, *Paterson*, which is heard thirteen times in a poem of 140 short-footed lines; but deliberate satire is outside Williams's range. Satire is born of an intolerable pain and anger at the foibles of the world, sometimes coupled with a desire to reform it. Williams accepted the world as he found it. He was not unaware of its short-comings and social injustices; he merely did not use it as a subject for poetry. In this respect he differed sharply from John Arbuthnot, and Tobias Smollett. Yet oddly, Arbuthnot's contemporaries praised him even as Williams's did him for his "sense of humanity." Therefore, it is not necessarily a sense of humanity that stays the poet's hand from satire; it may be a lack of aptitude for it. Williams wrote few poems of social criticism; one recalls the lamentable verses on Sacco and Vanzetti titled *Impromptu: The Suckers* (1927). I quote the third and fourth stanzas:

> Why in the hell didn't they choose some other
> kind of "unprejudiced adviser" for their
> death council? instead of sticking to that
> autocratic strain of Boston backwash, except
> that the council was far from unprejudiced
> but the product of a rejected, discredited
> class long since outgrown except for use in
> courts and school, and that they
> wanted it so—
>
> Why didn't they choose at least one decent
> Jew or some fair-minded Negro or anybody
> but such a triumvirate of inversion, the
> New England aristocracy, bent on working off
> a grudge against you, Americans, you
> are the suckers, you are the ones who will
> be going up on the eleventh to get the current
> shot into you, for the glory of the state
> and the perpetuation of abstract justice—[21]

Everyone who was anyone in 1926 and 1927 was writing about Sacco and Vanzetti, and Williams's polemics are not so disastrous as some of the ephemera of the period. My only cavil is why was he so uncritical as to include it in the New Directions book, *Selected Poems,* published in 1949. As a doctor, Williams may have buried his mistakes; as a poet, he published them.

There are also a few collateral remarks about labor problems and strikes in *Paterson,* but Williams cannot be considered a "social poet" in any sense. There is just about enough social conscience in his poems to show that he read the morning papers and knew when people were being mistreated.

Another element conspicuously lacking in Williams's poems is medical material. We get occasional whiffs of the medical world in "An old lady dying of diabetes," "By the road to the contagious hospital," and an occasional allusion to nurses or patients. But these notations merely represent the physical world Dr. Williams moved in. His poems are not about medicine, a disease, or the impact of illness on a given individual, real or hypothetic. True, Marin Marias (1656–1728), a French baroque composer, did write "Tableau de l'Operation de la Taille," a musical description of an operation for the stone, and George Onslow (1784–1853) an Anglo-French composer did compose "Le Quintette de la Balle," in which he describes his emotions after an accident in 1829 when he was hit in the side of the face by a spent bullet while hunting wolf. But these works are not artistically successful. I scarcely think that the A.M.A. would have commissioned Dr. Williams to write a set of verses in honor of National Gallbladder Week. One modest exception is a poem titled *Le Médecin Malgré Lui,* but its subject is the poet's role in life rather than the substance of medicine:

> Oh I suppose I should
> wash the walls of my office
> polish rust from my instruments and
>   keep them
> definitely in order
> build shelves in the laboratory
> empty out the old stains . . .
>
> Who can tell? I might be
> a credit to my Lady Happiness
> and never think anything
> but a white thought![22]

Williams reserved his medical material for his short stories. He published three collections of them: *The Knife of the Times* (1932), *Life Along the Passaic River* (1938), and *Make Light of It* (1950). The stories are in the form of short sketches and anecdotes, the characters are drawn with swift linear strokes, and the dialogue is "natural." Williams was a good observer of the daily life around him, had some insight into the motivation and manners of the lower and lower-middle classes in the Rutherford-Paterson mill-town area, and a good ear for their actual speech, much better than in his poems. Many of the stories deal with the sick, the damaged, the deranged, and the deviated. They show that Williams was a good doctor and knew his patients. They do not show that he was a very good short story writer; he had a knack for turning out the sort of short piece which was popular with editors in the avant-garde little magazine press of the late 1920s, 1930s, and even the 1940s. "The Use of Force" describes his efforts to get a six-year-old girl with suspected diphtheria to open her mouth so he can look down her throat; as a symbolic rape it fails to satisfy. Another story, "A Night in June," describes the delivery at her home of a stocky Italian multi-gravida with varicose veins. Their realism is obvious, but they do not rise above that level. One of the more interesting stories is titled "A Descendant of Kings." It deals with the misfortunes of a young man who had quite a career as a stud, but who became impotent after he was double-crossed by a schoolteacher from Boston. He managed to recover a moiety of his potency after he was gored by a bull. I suppose one is intended to read into this story some of the symbolism of Adonis gored by a boar, but the innumerable ordinary female bodies that this young man, named "Stewie," worked over are not quite surrogates for Venus, nor are his innumerable ordinary rough-and-tumble rolls in the hay quite sufficient in quality to be a votive offering to a latter-day goddess of beauty. The business of being gored by a bull suggests imperfectly assimilated and undigested Ernest Hemingway, somewhat watered down, and the information supplied somewhat gratuitously that "Stewie" had a partially successful career as a banjo player does not add stature to his image as a symbol; in fact, it lends a somewhat ludicrous note to the tale.

Nonetheless, one must infer that the reputation Williams had for his interest in people derives largely from these short stories and from the fact that reviewers and critics knew that he was a practicing physician. Van Wyck Brooks speaks of him as "insatiably interested in human nature" and also of "the doctor's tender sympathetic feeling." To digress briefly, during the late 1930s and early 1940s one of the common catch phrases was "Do you like people?" The socially desirable answer was "Yes, I like people!" We see this attitude reflected in such books as Carl Sandburg's *The People, Yes*. It was the era of the common man! Predictably Williams's "sense of humanity" was an approved value of that particular cultural trend. However, alternative views are possible. I can recall retorting to one psychologist who asked me whether I "liked people" with the blunt comment, "Some yes, others no!" I seriously question whether an indiscriminate liking for people is a virtue; it is, rather, a confession of uncritical acceptance. Yet this may be one reason why Williams went into general practice, and I became a pathologist. He was willing to accept the world and people in it as they were; I reserve the right to review them under the microscope and look daily at their weaknesses, faults, malformations, and diseases.

Let us consider briefly his two books which reputable critics praise most highly. The first is a book of prose titled *In the American Grain* and the second a long poem in five books titled *Paterson*. To write *In the American Grain*, Williams took off about nine months to a year from practice in 1923 to 1924. His stated purpose was "to give the impression, an inclusive definition, of what these men of whom I am writing have come to be for us. That they have made themselves part of us and that that is what we are. I want to make it clear that they are us, the American make-up, that we are what they have made us by their deeds and so remain in the American."[23] This is what he told his publisher, Charles Boni, who then added the word "grain."

In the American Grain can easily and accurately be called a poet's slices of historical life. Unlike the books of short lyric poems it cannot be considered as a collection of outbursts turned out on the typewriter in between patients and house calls. It was worked and reworked, and we must assume that its effects are deliberate. It would be puerile and superbly irrelevant to point out that history written by a poet is not the same thing as history written by a historian. One has no right to expect an increment to one's body of factual knowledge; one may legitimately expect new insights from a mind untrammeled by academic conventions. To some extent Williams delivers the goods. However, one must take into account that he himself was a first-generation American and was trying to determine his own national heritage. Put crudely, this is "what America means to me." Williams's canvas is contained in some twenty sketches or word pictures (I hesitate to call such lyric prose by the mundane label, essays) covering a rather idiosyncratic selection of characters. Again, the omissions are as revealing as the inclusions. Seven of the sections deal with the early explorers: Eric the Red, Columbus, Cortez, Ponce de Leon, DeSoto, Raleigh, and Champlain; three with early Massachusetts: the Pilgrims, Thomas Morton of Merrymount, and Cotton Mather; and six deal with the Revolution and early Federal period: Father Rales, Daniel Boone, George Washington, Benjamin Franklin, John Paul Jones, and Aaron Burr. Only two of the sections deal with nineteenth-century matters, a longish essay on Poe, and a single page on Abraham Lincoln. One looks in vain for Jefferson, Lewis and Clark, John Quincy Adams, Jonathan Edwards, Alexander Hamilton, John Marshall, and others. However, one cannot expect a systematic treatment of history or biography from a poet.

The result of a lack of system and a cubist's shifting eyepoint is a rather uneven book. The word picture titled "The Destruction of Tenochtitlan" dealing with Cortez and Montezuma is a splendid piece of lyrical exposition, certainly one of the most eloquent short pieces of its decade and a masterpiece of American prose. It is both informative and emotionally moving; it should be required reading for academic historians. However, the lyric piece on Sir Walter Raleigh has little information and is so excessively rhapsodic that it fails to convince or move. The piece on Eric the Red seems to arise from Williams's imagination; it is the scenario for a myth opera. Much of the chapters on Cotton Mather consist of excerpts from the witchcraft trials; the chapter on Benjamin Franklin includes nine and one-half pages from *Poor Richard's Almanac* followed by four and one-half pages of notes by Williams; the chapter on John Paul Jones is a reprint of his letter to Franklin, then our ambassador to Paris, after the battle between the *Bon Homme Richard* and the *Serapis*. It runs to fifteen pages and is presented plain without comment. It is pleasant to see that Dr. Williams can select significant passages for an anthology, but this is scarcely the task of a poet-historian.

One of the most stimulating chapters deals with Père Sebastian Rales, the French Jesuit (1689–1723). Williams points out clearly that the conflict between British and French colonists was largely based on religion, the Puritans against the Jesuits, religion tempered by commercial self interest. He does not quite say that it is the backbone of Boston, but that is an inescapable conclusion. Likewise, the chapter in defense of Aaron Burr is praiseworthy. One rarely hears the motivation of Burr's enemies called to question. These two chapters alone can be used as a text to illuminate the thesis that the victor manages to rewrite history in terms favorable to himself.

Many critics have praised the concluding piece on Abraham Lincoln. Frankly, I find it offensive. The key passage reads as follows: "It is Lincoln pardoning the fellow who slept on sentry duty. It is the grace of the Bixby letter. The least private would find a woman to caress him, a woman in an old shawl—with a great bearded face and a towering black hat above it, to give unearthly reality."[24] Accustomed as we are to metaphysical imagery, here we have two of the stock images of the American dream, Abe Lincoln and mother, fused into one. Somehow, I have never thought of Abe Lincoln as a mother figure. The two images are "yoked by violence together," but the yoking is so violent that it manages to garotte them both. Mercifully the piece on Lincoln is less than four hundred words long. It was written at the suggestion of Charles Boni, the book's first publisher.

It is not improper to emphasize that *In the American Grain* was not composed in bits and snatches; Williams took off time to write it. He moved into New York with his wife and worked hard at the library; he went up to Boston and Salem for the material on Cotton Mather and the witchcraft trials, using them again in his play *Tituba's Children* written in 1950. Yet despite the full application of his time, one still finds the deliberate use of a disjunctive style of exposition, almost like a nervous tic intruding itself into otherwise well-coordinated behavior. Some readers may find it a bit distracting to continuity, and I am old-fashioned enough to side with the latter.

Williams's most highly praised work is the long poem *Paterson*. It occupied a long period in his creative activity and represents the culmination of many years of thinking about the theme. Originally, the plan called for four books; these appeared in print from 1946 through 1951, but a fifth book was published in 1958, and fragments for a sixth were found in Williams's papers after his death. It is not easy to state in simple terms precisely what the subject of this magnum opus is. The framework is set for a free discursive treatment of the Paterson-Rutherford-Passaic area, its history, geography, some of its more interesting personages, and the poet's reactions to his local fragment of the cosmòs. However, it goes beyond these obvious limits into the uncharted spaces of his imagination. Time and space do not permit any analysis of the lengthy poem; however, its technic is that of alternating philosophic, or quasi-philosophic, and lyric passages of verse with prose passages. The prose passages may be anything Williams's fancy dictates: geographic notes, old newspaper stories, snatches of local history, anecdotes, letters received, and so on. It is an enormous canvas, and far more than any of his shorter poems it reveals the breadth of the man. His verbatim use of newspaper quotations recalls the method used in contemporary collages in which variously shaped pieces of the daily paper are cut out and pasted on the canvas as an integral part of the picture. Williams, the poet, identifies himself with Paterson, the place, and the numerous fragments do constitute his "dome of many-coloured glass," his set of particulars posed against his vision of the universal. One could cite any number of individual passages of great beauty and great strength. Nonetheless, it remains a defective masterpiece. Finely written as many sections are, the poem as a whole lacks cohesive organization, a defect in a work so long and so complex. One might paraphrase Williams's revealing line from *The Orchestra:* "Is there a sound addressed / not wholly to the ear?" and have him ask: Is there a thought addressed not wholly to the mind? I imagine that he would answer yes, and possibly this is his idea of the transformation of nature into poetry; the poet's ideas derived from nature, that is, the physical world around him, the people in it, and the diverse stimuli which daily assail his senorium, are worked on by the poet's imagination to produce a sequence of words and phrases (poetry) which contains something over and above the mental processes involved. It is a defensible attitude, even an admirable one. Yet, for a poem so long (the paperback edition contains 268 pages for the five completed books) some structural plan is a necessity.

I am not the only person to complain of an inability to grasp it. In Book IV, published in 1951, Williams quotes a letter to him signed by A. G., undoubtedly the young Allen Ginsberg, that other Paterson poet, who writes: "I seldom dig exactly what you are doing with cadences, line length, sometimes syntax, etc., and cannot handle your work as a solid object—which properties I assume you rightly claim. I don't understand the measure."[25] It was generous and perceptive of Williams to publish in full the letter of this young writer, then obscure, as part of the *res gestae* of his own poem. But it is not only a matter of cadence, line length, syntax. It is the "measure," using the word a bit more broadly than Ginsberg may have intended. It is very difficult to achieve a rounded view or even a perspective on *Paterson* to fit the various pieces into a unified pattern. One has the forlorn feeling that one will always know Williams's masterpiece better from passages quoted in critical glosses, sections culled for anthologies, than from reading and rereading the poem as he gave it to us.

I shall say nothing about Williams as a playwright, for I am not qualified to have an opinion. It should be recorded that *Many Loves* was successfully performed in 1959 by the Living Theatre led by Julian Beck and Judith Malina. It received considerable favorable notice even from the traditionally blasé New York drama critics. An earlier play, *Tituba's Children* (1950), based on the Salem witchcraft trials, preceded Arthur Miller's *The Crucible* on the same subject by three years. Never identified with any political movement, Williams was intelligent enough to recognize the dangers of security checks, McCarthyism, and inquisitorial methods.

It would be very easy to compare Williams to both Wallace Stevens and Charles Ives, two other American artists who wrote poems or composed music with some success (it came to Ives only after his death), but who earned their livings by work not related to or derived from their esthetic interests. They have certain features in common. Virgil Thomson discusses the economic determinism of musical style, pointing out that the work of a composer who lives by nonmusical jobs or earned income from nonmusical courses is marked by the absence of professionalism, is essentially naïf:

> The naïf makes up his music out of whole cloth at home. He invents his own esthetic. When his work turns out to be not unplayable technically, it often gives a useful kick in the pants to the professional tradition. The music of Modest Moussorgsky, of Erik Satie, and of Charles Ives did that very vigorously indeed.
>
> The naïfs show no common tendency in stylistic orientation. Their repertory of syntactical device is limited to what they can imitate plus what they make up for themselves. They are like children playing alone. . . . They put Dante to music, and Shakespeare, Dialogues of Plato, the Book of Revelation. They interpret these in terms of familiar folklore, remembered classics, and street noises. They derive their melodic material from hymns and canticles, from jazz-ways and darn-fool ditties. They quote when they feel like it. They misquote if they prefer. They have none of the professional's prejudices about "noble" material or about stylistic unity. . . . Its clarity is a shock to the professional mind. It doesn't hesitate about being lengthy or about being brief, and it neglects completely to calculate audience psychology. It is not made for audi-

ences. As Tristan Tzara said of Dada, it is "a private bell for inexplicable needs." It is beyond mode and fashion. It is completely personal.[26]

Mr. Thomson has already applied his remarks to Ives. To some extent, not completely, they can be applied to Williams and Stevens. They both invented their own "esthetic." They did kick tradition in the pants; in this they had good company among poets; Ives was quite alone among musicians at his time in this country. Neither Williams nor Stevens had any preconceived ideas about stylistic unity; Williams certainly did not hesitate to be very long *(Paterson)* or very brief (several hundred short lyrics). For both, poetry was a private bell for inexplicable needs, beyond fashion, completely personal. I question seriously the idea that their work was not made for audiences. It is a commonplace of sociology that the minority of today is the majority of tomorrow. True, neither Williams nor Stevens had audience reaction in mind, unless we include as audience a handful of friends and a few editors; but their poems, like Ives's music, can be read or played for audiences, and I think the audience is increasing. Time has a way of winnowing out those works which are relevant for the time of winnowing. Many of Williams's poems are ephemeral and deserve to be forgotten; however, a fair number are very fine poems indeed and will be remembered; the precise poems which will be valued in one decade may not seem so good in the next; others will take their place. The point Mr. Thomson does not quite make about the naïf is that his freshness and originality do have a value for all time. Such poetry or music is a countereddy in the stream of its times, valuable to the student of literary, musical, or pictorial movements, valuable in that some of its ideas and elements do become incorporated into the "main stream" of esthetic production of a later generation. Much as I take exception to Williams's lack of discipline, lack of self criticism, to the fact that he published many lesser poems when he did not depend on them for his livelihood, at his best he has an individual note of personal eloquence and a personal vision which will always be admired. However, pundits will always disagree on the particular, that is, which poems represent the best of Williams.

Needless to say the comparison with Ives can only be general; they worked in different media. The similarity with Stevens could be studied more closely, and it is not surprising that Stevens and Williams were good friends, each respecting the other's goals and methods, each noting privately his view of the other's subjectivism. However, it is obvious on casual inspection that Williams was more concerned with the external world, the here and the now, the daily experience, whereas Stevens was occupied with the landscape of his own imagination. I leave it to others more apt at detecting influences and interactions to dissect the details.

Williams was not the sort of man to write manifestos or issue pompous pronunciamentos about the nature of poetry. One very rarely finds him making the broad generalization or tacking his credo to a masthead. Even as one rereads the five issues of *Contact*, a magazine he edited with Robert McAlmon in 1920 to 1923, one fails to find evidence that he was ever willing to define a policy or set up a platform. One might even say that he "played by ear" and not be too far off the track. However, on one occasion, when his guard was down, he did write the following sentence: "To each thing its special quality, its special value that will enable it to stand alone. When each poem has achieved its particular form unlike any other, when it shall stand alone—then we have achieved our language. We have said what it is in our minds to say."[27] The remark occurs on the jacket of a phonograph record in which Williams reads some sixteen of his shorter poems. It is a statement of particularism, individual content determining form, and the subject matter determining the language.

I think we must remember that, although it now sounds strangely remote, when Williams first began writing poetry, there was a good deal of controversy about what was and what was not suitable thematic material. Even in the early years of this century conservative critics generally had the idea that some subjects were suitable to be treated poetically and others were not. Up to a generation previously the same argument was applied in painting. Manet's *Olympia* was a break with tradition not only in technic but in choice of subject. It is somewhat more difficult to date the concept of "free choice of subject matter" in literature. A novelist was accorded more latitude than a poet. Matthew Arnold's high seriousness was a widely held credo in both English and American schools of literary judgment at the turn of the century. The battle for freedom of choice of material in poetry was still to be fought and won. It was a good fight and I am glad it was won. Nowadays the idea that we judge a poem by how successfully it has fulfilled the poet's aims is so well entrenched that we forget how much ink was spilt over this right.

However, there is one very practical limitation to be considered. Unless a given poem has something new or important to say, has a new technic, a mode of statement that causes the reader to restructure his cognitive field, it will have a hard time rising above the limit set by its material. If one writes poems about the trivial, the mundane, the ephemeral, there is a high statistical probability or risk that the poem itself will be trivial, mundane, and ephemeral. The flame of poetic genius does not burn evenly; it is a series of sparks interspersed with some sputterings. Williams is not the only poet whose output is uneven. However, with few exceptions he avoided major themes and issues; he was deliberately particular, and his visual and intellectual range was usually limited to the world around him. It is not surprising that he should have a low batting average. Even in his most important poem, *Paterson,* there is a limitation inherent in the subject matter, the choice of a theme. Plainly, many readers are not especially interested in Paterson, New Jersey. A declining milltown and its purlieus, the minutiae of its local history, its landscape, even its people are not very edifying or exciting matters in and of themselves. Paterson is on a side road if not at the end of a blind alley; continuing the baseball analogy, singularly appropriate for a writer so self-consciously American, it is a Class D minor league town, and the Passaic River is not much more than an old millstream to most readers. That Williams can make Paterson exciting at all, even in part, is a tribute to his sympathy with his subject and his skill.

Perhaps one of Williams's most memorable passages comes from a late poem, *Asphodel, that Greeny Flower*

It is difficult
to get the news from poems
yet men die miserably every day
for lack
of what is found there.[28]

Clearly, the lack of what is found in poetry is not a medical cause of death; "apoiesis" would not be accepted by the Department of Health on a death certificate. Williams is concerned with emotional starvation and spiritual death, even as he was concerned with the emotional and spiritual well-being of his patients.

He is able to communicate a great deal of his own personal feeling about it as a place and his role as a poet in it. Likewise, in the dozen or two successful shorter poems he does make an occasional clean base hit, and in these poems he does speak with an authoritative original voice in them; he does manage to say what it is in his mind to say, and it would be a kindness to judge him on his best efforts. For the remainder, all one can say is that he was a warm genuine human being, a very nice man who enjoyed the act of writing.

Mark Linenthal speaks of Williams's "aesthetic proximity to his subject" as contrasted with the usual esthetic distance the poet or painter places between himself and his subject.[29] One might compare this intimacy with that of the doctor at his patient's bedside; the doctor is closely involved with his patient, engaged much as the poet with his poem, yet he must preserve at the same time a sense of detachment and objective judgment. Despite the risks inherent in such proximity, Linenthal is satisfied that Williams gives the reader "the moment of revelation, not the thing revealed."[30] Yet Williams was more concerned with the poetic process than the finished product. This is one reason why Williams is of paramount value to Professor Linenthal whose area is poetry in the workshop; the common reader is a consumer and is likely to form his judgment on the finished product: the container and the thing contained.

CHAPTER 8

The Earl of Rochester and Ejaculatio Praecox

Non nocet vitium minus, sed multos innocentos perditos stultosque virtū cognovi.—Quintillius

Sexual impotence in the male is a common complaint. After such organic factors as congenital malformation, trauma, and severe endocrine disturbance are excluded, Leonard Wershub stated that "more than 90 per cent of sexual impotence is dependent upon psychological conflict."[1] The two major symptoms are inability to achieve or maintain an erection and, less commonly, premature ejaculation. Occasionally, ejaculation may occur without erection. A third symptom, much less frequent, is inability to attain ejaculation even though erection is maintained and coitus proceeds. Ejaculatio praecox is not an uncommon event in the exploratory encounters of adolescents, but it is less often a cause for clinical complaint than failure to achieve erection in adult males whose pattern of sexual response has been established.

The literary representation of psychogenic male impotence is not voluminous. Even such outspoken writers of the generation just past as Ernest Hemingway and D. H. Lawrence make Jake Barnes in *A Farewell to Arms* and Clifford Chatterley in *Lady Chatterley's Lover* impotent as the result of injuries sustained in combat. So much inhibition and taboo surround the question of male impotence that it was not until 1963 that Roger Peyrefitte was able to publish *The Prince's Person,* giving the droll but pathetic circumstances surrounding the marriage of Don Vincenzo Gonzaga, prince of Mantua, with Margherita Farnese, granddaughter of the duke of Parma, which took place in 1581. The majority of poets, novelists, and dramatists are male, and the very idea of impotence provokes anxiety among them, nor do men, as a rule like to remind themselves of their *chagrin d'amour*. Also, it can be argued that impotence is nondramatic and uninspiring as a theme; male and female writers alike can reasonably claim that it does not lead to a fulfilling emotional experience which would serve as the substrate for literary expression. Even in simple genres, premature ejaculation interrupts the story line. Yet within the past few years, two works have appeared in which male impotence is a central element. A Czech film, *Closely Watched Trains*, depicts with great sympathy an episode of ejaculatio praecox in a young man, then his attempted suicide. In the recent novel, *Portnoy's Complaint*, the hero does not seek medical attention, despite two decades of psychoneurotic sexual behavior, until he finds himself unable to achieve erection with an attractive Israeli girl. Regrettably, the author fails to emphasize this important point and tries to make capital of the hero's masturbatory experiences and some stereotypic ethnic posturings.

Classical literature contains at least two accounts of psychogenic male impotence. Ovid's *Amores* (III, 7) relate an incident of impotence in a young lover ("Tacta tamen veluti gelida mea membra cicuta") with an attractive, much-desired girl. He describes recent successes with Childe (twice), Pitho (thrice), Libas (also thrice) and Corinna (nine times in one short night—*arcibravo!*), and attributes his inability to achieve erection to witchcraft ("quid vetat et vervos magicas torpere per artes"), adding that shame has aggravated his collapse. The disappointed maiden, somewhat piqued, stalks off, conceding that witchcraft might have been responsible, but more likely his failure is due to his previous sexual excesses ("aut te trajectis Aeaea venefica lanis/devovet aut alio lassus amore venis").

In an extended passage in the *Satyricon* (chaps. 128–40), Petronius describes the impotence of Encolpius, his bisexual narrator, first with Chrysis, then with his minion Giton ("Non tam intactus Alcibiades in praeceptoris sui lecto iacuit"). The psychopathology is continued by the narrator's transient impulses to self-castration, his prayer to Priapus to relieve him of his guilt, and his attempts to cure his loss of potentia first by receiving flagellation at the hands of an old woman, then by her insertion of a dildo in his rectum, the instrument having been lubricated with oil and seasoned with pepper and nettleseed ("Profert Oenothea scorteum fascinum, quod ut oleo et minuto pipere atque urtico trito circumdedit semine, paulatim coepit inserere ano meo").

Literary treatment of sexual impotence remained in abeyance for

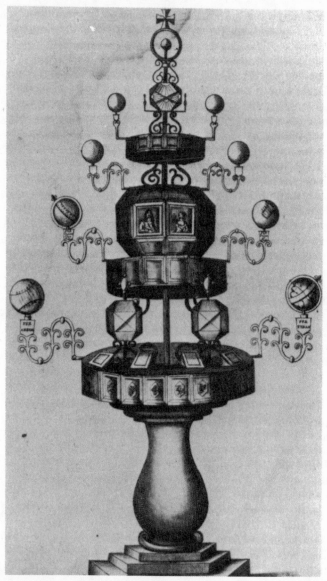

The set of dials and chronometer designed by Franciscus Linus for the King's Privy Garden at Whitehall. From *The Art of Dyalling*, by William Leybourn (2d ed., 1681)

fifteen centuries after Ovid and Petronius. Professor Richard Quaintance has segregated a group of ten poems written between 1577 and 1682 dealing with the topic.[2] Five of the poems are in French and five in English. Ovid's version of the failed amorous encounter is the archetype for the five French poems by Belleau, Regnier, Beys, de Morangle, and de Cantenac. Of the five poems in English, Etherege's "After a pretty amorous discourse" (1672) is a free translation of Beys's poem; Aphra Behn's "One Day the Am'rous Lisander" (ca. 1678) is a free translation of the first part of de Cantenac's poem, and the anonymous verses "It chanc'd Lysander, that unhappy man" (1682) is a close translation of de Cantenac's entire poem. They share a common tradition, the pastoral version of courtly love. In each, the unfortunate swain or shepherd is unable to achieve erection, and no attempt more profound to analyze the cause is made than Aphra Behn's apothegm "Excess of love his Love betray'd," implying that impotence results from too intense a passion. All five French poems and the three English translations are written in the third person and contain no hint that the experience is autobiographical.

Somewhat different, a subspecies of the genre, are two of the poems in English, one titled *The Imperfect Enjoyment* by John Wilmot, second earl of Rochester (1647–80), first appearing in his *Poems on Several Occasions* (1680), and beginning with "Naked she lay, claspt in my longing arms," the other bearing the same title but of anonymous authorship, first appearing in *A New Collection of Poems and Songs* (1674), its first line reading "Fruition was the Question in Debate." In both of these the mechanism of impotence is ejaculatio praecox, and they are both written in the first person, as if the poet were recounting his own experience and his reaction to it. This essay is designed to explore the relationship between Rochester's poem, and what is known of his life and psychosexual responses.

During the past two decades the efforts of several scholars have rehabilitated Rochester's reputation as a person and rectified, insofar as possible, the canon of his poetry. John H. Wilson has shown that it was not Rochester who was responsible for the cowardly beating given Dryden near Covent Garden in December 1679;[3] and somewhat earlier he established that Rochester's marriage to Elizabeth Malet was with that heiress's choice and consent, not the result of his carrying her off by force and fraud.[4] In his sympathetic biography, the late Professor Vivian de Sola Pinto presents a portrait of Rochester as a man who began his career as a hedonistic courtier but whose intellect and powers of dialectic developed so rapidly that, no longer concerned with mere physical pleasure, he became "the boldest spiritual adventurer" of his time, despite his untimely death at the age of thirty-three.[5] Professor Pinto also shows that despite his numerous extramarital exploits, even including his affair with Elizabeth Barry the actress, he did not abuse his wife, and they remained on terms of mutual respect and affection.

Rectifying the canon of Rochester's poetry was the result of a complex sequence of scholarly studies. During his lifetime he published nothing; as befitted a nobleman, his poems circulated in manuscript among his friends. After his death in 1680, a hastily collected volume titled *Poems on Many Occasions,* attributed on the title page to "the E. of R." was printed by a less than scrupulous publisher who not only included bawdy poems by other hands (as well as some by Rochester) but also marked it as having been printed in Antwerp. The sin of false attribution multiplied, and for almost two and a half centuries edition after edition appeared of "Rochester's poems," the number of ribald ones forever increasing. These poems coupled with his known rakish exploits as an unbridled young courtier—and spurious reports of dissolute conduct multipled as rapidly as false attributions of poems— led to his unenviable reputation as "the wicked Earl." In 1946, Rodney Baine showed that the grossly obscene play *Sodom* was probably written by Christopher Fishbourne, not Rochester.[6] James Thorpe's scholarly introduction and notes to the 1950 publication of a facsimile edition of the 1680 *Poems* analyzed many of the problems connected with both manuscript and early printed sources.[7] Individual scholars published short notes and articles clarifying specific points of authenticity, but the major rectification was accomplished by David M. Vieth.[8] His edition of the *Complete Poems* limits Rochester to seventy-six authentic, plus eight "possible," poems which have come down to us.[9] A striking feature of this volume is the list of one hundred seventeen poems incorrectly attributed to Rochester at one time or another, few of them having any merit, many being merely obscene or quasi-obscene facetiae.

Rochester's father was Henry Viscount Wilmot, a famous cavalier general, who accompanied Charles II into exile in France. He participated in the ill-fated expedition to Scotland in 1650 and helped the king escape after the rout at Worcester. While in exile, he was created earl of Rochester in 1652, paid a brief visit to England in 1655 to assist Royalist plots against the Commonwealth, and died at Sluys early in 1658. Whatever contact he had with his son and only child was brief. For all practical purposes, John Wilmot, who became second earl of Rochester at the age of eleven, was brought up by his mother, the former Anne St. John, daughter of a Wiltshire knight, with the assistance of a friendly neighbor, Sir Ralph Verney. In January 1660,

Rochester, not yet thirteen years old, was entered as a fellow commoner at Wadham College, Oxford. At that time Wadham represented the most advanced intellectual life in England, especially in
philosophy and natural science. The "experimental philosophicall
clubbe" at Wadham, where the redoubtable John Wilkins was master,
was one of the nuclei from which the Royal Society developed.

A few months later the monarchy was restored, and the entire
atmosphere of the university changed. The first evening Charles II
spent in London was at the home of Sir Thomas Morland, a scientist
and inventor; later that night he stayed with his mistress, Barbara
Palmer. This mixture of inquiring disbelief and sensuality is a fundamental orientation of Restoration life and thought. After the Restoration, revelry and gaiety soon took the place of Puritan austerity: stage
plays were once more produced; May games and morris dances were
encouraged; alehouses and taverns became the centers of social activity. Rochester's cicerone through this carnival was Robert Whitehall, a
fellow of Merton; notable for his capacity for claret, he not only
coached the young nobleman in his early efforts at writing poetry but
he also introduced him to the fleshpots of Oxford. We are told that
Whitehall "doted" on the precocious boy, and we may conjecture that
he seduced him into homosexual practices as well as the everyday
forms of drinking and whoring. Fatherless and the only child of his
mother, Rochester was certainly vulnerable, and we are told that he
"soon grew debauch'd."

Of some interest to a medical readership is a passage in one of
Rochester's early poems. Written at the tender age of twelve in a rather
conventional poem dedicated to the Queen Mother *On the Death of
Mary, Princess of Orange,* probably corrected by Whitehall, the lines
show an interest in and understanding of medical practice:

> In vain we blast the Ministers of Fate,
> And forlorn Physicians imprecate;
> Say they to Death new Poisons add, and fire;
> Art's Basilisks, that kill whom e'er they see,
> And truly write Bills of Mortality.[10]

Young Rochester took a dim view of doctors, possibly justified when we
consider how limited were their skills at diagnosis and treatment, and
he was surely sensitive to the notion of venality.

Rochester did not stay long at Oxford. He was awarded his M.A.
degree in September 1661 in a special ceremony conducted by the earl
of Clarendon, then lord chancellor of England and chancellor of the
University. This was a mark of royal favor; one of Charles II's more

praiseworthy traits was that he never forgot his obligation to those loyal to him during his years of exile. He granted prerogatives to them and their children with a generous hand. Even a few months previously, in February 1661, the king had given Rochester an annual pension of £500. Within a few weeks, he sent Rochester off on the Grand Tour under the guidance of Sir Andrew Balfour, M.D., then aged thirty, a man of parts who had studied at Saint Andrews, Oxford, Paris, Montpellier, and Padua, finally receiving his M.D. degree at Caen only two weeks after Rochester had received his M.A. at Oxford. The Grand Tour lasted from November 1661 through December 1664; Rochester may have learned something about medical methods and vocabulary from Balfour, although documentary accounts of their intellectual pursuits are fragmentary. When Rochester arrived at Whitehall on Christmas Day, 1664, he was ready to take his place as a courtier and play an active role in the social and literary life of his time.

Rochester's activities at court have been amply described elsewhere, and it is not necessary to recount the details. He was appointed a Gentleman of the Bedchamber. He served with gallantry in the naval war against the Dutch. In 1667 he married Elizabeth Malet, the heiress to a modest fortune. He became an intimate of such figures as Etherege, Buckhurst, Sedley, Shadwell, and Wycherley, soon becoming their leader in revels and amorous exploits. Not long after his arrival at court Rochester became a member of the Ballers, a clique of fast-living courtiers who patronized the establishment of "my Lady" Bennett. They soon came into conflict with the Farmers, a set of customs house officials who tried to prevent the Ballers from importing phallic instruments made of leather and called dildoes from France into England. By this time (ca. 1670) Rochester had been chosen "general" of the Ballers, and he led his noble troops to victory in this skirmish. The custom of taking one's sexual sport en masse in the company of one's peers is not uncommon in the history of mores among the British nobility and gentry. In the 1750s, Sir Francis Dashwood organized a group with similar interests at Medmenham; his Hell-Fire Club of "Franciscan" monks included John Wilkes, the parliamentary figure, Thomas Potter, son of the archbishop of Canterbury, and Charles Churchill, the poet, author of *The Rosciad*. Even before that, in 1732, the Most Ancient and Puissant Order of the Beggar's Benison and Merryland has been founded in Scotland. Its prized possession was a wig, said to have been made from the pubic hair of the mistresses of Charles II. In 1775, when the Lords Murray and Aboyne broke away from the Beggar's Benison, they took this wig and founded the Wig Club; whereupon the remaining members collected material for a new wig made from the pubic hair of George III's mistresses. In recent years, we have witnessed the Profumo affair in which many prominent figures were implicated in a variety of sexual activities often indulged in collectively.

Much of Rochester's pastoral and lyric poetry dates from this period. His wit and urbanity coupled with his physical charm attracted attention in both court and literary circles. He became one of Dryden's early patrons. The character of Dorimant in Etherege's *Man of Mode* (1676) was modeled after Rochester. Only occasionally did his probing, analytic mind pause to reflect that a wider meaning and purpose might underlie what was superficially an attractive way of life. Such moments of introspection usually came when he was in his cups or recovering from a spree. He also suffered from a venereal disease contracted as a youth, claimed to be syphilis. Though information regarding his symptoms is limited, we are told he had trouble with his eyes, conceivably syphilitic keratitis. He was also severely constipated; whether this was due to a postgonorrheal rectal stricture incurred by passive pederasty or due to a nonvenereal cause remains an open question. However, as time went on, his drinking bouts with noble and literary companions became less gay and lighthearted; he often became splenetic, and occasional violence marred the conclusion of the party.

In spite of open promiscuity, Rochester's relationship with his wife remained stable. After a few brief seasons at court she retired to their country home at Adderbury where she gave birth to four children: a daughter in 1669, a son, the future third earl, in 1671, then two more daughters in 1674 and 1675. When Rochester was not engaged in playing the courtier, he would return to peace and domesticity. He managed his estate prudently and was considered a benevolent landlord. His conduct on his native heath was, in general, good. There is no evidence that the countess reproached him for his infidelities at court; she probably accepted them as part of the moral code of the age. Rochester led a double life, "the wild poet and rake at Whitehall and Covent Garden, and the respectable country gentleman who had married a lady of his own class and lived the life of his ancestors, hunting, hawking and dancing among his neighbors."[11] In the spring of 1674 the king appointed him Ranger of Woodstock Forest, which carried with it the right to live in the Ranger's Lodge. He moved his wife and children there, and it soon became his favorite refuge from the tensions and exhausting social life of Whitehall. Sensitive to the emptiness and brutality of the court, he needed a base where he could keep in touch with warm human values. Few English writers with any poetic instinct have been able to survive without some contact with the reality of the countryside; even so cerebral a man as Pope had his elaborate grotto at Twickenham.

The price for such a double life, bivalent, but without fixed polarity, was soon exacted. One night in June 1675, Rochester went out carousing with Buckhurst, Fleetwood, Shepherd, and others; returning to Whitehall in the small hours of the morning, they lurched into the great Privy Garden in the middle of which was an elaborate set of dials and a chronometer devised by the Jesuit Franciscus Linus. The great Pyramidical Diall suggested to Rochester the shape of a phallus. "What," he is reported to have exclaimed, "Dost thou stand here to fuck Time?" Whereupon he and the noble lords set upon the expensive mechanisms and smashed them to pieces. Rochester had been on thin ice with King Charles on previous occasions; he had taken liberties with decorum no other courtier would have dared attempt. He had circulated his own scurrilous satires about the king, one of which, a lampoon titled *The History of the Insipids,* went far beyond the rough usage of satire permissible even in that day, castigating Charles not only for his vascillating foreign policy and double-dealing with Parliament (true enough, and fair comment) but also remarking on his many extramarital affairs and numerous bastards. The king must have been fond of Rochester to permit him such freedom, and in a sense Rochester may have looked on the king as a father image; much like an unruly child, he constantly tested the king's patience and tried to see how far he could go without incurring disciplinary disaster. The more permissive and passive the father, the more suppressive the superego of the boy; one may well wonder whether in the episode of the Privy Garden Rochester was not really testing the king to see if he would crack down.

Under the releasing influence of alcohol, in which the superego is traditionally soluble, Rochester revealed an important facet of his psychodynamic orientation. Not only did he destroy an object which he interpreted as a phallic symbol but one which belonged to the king. His ambivalence is clear: Rochester may have loved the king as a father and as a ruler, but he also saw through him in part as a fraud and libertine. In symbolically destroying the king's phallus, he was taking revenge for paternal castration threats. Later, when we consider his poem on ejaculatio praecox, it will become evident that the idea of a castration threat played a role in his impotence. Rochester's ambivalence took the form of a display of exaggerated masculine prowess, which may be interpreted as a defense, disguise, or denial of unconscious feminine identification. It is curious to note that the royal chronometer which he destroyed was phallic in shape but contained a timepiece; characteristically timepieces are female genital symbols because of their cyclicity. In this destructive act Rochester, a confused bisexual, was in effect destroying a symbolic hermaphrodite. In this sense his outburst may have represented more than a simple reprisal against the king-father; it was also an act of self-destruction. In addition, a stopped clock can be construed as a symbol of impotence, and one recalls the celebrated opening of *Tristam Shandy* (1760) in which the wife interrupts the husband in coitus to ask whether he has wound the clock.

The wanton incident in the Privy Garden was probably the straw that broke the camel's hump; Rochester had accumulated too many demerits. It was made plain to him that he was in disgrace, and he retired from the court. Not wishing to return home to Woodstock, Rochester removed to the area of Tower Hill with his servant, Thomas Alcock, and soon handbills proclaiming the skills of Dr. Alexander Bendo were being distributed throughout the neighbourhood. Although Tower Hill was only about five miles from Whitehall and Westminster, in those days communications between the City and the seat of government were poor; the City was a safe hideout.

The story of Rochester's fling at medicine has been preserved in a manuscript written by Alcock, now available at the University of Nottingham.[12] A reasonably accurate version of Rochester's handbill was printed as early in 1691 in Tonson's edition of Rochester's poems. Itinerant quacks were as common in Europe of the seventeenth and eighteenth centuries as the traveling snakebite remedy salesman in the American South and Southwest during the latter part of the nineteenth century. Rochester doubtless had encountered these charlatans while on the Grand Tour, but they were not unheard of the England. The model for Ben Jonson's disguise of Volpone as Scoto Mantuano probably came from an Italian mountebank who came to London early in the century. Alcock informs us that when Rochester posed as Dr. Bendo, he wore an old overgrown Green Gown, an item he may have borrowed from Sir Andrew Balfour.

The text of the broadside handbill is not without interest to the student of medical history as well as the student of literature. Pinto reads it as an elaborate irony playing between falsehood disguised as truth versus truth wearing the external guise of falsehood. Rochester compares the quack with the Politician:

The Politician (by his example no doubt) finding how the People are taken with Specious Miraculous Impossibilities, plays the same Game, protests, declares, promises I know not what things which he's sure can ne'er be brought about; the People believe, are deluded, and pleased. The expectation of a future good, which shall never befall them, draws their eyes off the present Evil: thus they are kept and established in Subjection, Peace, and Obedience, He in

Greatness, wealth, and Power: so you see the Politician is, & must be a Mountebank in State Affairs, and the Mountebank no doubt, (if he thrives) an errant Politician in Physick.[13]

The same ironic polarity between appearance and reality is the theme of Pirandello's plays. Oscar Wilde's epigram on Max Beerbohm is in the same vein: "Tell me, when you are alone with Max, does he take off his face and reveal his mask?" In this tenor Rochester, disgusted with himself for persisting from force of habit to seek satisfaction from empty pleasures, sick at heart with a meaningless society and his role in it, sought to assuage his anxiety, not only by an ironic treatment of the world's deceits but by adopting the guise of a healer, yet withal a false, unqualified healer, unfit to cure the ills of any man, not even his own. Rochester summarizes his own moral dilemma:

All I shall say for my self on this score, is this: If I appear to anyone like a Counterfeit, ev'n for the sake of that chiefly, ought I to be contrued as a true Man, who is the Counterfeit's Example, his Original, and that which he employs his Industry and Pains to imitate and copy: Is it therefore my fault, if the Cheat by his Wits and Endeavors makes himself so like me, that consequently I cannot avoid resembling of him?[14]

This is the disingenuousness born of a bivalent posture and a double life. Rochester had not really resolved his inner conflict: he was acting it out.

Soon, however, the climate at court changed. Rochester was advised that he was welcome there once more, and Dr. Alexander Bendo vanished as mysteriously and as suddenly as he came. Rochester continued his promiscuous behavior at court, compulsive sexual activity revealing an unresolved conflict rather than the simple pursuit of pleasure. Later that summer he was involved in a drunken brawl which ended fatally for one of his drinking companions who was killed in an affray with the constabulary. Failing health began to take its toll, and his appearances at court became less frequent as he nursed his decaying body at Woodstock. During the last four years of his life, so far as one can date them, he wrote his famous satires, the only escape open to him from the web in which he was irretrievably trapped. During the last two years of his life he entered into a series of conversations with Gilbert Burnet, a Scottish Anglican clergyman who had achieved great fame as a preacher. "Rochester's starting-point was that of a sceptical deist, Burnet's that of a liberal Anglican."[15] By this time Rochester was almost ready to admit to himself the expense of greatness he had made of his life. True to the scientific training he had received at Wadham, he tried to show that religious experience could be demonstrated by experiment, something as real and reproducible as physical experience. His body may have been trammeled by disease, but his mind was undimmed. Pinto characterizes him as a "daring and original explorer of reality . . . a memorable spiritual adventurer . . . who perceived the full significance of the intellectual and spiritual crisis of his age."[16] He rejected, almost intuitively, the oversimplified Cartesian-Newtonian orthodoxy of a well-reasoned mechanical world. The history of his ultimate conversion to faith has been memoralized by Gilbert Burnet.[17] Even discounting the account of a conversion by a clergyman as a self-serving declaration, it is none the less the record of a remarkable journey of the human soul. Rochester died at Woodstock in June 1680, at peace with himself and the world.

Alcock chose shrewdly when he labeled Rochester a pathologist. Although morbid anatomy and histopathology had not yet been born, Rochester had a deeper insight into social pathology and psychopathology than any writer of his age. Satire in the Latin tradition had been introduced into England earlier in the seventeenth century by Donne, Hall, and Marston; as a literary mode it embraced not only the ephemera of manners and the trivia of mores but extended to include politics, letters, religion, and philosophy. Effective social satire is not written by men contented with the status quo whose mental and bodily needs are satisfied by accepted means of gratification. The court of Charles II was noted for its emphasis on wit and libertinism; men rose by their levity and women by their willingness to comply with the law of gravity, shortly to be discovered. Rochester did not suffer fools gladly:

> 'Twas impotence did first this vice begin:
> Fools censure wit as old men rail of sin,
> Who envy pleasure which they cannot taste,
> And, good for nothing, would be wise at last.[18]

Rochester wrote in the convention of his period; he used the same vocabulary, the same tropes, the same verse forms as other Restoration poets. What distinguishes him from the herd and places him second only to Dryden is that he had something important to say. By the same token, Mozart wrote in the same musical vocabulary as Paisiello and Salieri but was their superior. Even though Rochester's contemporaries may have undervalued him, the judgment of more recent generations has been more perceptive. Take, for example, the incipit of his short poem attacking the Roman Catholic practice of selling indulgences (which had exercised Martin Luther so sorely a century and a half before—and to such great length):

> If Rome can pardon sins, as Romans hold,
> And if those pardons can be bought and sold,
> It were no sin t' adore and worship Gold.[19]

Deceptively simple and direct, it avoids the easy anticlericalism and penetrates to the essence of the moral problem. Sometimes it is the conscious sinner who can put best the difference between right and wrong.

Satire is born of anger. Like Swift, Rochester knew the intolerable pain of a perceptive mind enslaved by the needs and sensual drives of a decaying body. He alternately rebelled against and submitted to the tyranny of the orgasm. Acutely aware of how little reason could control passion, he began his much quoted *Satyr against Mankind* by stating as clearly as any poet ever succeeded the conflict between mind and body, reason and instinct:

> Were I (who to my cost already am
> One of those strange prodigious creatures Man,)
> A spirit free to choose for my own share
> What case of flesh and blood I pleased to wear,
> I'd be a dog, a monkey, or a bear,
> Or any thing but that vain animal
> Who is so proud of being rational.
> The senses are too gross, and he'll contrive
> A sixth to contradict the other five;
> And, before certain instinct, will prefer
> Reason, which fifty times for one does err.

It is the pious wish of all moral philosophers: If man's will were free, his choices would be rational. But Rochester knew the limits of reason and continued:

> Reason, an ignis fatuus in the mind,
> Which leaving light of nature, sense behind,
> Pathless and dang'rous wand'ring ways it takes,
> Through errors, fenny-bogs, and thorny brakes;
> While the misguided follower climbs with pain
> Mountains of whimseys, heaped in his own brain,
> Stumbling from thought to thought, falls headlong down
> Into Doubt's boundless sea, where, like to drown,
> Books bear him up a while, and make him try
> To swim with bladders of philosophy.[20]

This is not to be dismissed as the anti-intellectualism of an unlettered man nor the moral stance of a failed pagan hedonist. Rochester's pointed remark that "bladders of philosophy" are unequal to the task of supporting Reason in the swift undertow of "Doubt's boundless sea" is the insight of a voyager who knows the limits of his vessel and the force of the wind. Rarely does satire become so autobiographical, so lucid a statement of the poet's own paradox. In this and other satires Rochester achieved internal consistency; he had learned to balance his ambivalances. His best-known portrait shows him placing a laurel wreath on the head of a pet monkey (cf. line 5 of the *Satyr*). Few poets have been so conscious of the animal instinct.

Unlike most satirists who prefer to remain detached, Rochester did not hesitate to involve himself directly; his sense of plight was such that several of his most effective satires were directed by self-examination. Until Lord Byron, no English poet was so well qualified to write on the variety of sexual experiences, and possibly Rochester even outdid Byron in the realization of adolescent fantasies. Rochester was obsessed by coitus even as Swift was by excrement. It is in this vein that *The Imperfect Enjoyment* was written. Rochester was not abashed to deal with psychogenic impotence; his attitude was similar to that expressed by Petronius, "Foeda est in coitu et brevis voluptas," and he looked upon sexual experience with the pitiless eyes of youthful experience. It may well have been the brevity of that *voluptas* which disturbed him most, but his purview included not only the sexual performance of his contemporaries but his own as well.

It is a psychiatric truism that ejaculatio praecox is not a disease but a symptom, one which may reflect a considerable variety of intrapersonal conflicts and arise in many contexts. It is common in the early sexual encounters of adolescence; in such cases it may reflect castration anxiety as fear of reprisal from the father for forbidden sexual wishes toward the mother, or toward females generally. When ejaculatio praecox occurs in adults, it commonly reflects ambivalence toward the sexual object, not in the sense of Zerlina's "Vorrei, e non vorrei," but a difficulty in resolving a choice between two objects, for example, between a female and a male partner. It is reasonable to infer that, if *The Imperfect Enjoyment* is autobiographical, such an unresolved choice was at the bottom of Rochester's problem. Certainly, his relationship with a French youth bearing the callipygeous name of Baptiste de Belle Fasse (cf. *fesse*) leaves no doubt regarding the persistence of his homosexual conduct into adult life.

Quaintance has pointed out that the five French poems and the three

English poems based upon them are "not so much confessional as hedged by tradition."[21] By contrast, Rochester's *The Imperfect Enjoyment* and the anonymous "Fruition was the Question in Debate" are suited to the circumstances of the individual poet. Written in the first person, they have a greater sense of immediacy, more direct visual and tactile imagery, and "confessional" in the sense that they record the poet's private experience.[22]

The *Imperfect Enjoyment* first appeared in print in *Poems on Several Occasions* by the E. of R. in 1680; the anonymous poem on the same theme first appeared in *A New Collection of Poems and Songs* in 1674. But the date of publication cannot be used to assign priority of composition, for it was common practice for poems to circulate in manuscript. Vivid in imagery and blunt in language, Rochester's poem has rarely been printed in its original form. For example, in the Nonesuch Press edition of 1926, edited by John Hayward, thirteen of its seventy-two lines have been altered with an eye to the censor. Even as late as 1953, Pinto omitted the entire poem (as well as *A Ramble in St. James's Park*), stating in his preface that it "had to be omitted at the request of the publishers owing to the risk of prosecution in this country under the existing laws."[23] Presumably, he was referring to the laws in England and the request of a trade publisher. The same book was published in the United States by the Harvard University Press, and one would like to think that, operating as it does under the aegis of scholarship, it might have added *The Imperfect Enjoyment* on a tipped in page. But even two decades ago the Commonwealth of Massachusetts was not known for its tolerance of explicitly sexual literature. On balance, one prefers Pinto's forced omission to Hayward's bowdlerization. A correct text can always be retrieved from a scholarly library, but a corrupted text is deceitful and deceptive. Fortunately, Vieth's edition furnishes an accurate, accessible text, repunctuated to conform to modern usage.

Rochester's description of the actual event is plain enough:

> But whilst her busy hand would guide that part
> Which should convey my soul up to her heart,
> In liquid raptures I dissolve all o'er,
> Melt into sperm, and spend at every pore.

His partner wishes him to carry on:

> "Is there then no more?"
> She cries. "All this to love and rapture's due:
> Must we not pay a debt to pleasure too?"

But of course Rochester cannot continue and explains his dilemma:

> Eager desires confound my first intent,
> Succeeding shame does more success prevent,
> And rage at last confirms me impotent.

This takes us no further than Ovid's lover who also avers that shame has aggravated his collapse, but Rochester adds anger to his embarrassment as sealing his incapacity. Again, like Ovid's lover, he calls to witness his past successes:

> This dart of love, whose piercing point, oft tried,
> With virgin blood ten thousand maids have dyed.

Amusingly, in Hayward's bowdlerized text, ten thousand is reduced to one hundred. Probably the truth lies somewhere in between, but what benefit accures from reducing Rochester's metaphoric claim to a mere 1 percent of its number is difficult to judge. But Rochester, in his rage at the organ which failed him, gives us a clue to his ambivalence:

> Stiffly resolved, 'twould carelessly invade
> Woman or man, nor ought its fury stayed.

The almost casual admission of bisexual activities indicates that he did not gauge their importance correctly.

Rochester wrote more in anger than in sorrow. He is angry with himself for having failed to fulfill his image of himself as a creature of prodigious sexual prowess. Constructing the easy dichotomy between love and lust, he rationalized his premature ejaculation to the notion that his relationship to his present Corinna was based on true love as distinguished from a passing lecherous fancy, and he describes his penis as "So true to lewdness, so untrue to love," implying that he has been betrayed by his flesh, not by his spirit. So great is his chagrin that he barely apologizes to the lady in question; he contents himself with promising her excess gratification with other lovers. Obliquely, he refers to castration threats from the king-father:

> But if his King or country claim his aid,
> The rakehell villain shrinks and hides his head; . . .
> But when great Love the onset does command,
> Base recreant to thy prince, thou dar'st not stand.

And finally, in the rage of frustration he curses his own genital organ and invokes disease upon it:

> May strangury and stone thy days attend;
> May'st thou ne'er piss, who didst refuse to spend
> When all my joys did on false thee depend.[24]

Impairment of function, self-willed, is a form of self-castration. Rochester does everything but cast a pox on himself, and that disease he presumably had already contracted.

The anonymous author of "Fruition was the Question in Debate" has a strikingly different attitude toward ejaculatio praecox when that poem is compared with Rochester's. The poem is a third shorter, forty-eight lines long. Published texts show almost no evidence of bowdlerization apart from minor textual variants which do not affect meaning; Hayward's edition, for example, merely omits a single line, one of neutral content, probably the result of careless typesetting and proofreading. Other inaccuracies seem to be the result of transcription errors. The anonymous poem may have been inoffensive to self-appointed censors because its tone is more detached, the act and its consequences intellectualized, the poet himself involved at one remove. Rochester painted directly from life, the anonymous poet viewed the experience through a literary lens. Though his experience may have been real, he was able to cast both the event and his reaction to it into compartmentalized antitheses. By subjecting experience to rhetorical rules the anonymous poet purged much of the immediate emotion from the scene, and purgation by wit is a strong defense.

Rochester was almost exclusively preoccupied with his own subjective visceral reaction. By contrast, the anonymous poet takes some pains to establish the motivation and behavior of his lady love:

> she with freedom urg'd as my offence,
> To teach my Reason to subdue my Sense.

—an echo of the polarity found in *A Satyr against Mankind* and other poems of the period—and

> When of her breasts her hands the Guardians were....
> Nor could those Tyrant hands so guard the Coyn,
> But Love, where 't cannot purchase, my purloin.

But after these preliminary skirmishes:

> for on the Bed she sat,
> And seemed to covet what she seemed to hate:
> Heat of resistance had increased her fire,
> And weak defence is turn'd to strong desire.

Yet despite this promising prelude, ejaculatio praecox struck:

> Only too hastie zeal my hopes did foil,
> Pressing to feed her lamp, I spilt my Oil.

Having depicted a scene of seduction, overcoming his partner's reluctance, he attributes his failure more to a physical or mechanical cause than a psychological one, "too hastie zeal" contrasted with "strong desire," and expresses the hope that later triumphs will be marked by improved physical control:

> When next on such assaults I chance to be,
> Give me less vigour, more activitie.

Unlike Rochester, the anonymous poet does not attempt to rationalize his predicament by contrasting "true love" with lust. It is plain that love enters his equation only as part of a literary convention.

Whatever his limitations as a psychologist or reluctance to examine his own psychodynamics, we must be grateful to the anonymous poet for some well-turned phrases in the metaphysical tradition:[25]

> Like prudent Corporations, had we laid
> A Common Stock by, we'd improv'd our Trade.

A sound generalization about motivation, prefiguring the rational sensibility of a later generation, is found:

> And those delays do but advance delight
> As prohibitions sharpen appetite.

One cannot but admire the "modern" ring to the two "scientific" conceits: "Heat of resistance has increased her fire," an early statement of Ohm's law in a somewhat different setting, and the concluding line of the poem, its moral: "Love Chymistry thrives best in equal heat" is an axiom which can be construed as an early appreciation of the law of conservation of energy, a recognition that emotional reactions, like chemical ones, ultimately reach an equilibrium, or a strong plea for balanced equations. The metaphysical poet snatched victory from defeat by turning his failed sexual encounter into a game of wits. Rochester was left with his *chagrin d'amour*. One speculates that should the anonymous poet one day be identified, he might prove to be a soldier and diplomat, the sort who could lose battle after battle yet win the peace treaty, a recognizable type in the history of English letters, still to be found in Whitehall today. Conversely, Rochester had the character of a man who won or lost on the battleground, be it one of love or of rational debate. He lost the battle in *The Imperfect Enjoyment* and, crestfallen, retired from the field. Perhaps, considering his deathbed repentance and conversion, it was a battle he was unconsciously pre-pared to lose.

Caught in a conflict between female and male object-choice, Roches-ter's psyche demanded retreat to infantile behavior in the form of premature ejaculation. There is congruence between this form of regression and his aggression toward the bisexual clock and dialls in the Privy Garden. Abraham has pointed out the similarity between ejaculatio praecox and urination.[26] Perhaps Rochester's premature ejaculation was a form of urethral aggression toward a female object he consciously desired but unconsciously rejected. He was the son of an absent father, and, to use a demotic phrase, his mother was "mother and father to him." Such fusion or blurring of the parental image might explain his later difficulty in attaining a firm heterosexual ad-justment, why he persisted in ambivalences not only in sexual choices but in other decisions, why he chose to lead a double life between Woodstock and Whitehall. Perhaps in *The Imperfect Enjoyment* (the very title connotes ambivalence), he unconsciously identified his unnamed female partner with some aspect of his mother, responding by urethral behavior comparable to the satisfaction a child obtains in urination, denying at the same time to his partner an equivalent satisfaction. In that respect, as well as in exposing his personal failure, Rochester stood outside the accepted convention of Restoration amatory poetry. Fredelle Bruser has summarized the majority view: "Reading collec-tions of the period, one is struck by the recurrence of the theme tersely formulated by Dryden: *the chase has a beast in view.* Love is to be pursued, if possible, with detachment and amused contempt, and always with the knowledge that possession takes from love its final charm."[27] Cer-tainly Rochester was aware of the ultimate defeat of lust by satiety, but he still pursued "the right true end of love," driven as he was by ambivalent instincts and passions. Though he expressed a minority view, as in *The Imperfect Enjoyment,* he was still subject to the demands of the flesh.

Rochester, who touches and transcends so many contemporary modes of thought, returns again and again to the paradoxical frustration which is in possession. ... Pursuing the various joys of wine, women, and wisdom, Rochester could not help reminding himself, constantly and with a furious masochism, that the end proposed was self-destructive. It is only distance which lends enchantment to the view of woman:

"Perhaps in Rowing you may take a Pride;
The Pleasure flyes, when to the Oar you're tyed."[28]

Distance yes, and also time! For Rochester the paradox was purely an
intellectual one; his frustrations were only temporary. When the latter
cut deeply enough into his emotions, he expressed them clearly in his
poetry. One suspects that other contemporary poets either lacked his
insight or were reluctant to reveal either their frustrations or their
genesis too freely. As a class, Restoration poets were pleased to lift the
curtain on the act of love; few were willing to bare their own hearts as
well, hence the detachment and amused contempt. None the less, both
poets and lovers are trapped whichever extreme they espouse: "The
coy mistress is the symbol at once of both the fascination and the
inevitable betrayal of the flesh."[29] There is more than one way to betray
the flesh; the majority opted for denial of fruition to the male by the
female. On one occasion at least Rochester reversed that role and
denied the female his own flesh.

CHAPTER 9

Thomas Shadwell: His Exitus Revis'd

Thomas Shadwell has suffered from a bad press. We remember him, if at all, as the subject of Dryden's *MacFlecknoe,* the Prince of Dullness. Among the poets and playwrights of his period

> The rest to some faint meaning make pretence,
> But Shadwell never deviates into sense.

Keats's life may have been "snuff'd out by an article," but Shadwell's literary reputation was stabbed by Dryden's couplet. Even the subtitle of MacFlecknoe, proclaiming Shadwell as "the True Blue Protestant Poet, T.S." has been usurped; most readers of our generation would supply the surname Eliot after the initials T. S. and the imputation of denominational fervor. Dryden's charge of nonsense is, of course, an exaggeration. Shadwell's plays are as coherent as any other Restoration comedies. Not only are *The Squire of Alsatia* and *Bury-Fair* pointed comedies of manners, but *The Virtuoso* remains a durable satire on the "new science" then being explored by the Royal Society, and *The Libertine* is an important retelling of the Don Juan legend. A rough measure of Shadwell's poetic stature is that it was the prosaic William III who made him poet laureate in 1689.

Shadwell's twentieth-century biographers seem to have accepted uncritically the story that he died of an accidental, self-administered overdose of opium. Michael Alssid relates simply that "it is assumed that he died of an overdose of opium to which he was addicted."[1] Albert Borgman supplies the additional information that Shadwell suffered from ill health and used opium for its analgesic properties: "Troubled by painful illness for at least four years, Shadwell formed the habit of taking opium, an overdose of which is believed to have caused his death."[2] Kenneth Hopkins specifies a date and hints at a time interval between the self-medication and the time of death: "On November 19th, 1692 he took opium, as his habit was, to relieve the pain: but the dose was a fatal one, and on the following day he died."[3] If the date Hopkins assigns is correct, presumably Shadwell took the opiate on the evening of the nineteenth and died the next morning; it is unlikely that death after an overdose would be delayed more than ten or twelve hours. But Montague Summers, after supplying voluminous conjectural details, offers a different time of day: "On the morning of November 20, 1692, after an unusually severe bout of pain, he had recourse to the opium for the last time, for he absorbed so exceptional a quantity of drug that when some hours later his wife and attendant entered the room it was found that he had passed away in his sleep."[4] Alssid and Borgman qualify their statements by "it is assumed" and "it is believed," but Hopkins and Summers assert opium overdosage as the cause of death as if it were an established fact. None of these four twentieth-century writers cites a source for this claim.

Whether Shadwell died of an overdose or not, evidence from his contemporaries leaves no doubt that he had been *using* opium, presumably as laudanum, for at least ten years before he died. In the second part of *Absalom and Achitophel* (1682) Dryden directs Og (Shadwell) to "Eat opium, mingle arsenic in thy drink, / Still thou mayst live, avoiding pen and ink." In a passage in *MacFlecknoe* (published in 1682 but circulated in manuscript as early as 1678) he describes Shadwell's coronation as the Prince of Dullness:

> In his sinister hand, instead of Ball,
> He plac'd a mighty Mug of potent Ale . . .
> His Temples last with Poppies were o'erspread,
> That nodding seem'd to consecrate his head.

Shadwell neither denied nor took umbrage at Dryden's comment on his use of opium; we may infer it was widely known. Shadwell had no reason for concealment or pudency; if he took opium as an anodyne for the pain of gout, that was a legitimate medical indication. At the time, laudanum was widely used, available without prescription, and free from social stigma. Neither Dryden nor Tom Brown, who wrote a mock epitaph on Shadwell, considered him an addict, nor did they suggest his use of opium had any effect on him or his readers but a

He has several Poems extant, but because his Name is not affix'd to them, I shall mention but Three; *viz. The tenth Satyr of* Juvenal, translated with Notes, printed 4°. *Lond.* 1687. *A Congratulatory Poem on his Highness the Prince of* Orange, *coming into* England: and another to the most Illustrious Q. *Mary,* upon her Arrival; both printed 4°. *Lond.* 1689.

William SHAKESPEARE.

One of the most Eminent Poets of his Time; he was born at *Stratford* upon *Avon* in *Warwick-shire*; and flourished in the Reigns of Queen *Elizabeth,* and King *James* the First. His Natural Genius to *Poetry* was so excellent, that like those Diamonds (¹), which are found in *Cornwall,* Nature had little, or no occasion for the Assistance of Art to polish it. The Truth is, 'tis agreed on by most, that his Learning was not extraordinary; and I am apt to believe, that his Skill in the *French* and *Italian* Tongues, exceeded his Knowledge in the *Roman* Language: for we find him not only beholding to *Cynthio Giraldi* and *Bandello,* for his Plots, but likewise a Scene in *Henry* the Fifth, written in *French,* between the Princess *Catherine* and her Governante: Besides *Italian* Proverbs scatter'd up and down in his Writings. Few Persons that are acquainted with *Dramatick Poetry,* but are convinced of the Excellency of his Compositions, in all Kinds of it; and as it would be superfluous in me to endea-

(1) Dr. *Fuller* in his Account of *Shakespear.*

soporific one: "Tom writ, his readers still slept o'er his book, / For Tom took Opium, and Opiates they took."[5] Neither the subject matter nor its treatment in any of Shadwell's eighteen plays and assorted poems betrays any effect of narcotic addiction on his ideation or imagery; there is no record that he suffered from dreams of terror or hallucinations.

Nicholas Brady, who preached Shadwell's funeral sermon, had no hesitation in mentioning his use of opium and took that fact as a point of departure for a comment on the decreased laureate's piety: "His Death seized him suddenly, but not unprepared, since (to my own certain knowledge) he never took his Dose of Opium, but he solemnly recommended himself to God by Prayer, as if he were then about to resign up his soul into the hands of his faithful Creator."[6] Brady is best remembered as the senior author of Brady and Tate's metrical version of the Psalms, and his comment on Shadwell's habit of prayer before downing a dose of laudanum has all the pietistic plausibility of "If I die before I wake, / I pray the Lord my soul to take." Yet the comment of this divine, taken with other contemporary evidence, establishes opium usage.

Although Brady's sermon was preached when the event was fresh in the minds of his audience, he made no allusion to the events of November 19 and 20, 1692, and is silent about the immediate cause of Shadwell's death. The question of opium overdose is not raised; there is nothing in the sermon to justify Wiltshire Austin and John Ralph's statement made 160 years later: "The report that his death was caused by an over-dose of laudanum was authoritatively contradicted by Brady who preached his funeral sermon."[7] As one tries to determine the origin of the charge, a number of perplexing problems arise. Transmission of factual data seems to have been neither direct nor linear, and several authors, Summers being the chief romanceur, have introduced details that—to be charitable—cannot be corroborated.

Despite their probative value to establish usage, the accumulated statements have but little forensic substance. They tell us nothing about the form in which Shadwell took opium, its strength, his customary dose, nor the frequency of medication. To accept the presumptive diagnosis of gout does not greatly tax credulity. Although many painful affections of bones and joints can be mistaken for gout, it is a disease known since antiquity and was probably diagnosed with reasonable accuracy in the seventeenth century. Opium (as laudanum) was often prescribed for the pain of podagra. All Shadwell's biographers agree that he suffered for many years from a recurrent disorder accompanied by severe pain, but none of them specifies the location of the pain. There is unanimity that Shadwell became seriously ill in the summer of 1688, shortly after the successful production of *The Squire of Alsatia*. The dedication of his next play, *Bury-Fair*, produced in April 1689, includes the phrase, "it was written during eight months painful sickness." Whatever its nature, this illness was severe, and Shadwell seems never to have fully regained his health. But Summers's assertion that he suffered from deep depression and took opium in greater and more frequent doses remains undocumented, a sheer speculation. That tolerance to opium increases and that addicts often increase dosage progressively are common knowledge, but there is no evidence that Shadwell was addicted nor that he ever took opium for any purpose other than analgesia.

The first editions of both Gerard Langbaine's *English Dramatick Poets*[8] and Anthony à Wood's *Athenae Oxoniensis*[9] appeared in 1691, the year before Shadwell died. Charles Gildon's revision of Langbaine was published in 1699, but the entry for Shadwell is shorter than in the first edition and says nothing about the cause of death.[10] The second edition of *Athenae Oxoniensis* was not printed until 1721, purportedly enlarged from notes left by Wood at his death in 1695.[11] We are told that "The said Tho. Shadwell died suddenly (of an apoplexy) at Chelsea near London in Nov., 1692." The day of the month is not given, and the placement of the cause of death in parentheses may indicate either uncertainty or that Wood's knowledge was not first hand, but the statement is closest in time to Shadwell's death and cannot be casually dismissed. Wood's information may have come from John Aubrey, who died in 1697 and knew Shadwell personally, but Aubrey's *Brief Lives* contains no entry for Shadwell nor any collateral comment on the cause of his death. The short life prefixed to the collected edition of Shadwell's plays published in 1720, the year before the second edition of *Athenae Oxoniensis*, mentions neither opium usage nor assigns a putative cause of death.[12] Thomas Birch's article on Shadwell in Bayle's *General Dictionary, Historical and Critical* (1734–39) is likewise uninformative. It served as the major source for the entry in *Biographia Britannica*[13] which repeats the information from Wood, crediting that source, but there is no relevant information in Whincop's *Dramatic Lists* (1747) nor Baker's *Biographia Dramatica* (1764).

The first written comment implicating opium in Shadwell's death was an annotation by William Oldys[14] in the copy of Langbaine[15] that he had bought in 1727. His marginal note was written between that date and 1761, when he died. Birch purchased Oldys's volume; the marginalia were transcribed by several scholars and widely circulated among literary antiquarians, but they were not printed until 1861.[16]

Oldys's note on the cause of Shadwell's death is firmly equivocal: "Tom Shadwell died suddenly of an apoplexy (or by taking too large a dose of opium given him by mistake) at Chelsea, near London, Nov. 20, 1692." Here we find that opium is placed in parentheses instead of apoplexy, and there is no guide as to which alternative to chose. Also, for the first time there is a suggestion that someone else gave Shadwell the fatal draught. Was it his wife? Was it the attendant Summers summoned from the vasty deep? Oldys was generally an accurate recorder, not given to supplying fictions of his own devising. If he did not secure his information from a written source, he must have heard it from someone whom he considered reliable. Like so many rumors, it persisted; in the next century Austin and Ralph were able to misquote Brady with equanimity in an effort to refute it. But, by the turn of the nineteenth century we hear no more about apoplexy. Saintsbury's *Introduction* to a selection of Shadwell's plays in the Mermaid Series describes him as "dying (perhaps of an overdose of opium) on November 19, 1692, at the age of fifty-two."[17] Opium still remains in parentheses and is qualified by "perhaps," but by 1924 the "perhaps" had vanished, and F. H. H. Guillemard states baldly: "Died at Chelsea, Nov. 20, 1692, from an overdose of opium."[18] Even overlooking the indecision as to the date, it is evident that rumor had solidified into accepted fact, and the four biographies written since have maintained that position.

Having examined the contradictory reports by literary historians about the cause of Shadwell's death, let us apply medical reasoning to the problem. In the absence of clinical details recorded by a competent observer, the results of such ratiocination will perforce be conjectural, but they may help reconcile conflicting statements. Armchair diagnosis, an attempt to reconstruct a medical problem at a remove of almost three centuries, is inherently speculative. The plain fact is that we do not know the cause of Shadwell's death and can only come to an "educated guess." There is no room for doubt that Shadwell had used opium for at least ten years to relieve the pain of a recurrent, episodic illness, then diagnosed as gout. By November 1692, when he was in his fifty-first to fifty-third year (his date of birth is variously given), he had been in poor health for over four years. The nature of his serious illness in 1688 to 1689 is not clear; Summers claims it kept him housebound in Chelsea for several months and was accompanied by pain in anatomic sites unspecified. We have abundant contemporary evidence that Shadwell was corpulent and that he ate and drank to excess. In *MacFlecknoe* Dryden describes him as having a "mountain belly," and in *Absalom and Achitophel* we see Shadwell as "round as a globe, and liquor'd ev'ry chink." Other citations might be added, but these will suffice to indicate that he continued to gormandize and guzzle long after the onset of gout. We picture him as a paunchy, rubicund old tosspot, jesting coarsely with the nearest barmaid, the Falstaff of the Restoration. Even before present-day knowledge about purine metabolism, dietary restriction was the common method used to control recurrent episodes of gouty arthritis. Shadwell's modus vivendi (et bibendi) was one calculated to do him the least amount of good and to accelerate the systemic effects of his underlying metabolic disease.

The systemic effects and visceral complications of gout are limited and predictable. According to John H. Talbott, "Kidney impairment, with varying severity of hypertension and arteriosclerosis, is the only critical complication of gout . . . [yet] in only a small percentage of cases does it result in uremia and premature death."[19] There is nothing to suggest that Shadwell died in uremia, but his regimen of gluttony and inebriety may well have accelerated the development of hypertensive and arteriosclerotic cardiovascular disease. With untreated gout of at least ten years' duration, Shadwell may have had mild renal damage, not clinically detectible but accompanied by moderate hypertension.

In patients over age fifty it is difficult to separate the arteriosclerosis due to gout from that which occurs in nongouty subjects. Talbott states that in his experience patients with gout are no more prone to develop coronary artery disease than those without gout, but Arthur Hall did find that hyperuricemia (increased blood uric acid levels) did influence the subsequent development of heart disease. Patients with gout usually have high blood uric acid levels. But the converse is not necessarily true.[20] Talbott's experience is based on *patients,* who presumably had the benefit of twentieth-century dietary regimens and modern drugs. Hall's observations stem from a prospective study of apparently healthy individuals. It seems reasonable to infer, albeit data for the specific prediction are not available, that individuals with untreated gout or patients who abuse their constitutions may be more susceptible to developing arteriosclerosis, specifically coronary sclerosis. Empirical observations by Talbott indicate that the youngest patient in his series to die of coronary heart disease was fifty-eight years old. Shadwell was somewhat younger, but he must be reckoned as an untreated case. Recently, Francis Viozzi and associates have reported six cases of myocardial infarction in ninety-one nonhypertensive, nondiabetic patients under age fifty who had had gout before the arterial thrombosis, for an incidence about seven times higher than nongouty individuals.[21] They concluded that elevated serum uric acid levels predisposed patients to arterial thrombosis, usually in the form of coronary or cerebrovascular occlusion.

Can we perhaps reconstruct the events of that dark, chilly evening of November 19, 1692, or the equally dark, chilly morning of November 20 as follows: Shadwell, in failing health, was about to retire (or had awakened) feeling ill, sicker than usual. Although accustomed to attacks of pain, he may have felt this one was more severe, more ominous than usual. We are not told precisely what his symptoms were. He may have had pain in an extremity, in the abdomen or flank, in the chest, or even headache. If he awakened with pain, he may have decided to take a somewhat larger dose of laudanum than usual, sleep away the morning, then proceed about his business as usual. If the onset of symptoms was in the evening, he may have taken a larger draught in the hope of obtaining a good night's sleep. If he was taking laudanum—that is, tincture of opium—he might have taken his dose from a bottle that had been left unstoppered for a while, resulting in evaporation of some of the alcohol and leaving a more concentrated solution; if so, a larger dose of a more highly concentrated narcotic might have been sufficient to be lethal. But he was a reasonably regular user of laudanum, and it is more likely that the solution in the bottle was of ordinary strength. In view of the fact that he was already quite habituated to the drug, it is unlikely that a double dose of it in ordinary concentration would have proved fatal.

The cause of death? Deliberate self-overdosage with suicidal intent seems unlikely. No credence can be given to Summers's statement that his illness of 1688 and 1689 had left him depressed. He may have been worried about his health, but he had been created poet laureate only three years before, and his position in the literary world was as high as it had ever been. Suicide seems out of character for this jolly writer of Restoration comedies. There is no medical evidence to point to uremia as a cause of death. If the attack of pain that necessitated a larger dose of opiate than usual was in an extremity, it would probably have been a recrudescence of gouty arthritis and would not have been fatal. The usual conditions that produce pain in the abdomen or flank—renal colic, biliary colic, perforated peptic ulcer, acute cholecystitis, acute pancreatitis, mesenteric thrombosis, and so forth—would likewise not have resulted in death a few hours later. It seems more probable, in view of the short interval between the onset of symptoms and death, that Shadwell died of a major vascular accident, dying in his sleep after taking an opiate to relieve the prodromal symptoms.

The vascular accidents most likely to prove fatal in a matter of hours are rupture of an aneurysm, either of the aorta or, statistically less frequent, some other major vessel; massive intracerebral hemorrhage; or occlusion of a major coronary artery. There is no clinical evidence to permit a firm choice among these possibilities. If we had any information about Shadwell's illness in 1688 to 1689, that might point more decisively in one direction than another. If we assume, however, that the natural history of arteriosclerotic disease has not materially altered since the end of the seventeenth century, it is reasonable to point out that both ruptured aortic aneurysms and massive intracerebral hemorrhages are more common after the age of sixty, whereas occlusion of major coronary arteries is not uncommon in the early fifties. The most probable sequence of events is that Shadwell's premonitory symptom was either chest pain or substernal oppression, that he took a somewhat larger dose of opium than usual, intending it as an analgesic and soporific, but succumbed in his sleep to a major coronary artery occlusion.

CHAPTER 10

Did Socrates Die
of Hemlock Poisoning?

The twentieth-century retinal image of the death of Socrates is conditioned by Jacques Louis David's famous depiction (1787) of the scene. We are familiar with it because it was reproduced in so many textbooks we studied in our youth, but probably few of us have tried to reconcile its content with the account given by Plato in the *Phaedo*.[1] To be sure, David's neoclassical approach to painting historic scenes did not pretend to verisimilitude. What he chose to dramatize is the moment when the jailer, his eyes averted, is handing Socrates the kylix with the lethal draught. Socrates is shown in midsentence, his left arm raised with the hand in an oratorical gesture, his right hand reaching for the cup. The prison cell seems quite spacious. There is room for six of Socrates' friends to stand in various attitudes of grief at the head of his couch, while another sits in dejection at the foot, and yet an eighth stands sobbing against the wall of the passageway leading to the cell. Seen in the background are three more friends departing in sorrow before the final moment.

Whether David had read the *Phaedo* closely we do not know, but Plato lists fourteen of Socrates' disciples as being present; David had room for only eleven in his composition. One also observes that the kylix is without the customary two handles, but perhaps a simpler utensil was used when prisoners were put to death. But the disturbing feature of David's painting is its sense of space. To be sure, we do not have floor plans of the jail at Athens, but as a general rule rooms in Greek buildings and houses were smaller than rooms used for similar functions today, and there is no reason to believe that the ancient

Greeks offered spacious and gracious quarters to their convicted felons. It is difficult for anyone familiar with prisons in any period to imagine a cell commodious enough to hold the prisoner, the jailer, and eleven or fourteen witnesses. A possible solution is that the execution took place in a special chamber, one in which there would be room for such an assembly and for the condemned man to walk around to hasten the effects of the toxin, as we are told Socrates did. But we are not told that there was such a chamber, and indeed, when we examine Plato's account, we will discover that several items of information are not given.

Plato is careful to let us know that he was not present at the execution. He was sick. Whether this was a diplomatic illness or not, we shall never know. But if we consider the nature of Socrates' trial and the temper of the times, there is good reason why a prudent man might not wish to seem too closely associated with him. The important facts in the case are known, not only from Plato's account but from Xenophon's independently written version supplemented by our general information about the antecedent political events and the Athenian code of justice. But Xenophon's evidence is based on hearsay; absent in Asia at the time, he wrote his account many years later.

Socrates was indicted and tried in 399 B.C. when he was seventy years old. Athens had finally lost the Peloponnesian War in 404 B.C. One major event had been the loss of a naval battle at Notium in 407 for which Alcibiades, who had not even been present, was unjustly blamed. He felt public disgrace keenly and retired to a castle on the Hellespont. Socrates, his tutor and friend, incurred only transient unpopularity; he was still held in sufficient esteem in 404 to be elected one of the proedri of the senate. He had the ill luck to be chosen by rota to be epistates, that is, presiding officer of the Prytaneis, the senate's leading committee, election to which was by lot, on the day a motion was brought to condemn to death the eight commanders blamed for losing the naval battle off Aegospotami in the summer of 405, after which Athens was invested. Socrates opposed the motion on grounds of conscience and incurred public disfavor thereby. It was an empty gesture, for the eight hapless naval officers were condemned and executed. Later in 404 the Spartans led by Lysander demolished fortifications at Piraeus, and reduction of Athenian power was complete.

Following this debacle Athens was governed by an oligarchy of thirty led by Critias, another of Socrates' former pupils. The period proved to be a reign of terror. Even though Socrates had not publicly denounced the political murders committed by Critias and his henchmen, Athenians who had been willing to overlook his influence on

Alcibiades began to feel that his political teachings did not produce the sort of democratic leadership they wanted. The unjust satire in Aristophanes' *Clouds* (425 B.C.) was revived and took effect.

We are not told how sentiment hostile to Socrates developed during the five years from 404 to 399 B.C., but by the latter date his enemy Anytus, who had gained considerable political influence from his sufferings under the oligarchy and zeal for democracy, felt he could muster enough votes against him. Charges were officially brought by Meletus, an obscure poet, and seconded by Lycon, a rhetorician. The nature of the charge is familiar: not believing in the gods of the city, introducing new gods, and corrupting the youth. One can trace them back to Aristophanes' *Clouds*. Atheism and worship of strange gods formed a stock accusation against the physical philosophers, and corrupting the minds of the young was likewise a stock accusation against the Sophists. The indictment was general; it alleged no specific felonious act by Socrates. In effect it was like an accusation of sedition, which can mean anything the party in power wants.

We are not given the details of Meletus's speech before the 501 dicasts (jurymen); we can only infer its substance from Plato's *Apology*. But the *Apology*, written some years after the trial, is not a complete account of the judicial proceedings. However, Socrates' uncompromising defense was not designed to win sympathy from a jury. He refused to appeal to their compassion, urging them to decide the case on its merits and according to law. As legal strategy in adversary proceedings, this was not prudent, and Socrates was condemned by a vote of 281 to 220. This did not mean that a majority of his fellow citizens desired his execution. In all likelihood they viewed him not so much as a danger to the security of the state but as a tiresome and argumentative old man who would never admit that he was wrong. He was also in the habit of giving his neighbors information they did not wish to hear. All too often cases are decided not on the issues of law but as popularity contests. The dicasts probably felt that when Socrates proposed an alternative sentence, as was his right, the mandatory death sentence would be mitigated to exile, from which point they would no longer have to listen to him.

The foregoing summary of the familiar sequence of events makes it plain that Socrates was condemned in a period of Athenian history characterized by political and civil unrest. A crushing military defeat had been followed by a tyrannical oligarchy that ruled by terror, and which was replaced by a government with only superficial pretenses to democracy. As one follows Greek history from that time to the present, the risks of political life seem not to have changed materially. During

Jacques Louis David's *The Death of Socrates* (1787). Reproduced by courtesy of the Metropolitan Museum of Art

recent decades similar trials have been held in Athens; the choice of individuals to suffer exile, imprisonment, or execution depends on which faction has most latterly managed to seize power. Although we pay homage to Athens as the cradle of democracy, despite its valued unique word *parresia,* when it came to practice, that city never was nor is it now the cradle of free speech and expression.

Plato's dialogues were written many years after the fact. It is universally accepted that they do not contain Socrates' ipsissima verba but that they do embody the substance of his ideas and his way of arriving at them by question and answer. Later readers are willing to accept Plato's reconstruction as real when the dialogues deal with philosophical ideas, but there is also a tendency to consider them factual when they deal with actual events, notably the trial and death of Socrates. We have already seen that Plato was not present at the execution. His account is secondhand, based on hearsay from men whose emotional involvement was intense. Any critical reading must put cautionary value on the details in such depositions, even though they were given with the best intentions. Another limitation is that the dialogues are written in a literary form tantamount in its day to a philosophical novel, the tension of each dialogue mounting to a climax. Socrates is the hero and never loses an argument. We are reminded of a popular television series in which a clever lawyer always outwits a bumbling prosecution by adroit cross-examination of witnesses. The conventions of the literary form of the dialogues were tacitly understood by Plato and his contemporary readers. Omissions, interpolations, and embellishments by the writer were permissible. No one mistook them for reportage, nor was Plato's intention to represent events *wie eigentlich gewesen.* The death scene is, perhaps, the best case in point.

We can, however, accept as fact the denial of Socrates' plea for mitigation of sentence. At no point did he appear contrite or apologetic. His first proposal that he be given free lodging and board at the town hall and his later offer to pay a fine of one mina (raised by his friends to thirty-nine minae) were insults to the dignity of the court. Such behavior hardened the attitude of those who might have settled for a lesser sentence. We may also accept as fact that Socrates was not executed on the day following the verdict, as was the custom. He was kept in prison awaiting execution until the sacred ship returned from its ritual journey to Delos, a period in the calendar during which many civil functions were prorogued.

But the inevitable hour drew near, and the *Phaedo* describes Socrates' last day on earth. It is an eloquent and moving account of his resolute attitude and serene approach to death. Much of the dialogue is given over to a discussion of what death means, and Socrates expresses his conviction that it is merely the separation of the soul (psyche) from the body. Plato's prose, at least as we read it in translation (and few of us can do more), is so beguiling that it is easy for us to suspend our disbelief and not examine carefully his description of the final moments. Perhaps one reason why Socrates is so much more popular in the Christian era than any other Greek philosopher is that he faced death firmly and calmly rather than renounce his principles, thereby prefiguring the death of Christ, his disciples, and many generations of Christian martyrs. But the analogy is not exact. Socrates submitted to the exaction of the law surrounded by his friends; when Christ was arrested, his disciples went underground. Socrates had an opportunity to bargain his sentence; once the Christian martyrs fell into the hands of civil authority they had no more options than the Marrano Jews who fell into the clutches of the Inquisition. And we are told that Christian martyrdom is never an accident; it is not the will of man but the design of God. We also recall that Galileo recanted, but his reputation has not suffered therefore.

Toward sunset of the appointed day the jailer brought Socrates the cup of hemlock. Socrates asked him for instructions how best to proceed. The jailer advised him to walk about until his legs felt heavy, then to lie down, and the poison would act. Socrates took the cup and asked whether he might make a libation to any god. One construes the remark to indicate that his mind was set to observe the proprieties of the solemn occasion and that his stated desire to make such a ritual gesture would support his claim to innocence of the charge of atheism. The jailer informed him that the cup held just enough to constitute a lethal dose. Socrates asked the gods to prosper his journey to the other world, and then "raising the cup to his lips, quite readily and cheerfully drank off the poison."[2]

At this juncture we must ask ourselves just what was in that kylix. Presumably it was an infusion of the leaves and possibly the root of the umbelliferous plant *Conium maculatum* which looks something like a carrot but has a white root. Its leaves have been mistaken for parsnip, parsley, or celery. But it is not to be confused with fool's parsley, *Aethusa cynapium,* nor, of course, with the familiar evergreens of the genus *Tsuga. Conium maculatum* is most commonly known as spotted hemlock because of the purple spots on its stem, but a number of regional synonyms exist. It contains the neurotoxic alkaloid coniine (cf. κςνειον), 2-propyl-piperidine, which is more highly concentrated in the root than in the leaves.

Nicander was the first to record the symptoms of hemlock poisoning.

As expected, he mentions numbness in the legs, but he also records rolling eyes, choking in the throat and trachea, the gasping respiration of asphyxia, such as "the victim draws his breath like one swooning," and disturbed consciousness.[3] More modern writers report that the toxin acts rapidly, and, depending on dosage, death occurs in a matter of minutes to less than three hours.[4] Clinton Thienes and Thomas Haley give the toxic dose as 60 mg. and the fatal dose as 150 to 300 mg. (2 to 5 gr.).[5] All authorities agree that ascending motor paralysis is the most prominent feature of coniine poisoning and that death is due to asphyxia when the muscles of respiration and the medullary centers are involved.[6] This coincides with the account of Socrates walking around his cell until his legs began to fail. But when we are told that the jailer pressed his foot hard and could elicit no sensation, we search in vain for reports of coniine producing peripheral anesthesia. Yet the text of the *Phaedo* emphasizes the point: "and then his leg, so upwards and upwards, and showed us that he was cold and stiff." This certainly does not resemble the flaccid paralysis of coniine acting on motor nerve ends. However, we ought not take literally the next statement that "When the poison reaches the heart, that will be the end." The Greeks did not know about neural control of respiration, and we must reinterpret the sentence as a description of the sense of oppression in the chest that accompanies asphyxia.

But there is more to coniine poisoning than simple ascending motor paralysis. Sydney Smith and Frederick Fiddes describe "first a burning pain in the mouth and abdomen with nausea and vomiting due to local irritant action. . . . Sometimes convulsions occur, but dyspnoea with cyanosis and progressive muscular weakness are the prominent features."[7] The most recent description is by Wolfgang von Oettingen and is more detailed:

Coniine poisoning usually takes a very rapid course. During the first half-hour the symptoms consist mainly of salivation, nausea, vomiting, and irritation of the pharynx. Later the mouth becomes dry, the patient suffers from thirst, and he is unable to swallow. These symptoms are followed by convulsion, weakening of the lower extremities, and paralysis of the skeletal muscles, those regulating the respiratory movements being the last to be affected. The pupils are nearly always dilated, and the patient may suffer from diplopia and amblyopia and impaired hearing . . . but consciousness is preserved up to the end.[8]

It is difficult to reconcile such description with the serene and peaceful death Plato describes thus: "he uncovered his face, for he had covered himself up, and said—they were his last words—'Crito, I owe a cock to Aesculapius; will you remember to pay the debt?' . . . in a minute or two a movement was heard, and the attendants uncovered him; his eyes were set, and Crito closed his eyes and mouth." Plato did not describe the burning sensation in the mouth and stomach, nor diplopia and amblyopia, thirst and inability to swallow; these, after all, are subjective sensations, and Socrates may not have complained of them aloud. But Plato does not mention salivation, nausea, retching, or vomiting. Nor is there any mention of tremors, clonic movements of a limb, let alone a generalized convulsion. Nor is there any description of cyanosis or the dyspnea and gasping respiration of terminal asphyxia. We can only conclude that the witnesses did not give Plato an accurate description or that Plato chose to omit such details as he felt were unpleasant or would detract from the image of Socrates facing death bravely and dying peacefully. It is unlikely that the witnesses were inaccurate; enough of their contemporaries had been given hemlock for them to be familiar with the more gruesome aspects of death by that means. It is almost certain that Plato, relating the event some years after it took place, chose to edit the facts and present a literary version which was in harmony with Socrates' philosophical ideas.

When one tampers with the facts, ambiguities are bound to arise for later readers. For example, scholarly tradition requires us to interpret Socrates' last words, "Crito, I owe a cock to Aesculapius" as ironic, suggesting that death was about to cure him of the sickness of life. Why indeed should a man who has already swallowed poison ask a friend to make a sacrifice in his name to the god of health? But the second part of the sentence suggests a different interpretation: "Will you remember to pay the debt?" Surely, even if Crito was known to be absent-minded, this was no occasion to tease him. More likely, Socrates, then seventy years old, had suffered from some minor, undisclosed ailment, had prayed to the god, but because of his trial and imprisonment had not had time to fulfill his vow. If we interpret his offer to pour a libation as evidence that he wanted to play his last scene with strict adherence to form, surely his exit line ought to be interpreted in the same way. But, understanding that Plato has doctored the story, can we be sure that these really were Socrates' last words? Could they have been supplied for rhetorical effect? Perhaps David's neoclassical rendition of the scene is no farther from the truth than Plato's account.

What could have been Plato's motive for such a *suppressio veri?* The simplest answer is that he wanted to preserve the noble image of his friend and teacher, "the wisest and justest and best," and that he wanted no undignified details to obscure the heroic manner of his death. He was writing literature, not an historical annal. He was also writing philosophy, and Christopher Gill, who has examined the question from a philosopher's point of view, interprets Plato's free rendering of the death scene as an elaboration of the theme of the purification of the psyche from the body: "The final movement of Socrates' body is the last index of the *psyche*'s presence, perhaps the movement of its actual departure. The quietness, the calmness, the regularity of the effects of the penetration of poison into Socrates' body (so different from the chaos, squalor, and collapse described by Nicander and modern toxicologists) is the quietness of a ritual, the *katharmos* or purification of the soul from the prison of the body."[9]

Plato's treatment of the scene, transforming an historical event into a philosophical idea, has proved effective as mythopoesis, so much so that the received account is generally taken for fact. When we return to the question put in the title of this chapter, "Did Socrates Die of Hemlock Poisoning?" the answer must be yes. But we know this more from our acquaintance with the practices of the ancient Greeks and their penal code than from Plato's description of Socrates' signs and symptoms. Yet who would change a word of the *Phaedo* in the name of accuracy? Nonetheless, when one rereads the printed page in the cold light of the North Library, taking refuge from the smoke and fog of a December afternoon, one cannot wholly forget that the *Phaedo* is cast as an art form and that a satisfactory death for Socrates is its necessary and climactic metaphor. Perhaps Plato's unconscious parricidal wishes were displaced onto his teacher and he has taken the circumstances of Socrates' legally sanctioned death to neutralize his own guilt feelings which may have accounted for his not being there. The inevitable distortions needed to transform this life experience safely into art account for its success as a sublimating and cathartic drama.

NOTES

CHAPTER 1 BOSWELL'S CLAP

1. Most of the references cited in the text are to the trade edition of Boswell's journals. These have been edited and published and cover the years 1762 through 1776. Most of the references to events after 1776 are taken from the privately printed edition, limited to 570 copies, of the collection of Boswell's papers made by the late Col. Ralph Isham. Boswell wrote his journals in bound volumes, the entries being based on informal notes and memoranda. The trade edition combines journal entries and dated notes and memoranda in a coherent sequence. The Isham papers are a chronological record of individual items. The distinction between notes and memoranda is somewhat arbitrary, the former being somewhat more fully written out and dated, the latter often in the form of jottings on scraps of paper.

See Geoffrey Scott and Frederick A. Pottle, eds., *Private Papers of James Boswell from Malahide Castle in the Collection of Lt.-Colonel Ralph Heyward Isham*, 18 vols. (New York: privately printed, 1928–34; index vol., 1937); Frederick A. Pottle, ed., *Boswell's London Journal, 1762–1763* (New York: McGraw-Hill, 1950); Frederick A. Pottle, "The History of the Boswell Papers," in *Boswell's London Journal, 1762–1763*, deluxe ed. (London: Heinemann, 1951), pp. xi–xlii; Frederick A. Pottle, ed., *Boswell in Holland, 1763–1764* (New York: McGraw-Hill, 1952); Frederick A. Pottle, ed., *Boswell on the Grand Tour: Germany and Switzerland, 1764* (New York: McGraw-Hill, 1953); Frank Brady and Frederick A. Pottle, eds., *Boswell on the Grand Tour: Italy, Corsica, and France, 1765–1766* (New York: McGraw-Hill, 1955); Frank Brady and Frederick A. Pottle, eds., *Boswell in Search of a Wife, 1766–1769* (New York: McGraw-Hill, 1957); William K. Wimsatt, Jr., and Frederick A. Pottle, eds., *Boswell for the Defense, 1769–1774* (New York: McGraw-Hill 1959); Frederick A. Pottle and C. H. Bennet, eds., *Boswell's Journal of a Tour to the Hebrides with Samuel Johnson, LL.D., 1773* (New York: McGraw-Hill, 1961); Charles Ryskamp and Frederick A. Pottle, eds., *Boswell: The Ominous Years, 1774–1776* (New York: McGraw-

Hill, 1963); Frederick A. Pottle, *James Boswell: The Earlier Years, 1740–1769* (New York: McGraw-Hill, 1966).

2. *Boswell: The Earlier Years*, p. 47.

3. Ibid., p. 50.

4. Chauncey B. Tinker, ed., *Letters of James Boswell* (London: Oxford Univ. Press, 1924) I, 8.

5. *Boswell: The Earlier Years*, p. 53.

6. "James Boswell, Journalist," in *The Age of Johnson: Essays Presented to Chauncey Brewster Tinker*, ed. Frederick W. Hilles and Wilmarth S. Lewis (New Haven: Yale Univ. Press, 1949), pp. 15–25.

7. *Boswell's London Journal*, pp. 49–50.

8. *Boswell: The Earlier Years*, pp. 483–84.

9. *Boswell's London Journal*, p. 117.

10. Ibid., p. 139.

11. Paul Fussell, "The Memorable Scenes of Mr. Boswell," *Encounter*, 28 (1967), 70–77.

12. *Boswell's London Journal*, p. 145.

13. Ibid., p. 149.

14. Ibid., p. 155.

15. Ibid., pp. 155–58.

16. Ibid., p. 160.

17. Ibid., p. 161.

18. Ibid., p. 175.

19. Ibid.

20. *Boswell: The Earlier Years*, p. 2.

21. *Boswell's London Journal*, p. 231.

22. Ibid., pp. 255–56.

23. Memoranda, Yale MS. J3.

24. *Boswell on the Grand Tour: Germany and Switzerland*, p. 91.

25. Ibid., p. 254.

26. Ibid.

27. Yale MS. A34.

28. *Boswell on the Grand Tour: Italy, Corsica, and France*, p. 74.

29. Memorandum, June 27, 1965.

30. *Boswell on the Grand Tour: Italy, Corsica, and France*, p. 11.

31. Ralph S. Walker, ed., *The Correspondence of James Boswell and John Johnston of Grange* (New York: McGraw-Hill, 1966), p. 174.

32. Memorandum, August 22, 1765, Yale MS. J6.

33. *Boswell on the Grand Tour: Italy, Corsica, and France*, p. 272.

34. *Boswell in Search of a Wife*, p. 37.

35. Ibid., p. 76.

36. Ibid., p. 80.

37. *Boswell: The Earlier Years*, p. 321.

38. *Boswell in Search of a Wife*, p. 117.

39. Ibid., p. 121.

40. Ibid., p. 150.

41. *Correspondence of Boswell and Johnston*, p. 174.

42. *Letters of Boswell*, I, pp. 153–54.

43. *Boswell in Search of a Wife*, p. 167.

44. Norman E. Himes, *Medical History of Contraception* (New York: Gamut, 1963), pp. 194–200.

45. *Boswell in Search of a Wife,* p. 207.

46. Ibid., p. 290.

47. Ibid., p. 317.

48. *Boswell for the Defense,* p. 35.

49. Ibid., p. 140.

50. *Boswell: The Ominous Years,* p.. x.

51. Ibid.

52. *Boswell: The Ominous Years,* p. 326.

53. A letter to Boswell from West Digges, the actor, dated February 18, 1763, does give a prescription for a urethral irrigant: "take care of falling under the Displeasure of Dame Venus. If you are ever sous'd again I transmit you a receipt for an Infection (Gratis) Rx: Aq. Ros. sub. 1 tbsp. / Trochii alb. Rhazii 2½ drams[.] Any sensible apothecary will tell you what quantity of white vitriol should be added.—N.B. A *Pewter* Syringe is the best. Eheu!" (Yale MS. C1042.)

White vitriol is zinc sulfate, which is relatively bland, and the white troches of rhases with rose water could not have done much harm (or good). A comparable recipe is to be found in James's *Pharmacopoeia Universalis* as a specific irrigant for gonorrhea:

"Take Compound Powder of Ceruse, three drams; Camphire, a Scruple. Dissolve them in twelve Ounces of Spring water for an Injection, or Take the Root of Marshmallows and Linseed, each of two Drams. Boil them in a pint of Water to the Consistence of a Syrup. Then strain it off for an Injection. Either of these Compositions, used two or three times a day, will be very servicable in a Gonorrhea, in order to supple the Urethra, allay the heat of Urine, . . . and prevent a Cordee." Ceruse is white lead ($2PbCO_3.Pb[OH]_2$), but the other ingredients are all of vegetable origin (Robert James, *Pharmacopoeia Universalis: or, A New Universal English Dispensatory,* . . . 2d ed. [London: Hodges, 1752], p. 747).

54. *Private Papers of Boswell,* XIII, 88; XIV, 93–94.

55. Ibid., XIII, 89.

56. Ibid., p. 90.

57. Ibid., pp. 93, 99.

58. Ibid., p. 107.

59. Ibid., XIV, 93.

60. Ibid., p. 94.

61. Ibid., pp. 120, 153.

62. Ibid., p. 211.

63. Ibid., pp. 222, 226.

64. Ibid., pp. 230–31.

65. Ibid., XV, 11.

66. Ibid., XVI, 15

67. Ibid., pp. 16–24.

68. Ibid., p. 30.

69. Ibid., p. 86.

70. Ibid., p. 89.

71. Ibid., p. 128

72. Ibid.
73. Ibid., p. 102.
74. Ibid., pp. 103, 105.
75. Ibid., p. 131.
76. *Boswell: The Ominous Years,* pp. 352–55.
77. *Private Papers of Boswell,* XVI, 167.
78. Ibid., p. 169.
79. Ibid., p. 184.
80. Ibid., p. 185.
81. The traditional English taste for port dates back to 1703 when the treaties negotiated by John Methuen provided that English cloth would be admitted to Portugal at a low tariff while Portuguese wines could enter England at rates one-third below those charged for French wines. Claret, an English favorite since the days of Henry II, was being rivaled if not supplanted in popular consumption by port during Boswell's lifetime as a result of economic and political factors.
82. *Private Papers of Boswell,* XVIII, 71.
83. Ibid., p. 26.
84. Ibid., pp. 29, 32.
85. Ibid., p. 48.
86. Ibid., pp. 53–56.
87. Ibid., pp. 60–61.
88. Ibid., p. 56.
89. Ibid., pp. 65, 68.
90. Ibid., pp. 81–86.
91. Boswell may have been attempting a mild pun. "Pleasance" was a slum area in Edinburgh, the environs of a pre-Reformation Fransican convent, a branch of Santa Maria di Campagna in Piacenza (Placentia), in Parma. "Pleasance" is a corruption of Placentia.
92. *Private Papers of Boswell,* XIII, 271; ibid., XIV, 3, 39.
93. Ibid., XVI, 60; ibid., XVIII, 176, 188.
94. James Grieg, ed., *The Farington Diary by Joseph Farington, R. A.,* 2d ed. (London: Hutchinson, 1922), I, 95.
95. *Letters of Boswell,* II, 466.
96. Ibid., pp. 466–67.
97. *Papers of Boswell,* XVIII, 276. MS. in collection of J. Pierpont Morgan Library, New York, N.Y.
98. *Letters of Boswell,* II, 465.
99. Ibid., p. 464.
100. Ibid., p. 465.
101. In his anxiety about his father's condition, James, Jr., misdated the quarto half sheet bearing his father's last scrawl and his own footnote; he wrote April 8, but the events described clearly took place in the first week of May.
102. Unpublished MS. in collection of J. Pierpont Morgan Library, New York, N.Y.
103. *Letters of Boswell,* II, 467.
104. Ibid., pp. 467–68.
105. Ibid., p. 468.
106. Ovid, *Amores* I, ix, 4.
107. *Private Papers of Boswell,* XIII, 178.

108. *Boswell in Search of a Wife,* p. 108.
109. Ps. 119:9.
110. *Boswell's London Journal,* pp. 53–54.
111. *Boswell: The Earlier Years,* p. 4.
112. Ibid., p. 30.
113. Ibid.
114. *Boswell on the Grand Tour: Germany and Switzerland,* p. 285.
115. Letters of Boswell, I, 7.
116. *Boswell's London Journal,* p. 244.
117. Memoranda, Yale MS. J7; *Boswell on the Grand Tour: Germany and Switzerland,* p. 130.
118. p. 11.
119. *Private Papers of Boswell,* XIII, 81.
120. Ibid., XV, 122.
121. *Boswell: The Earlier Years,* pp. 203, 376–77; *Boswell: The Ominous Years,* pp. 304–7.
122. *Boswell: The Ominous Years,* p. 74.
123. Margaret Boswell's obstetrical record is as follows: 1) term delivery followed by neonatal death, August 28, 1770; 2) spontaneous abortion, March 3, 1772; 3) term delivery, Veronica, born March 15, 1773; 4) term delivery, Euphemia, born May 20, 1774; 5) term delivery, Alexander, born October 9, 1775; 6) term delivery, David, born November 15, 1776 (died March 29, 1777, age 4½ months); 7) spontaneous abortion, July 29, 1777; 8) term delivery, James, Jr., born September 15, 1778; 9) term delivery, Elizabeth, born June 15, 1780. There is no written evidence of a pregnancy between 1770 and 1772. This interruption in the cycle of annual pregnancies may have been the sequel of a slow healing of lacerations incurred at her first delivery, which was difficult and traumatic. After 1780 she was in poor health most of the time, and one must infer that marital relations became progressively less frequent.
124. *Private Papers of Boswell,* XVI, 19.

CHAPTER 2   SWINBURNE'S MASOCHISM: NEUROPATHOLOGY AND PSYCHOPATHOLOGY

1. All poems and other works by Swinburne cited in this chapter are identified by their first date of publication; however, like many authors and poets of his day, Swinburne delayed the publication of many of his works until several years after they had been written. For certain works, when appropriate or necessary for chronology, I shall cite the dates they were written and/or their publishing history.
2. Louis J. Bragman, "The Case of Algernon Charles Swinburne: A Study in Sadism," *Psychoanalytical Review,* 21 (1934), 59–74; Terence V. Moore, "A Study in Sadism: The Life of Algernon Charles Swinburne," *Character and Personality,* 6 (1937), 1–15.
3. Cecil Y. Lang, ed., *The Swinburne Letters,* VI (New Haven: Yale Univ. Press, 1962), 238–48.
4. Edmund Gosse, *The Life of Algernon Charles Swinburne* (London: Macmillan, 1917).

5. Elaine Caruth, "The Onion and the Moebius Strip," *Psychoanalytical Review*, 55 (1968), 415–25.

6. Sigmund Freud, "A Child is Being Beaten," *Collected Papers*, (London: Hogarth Press, 1933), II, 195–96.

7. Bradford A. Booth, ed., *The Letters of Anthony Trollope* (New York: Oxford Univ. Press, 1951), p. 17.

8. Panshanger MSS., Box 18, undated but probably between 1828 and 1832.

9. C. R. Strother, "Minimal Cerebral Dysfunction: A Historical Overview," *Annals of the New York Academy of Science,* 205 (1973), 8.

10. Herbert G. Birch, "The Problem of 'Brain Damage' in Children," in *Brain Damage in Children—The Biological and Social Aspects,* ed. H. G. Birch (New York: Williams and Wilkins, 1964), p. 8.

11. Cecil Y. Lang, ed., *The Swinburne Letters,* IV (New Haven: Yale Univ. Press, 1960), 12. This assertion was denied some years after Swinburne's death by his younger cousin, Mrs. Disney Leith (nee Mary Gordon), but she denied so many demonstrably true intrafamilial matters that she cannot be considered a reliable spokesman. However, Mrs. Leith was three years younger and may not have been informed that her favorite cousin had suffered neonatal distress.

12. C. Keith Conners, "The Syndrome of Minimal Brain Dysfunction: Psychological Aspects," *Pediatric Clinics of North America,* 14 (1967), 749–66; Abraham Towbin, "Organic Causes of Minimal Brain Dysfunction: Perinatal Origin of Minimal Cerebral Lesions," *Journal of the American Medical Association,* 217 (1971), 1207–14; Bennett M. Derby, "Minimal Brain Dysfunction and the Hyperkinetic Child: Structural Basis," *New York State Journal of Medicine,* 72 (1972), 2061–62.

13. Edmund Gosse, "Swinburne's Agitation," in *The Swinburne Letters,* VI, ed. Cecil Y. Lang (New Haven: Yale Univ. Press, 1962), 238–48.

14. *Life of Swinburne,* p. 26.

15. Ibid., pp. 66–67.

16. Ibid., p. 296.

17. A. C. Benson, "Theodore Watts-Dunton," in *English Critical Essays: Twentieth Century,* ed. P. M. Jones (London: Oxford Univ. Press, 1933), pp. 132, 133.

18. Ibid., p. 136.

19. Mrs. Disney Leith, *The Boyhood of Algernon Charles Swinburne: Personal Recollections of His Cousin Mrs. Disney Leith with Extracts from Some of His Private Papers* (London: Chatto & Windus, 1917), p. 5.

20. *Life of Swinburne,* p. 14.

21. Cecil Y. Lang, ed., *The Swinburne Letters,* I (New Haven: Yale Univ. Press, 1959), 63.

22. *Boyhood of Swinburne,* p. 38.

23. *Life of Swinburne,* pp. 314–15.

24. Ibid., p. 70.

25. Birch, "Problem of 'Brain Damage' in Children."

26. *Boyhood of Swinburne,* p. 3.

27. "Swinburne himself gave '1862–63' as the period in which he wrote *Love's Cross-Currents* (in a passage where he called it his 'maiden attempt at a study of contemporary life and manners')" (Randolph Hughes, *Lesbia Brandon by Algernon Charles Swinburne* [London: Falcon Press, 1952], p. 197). Georges

Lafourcade states it was first published in 1877 in *The Tatler* under the original title *A Year's Letters* and then under the new title *Love's Cross-Currents* in 1905.

28. Tracing the history of *Lesbia Brandon* is like reading a mystery story, presented *in toto* and in detail by Hughes, who first published the novel. However, brief recital of some of that history here may be useful. Swinburne's first reference to the novel was in a letter to Mary Gordon in October 1864. Sometime in the early 1870s, he sent the unfinished manuscript to his publisher, John Camden Hotten, for his appraisal. However, when Hotten died in 1873, Watts-Dunton, in trying to straighten out the poet's business affairs with that publisher, wrote to Swinburne " 'that there are two novels of yours in manuscript lying at Hotten's place.' . . . They could only have been *Love's Cross-Currents* and *Lesbia Brandon*. . . . it is very probable that had he [Hotten] lived longer he not only would have brought out *Love's Cross-Currents*, but would have encouraged Swinburne to complete *Lesbia Brandon*. . . . His death at this stage was almost unquestionably a setback to the fortunes of these two works, and in the . . . [case] of *Lesbia Brandon* a very serious one that was never retrieved" (Hughes, *Lesbia Brandon*, pp. 205–9). What was left of the work was placed in the British Museum and was not published until 1952, even though "Swinburne himself [considered] the work . . . one of his dearest, most important, undertakings . . . [in fact] he stated categorically . . . that he 'certainly meant to complete' it at some time in the future. . . . [However] The chief, if not the only, reason for the hold-up was apparently, and even evidently, very cautelous opposition on the part of Watts-Dunton. . . . he obstinately failed over some four years, in spite of reiterated urgent demands from Swinburne, to return parts of the work which had been lent to him. . . . The reason could only have been that he strongly disapproved of certain of the themes of the novel and Swinburne's treatment of them. The disabling loss of the missing parts, then, would go to explain why Swinburne never carried out his firmly-expressed intention of completing the novel" (ibid., pp. 230–40).

29. Georges Lafourcade, *Swinburne: A Literary Biography* (New York: William Morrow & Co., 1932), p. 10.

30. *Swinburne Letters*, I, 82.

31. Cecil Y. Lang, ed., *The Swinburne Letters*, III (New Haven: Yale Univ. Press, 1960), 12.

32. Hughes, *Lesbia Brandon*, p. 18.

33. Ibid., p. 10.

34. Jean Overton Fuller, *Swinburne: A Biography* (New York: Schocken Books, 1968).

35. *Swinburne Letters*, I, 109–10.

36. F. A. C. Wilson, "To the Editor: Swinburne and Mary Gordon," *Times Literary Supplement*, 16 Jan. 1969, p. 62.

37. *Boyhood of Swinburne*, p. 27.

38. *Swinburne Letters*, I, 256.

39. Ibid., pp. 259–60.

40. Ibid., p. 265.

41. *Swinburne: A Biography*, p. 260.

42. See Lafourcade, *Swinburne: A Literary Biography*, p. 47.

43. To my knowledge, this work has never been published.

44. Fuller, *Swinburne: A Biography*, p. 50.

45. See Gosse, *Life of Swinburne;* Fuller, *Swinburne: A Biography;* and Philip Henderson, *Swinburne: The Portrait of a Poet* (London: Routledge & Kegan Paul, 1974).

46. *Swinburne Letters,* I, 54–55.

47. Ibid., p. 56.

48. Ibid., pp. 121–22.

49. Ibid., p. 125.

50. Ibid., pp. 74–75.

51. Ibid., III, 191–92.

52. Ibid., II, 297.

53. Ibid., VI, 179.

54. Ibid., I, 123.

55. Ibid., p. 166.

56. *Pre-Raphaelite Twilight: The Story of Charles Augustus Howell* (London: Richards Press, 1954).

57. *Swinburne Letters,* II, 180.

58. Gosse, "Swinburne's Agitation," *Swinburne Letters,* VI, 245.

59. Ibid., p. 246.

60. *Swinburne Letters,* II, 75–76.

61. Ibid., pp. 126–28.

62. Ibid., pp. 133–34.

63. *Swinburne Letters,* I, 109–10.

64. Fuller, *Swinburne: A Biography.*

65. See *Swinburne Letters,* II, letter numbers 310, 310a, 318, 346, 386, 387, 400, 445.

66. William R. Rothenstein, *Men and Memories: Recollections of William R. Rothenstein* (London: Faber & Faber, 1931).

67. The first published account of this incident was in the Goncourt's journals; apparently William Rothenstein related it to Edmond Goncourt, telling him he had it on Whistler's authority. Georges Lafourcade repeated the anecdote, and it seems to have been accepted as part of the canon. Mario Praz (*The Romantic Agony,* 2d ed., tr. Angus Davidson [New York: Oxford Univ. Press, 1951]) recalls that Laurence Binyon, who befriended Solomon in his last years, informed him that in addition he and Swinburne daubed or splattered each other with red ink, presumably to simulate the marks of the birch.

68. *Swinburne Letters,* I, 305.

69. Ibid., II, 232.

70. Ibid., p. 12.

71. Ibid., p. 20.

72. Derek Hudson, *Munby: Man of Two Worlds. The Life and Diaries of Arthur J. Munby, 1828–1910* (London: John Murray, Ltd., 1972), p 270.

73. Ibid., p. 238.

74. Gosse, "Swinburne's Agitation," *Swinburne Letters,* VI, 245. In a footnote to Gosse's manuscript, Lang identified the address of this establishment as 7 Circus Road, St. John's Wood, N.W. The Greater London Council will not likely honor this structure with one of its blue tile medallions as a national monument.

75. *Swinburne Letters,* I, 136.

76. Ibid., p. 187.

77. Ibid., IV, 42–43.

78. Ibid., VI, 201–2.

79. Ibid., pp. 213–14.

80. Mollie Panter-Downes, "At the Pines. II. When I Had Wings, My Brother," *New Yorker*, 30 Jan. 1971.

81. *Swinburne Letters*, VI, 71–72.

82. James Joyce, *Ulysses* (New York: Random House, 1934), p. 459.

83. *The Rodiad* (1871) was published by John Camden Hotten (Swinburne's publisher at the time), even though the title page gives the bogus information that the author is "George Coleman [sic]," that the publisher is Cadell and Murray of Fleet Street, and that the date of publication is 1810. To use Colman's name as author was no doubt an advertising gimmick. H. Spencer Ashbee, whose bibliographies or erotica up to 1885 were based on firsthand knowledge, asserts that Hotten had pirated *The Rodiad* from a manuscript copy and that its author was an unnamed client of a flagellatorium managed by one Sarah Potter. If so, Swinburne had easy access to it, since he was supplying Hotten with material for such books as *Flagellation and the Flagellants: A History of the Rod* and the even less pseudoscholarly *Romance of Chastisement: Or Revelations of the School and the Bedroom.* Fuller speculates that Milnes (Lord Houghton) was the author and that *The Rodiad* was Milnes's part of a "covenant" Swinburne and he had made to exchange "flagellant fiction" (*Swinburne Letters*, I, 66–67).

84. See Lafourcade, *Swinburne: A Literary Biography*, p. 47.

85. "Swinburne's Agitation," *Swinburne Letters*, VI, 244.

86. *The Romantic Agony*, p. 218.

87. *Swinburne Letters*, I, 175 n.

88. Ibid., p. 232 n.

89. Ibid., p. 233.

90. Ibid.

91. Ibid., III, 13–14.

92. Harold Nicolson, *Swinburne and Baudelaire* (The Zaharoff Lecture) (London: Oxford Univ. Press, 1930).

93. "Charles Baudelaire: Les Fleur du Mal," *The Spectator*, 35 (Sept. 1862), 998.

94. Ibid., p. 999.

95. Ibid.

96. "Baudelaire," in *Do What You Will: Essays by Aldous Huxley* (London: Chatto & Windus, 1929), p. 199.

97. *The Overreacher: A Study of Christopher Marlowe* (Cambridge, Mass.: Harvard Univ. Press, 1952), p. 102.

CHAPTER 3   LADY CHATTERLEY'S *WHAT?*

1. *Thirteen Famous Patients* (Philadelphia: Chilton Co., 1960), pp. 116–27.

2. Personal communication.

3. Harry T. Moore, *The Intelligent Heart* (New York: Grove Press, 1962), esp. pp. 84, 470–72; Richard Aldington, *D. H. Lawrence: Portrait of a Genius, But . . .* (New York: Duell, Sloan, & Pearce, 1950), esp. pp. 54, 76, 125–26, 246.

4. Charles Rembar, *The End of Obscenity* (New York: Random House, 1968).

5. C. H. Rolph, ed., *The Trial of Lady Chatterley* (Harmondsworth, England: Penguin Books, 1961), esp. pp. 57–58, 92, 99–100.

6. D. H. Lawrence, *Apropos of "Lady Chatterley's Lover"* (London: Mandrake Press, 1930).

7. Bryan, *Grove Press Inc. and Reader's Subscription Inc. v. Robert K. Christenberry, individually and as Postmaster of the City of New York*, U.S. District Court, Southern District, Civil, 147–87 (1959).

8. "An Obscenity Symbol," *American Speech*, 9 (1934), 264.

9. *The Trial of Lady Chatterley*, pp. 144–45.

10. Aldous Huxley, ed., *The Letters of D. H. Lawrence* (London: William Heinemann Ltd., 1932).

11. Lawrence: Portrait of a Genius, p. 126.

12. Ibid., p. 246.

13. *Two or Three Graces* (London: Chatto & Windus, 1926), p. 119–20.

14. *The Intelligent Heart*, p. 471–72.

15. Penguin Books Edition (1960), p. 231; subsequent references are to this edition.

16. Ibid., p. 259.

17. *Trial of Lady Chatterley*, pp. 57–58.

18. Ibid., p. 92.

19. Ibid., pp. 99–100.

20. "An Obscenity Symbol," p. 264.

21. Harry T. Moore, "Richard Aldington in His Last Years," *Texas Quarterly*, 6 (Autumn 1963), 60.

22. *Lady Chatterley's Lover*, p. 17.

23. Ibid., pp. 278–82.

24. Ibid., p. 10.

25. Ibid., p. 181.

26. D. H. Lawrence, *Sons and Lovers* (New York: Modern Library, 1922), esp. Preface by John Macy, p. viii and pp. 82, 211, 328, 427.

27. "The Idea of Nostalgia," *Diogenes*, 54 (1967), 81.

28. *Sons and Lovers*, p. 82.

29. Psychoanalysts began commenting on *Sons and Lovers* soon after it was published (see A. B. Kuttner, *Psychoanalytical Review*, 3 (1916), 295–317). Lawrence ultimately rejected close identification with the developing psychoanalytical movement (see F. J. Hoffmann, "Lawrence's Quarrel with Freud," in *The Achievement of D. H. Lawrence*, ed. Harry T. Moore (Norman: Univ. of Oklahoma Press, 1953).

30. *Sons and Lovers*, p. 211.

31. Ibid., p. 328.

32. "Richard Aldington in His Last Years," p. 64.

33. D. H. Lawrence, *The White Peacock* (London: William Heinemann, 1911) p. 340.

34. Moore, *The Intelligent Heart*, p. 84.

35. Malcolm Muggeridge and Helen Corke, "The Dreaming Woman— Helen Corke, in Conversation with Malcolm Muggeridge, Tells of Her Relationship with D. H. Lawrence," *Listener*, 80, No. 2052 (July 1968), 104.

36. *Lady Chatterley's Lover*, p. 212.

37. Ibid., p. 225.

38. *The Image of Childhood* (Harmondsworth, England: Penguin Books, 1967), pp. 258–59.

39. "Regina v. Penguin Books: An Undisclosed Element in the Case," in *Controversial Essays* (London: Faber and Faber, 1966); first published in *Encounter*, 18, No. 35 (Feb. 1962). Andrew Shonfield was the first to suggest that there were cryptic hints of perverted sexual practices in the novel ("Lawrence's Other Censor," *Encounter*, 17, No. 63 [Sept. 1961]), and a few months after the appearance of this article Sparrow analyzed the literary evidence in detail. His view has been supported by independent observations by G. Wilson Knight ("Lawrence, Joyce, and Powys," *Essays in Criticism*, 11 [Oct. 1961], 403) and William Empson ("Lady Chatterley Again," *Essays in Criticism*, [Jan. 1963], 101).

40. *Lady Chatterley's Lover*, p. 232.

41. Ibid., p. 258.

42. Ibid., p. 280.

43. Personal communication.

44. Knight, "Lawrence, Joyce, and Powys," p. 406.

45. "Portraits from Memory. III. D. H. Lawrence," *Listener*, 48, No. 1221 (July 1952), 135.

46. Sparrow, "Regina v. Penguin Books," pp. 53–54.

47. *Lawrence: Portrait of a Genius*, p. 76.

48. Ibid., p. 103.

49. Sparrow, "Regina v. Penguin Books," p. 53.

50. *Sons and Lovers*, p. 427.
427.

51. "D. H. Lawrence and *Women in Love*," in *Pelican Guide to English Literature*, Vol. 7, *The Modern Age* (Harmondsworth, England: Pelican Books, 1961), p. 282.

52. "Four-Letter Words," *Critical Quarterly*, 3 (1961), 122.

53. "Lady Chatterley in America," in *Contemporaries* (Boston: Atlantic-Little, Brown Co., 1962), pp. 107–12.

54. "Advocate for Eros: Notes on D. H. Lawrence," *American Scholar*, 30 (1961), 191.

CHAPTER 4   DROWSED WITH THE FUME OF POPPIES: OPIUM AND
JOHN KEATS

1. "The Effects of *Anhalonium lewinii* (the Mescal Button)," *British Medical Journal*, 2 (1896), 1625–29.

2. "Mescal, the Study of a Divine Plant," *Popular Science Monthly*, 41 (1902), 52–71.

3. *The Milk of Paradise* (Cambridge, Mass: Harvard Univ. Press, 1934).

4. "Le Club des Haschischiens," *Feuilleton de la Presse Médicale*, 10 (1834), 7.

5. *Les Paradis Artificiels* (Paris: Poulet-Malassis, 1860).

6. *Opium: The Diary of an Addict*, tr. E. Boyd (London: Longmans, 1932).

7. *The Doors of Perception* (New York: Harpers, 1954); *Heaven and Hell* (New York: Harpers, 1956).

8. *Les opiomanes: mangeurs, buveurs, et fumeurs de l'opium* (Paris: Felix Alcan, 1912).

9. *Doors of Perception*, p. 25.

10. "Mescal," p. 64.

11. *George Crabbe and His Times*, tr. F. Clarke (London: John Murray, 1907), p. 374.

12. John C. Reid, *Francis Thompson, Man and Poet* (Westminster, England: Newman, 1960), p. 3.

13. Ibid., p. 11

14. Ibid., p. 203

15. Ibid., p. 151

16. Ibid., p. 116

17. *John Keats* (Cambridge, Mass: Harvard Univ. Press, 1963), p. 465.

18. Hyder E. Rollins, ed., *The Letters of John Keats*, 2 vols. (Cambridge, Mass.: Harvard Univ. Press, 1958), II, 78–79.

19. At this point in the letter Keats added a footnote: "Especially as I have a black eye."

20. *Letters of Keats*, II, 79.

21. Ibid., 91.

22. Charles Armitage Brown, *Life of John Keats*, ed. D. H. Bodurtha and W. B. Pope (London: Oxford Univ. Press, 1937), pp. 63–64.

23. *Letters of Keats*, II, 372.

24. *Life of Keats*, pp. 53–54.

25. The original manuscript in the Fitzwilliam Museum at Cambridge shows that Keats's first approximation of the opening line read "My heart aches and a painful numbness falls"—an incipit which he quickly rejected.

26. The name Hippocrene is derived from the Greek, *hippo*, horse + *krene*, meaning fountain or stream. The legend has it that Pegasus stamped his hoof upon the ground and at that place a sparkling stream arose, hence the name, and hence its attribution as a source of poetic inspiration. Possibly Keats was confusing Hippocrene with hippocras, the "wine of Hippocrates," a cordial made of wine flavored with spices, usually strained through a conical sieve or a bag of linen or flannel. Hippocras was known to Chaucer, who mentions it in *The Merchant's Tale:* "He drynketh Ypocras Clarree and Vernage / Of spices hoote tencressen his corage." The comparative endocrinologist must avoid the pitfall of deriving Hippocrene from *hippo*, horse + *krinein*, to secrete, the latter being the root for exocrine, endocrine, and allied terms. Horses do have many secretions, some of particular interest to endocrinologists, but none of them is purplish. The only potable which might qualify would be Hospices de Beaune, a decent Burgundy, but Keats, like Chaucer's merchant, was fond of claret. In any case, Hippocrene is not purple; Keats's imagination (or vision) endowed it with that tinctorial quality.

27. "Synaesthetic Imagery and Keats," in *Keats, a Collection of Critical Essays*, ed. Walter Jackson Bate (Englewood, N.J.: Prentice-Hall, 1964), pp. 41–50.

28. Arthur Pollard, ed., *New Poems by George Crabbe* (Liverpool: Liverpool Univ. Press, 1960).

CHAPTER 5 MADNESS AND POETRY: A NOTE ON COLLINS, COWPER, AND SMART

1. *The Name and Nature of Poetry* (Cambridge: Cambridge Univ. Press, 1933), p. 21.

2. *Criterion* (January 1934), XIII, p. 222.

3. Clarence Tracy, ed., *The Poetical Works of Richard Savage* (Cambridge: Cambridge Univ. Press, 1962), p. 3.

4. J. S. Cunningham, ed., *William Collins: Drafts and Fragments of Verse* (Oxford: Clarendon Press, 1956).

5. Joseph Warton (1722–1800) was the elder son of Thomas Warton (1688–1745), professor of poetry at Oxford from 1718 to 1728, and older brother of Thomas Warton (1728–90), professor of poetry at Oxford from 1757 to 1767, author of *The History of English Poetry*, created poet laureate in 1785. Joseph Warton returned to Winchester in 1755 as master, became headmaster in 1766, and served in that post to 1798. He is best known for his *Essay on the Writings and Genius of Pope* (2 vols., 1956, 1782).

6. *Lives of the Poets* (London: Oxford Univ. Press, 1961) II, p. 383.

7. Oswald Doughty, *William Collins* (published for the British Council and the National Book League [London: Longmans, Green, 1964]), p. 13.

8. Edmund Blunden, ed., *The Poems of William Collins, Edited with an Introductory Study* (London: Etchells & MacDonald, 1929), p. 32.

9. Ibid., pp. 27–28.

10. H. W. Garrod, *The Poetry of Collins*, Warton Lecture on English Poetry, from *Proceedings of the British Academy*, Vol. 14 (London: Humphrey Milford, 1928).

11. *Odes on Various Subjects* (London: J. Dodsley, 1746), Advert.

12. Paget Toynbee and Leonard Whibley, eds., *The Correspondence of Thomas Gray* (Oxford: Clarendon Press 1934–50) I, 261.

13. *The Poetry of Vision* (Cambridge, Mass.: Harvard Univ. Press, 1967).

14. *The Primary Language of Poetry in the 1740's and 1840's,* University of California Publications in English, 19 (1950), 161–382.

15. Spacks, *Poetry of Vision*, p. 72.

16. David Cecil, *The Stricken Deer* (London: Constable, 1929).

17. Charles Ryskamp, *William Cowper of the Inner Temple, Esq.* (Cambridge: Cambridge Univ. Press, 1959).

18. Maurice J. Quinlan, "Memoir of William Cowper, an Autobiography Edited With an Introduction," *Proceedings of the American Philosophical Society*, 97 (1953), 359–82.

19. Ibid., p. 366–67.

20. Lytton Strachey and Roger J. Fulford, eds., *The Greville Memoirs*, 8 vols. (London: Macmillan, 1937–38), III, 85.

21. *Table Talk*, line 764.

22. "Memoir of William Cowper," p. 360.

23. Ibid., p. 371.

24. Ibid., p. 377.

25. Denis Leigh, "The Form Complete," *Proceedings of the Royal Society of Medicine*, 61 (1968), 375–84.

26. *DNB*, (1921–22), IV, 1232.

27. "Memoir of William Cowper," p. 380.

28. *William Cowper* (published for the British Council and the National Book League [London: Longmans, Green, 1960]), 17.

29. The numbering of the hymns follows that used in Cowper's *Poetical Works*, ed. H. S. Milford, English Standard Authors' series, 4th ed. (New York: Oxford Univ. Press, 1934).

30. III.ii.67–71.

31. *William Cowper* (1960), p. 16.

32. Michael Holroyd, *Lytton Strachey, A Critical Biography* (New York: Holt, Rinehart and Winston, 1968). II, p. 545.

33. *William Cowper* (London: Lehmann, 1951), pp. 7–8.

34. Ibid., p. 165.

35. "William Cowper," in *The Age of Johnson,* ed., Frederick W. Hilles (New Haven: Yale Univ. Press, 1949), pp. 257–67.

36. "Toward Defining an Age of Sensibility," in *Fables of Identity* (New York: Harcourt, Brace, 1963), pp. 130–37.

37. James Boswell, *The Life of Samuel Johnson, LL.D.,* ed. George B. Hill, rev. and enl. by Lawrence F. Powell (Oxford: Clarendon Press, 1934–50), I, 397.

38. Paget Toynbee and Leonard Whibley, eds., *The Correspondence of Thomas Gray* (Oxford: Clarendon Press, 1935), I, 273–75.

39. *Christopher Smart, Scholar of the University* (Ann Arbor: Michigan Univ. Press, 1967).

40. Robert Anderson, *The Works of the British Poets* (London: Arch, 1795), XI, 117.

41. *Poor Kit Smart* (London: Hart-Davis, 1961).

42. Donald J. Greene, "Smart, Berkeley, the Scientists and the Poets, a Note on Eighteenth-century Anti-Newtonianism," *Journal of Historical Ideas,* 14 (1953), 327–52.

43. *The Rhetoric of Science* (Berkeley: Univ. of California Press, 1966), p. 164.

44. Ibid., p. 43.

45. Sherbo, *Christopher Smart,* pp. 111–12.

46. Ibid., p. 130.

47. *Boswell's Life of Johnson,* Oxford Standard Edition (New York: Oxford Univ. Press, 1933), I, 265.

48. *Thraliana,* 2d ed., ed. Katharine C. Balderston (Oxford: Clarendon Press, 1951), p. 728.

49. Christopher Smart, *Rejoice in the Lamb, a Song from Bedlam,* ed. William F. Stead (New York: Holt, 1939).

50. Christopher Smart, *Jubilate Agno,* ed. William H. Bond (London: Hart-Davis, 1954), pp. 17, 20.

51. Ibid., pp. 14–15.

52. "The Apocalypse of Christopher Smart," in *Studies in the Eighteenth Century,* ed. R. F. Brissenden (Toronto: Univ. of Toronto Press, 1968), p. 271.

53. Ibid., p. 274.

54. Ibid., p. 269.

55. "The Structure of Smart's *Song to David,*" *Review of English Studies,* 14 (1938), 178–82.

56. *The Case of Christopher Smart,* English Association Pamphlet No. 90 (London, 1934).

57. *Poetry of Vision,* p. 121.

58. *Christopher Smart as a Poet of His Time, a Reappraisal* (The Hague and Paris: Mouton, 1966), p. 123.

59. *The Collected Poems of Christopher Smart,* ed. Norman Callan, 2 vols. (Cambridge: Harvard Univ. Press, 1967), I, xxxi.

60. Bond, ed., *Jubilate Agno,* p. 15.

CHAPTER 6   CHEKHOV AMONG THE DOCTORS: THE
            DOCTOR'S DILEMMA

1. Lillian Hellman, ed. and Sidonie K. Lederer, trans., *The Selected Letters of Anton Chekhov* (New York: Farrar, Strauss, and Cudahy, 1955), p. 78 (letter to Suvorin, 9 Jan. 1889).

2. Ernest J. Simmons, *Chekhov: A Biography* (Boston: Little, Brown, 1962), p. 96 (letter to Suvorin, 11 Sept. 1888).

3. Michael Henry Heim, trans., in collaboration with Simon Karlinsky, *Letters of Anton Chekhov* (New York: Harper & Row, 1973), p. 107 (letter to Rossolimo, 11 Oct. 1889).

4. Simmons, *Chekhov,* p. 479.

5. Ibid., p. 480.

6. Ibid., p. 166.

7. Ronald Hingley, *A New Life of Chekhov* (New York: Knopf, 1976), p. 128.

8. Simmons, p. 345.

9. Ronald Hingley, *Chekhov, a Biographical and Critical Study* (London: Allen & Unwin, 1950), p. 233.

10. Ann Dunnigan, trans., *Anton Chekhov: Ward Six and Other Stories* (New York: New American Library, 1965), p. 52.

11. Ann Dunnigan, trans., *Anton Chekhov: The Major Plays* (New York: New American Library, 1965), *The Sea Gull,* Act I, p. 122.

12. Ibid., p. 123.

13. Ibid., *Uncle Vanya,* Act I, p. 182.

14. Ibid., Act IV, p. 222.

15. Ibid., *The Three Sisters,* Act IV, p. 297.

16. Ibid., p. 301.

CHAPTER 7   WILLIAM CARLOS WILLIAMS, M.D.: PHYSICIAN AS
            POET

1. William Carlos Williams, *Autobiography* (New York: Random House, 1951), p. 3.

2. Ibid., p. 106.

3. Ibid., p. xii.

4. Ibid., p. xiii.

5. Kenneth Burke, "Heaven's First Law," *The Dial,* No. 72 (1922), p. 197.

6. *Autobiography,* pp. 288–89.

7. *Raindrops on a Briar,* in William Carlos Williams, *Collected Later Poems* (New York: New Directions, 1962), p. 99.

8. Ibid.

9. *Collected Earlier Poems* (New York: New Directions, 1951), p. 106.

10. Ibid., p. 159.

11. *Collected Later Poems*, p. 10.

12. *Collected Earlier Poems*, p. 111.

13. *The Desert Music and Other Poems* (New York: Random House, 1954), p. 90.

14. William Carlos Williams, "An Approach to the Poem," in *English Institute Essays 1947* (New York: Columbia University Press, 1948), p. 57.

15. Ibid., p. 58.

16. *The Desert Music and Other Poems*, pp. 72–73.

17. *Collected Later Poems*, p. 267.

18. *The Desert Music and Other Poems*, pp. 12–16.

19. *Collected Earlier Poems*, p. 217.

20. *Collected Later Poems*, p. 60.

21. *Collected Earlier Poems*, p. 315.

22. Ibid., p. 36.

23. *Autobiography*, p. 236.

24. William Carlos Williams, *In the American Grain* (New York: New Directions, 1956), p. 234.

25. William Carlos Williams, *Paterson, Book IV* (New York: New Directions, 1963), pp. 204–6.

26. Virgil Thomson, *The State of Music*, 2d ed. (New York: Vintage, 1961), pp. 85–86.

27. *William Carlos Williams Reads His Poetry* (New York: Caedmon Records, TC-1047), recorded 6 June, 1954.

28. *Asphodel, that Greeny Flower*, In *Pictures from Brueghel and Other Poems* (New York: New Directions, 1962), p. 161.

29. Mark Linenthal: personal communication.

30. Ibid.

CHAPTER 8   THE EARL OF ROCHESTER AND EJACULATIO PRAECOX

1. Leonard P. Wershub, *Sexual Impotence in the Male* (Springfield, Ill.: C C Thomas, 1959), p. 12.

2. Richard F. Quaintance, "French Sources of the Restoration 'Imperfect Enjoyment' Poem," *Philological Quarterly*, 42 (1963), 190–99.

3. John H. Wilson, "Rochester, Dryden, and the Rose-Street Affair," *Review of English Studies*, 15 (1939), 294–301.

4. John H. Wilson, "Rochester's Marriage," *Review of English Studies*, 19 (1943), 399–403.

5. Vivian de Sola Pinto, *Enthusiast in Wit* (London: Routledge & Kegan Paul, 1962).

6. Rodney M. Baine, "Rochester or Fishbourne: A Question of Authorship," *Review of English Studies*, 22 (1946), 201–6.

7. James Thorpe, ed., *Rochester's Poems on Several Occasions* (Princeton: Princeton Univ. Press, 1950).

8. David M. Vieth, *Attributions in Restoration Poetry* (New Haven: Yale Univ. Press, 1968).

9. David M. Vieth, *The Complete Poems of John Wilmot, Earl of Rochester* (New Haven: Yale Univ. Press, 1968).

10. Ibid., p. 158.

11. Pinto, *Enthusiast in Wit*, p. 138.

12. Thomas Alcock and John Wilmot, *The Famous Pathologist, or the Noble Mountebank*, ed. Vivian de Sola Pinto (Nottingham: Sisson & Parker, 1961).

13. Ibid., p. 34.

14. Ibid., p. 33.

15. Vivian de Sola Pinto, ed., *Poems by John Wilmot, Earl of Rochester* (London and Cambridge: Routledge & Kegan Paul, Harvard University Press, 1953), p. xxxiii.

16. Ibid., p. xxxix.

17. Gilbert Burnet, *Some Passages of the Life and Death of the Right Hon. John, Earl of Rochester* (London, 1680).

18. Vieth, *Complete Poems*, p. 140.

19. Ibid., p. 161.

20. Ibid., pp. 99–101.

21. Quaintance, "French Sources of the Restoration 'Imperfect Enjoyment' Poem," *Philological Quarterly*, 42 (1963), 190–99.

22. Rochester presents it as an isolated incident, but I suspect he experienced ejaculatio praecox more than once and that the poem crystallizes such debacles. There is little evidence that his drinking habits played a role. Conventionally, alcohol "provokes the desire but it takes away the performance"; but when it does so, failure to achieve erection is far more likely than premature ejaculation. There is nothing in the setting of the poem to indicate an amorous encounter bred from a drinking spree. Venereal disease cannot be blamed; syphilis does not affect potentia until its most advanced stages. The poem was written before 1671, a few years before Rochester's health failed. Parenthetically, the imputation that Rochester had syphilis lacks any substantive medical documentation. His promiscuity certainly entitled him to it, and one cannot exclude the diagnosis. But the little we know of his last illness does not suggest syphilis. That his mental faculties were not impaired during his last days almost surely rules out syphilis involving the central nervous system. The absence of shortness of breath and dropsy likewise makes cardiovascular syphilis improbable. Rupture of a syphilitic aneurysm would have led to sudden death. The evidence suggests a disease of insidious onset with exacerbations and remission over a four-year period, its prominent features being progressive weakness, probably some weight loss, and intermittent episodes of fever lasting for several days. Far more probable than syphilis would be tuberculosis, Hodgkin's disease, or some form of lymphoma or leukemia. Cirrhosis of the liver or one of the many forms of glomerulonephritis cannot be excluded, though these might be expected to produce some degree of peripheral edema or "dropsy." Rochester had many enemies, and it was thoroughly in keeping with the mores of the times to calumniate a rival by insinuating that he had the pox. But there is no affirmative medical evidence that such was the case. Any statement about the nature of Rochester's final illness would be purely speculative, and I leave the question open to a more temerarious diagnostician.

23. Pinto, ed., *Poems,* p. xlix.

24. Vieth, *Complete Poems,* pp. 37–40.

25. *The Miscellaneous Works of the Right Honourable the Late Earls of Rochester and Roscommon* (London: R. Bragge, 1707), pp. 15–16.

26. K. Abraham, "Über Ejaculatio praecox." *International Zeitschrift für Psychoanalyse,* 4 (1917) 171–86.

27. Fredelle Bruser, "Concepts of Chastity in Literature, Chiefly Non-dramatic, of the English Renaissance," Diss., Radcliffe College, 1948.

28. Ibid.

29. Ibid.

CHAPTER 9   THOMAS SHADWELL: HIS EXITUS REVIS'D

1. *Thomas Shadwell* (New York: Twayne Publishers, Inc., 1967), p. 21.

2. *Thomas Shadwell, His Life and Comedies* (New York: New York Univ. Press, 1928), p. 87.

3. *The Poets Laureate* (London: The Bodley Head, 1954), p. 43.

4. *The Complete Works of Thomas Shadwell,* ed. Montague Summers, 5 vols. (London: Fortune Press, 1929), I, ccxxxii–xxxiii.

5. Tom Brown, *Collected Works,* 5th ed., 5 vols. (London: Sam Briscoe, 1720), IV., 105–6.

6. *Complete Works of Shadwell,* I, ccliv.

7. *The Lives of the Poets-Laureate* (London: Richard Bentley, 1853), p. 192.

8. *An Account of the English Dramatick Poets* (Oxford: G. West & H. Clements, 1691).

9. *Athenae Oxonienses* (London: Tho. Bennet, 1691).

10. *The Lives and Characters of the English Dramatick Poets,* ed. Charles Gildon (London: Nicholas Cox & William Turner, 1699).

11. *Athenae Oxonienses,* 2d ed. (London: B. Knaplock, D. Midwinter, J. Tonson, 1721).

12. *Dramatick Works,* 4 vols. (London: J. Knapton & J. Tonson, 1721).

13. *Biographia Britannica,* VI (1763), 3626.

14. "William Oldys (1696–1761)," in *Dictionary of National Biography,* XLII (1895), 119–23.

15. British Museum shelf mark C.28.g.l.

16. *Notes & Queries,* 2d ser., XI (9 Mar. 1861), 182.

17. *Introduction to Shadwell's Plays,* Mermaid Series (London: T. Fisher Unwin, 1899), p. xv.

18. *Notes & Queries,* 13th ser., CXLVI (22 Mar. 1924), 217.

19. John H. Talbot, *Gout,* 3d ed. (New York: Grune & Stratton, Inc., 1967), p. 148.

20. Arthur P. Hall, "Correlations Among Hyperuricemia, Hypercholesterolemia, Coronary Disease and Hypertension," *Arthritis & Rheumitism,* 8 (1965), 846–52.

21. Francis J. Viozzi et al., "Coexistence of Gout and Arterial Thrombosis," (abstract), *Arthritis & Rheumitism,* 13 (1970), 355–56.

CHAPTER 10   DID SOCRATES DIE OF HEMLOCK POISONING?

1. Plato, *Phaedo*, in *The Dialogues of Plato*, tr. Benjamin Jowett (New York: Random House, 1937), I, 441.

2. Ibid.

3. Nicander, *Alexipharmaca*, in *Poems and Poetical Fragments*, tr. and ed. A. S. F. Gow and A. F. Scholfield (Cambridge: Cambridge Univ. Press, 1953), p. 107.

4. Rudolph A. Witthaus and Tracy C. Becker, *Medical Jurisprudence, Forensic Medicine, and Toxicology*, 2d ed. (New York: William Wood, 1911), IV, 920; Frederick Peterson, Walter S. Haines, and Ralph W. Webster, *Legal Medicine and Toxicology* 2d ed. (Philadelphia: W. B. Saunders, 1923), II, 487.

5. *Clinical Toxicology*, 2d ed. (Philadelphia: Lea & Febiger, 1948), p. 33.

6. In addition to references cited in nn. 4 and 5, see Albert H. Brundage, *A Manual of Toxicology*, 15th ed. (New York: Appleton-Century, 1926), p. 130; John Glaister, *Medical Jurisprudence and Toxicology*, 7th ed. (Baltimore; Williams & Wilkins, 1942), p. 604.

7. *Forensic Medicine*, 9th ed. (London: J. & A. Churchill, 1949), p. 547.

8. *Poisoning* (New York: Paul B. Hoeber, 1952), p. 317.

9. "The Death of Socrates," *Classical Quarterly*, 23 (1973), 25.